Edith Penrose's Legacy

Edith Penrose is best known for *The Theory of the Growth of the Firm*, originally published in 1959, but she made major contributions in other fields, including patents, the oil industry, and development economics. This book explores her work and legacy, not just on economics – she was the founding Head of the Department of Economics at SOAS University of London – but also on the related fields of management and political economy where her contribution has had significant impact.

Penrose challenged the conventional wisdom of economics by opening up the 'black box' view of the firm to explore what goes on inside, in particular how resources are managed and renewed to influence growth and innovation. Her analysis was cognisant of the wider political economy context in which firms operate, recognising the different impact of large international firms on developing and developed countries. Penrose's work has shaped modern theories of strategic management including the resource-based view of the firm and the dynamic capabilities approach.

The chapters in this volume, from leading economists and management scholars, cover a range of topics including innovation, collaboration between firms and universities, and the practice and consequences of share buy-backs, highlighting the value of a Penrosian perspective and the extent of her legacy. This book will be relevant to students and scholars of economics, management, and political economy.

This book was originally published as a special issue of the *International Review of Applied Economics*.

Jonathan Michie is Professor of Innovation and Knowledge Exchange at the University of Oxford, where he is also Pro-Vice-Chancellor and President of Kellogg College. He is the managing editor of the *International Review of Applied Economics*, and Chair of the Universities Association for Lifelong Learning.

Christine Oughton is Professor of Management Economics at SOAS University of London and Fellow of the Academy of Social Sciences. Her research focuses on innovation, environmental management and economics, corporate governance, financial inclusion, and growth.

Edith Penrose's Legacy
Shaping Economics, Management, and Political Economy

Edited by
Jonathan Michie and Christine Oughton

LONDON AND NEW YORK

First published 2025
by Routledge
4 Park Square, Milton Park, Abingdon, Oxon OX14 4RN

and by Routledge
605 Third Avenue, New York, NY 10158

Routledge is an imprint of the Taylor & Francis Group, an informa business

Preface, Chapters 3, 5, 6, 10, 12 and 13 © 2025 Taylor & Francis
Chapter 1 © 2024 Jonathan Michie and Christine Oughton. Originally published as Open Access.
Chapter 2 © 2024 Kofi Adjepong-Boateng and Christine Oughton. Originally published as Open Access.
Chapter 4 © 2022 Mariana Mazzucato. Originally published as Open Access.
Chapter 7 © 2023 Damian Tobin. Originally published as Open Access.
Chapter 8 © 2024 Juana Paola Bustamante Izquierdo. Originally published as Open Access.
Chapter 9 © 2022 Chia Huay Lau and Jonathan Michie. Originally published as Open Access.
Chapter 11 © 2022 Michael Joffe. Originally published as Open Access.
Chapter 14 © 2024 Jonathan Michie. Originally published as Open Access.

With the exception of Chapters 1, 2, 4, 7, 8, 9, 11 and 14, no part of this book may be reprinted
or reproduced or utilised in any form or by any electronic, mechanical, or other means, now known
or hereafter invented, including photocopying and recording, or in any information storage or
retrieval system, without permission in writing from the publishers. For details on the rights for
Chapters 1, 2, 4, 7, 8, 9, 11 and 14, please see the chapters' Open Access footnotes.

Trademark notice: Product or corporate names may be trademarks or registered trademarks, and are
used only for identification and explanation without intent to infringe.

British Library Cataloguing in Publication Data
A catalogue record for this book is available from the British Library

ISBN13: 978-1-032-95909-2 (hbk)
ISBN13: 978-1-032-95911-5 (pbk)
ISBN13: 978-1-003-58713-2 (ebk)

DOI: 10.4324/9781003587132

Typeset in Minion Pro
by Newgen Publishing UK

Publisher's Note
The publisher accepts responsibility for any inconsistencies that may have arisen during the
conversion of this book from journal articles to book chapters, namely the inclusion of journal
terminology.

Disclaimer
Every effort has been made to contact copyright holders for their permission to reprint material
in this book. The publishers would be grateful to hear from any copyright holder who is not
here acknowledged and will undertake to rectify any errors or omissions in future editions of
this book.

Contents

Citation Information		vii
Notes on Contributors		x
Preface – Edith Penrose: Legacy and impact		xi
Jonathan Michie		

1 Edith Penrose's influence on economic analysis, strategic management
and political economy 1
Jonathan Michie and Christine Oughton

2 Edith Penrose and the Penrose Lectures 11
Kofi Adjepong-Boateng and Christine Oughton

3 Patents, innovation, and development 16
Bronwyn H. Hall

4 Collective value creation: A new approach to stakeholder value 42
Mariana Mazzucato

5 Is the most unproductive firm the foundation of the most efficient
economy? Penrosian learning confronts the neoclassical fallacy 57
William Lazonick

6 The story of flight 89
John Kay

7 Captive markets and climate change: Revisiting Edith Penrose's analysis
of the international oil firms in the era of climate change 103
Damian Tobin

8 Complementarities between product and process innovation and their
effects on employment: A firm-level analysis of manufacturing firms
in Colombia 128
Juana Paola Bustamante Izquierdo

CONTENTS

9 Penrose's theory of the firm in an era of globalisation 154
Chia Huay Lau and Jonathan Michie

10 Necessary and sufficient conditions for the absorptive capacity of firms that interact with universities 174
Júlio Eduardo Rohenkohl, Andreia Cunha da Rosa, Janaina Ruffoni and Orlando Martinelli

11 Profit rate dynamics in US manufacturing 193
Michael Joffe

12 What is Edith Penrose's legacy for the theory of the firm? 223
Irene Roele and Sonja Ruehl

13 Regulating stock buybacks: The $6.3 trillion question 242
Lenore Palladino and William Lazonick

14 The life and times of Edith Penrose 267
Jonathan Michie

Index 276

Citation Information

The chapters in this book were originally published in the *International Review of Applied Economics*, volume 38, issue 1–2 (2024). When citing this material, please use the original page numbering for each article, as follows:

Preface
Double special issue on Edith Penrose
Jonathan Michie
International Review of Applied Economics, volume 38, issue 1–2 (2024), p. 1

Chapter 1
Edith penrose's influence on economic analysis, strategic management and political economy
Jonathan Michie and Christine Oughton
International Review of Applied Economics, volume 38, issue 1–2 (2024), pp. 2–11

Chapter 2
Edith Penrose and the Penrose Lectures
Kofi Adjepong-Boateng and Christine Oughton
International Review of Applied Economics, volume 38, issue 1–2 (2024), pp. 12–16

Chapter 3
Patents, innovation, and development
Bronwyn H. Hall
International Review of Applied Economics, volume 38, issue 1–2 (2024), pp. 17–42

Chapter 4
Collective value creation: a new approach to stakeholder value
Mariana Mazzucato
International Review of Applied Economics, volume 38, issue 1–2 (2024), pp. 43–57

Chapter 5
Is the most unproductive firm the foundation of the most efficient economy? Penrosian learning confronts the neoclassical fallacy
William Lazonick
International Review of Applied Economics, volume 38, issue 1–2 (2024), pp. 58–89

Chapter 6
The story of flight
John Kay
International Review of Applied Economics, volume 38, issue 1–2 (2024), pp. 90–103

Chapter 7
Captive markets and climate change: revisiting Edith Penrose's analysis of the international oil firms in the era of climate change
Damian Tobin
International Review of Applied Economics, volume 38, issue 1–2 (2024), pp. 104–128

Chapter 8
Complementarities between product and process innovation and their effects on employment: a firm-level analysis of manufacturing firms in Colombia
Juana Paola Bustamante Izquierdo
International Review of Applied Economics, volume 38, issue 1–2 (2024), pp. 129–154

Chapter 9
Penrose's theory of the firm in an era of globalisation
Chia Huay Lau and Jonathan Michie
International Review of Applied Economics, volume 38, issue 1–2 (2024), pp. 155–174

Chapter 10
Necessary and sufficient conditions for the absorptive capacity of firms that interact with universities
Júlio Eduardo Rohenkohl, Andreia Cunha da Rosa, Janaina Ruffoni and Orlando Martinelli
International Review of Applied Economics, volume 38, issue 1–2 (2024), pp. 175–193

Chapter 11
Profit rate dynamics in US manufacturing
Michael Joffe
International Review of Applied Economics, volume 38, issue 1–2 (2024), pp. 194–223

Chapter 12
What is Edith Penrose's legacy for the theory of the firm?
Irene Roele and Sonja Ruehl
International Review of Applied Economics, volume 38, issue 1–2 (2024), pp. 224–242

Chapter 13

Regulating stock buybacks: the $6.3 trillion question
Lenore Palladino and William Lazonick
International Review of Applied Economics, volume 38, issue 1–2 (2024), pp. 243–267

Chapter 14

The life and times of Edith Penrose
Jonathan Michie
International Review of Applied Economics, volume 38, issue 1–2 (2024), pp. 268–276

For any permission-related enquiries please visit:
www.tandfonline.com/page/help/permissions

Notes on Contributors

Kofi Adjepong-Boateng, Chair of the Penrose Lectures Committee, SOAS University of London, UK.

Juana Paola Bustamante Izquierdo, Department of Economics and Finance, University of Rome Tor Vergata, Rome, Italy.

Andreia Cunha da Rosa, Economics, Unisinos University, Porto Alegre, Brazil.

Bronwyn H. Hall, University of California, Berkeley, CA, USA; National Bureau of Economic Research, Institute for Fiscal Studies, London; Max Planck Institute for Innovation and Competition, Munich.

Michael Joffe, Department of Epidemiology & Biostatistics, Imperial College London, UK.

John Kay, Economics, St John's College, Oxford, England, UK.

Chia Huay Lau, Kellogg College, University of Oxford, UK.

William Lazonick, The Academic-Industry Research Network, Cambridge, MA, USA.

Orlando Martinelli, Economy and International Relations Department, Federal University of Santa Maria, Santa Maria, Brazil.

Mariana Mazzucato, Institute for Innovation and Public Purpose, University College London, UK.

Jonathan Michie, Kellogg College, University of Oxford, UK.

Christine Oughton, School of Finance and Management, SOAS University of London, UK.

Lenore Palladino, Economics & Public Policy, University of Massachusetts Amherst, Amherst, MA, USA.

Irene Roele, Alliance Manchester Business School, The University of Manchester, UK.

Júlio Eduardo Rohenkohl, Economy and International Relations Department, Federal University of Santa Maria, Santa Maria, Brazil.

Sonja Ruehl, School of Finance and Management, SOAS University of London, UK.

Janaina Ruffoni, Economics Graduate Program, Unisinos University, Porto Alegre, Brazil.

Damian Tobin, Department of Management and Marketing, Cork University Business School, University College Cork, Cork, Ireland.

Preface – Edith Penrose: Legacy and impact

Jonathan Michie

Edith Penrose was a major figure in economics and also played a key role in the field of management and business. Penrose is best known for her classic book *The Theory of the Growth of the Firm*, originally published in 1959, but she also made major contributions in other fields, including patents, the oil industry and development economics.

As described by Adjepong-Boateng and Oughton in their article, Penrose was appointed Professor of Economics at SOAS University of London, where an annual lecture series has been inaugurated in her honour. This double issue of the *International Review of Applied Economics* publishes the contributions from three of these Penrose lecturers, along with a range of articles from other academics who explore various aspects of Penrosian economics.

Together, these articles represent a compelling testament to the continued relevance of Penrose's key messages, around the importance of managerial capabilities; of knowledge, learning and innovation; and the development of organisational capacity and firm growth.

ⓐ OPEN ACCESS

Edith Penrose's influence on economic analysis, strategic management and political economy

Jonathan Michie and Christine Oughton

ABSTRACT
Edith Penrose is best known for her classic book *The Theory of the Growth of the Firm*, originally published in 1959, but she also made major contributions in other fields, including patents, the oil industry, and development economics. This special double issue of the *International Review of Applied Economics* publishes recent research from a range of leading economists and management scholars from across the world, either explicitly analysing Penrose's contribution, or else analysing topics from firms' collaborations with universities through to the practice and consequences of share buy-backs, which demonstrate that a Penrosian perspective helps to illuminate the reality of such processes.

1. Introduction

In this article we consider Penrose's influence on economics, management, political economy, development and methodology as a backdrop to the papers in this special issue. We start by considering in Section 2 her ground-breaking work on firm growth and her methodological approach before considering her work on large international firms, patents, development and political economy in Section 3. Section 4 then provides an overview of the papers in this double special issue, and Section 5 concludes.

2. *The Theory of the Growth of the Firm*: applied economics, theory and methodology

Penrose's, (1959/2009) book *The Theory of the Growth of the Firm* provided a new approach to analysing business behaviour and performance based on an explicit consideration of the internal organisation of the firm and its managerial capabilities. Penrose was keen to understand the limits to firm growth and the interaction between internal resources and market opportunities. Her study explored how firms' resources are managed, acquired, transformed, created and re-created to shape business performance and competitive advantage. Penrose's work led to a new theory of firm growth and to the resource-based view of the firm. Both have been highly influential in the fields of

---

This is an Open Access article distributed under the terms of the Creative Commons Attribution License (http://creativecommons.org/licenses/by/4.0/), which permits unrestricted use, distribution, and reproduction in any medium, provided the original work is properly cited. The terms on which this article has been published allow the posting of the Accepted Manuscript in a repository by the author(s) or with their consent.

economics and management, the first as an alternative to the neoclassical theory of the firm and the second as a foundation for modern theories of strategic management.

What is pertinent for this special issue of the *International Review of Applied Economics* is that Penrose (1959) regarded theory *and* applied analysis as necessary and complementary elements in advancing our understanding of firm behaviour and performance, bridging the divide that had come to exist between the theory of the firm and empirical research:

> In the literature of economics, the firm of the 'real world' has long lived in that uncomfortable no-man's-land between the high and dry plateaus of 'pure theory' and the tangled forests of 'empiric-realistic' research. (Penrose, 1959, p. x)

Penrose looked at the firm from the inside out, having gained deep insight into the operations of the Hercules Powder Company (HPC) as a college-business fellow attached to HPC while working on a research project on *Advancement of Financial Knowledge* led by Fritz Machlup (A. Penrose 2018, 120) at John Hopkins University. Penrose chose to work on the theory stream of the project and used her case study of the HPC to inform the development of theory. The case study of HPC was initially to be included in her book *The Theory of the Growth of the Firm* but was later extracted and published separately (as E. Penrose 1960). Still, her combination of applied and theoretical work was built into *The Theory of the Growth of the Firm* from the start.

Her approach was to redefine the firm to enable the development of a new theory of firm growth. In a reflective lecture, 'The Theory of the Growth of the Firm Twenty-Five Years After' given at Uppsala University in 1984, Penrose argued:

> Few economists thought it necessary to enquire what happened inside the firm – indeed their firm had no 'insides', so to speak. I do not say they were wrong, only that, being theoretical economists they saw reality differently from other people. The question I wanted to answer was whether there was something inherent in the very nature of any firm that necessarily limited its rate of growth. Clearly a definition of a firm that did have 'insides' was required. (Penrose, 1984, cited in A. Penrose 2018, 253)

Penrose conceptualised the firm as a collection of productive resources or capabilities. Technology, knowledge and human capital are key, but it is the firm's managerial capabilities and their capacity to combine and renew resources that is central to enabling the firm to innovate and grow. Penrose analysed growth as a *process* that emanates from the ability of managers to fully utilise and enhance the productive potential of the internal resources currently at their disposal, and to integrate new resources,

> Physically describable resources are purchased in the market for their known services; but as soon as they become part of a firm the range of services they are capable of yielding starts to change. The services that resources will yield depend on the capacities of the men using them, but the development of the capacities of men is shaped partly by the resources men deal with. The two together create the special productive opportunity of a particular firm. The full potentialities for growth provided by this reciprocal change will not necessarily be realized by any given firm, but in so far as they are realized, growth will take place which cannot be satisfactorily explained with reference to changes in the *environment* of the firm. (E. Penrose 1959/2009, 69–70)

According to Penrose, firms differ significantly in terms of the resources they possess and the way they are configured and utilised. Hence, for Penrose, the neoclassical approach of modelling the behaviour of a single representative firm and then replicating that to explain the behaviour of many identical firms in an industry or an economy, was wholly inadequate. Innovation, knowledge, especially firm-specific knowledge, and learning are unique to firms and shape their growth. Managerial resources and capacity are particularly important, as Penrose saw managerial capabilities as the main limit to firm growth.

Managerial capabilities can be expanded by developing both existing resources, via enhancing knowledge, learning, and experience, and by employing new staff. However, Penrose argues that new hires, especially new managerial staff, will not immediately be at their most productive. It takes time for new managers and employees to gain the firm-specific knowledge and experience that is necessary for their capabilities to be fully utilised in combination with the firm's existing technological knowledge and human capital. It is the process of combination and renewal of resources that generates growth.

In many ways Penrose's analysis of managerial capabilities and the innovative firm was ahead of the curve and her theory of the innovative enterprise is more relevant today than it was when first published in 1959. The increasing importance of knowledge, technology and human capital, moves management of the firm's capabilities, particularly its intangible knowledge and human capital, centre stage. Indeed, Penrose's theory of the growth of the firm may help explain the UK 'productivity puzzle' that has emerged since the financial crisis. As noted by the UK Office for National Statistics, labour productivity,

> has demonstrated weak growth since the 2008 economic downturn, while in the previous 10 years it was close to historical long-term average growth rates of 2.0% per year. This sustained period of minimal labour productivity growth has been labelled the UK's 'productivity puzzle', and it is arguably the defining economic question of our age. (Office for National Statistics 2019, 3)

The productivity puzzle is captured by the fact that while UK output and employment have recovered since the financial crisis of 2007–2008 and the consequent global recession of 2009, productivity growth, as measured by output per employee, has remained flat, and below levels observed before the financial crisis. Penrosian theory points to managerial capabilities, in particular the ability of management to utilise and enhance the resources within the firm (knowledge, financial resources for investment in capital, research and development and human capital) and managers' capacity to combine their existing resources with new resources, such as newly recruited employees. Relaxation in labour protection laws may play a role as it has become easier to shed staff with valuable firm-specific knowledge. While new recruits have been hired in the recovery phase after the great recession, it takes time for managers to utilise the full potential of newly employed resources (capital, labour and knowledge), which by virtue of their 'newness' are less productive than existing internal resources. Penrose's approach also explains why firms may choose not to shed staff during a downturn in order to retain firm-specific, institutional knowledge that is valuable to the firm and its future growth.

2.1. Penrose's methodology

As discussed above, the methodology underlying *The Theory of the Growth of the Firm* was grounded in insights gained from a detailed case study to inform a new theoretical approach. In this section we consider three aspects of Penrose's methodological approach that are relevant to the subject matter and content of the *International Review of Applied Economics*: (i) pluralism and multi-disciplinarity, (ii) rationality and biological analogies; and (iii) complexity.

Penrose was open to pluralism in method and multi-disciplinarity, seeing neoclassical economics as unduly constrained by a desire to convey 'scientific' rigour yet unable to embrace the complexity required by acknowledging firm diversity:

> Because of its complexity and diversity, a firm can be approached with many different types of analysis—sociological, organizational, engineering, or economic—and from whatever point of view within each type of analysis seems appropriate to the problem in hand. Within economics itself there are several different approaches to the study of the firm, and one type—the so-called 'theory of the firm'—continues to hold the field in spite of vigorous attacks; of all the approaches it is probably the most often misunderstood and misapplied by both its defenders and its attackers. (E. Penrose 1959/2009, 9)

At the time she was writing, economics was dominated by the neoclassical theory of the firm. Applied industrial economics and business studies, which did draw on a wider set of disciplines – in her 1984 lecture, Penrose approvingly cites sociology, institutional theory, behavioural psychology and business analytics – met with some resistance from within mainstream economic departments. Penrose recognised the methodological limitations of the dominant neoclassical theory and its methodological approach, but chose not to tackle that issue head on:

> Educated laymen as well as economists studying the vagaries of actual business behaviour often show an understandable impatience with the 'theory of the firm', for they see in it little that reflects the facts of life as they understand them. It is therefore worth a little trouble, perhaps, to discuss at the very beginning the nature of the 'firm' in the 'theory of the firm', to indicate why it provides an unsuitable framework for a theory of the growth of firms, but at the same time to make clear that we shall not be involved in any quarrel with the theory of the 'firm' as part of the theory of price and production, so long as it cultivates its own garden and we cultivate ours. Much confusion can arise from the careless assumption that when the term 'firm' is used in different contexts it always means the same thing. (E. Penrose 1959/2009, 2)

For Penrose, the term 'firm' was used to mean an actual firm; for mainstream economics, it meant something else. One explanation of why Penrose chose to sidestep, rather than engage in debate around the static, neoclassical theory of the firm is that it would no doubt have detracted from the development of her own theory, thereby contributing to a continued lack of pluralism. To use an expression of Keynes, it would have made the 'struggle to escape' existing modes of thought more difficult.[1]

For Penrose, the neoclassical theory of the firm was designed as a theory regarding prices and quantities ('their garden'), but was of limited use for other purposes. In particular, it did not address the more interesting and challenging question of how firms grow over time and why they grow at different rates. Distinguishing the different objectives of neoclassical theory and her own approach paved the way for Penrose to develop her own approach and theory without becoming engulfed in unnecessary arguments over the mainstream theory.

The second and third aspects of Penrose's methodological approach concern the way she handled rationality and complexity. For Penrose, the idea of a representative firm was a nonsense. Firms are not identical: they differ in important ways in terms of their resources, and over the way in which those resources are configured and utilised. Innovation, knowledge – especially firm-specific knowledge – and learning are part of this approach, as is path dependency. Moreover, managers do not necessarily share a single common motivational goal (e.g. profit maximisation or growth maximisation); rather, their objectives and decision-making behaviours will differ from one manager to another, and this therefore needs to be explicitly considered:

> In addition to the traditional approaches, there have been sporadic attempts to develop theories of the growth of firms using biological analogies and treating firms as organisms whose processes of growth are essentially the same as those of the living organisms of the natural world. There are many difficulties with this type of analysis, one of the most serious being the fact that human motivation and conscious human decision have no place in the process of growth. This alone, I believe, is sufficient ground for rejecting such theories of the growth of firms. All the evidence we have indicates that the growth of a firm is connected with attempts of a particular group of human beings to do something; nothing is gained and much is lost if this fact is not explicitly recognized. (Penrose, 1959, p. 2)

Penrose thus rejected biological analogies in *The Theory of the Growth of the Firm* as they preclude consideration of varieties of human motivation.

> The purpose of analogical reasoning in which we consciously and systematically apply the explanation of one series of events to another very different series of events is to help us better to understand the nature of the latter, which presumably is less well understood than the former. If the analogy has really helpful explanatory value, there must be some reason for believing that the two series of events have enough in common for the explanation of one, *mutatis mutandis*, to provide at least a partial explanation of the other. (Penrose, 1959, pp. 806–807)

Biological analogies applied to the growth processes of firms do not share sufficient common series of events to be helpful. Penrose wanted to incorporate complexity and diversity in firm behaviour and resources – something that is now being tackled using agent-based modelling and computer-based simulations.

3. Patents, large international firms, development, and policy

While Penrose is best known for her book *The Theory of the Growth of the Firm*, she also made major contributions to the analysis of patents, large international firms, and economic development, as well as having played a major role in shaping economic policy. As Michael Best and Elizabeth Garnsey have argued:

> Edith did not pursue the growth of the firm research agenda or lecture on related subjects. In fact she made little subsequent reference to her theory of the growth of the firm until writing and speaking invitations to do so poured in during the last years of her life. At LSE and SOAS her concerns focused on economic development. (Best and Garnsey, 1999, p. 199)

Prior to her book *The Theory of the Growth of the Firm*, Penrose worked on innovation and patents. In 1950 she co-authored a paper on patents with Fritz Machlup that provides a systematic account of the patent controversy in the nineteenth century – a controversy between those who were in favour of abolishing the patent system and those who wanted to preserve and/or extend the use of patents. The article is outstanding in its careful and precise marshalling of economic arguments on both sides of the debate, but what is more remarkable is that the paper shows that these economic arguments were set against a wider backdrop of social, legal and political arguments which allowed Machlup and Penrose to understand that the question of the patent controversy was not solved by academic arguments but by political arguments, 'propaganda' (to use their term) and legislation – the academic controversy died down once the political controversy was resolved, although we note that it has resurfaced in the era of COVID-19 and climate change. In other words, Penrose's analysis was very much in the tradition of political economy, and she recognised that economic problems do not exist outside of wider social and political controversies, influenced by a legal and institutional setting. In a later article (E. Penrose 1973) she addressed the questions of patents and economic development.

Her analysis both of large international firms (E. Penrose 1968) and of the oil industry was also conducted very much within a political economy approach, covering the impact of foreign investment by large international corporations in the oil industry on the economies of the low-income countries as well as issues related to competition, monopoly power, dumping, and unfair competition. She made a number of recommendations for policies regarding large international firms, designed to address the uneven spread of any potential benefits from foreign investment.

4. Overview of papers

The importance of Penrose's work, as indicated above, was the spur for crafting and launching an annual series of lectures at SOAS University of London on Penrose and her contributions to the academy as well as to the worlds of policy and practice. All this is described in the first article below, by Kofi Adjepong-Boateng and Christine Oughton on 'Professor Edith Penrose and the Penrose Lectures'. One of the lecturers who was not able to publish in this Special Issue was Professor Rita McGrath of Columbia Business School, and Adjepong-Boateng and Oughton therefore include a brief synopsis of the key points McGrath made in her Penrose lectures, on financialisation and the innovative capacity of firms, as well as on the implications of digitisation for firm growth.

The first substantive article in this Special Issue collection is by Professor Bronwyn Hall, one of the Penrose Lecturers, on 'Patents, Innovation, and Development' in which she surveys recent research on the role of patents in encouraging innovation and growth in developing economies, beginning with a brief history of international patent systems and facts about the current use of patents around the world. Hall discusses research on the implications of patents for international technology transfer and domestic innovation, and reports on her own work (with co-authors) on regional patent systems, and the impact of patents on firm performance, on pharmaceutical patenting, and on domestic innovation. Hall concludes that patents may be relatively unimportant in development, even for middle income countries.

Next, another of the Penrose Lecturers, Professor Mariana Mazzucato discusses 'Collective Value Creation: a new approach to stakeholder value', arguing that 'The corporate community has rediscovered an old idea: stakeholder value', and that the concept's history is rooted in the literature on varieties of capitalism. Within that scholarship, Mazzucato argues, the concept of stakeholder value has served to delineate institutional and relational differences between capitalist systems and forms of corporate governance, and is currently being used to argue for the redirection of capitalism to deliver on key goals related to inclusion and sustainability. In her paper, Mazzucato argues that the concept of stakeholder value – and the related endeavours to change capitalism – will remain weak unless it goes to the centre of how we create value. Moralistic exhortations to business leaders, Mazzucato argues, will not be enough to bring about a true stakeholder form of capitalism, for which we would need to have a stronger base in both theory and practice regarding how to restructure finance, production, and public-private partnerships in new ways that recognise the state's market-shaping role, and that would support an equitable distribution of value across stakeholders.

In 'Is the most unproductive firm the foundation of the most efficient economy? Penrosian learning confronts the neoclassical fallacy', William Lazonick – another of the Penrose Lecturers – argues that Edith Penrose's *The Theory of the Growth of the Firm* provides an intellectual foundation for a theory of innovative enterprise, which is essential to any attempt to explain productivity growth, employment opportunity, and income distribution. Penrose's theory of the firm is also, Lazonick argues, an antidote to the 'absurdity' that has been taught by economists to millions of college students for over seven decades that 'the most unproductive firm is the foundation of the most efficient economy'. The dissemination of this 'neoclassical fallacy' to a mass audience began, Lazonick goes on to argue, with Paul A. Samuelson's textbook, *Economics: An Introductory Analysis*, first published in 1948, following which this 'neoclassical fallacy' has persisted through eighteen revisions of Samuelson's *Economics* and in its countless 'economics principles' clones. Lazonick challenges the intellectual hegemony of neoclassical economics by exposing the illogic of its foundational assumptions about how a modern economy operates and performs, arguing that to get beyond the neoclassical fallacy, economists must be trained in a 'historical transformation' methodology that integrates history and theory, in which theory serves as both a distillation of what we have learned from the study of history and a guide to what we need to learn about reality as the 'present as history' unfolds.

In 'The story of flight', John Kay uses the history of commercial aviation – from the earliest attempts at flight to the modern civil aircraft – to illustrate the central role of the evolutionary progress of collective knowledge in what is loosely described as technical progress. No individual knows how to build an airbus – ten thousand people working together do. Kay's emphasis on collective intelligence as a means of solving problems builds on Penrose's insight that the firm is best viewed as a collection of capabilities, to develop a template for the modern corporation that recognises the development of 'capital as a service' and the importance of 'hollow corporations', franchises, and platforms in the twenty-first century economy.

Penrose's work on international oil firms is discussed by Damian Tobin in 'Captive markets and climate change: revisiting Edith Penrose's analysis of the international oil firms in the era of climate change', in which he argues that Edith Penrose's analysis of the investments of the international oil companies stemmed from her interest in the economics of the large international firm and its implications for developing economies. Tobin argues that Penrose's approach highlights the endogenous factors shaping the growth of the large firm, and cautions against viewing it as a neutral technocracy where investment automatically responds to price incentives. Drawing on Penrose's concept of a captive market in oil products, this research develops Penrose's ideas around motive, profit, self-financing and the international firm to explain why the institutional environment still favours investment in fossil fuels. Tobin reports on country and firm level data on investment and production in downstream petrochemical refining which show a connection between the captive market and the strategies of the large oil firms in expanding refining capacity as a strategic hedge against regulatory policies to limit climate change. This locks society into a carbon intensive infrastructure, reduces the motivation for investment, and adds to global CO_2 emissions. Tobin's findings indicate, he argues, that the oil companies need to take greater risks on green investments with their retained earnings, and that governments need to direct this investment towards socially useful purposes using coordinated regulatory pressure.

In 'Complementarities between product and process innovation and their effects on employment: a firm-level analysis of manufacturing firms in Colombia', Juana Paola Bustamante Izquierdo considers the effects of innovation on employment growth at the firm level using a framework that draws on Penrose's insight's regarding the importance of the availability of managerial and planning resources at the firm level.

In 'Penrose's theory of the firm in an era of globalisation', Chia Huay Lau and Jonathan Michie analyse the consulting engineering sector that in Edith Penrose's day operated almost exclusively domestically, and consider why firms in this sector are now increasingly operating internationally, and whether the factors identified – by Penrose and others – as causing firms to grow are also relevant to the expansion of these firms overseas. Their findings support Penrose's resource-based theory that unique strategic resources that are inimitable and non-substitutable can provide firms with competitive advantages, with internationalisation providing consulting engineering firms with opportunities to obtain different kinds of expertise and resources from other regions. With a larger pool of expertise to draw from, firms can develop their firm-specific strategic assets and technical advantages along the lines that Penrose suggested.

In 'Necessary and sufficient conditions for the absorptive capacity of firms that interact with universities', Júlio Eduardo Rohenkohl, Andreia Cunha da Rosa, Janaina Ruffoni and Orlando Martinelli consider firms that interact with universities in their search for external knowledge, aiming to identify the necessary and sufficient conditions for these firms to reach certain levels of absorptive capacity. They argue that their results are consistent with Penrose's theory of the firm, both as regards the importance to the firm of sourcing knowledge resources externally and then absorbing these resources successfully within the firm, and also as regards the diversity of firms when it comes to the managerial capabilities to deliver all this successfully.

In 'Profit rate dynamics in US manufacturing', Michael Joffe argues that Edith Penrose took agency, managerial capabilities, heterogeneity and open-endedness as characteristic of the economy, while neoclassical theory, in contrast, envisages convergence to a standard rate of return, invoking inter-industry capital flows and diminishing returns as the main mechanism. Joffe analyses data on US manufacturing for 1987 to 2015, finding that the features of the distribution confirm Penrose's view, while neoclassical theory fared poorly: the data did not support 'a standard rate of return', and there were no plausible macro shocks that could have produced the observed dispersion. Penrose's conception of heterogeneous managerial capacity, on the other hand, refers to a concept of economic power distinct from market power, corresponding to differential *ex ante* strength; differential profit outcomes represent *ex post* strength.

Irene Roele and Sonja Ruehl ask 'What is Edith Penrose's legacy for the theory of the firm?', and consider the continuing usefulness of Penrose's perspective for strategic management, from the point of view of the practitioner, the management educator and to the development of the academic field of strategic management. Roele and Ruehl draw on methods originating with Penrose's pioneering case study methodology by framing illustrative 'vignettes' or case examples for analysis and discussion, including that of Tesco, which draws on extensive participant observation as well as theory, concluding that:

> The business world has changed and will change in specific ways which Edith Penrose could not have foreseen but, nevertheless, her approach continues to be extended and remains applicable.

> Of continuing relevance are themes which Penrose explicitly foresees: that enterprises making better use of unused resources will be 'vast', that knowledge generation and organisational learning are key to firm survival and expansion and that ideas, imagination and willingness to experiment on the part of managements are continually required.

In 'Regulating stock buybacks: the $6.3 trillion question' Lenore Palladino and William Lazonick argue that 'shareholder primacy' as a theory of corporate governance is embedded in the neoclassical model of the firm, which lacks a theory of how corporations innovate over time as set out by Penrose. This is a problem because corporate resource allocation decisions shape business investment, income distribution, and productivity growth, with 'stock buybacks'--when a corporation repurchases its own shares on the open market--manipulating stock prices and enriching senior corporate executives and hedge fund managers. Palladino and Lazonick argue that the growing distribution of corporate funds to share-sellers via stock buybacks is a source of productivity fragility in the US economy, which requires policies to curb the excessive use of corporate funds on stock buybacks.

Finally, in 'The Life and Times of Edith Penrose', Michie reports on and discusses the biography of Edith Penrose, written by her daughter-in-law Angela Penrose. The book – and review article – cover many of the points made by the various authors referred to above regarding Penrose's contributions to theory and practice, and also much else besides regarding her personal life, which is equally impressive, from opposing fascism before the Second World War, then contributing greatly to the war effort in Britain, including by advising on how food rationing might best be organised, through to her courageous opposition to McCarthyism in the U.S., which led to her and her husband abandoning America and moving to Britain.

Note

1. Keynes wrote in the Preface to his *General Theory of Employment, Interest and Money* that 'The composition of this book has been for the author a long struggle of escape, and so must the reading of it be for most readers if the author's assault upon them is to be successful - a struggle of escape from habitual modes of thought

and expression. The ideas which are here expressed so laboriously are extremely simple and should be obvious. The difficulty lies, not in the new ideas, but in escaping from the old ones, which ramify, for those brought up as most of us have been, into every corner of our minds' (Keynes, 1936, p. viii).

Disclosure statement

No potential conflict of interest was reported by the author(s).

References

Best, M., and E. Garnsey. 1999. "Edith Penrose, 1914–1996." *The Economic Journal* 109 (453): 187–201. https://doi.org/10.1111/1468-0297.00408.

Keynes, J. M. 1936. *The General Theory of Employment, Interest and Money*. London: Macmillan.

Office for National Statistics. 2019. "Labour Productivity, UK: October to December 2019." *Statistical Bulletin* 1–13. https://www.ons.gov.uk/employmentandlabourmarket/peopleinwork/labourproductivity/bulletins/labourproductivity/januarytomarch2019.

Penrose, A. 2018. *No Ordinary Women: The Life of Edith Penrose*. Oxford: Oxford University Press.

Penrose, E. 1959/2009. *The Theory of the Growth of the Firm*. Oxford: Oxford University Press.

Penrose, E. 1960. "The Growth of the Firm—A Case Study: The Hercules Powder Company." *Business History Review* 34 (1): 1–23. https://doi.org/10.2307/3111776.

Penrose, E. 1968. *The Large International Firm in Developing Countries: The International Petroleum Industry*. London: George Allen and Unwin Ltd.

Penrose, E. 1973. "International Patenting and Less-Developed Countries." *The Economic Journal* 83 (331): 768–786. https://doi.org/10.2307/2230670.

8 OPEN ACCESS

Edith Penrose and the Penrose Lectures

Kofi Adjepong-Boateng and Christine Oughton

ABSTRACT
This article summarises Edith Penrose's career and impact on two disciplines - economics and management. The extent of her influence can be gauged by scanning the pages of leading publications in both fields, where copious references to Penrosian Theory, the Penrose Effect, the Penrosian Firm, Penrosian Analysis, the Penrosian Perspective, Penrosian Dynamics are standard. Penrose also played a major role in a variety of economics associations, policy bodies and government inquiries. This article considers the nature of her achievements and the fact that they are all the more remarkable for having been made at a time when economics was even more male dominated than it is today. Perhaps it is because she was a woman that her major contribution – The Theory of the Growth of the Firm - modelled firms as collections of people rather than as anonymous automata. We show how her contributions are honoured today via the annual Penrose Lectures; two lectures given each year at SOAS University of London, on a topic in economics, management or political economy. One of the objectives of the Penrose Lecture series is to showcase the work of leading women working in the fields of economics and management.

Academics seldom shape their discipline to the extent that their name becomes a byword for theory, practice and policy. Keynes is a noteworthy example, leaving a legacy of Keynesian economics and policy that shaped the international economic order, underpinned the golden age of economic growth, helped to create a central bank in India and led a US President to declare himself a 'Keynesian' in 1971.

Even fewer academics have achieved such acclaim across two disciplines. Edith Penrose, however, is one of them, her influence spanning the disciplines of economics and management. Her achievement is all the more remarkable given the lack of representation and recognition of women in economics, both then and now.

The absence of women in the economics profession has not gone unnoticed, at least by the *Financial Times* (FT), *The Economist* and other media outlets. Both (Coyle 2017) and (Tetlow 2018) have highlighted this problem in the *FT*. In her article, Gemma Tetlow

---

This is an Open Access article distributed under the terms of the Creative Commons Attribution License (http://creativecommons.org/licenses/by/4.0/), which permits unrestricted use, distribution, and reproduction in any medium, provided the original work is properly cited. The terms on which this article has been published allow the posting of the Accepted Manuscript in a repository by the author(s) or with their consent.

pointed out that in 2018 Elinor Ostrom was still the only woman at that time to have been awarded the Nobel Prize in Economics; and in 2019 Rachel Griffith, Professor of Economics at Manchester University, was only the second female president of the Royal Economic Society since its creation in 1890.

Moreover, a list of influential economists published in *The Economist* in 2014 attracted much attention, a fair bit of which was critical. One of the criticisms was the total absence of any women. In a more recent article in the same publication, it was argued that the gender problem in economics results in fewer ideas to benefit the discipline and the consequent disadvantage of a skewed point of view.

Writing in the New Statesman in 2017, as the winner of the (Weetman 2017) Virago/New Statesman Women's Prize for Politics and Economics, Weetman observed:

> Economics has a problem with women. I write this as a woman who has studied, worked in and is now writing about the subject. The data bears this out. Across the UK, just a quarter of undergraduate economics students are women. This is about the same proportion as the economics teaching and research academics at the University of Cambridge: by contrast, women make up 43 per cent of the Cambridge psychology faculty ... Where are all the women? Why does economics fail to attract women in the way that other social sciences do? ... Perhaps they are discouraged from joining the world of economics as it doesn't seem likely to reward them with career prospects. According to a 2014 paper by the economists Donna K Ginther and Shulamit Kahn, working with the psychologists Stephen J Ceci and Wendy M Williams, once you control for productivity (which they measured by the number of published research articles), men and women have the same promotional outcomes in most academic fields – but not in economics.

So, while progress has been made since Penrose's time, the problem remains and one of the aims of the Penrose Lectures, held annually at SOAS University of London, is to showcase the work of leading scholars in the fields of economics, management and political economy. To ensure that the work of women scholars is recognised appropriately, a founding principle of the Penrose Lectures is that at least half of the lectures should be given by women. The lectures have been supported by the *Financial Times* and ties in with their *Women in Economics, FT Collection*. To set the lectures and this special issue in context it is instructive to consider briefly the career and contribution of Edith Penrose, not just as a pioneering woman economist, but also as an outstanding and original theorist, thinker and contributor to academic and policy debates. Those interested in more detail will find Angela Penrose's (2018) biography of Edith Penrose invaluable; we draw on her biography and our discussions with Angela Penrose below.

After graduating with a degree in economics from the University of California at Berkeley, and completing her PhD in economics at John Hopkins University, Penrose held a joint Readership at two University of London Colleges – the London School of Economics and the School of Oriental and African Studies (SOAS), before becoming in 1964 the first woman to be appointed to a Chair in economics at SOAS.

Penrose worked in the field of economics until she retired from SOAS in 1978; yet her contribution is equally, if not more widely recognised by management scholars and practitioners. Indeed, after retiring from SOAS in 1978 she became Professor of Political Economy at INSEAD – one of the world's leading business schools (Penrose 2018).

Her best-known work, *The Theory of the Growth of the Firm*, was originally published in 1959, and remains in print to this day. The book probed inside the conventional 'black box' model of the firm to look at the way in which the combination and renewal of resources within firms shaped their growth. This analysis provided fertile ground upon which to sow new theories of firm behaviour, dynamic business performance and strategic management, leading to the development of the *resource-based view* of the firm and the approaches of *dynamic capabilities* in strategic management. Firms are important to our livelihoods by being the primary engine of economic growth and prosperity across nations. For this reason, an analysis of what drives the success of firms is of critical importance and it is what keeps Penrose's work relevant.

To gauge the extent of her impact in the fields of both economics and management, one need only scan the pages of leading publications in both fields, where copious references to *Penrosian Theory, the Penrose Effect, the Penrosian Firm, Penrosian Analysis, the Penrosian Perspective, Penrosian Dynamics*, and so on, are standard.

Penrose's work laid the foundation for a new general theory of the growth of firms. Rather than seeking to explain the optimal size and efficiency of firms, something that had preoccupied much of economic theory since Marshall, Penrose focused on a different question: why, faced with the same market conditions, do some firms grow while others stagnate? Her answer identified the key role of firms' managerial, or entrepreneurial capacity to create and renew the resources required to generate new products, new processes and new market demand.

Throughout her career, Penrose slipped easily between academia and policy, using her research to inform economic policy, political economy and wider humanitarian issues. She witnessed many major events of the 20th century, including the Depression in the US and the Second World War. During this, she worked as a special adviser to the US Ambassador in London, and on food planning with her husband in England and in Switzerland to help Jews escape from Germany. During the post-war reconstruction, she helped Eleanor Roosevelt with the drafting of the Universal Declaration of Human Rights; and lived through the oil crisis of the 1970s. Her work as an economist made its mark in several areas of which she had direct experience – the patent system, the theory of the firm, multinational enterprises, the oil industry, and the economics of the Middle East.

It is worth noting, too, that during her time at SOAS, as Visiting Professor at the University of Dar es Salaam in 1972, she participated in a sensitive mission to University College, Rhodesia where she openly expressed her contempt for the College's collusion with racial segregation.

Professor Penrose also held a number of positions outside academia, including membership of the UK Government Committee of Inquiry into the Relationship of the Pharmaceutical Industry with the National Health Service (the Sainsbury Committee) from 1965 to 1967 and the Medicines Commission in 1975–78. She was an advisor to the UK Monopolies Commission from 1968–1970 and also served on a variety of associations of economists: chairing the Economic Committee of the SSRC/ESRC from 1970 to 1976; on the Council of the Royal Economic Society from 1975 to 1980; as a Director of the Commonwealth Development Corporation from 1975 to 1978; and as a member of the Overseas Development Institute from 1992 to 1994.

Edith Penrose was a truly remarkable person and the Penrose Lectures were established in recognition of her work and legacy. Few women have had as distinguished and influential a career in economics as hers. She was influential in the affairs of many countries and her ground-breaking ideas in the fields of management, patents and petroleum, as well as her work as a writer, as a member of committees and as a university professor, all set her apart. The goal of the Penrose Lecture series is to bring her work and the work of many other outstanding economists and management scholars who have continued to expand on her thinking to a wider audience of faculty, students, practitioners and the general public. However, the lectures are not confined to Penrosian themes or to the work of Penrose, rather they celebrate her life's work in the areas of economics, management and political economy and can be on any topic in those fields.

The inaugural Penrose Lectures were given in 2018 by Professor Bronwyn H. Hall, one of the world's foremost authorities on R&D, innovation, patents, productivity and industrial policy. Professor Hall is Emerita Professor at the University of California at Berkeley, a Research Associate of the National Bureau of Economic Research and the Institute for Fiscal Studies, London, and a Visiting Fellow at NIESR, London. Hall's lecture covered her work on the economics and econometrics of technical change and innovation. She presented it in the context of Penrose's work on innovation as a source of a firm's profits and the enhancement of profitability through learning at firm level, partly through developing new applications of its current resources (Cantwell 2002). An article based on her Penrose Lectures is included in this Special Issue.

In 2019 the Penrose Lectures were given by Professor Rita McGrath a world-renowned leader of management theory and an expert on leading innovation and growth in times of uncertainty a professor at Columbia Business School. In her first lecture on 'Financialisation and the Innovative Capability of Firm', McGrath (2019a) highlighted the contemporary relevance of Penrose's analysis,

> "Penrose sounded an early warning in the 1995 introduction to *The Theory of the Growth of the Firm*. She expressed concern that we are now contemplating conditions in which corporate leaders 'may well be more interested in their own financial rake-offs through high salaries, stock options, golden handcuffs, bonuses, etc. than in the growth of their firms'. Financialisation undermines growth, both of firms and of the overall economy, in ways that are entirely predictable given Penrose's theory. Those in the financial sector find it more lucrative in the near term to invest in other financial assets or in assets (such as real estate, stocks and bonds) that already exist, not in the creation of new resources. Executives stand to earn more for themselves (and for shareholders) by extracting value from firms rather than investing in long-term capability building. And when incentives are to engage in financial engineering rather than entrepreneurial activity, it is no surprise that we get more of the former and less of the latter. Proposed remedies would do well to build on what Penrose has taught us.

McGrath's second lecture (McGrath 2019b), 'From Firms to Markets: How Digitisation is Changing our Theories of Firm Level Growth' considers the role of asset ownership in an era of digitalisation,

> Today, digitization has made it entirely possible for firms to grow without owning any assets to speak of. Instead, they utilize the services of assets owned by others. Penrose actually anticipated something like this – pointing out that it was not the resources of a firm that gave it an advantage but the 'services' executives extracted

from those resources. … Essentially, digital technologies have relaxed the constraints that more traditional firms operate under, creating an inflection point in the nature of what growth is possible and how we should understand the limits to firm growth.

In 2020 the lectures were not held due to COVID-19; instead, a Penrose Lectures Special Event Panel was held online with contributions from Angela Penrose, Kofi-Adjepong-Boateng, Jonathan Michie, Christine Oughton and William Lazonick. In 2021 Professor Mary O'Sullivan Professor Mary O'Sullivan delivered lectures on 'Profit, Power and Patents in Late 18th Century Capitalism', published in *Past and Present* (2023), and 'Capitalism and Crisis: the Real Problem of the Great Depression', published in *Economic History Review* (O'Sullivan 2022). The 2022 Lectures were given by Professor Mariana Mazzucato entitled 'From Market Fixing to Market Shaping' and 'A Challenge Led Approach to Industrial Strategy'. An article based on the lectures is included in this Special Issue. Professor William Lazonick gave the 2023–24 lectures on two inter-related themes, the first dealing with fundamental weaknesses in the neoclassical theory of the firm, and the second exposing the effects of shareholder value on innovation, sustainability, equity and growth. These issues are discussed in his article in this Special Issue.

Disclosure statement

No potential conflict of interest was reported by the author(s).

References

Cantwell, J. 2002. "Innovation, Profits and Growth: Penrose and Schumpeter." In *The Growth of the Firm: The Legacy of Edith Penrose*, edited by Christos Pitelis, 215–248. Oxford: Oxford University Press.

Coyle, D. 2017. "Economics Has a Problem with Women." *Financial Times*. Accessed August 28, 2017. https://www.ft.com/content/6b3cc8be-881e-11e7-afd2-74b8ecd34d3b.

McGrath, R. 2019a. "Financialisation and the Innovative Capability of Firm." *Penrose Lecture 1*. SOAS University of London

McGrath, R. 2019b. "From Firms to Markets: How Digitisation Is Changing Our Theories of Firm Level Growth." *Penrose Lecture 2*. SOAS University of London

O'Sullivan, M. 2021. "Machines in the Hands of Capitalists: Power and Profit in Late Eighteenth-Century Cornish Copper Mines." *Past and Present* 260 (1): 71–122. https://doi.org/10.1093/pastj/gtac039.

O'Sullivan, M. 2022. "History As Heresy: Unlearning the Lessons of Economic Orthodoxy." *The Economic History Review* 75 (2): 297–335. https://doi.org/10.1111/ehr.13117.

Penrose, A. 2018. *No Ordinary Woman: The Life of Edith Penrose*. Oxford: Oxford University Press Oxford.

Penrose, E. 1959. *The Theory of the Growth of the Firm*. 4th ed. Oxford: Oxford University Press.

Tetlow, G. 2018. "Where Are All the Female Economists." *Financial Times*. Accessed April 12, 2017. https://www.ft.com/content/0e5d27ba-2b61-11e8-9b4b-bc4b9f08f381.

Weetman, F. 2017. "Where Are All the Women Economists?" New Statesman. Accessed April 3, 2017. https://www.newstatesman.com/politics/feminism/2017/02/where-are-all-women-economists.

Patents, innovation, and development

Bronwyn H. Hall

ABSTRACT

I survey some recent research on the role of patents in encouraging innovation and growth in developing economies, beginning with a brief history of international patent systems and facts about the current use of patents around the world. I discuss research on the implications of patents for international technology transfer and domestic innovation. This is followed by a review of recent work by myself and co-authors on regional patent systems, the impact of patents on firm performance, and the impact on pharmaceutical patenting and domestic innovation. The conclusion suggests that patents may be relatively unimportant in development, even for middle income countries.

1. Introduction

In her 1951 thesis on the international patent system, Edith Penrose concluded with the following statement:[1]

> "Up to the present, the regime for the international protection of patent rights has been developed primarily in the interest of patentees. The gains to be derived from an extension of the patent system have been stressed, but the concomitant increase in social costs has been seriously neglected. So far as it goes, the International Convention has not been to any important extent incompatible with the best interests of the world economy. Nonetheless, the Convention in no way helps to alleviate the restrictions on trade and industrial activity which unregulated international patenting permits. A reconsideration of its provisions from this point of view is in order." (Penrose 1951, 233.)[2]

Since the time she wrote this passage, there has been an enormous growth of patenting around the world, some of it clearly coincidental with the development process, especially in East Asian countries (Fink, Khan, and Zhou 2016). However at the present time, if we replace the words 'International Convention' with 'TRIPS (The Agreement on Trade-Related Aspects of Intellectual Property Rights)', the uneven distribution of the benefits and costs suggested by this paragraph is as true as ever. Again in her 1973 *Economic Journal* article Penrose highlighted the disadvantages of a one-size-fits-all patent system for developing countries and many of her concerns remain valid today.

As a consequence of reservations similar to those expressed by Penrose, a large amount of research on the relationship between patents, innovation, and development has been produced over the past few decades, much of it empirical in nature. The conclusions from the theoretical literature on the choice of IP system are fairly clear: in the absence of any kind of coordinated action, more developed countries will have stronger IP protection than less developed (Grossman and Lai 2004; Angeles 2005). In addition, harmonization generally leads to levels of IP protection that are higher than the social optimum, at least in the less developed countries (Scotchmer 2004). As these models predict, the tendency is for IP protection strength to harmonize upward rather than downward. However, the theory is less clear about the consequences of different levels of IP protection for development. As Fink and Maskus stress in the introduction to their edited volume on the topic, ' . . . many effects of stronger IPR standards are theoretically ambiguous and thus need to be subjected to empirical analysis'. (Fink and Maskus 2005, 2)

Two additional edited books on the topic have recently been published: (Ann, Hall, and Lee 2014; Cimoli et al. 2014). It is worth noting that although the titles of these books contain the phrase 'intellectual property', the majority of the papers they contain concern patents rather than other forms of intellectual property. This reflects both data availability and the relative importance of patents in the thinking of many policymakers and firms. The present paper is no exception to this rule, although later on it will become obvious that the use of trademarks by domestic entities may be a more important form of IP in the course of development.

A patent system is one of the components of what is sometimes referred to as a 'national innovation system', although that term suggests a level of organized planning that does not characterize the performance of innovation in most countries (Nelson 1993). It is probably not the most important, as its primary function is to provide incentives for invention and possibly to promote the diffusion of knowledge.[3] Incentives are helpful but not sufficient without inventors so other factors such as the quality of the higher education system and basic research provision will matter. Translating new inventions into successful innovation requires financing (either a developed financial system or government-provided), the presence of demand for the innovation, and in many cases the development of new or improved infrastructure to support the use of the innovation.

Given the ample coverage of this broad topic in the volumes cited above, the present article offers a only a brief and selective review of what economists have learned about the relationship between the international patent systems and the development of economies during the decades since Penrose's work. The review is coupled with a more detailed look at the research output of three new empirical investigations by the author and her co-authors into the role of patents in middle-income economies: 1) What happens to patenting and innovation when middle-income countries join a regional patent system? (Hall and Helmers 2019); 2) Are patents and other IP related to firm performance in a rapidly developing economy? (Fink, Hall, and Helmers 2018, 2021); and 3) Do pharmaceutical patents in a middle-income country play a positive role in pharmaceutical innovation in that country? (Abud-Sittler, Hall, and Helmers 2015).

2. A brief patent primer[4]

Patents have a long history, although some of the earliest patents are simply the grant of a legal monopoly in a particular good rather than protection of an invention from imitation. Early examples of technology-related patents are Brunelleschi's patent on a boat designed to carry marble up the Arno River, issued by the Florentine government in 1421 (Prager 1946), the Venetian patent law of 1474 (Comino, Galasso, and Graziano 2017), and various patent monopolies granted by the English crown between the 15th and 17th centuries. The modern patent, which requires a working model or written description of an invention, dates from the 18th century, first in Britain (1718) and then in the United States (1790), followed closely by France (in both the latter two cases one of the consequences of a popular revolution).[5] Many other Continental European countries introduced patents during the 19th century, as did Japan (JPO, 2007) and India (James 2007). During the 20th century, the use of patent systems became almost universal and the signing of the TRIPS agreement has ensured that all countries who are members of the World Trade Organization will have at least a minimal level of patent protection.

In 1883 the Paris Convention for the Protection of Industrial Property guaranteed national treatment of patent applicants from any country that was a party to it. Its most important provision gave applicants who were nationals or residents of one member state the right to file an application in their own country and then, as long as an application was filed in another country that was a member of the treaty within a specified time (now 12 months) to have the date of filing in the home country count as the effective filing date in that other country (the 'priority date'). This is an important feature of the patent system, as it enables worldwide priority to be obtained for an invention originating in any one country, in addition to ensuring that in principle all inventors are treated equally by the system, regardless of the country from which they come.[6]

Although the process for granting a patent varies slightly according to the jurisdiction for which protection is desired, the adoption of the TRIPS agreement in 1995 ensures that it is approximately the same everywhere in the world. This agreement requires its member countries to make patent protection available for any product or process invention in any field of technology with only a few specified exceptions. It also requires them to make the term of protection available for not less than a period of 20 years from the date of filing the patent application. As of February 2020, 164 countries are signatories to this agreement and 28 countries are designated as 'observers'.

The World Intellectual Property Organization (WIPO) has even more (almost 200) member states and lists an equivalent number of national patent offices and industrial property offices on its website. In general, a patent right extends only within the border of the jurisdiction that has granted it (usually but not always a country). An important exception to this rule is the European system, where it is possible to file a patent application at the European Patent Office (EPO) that will become a set of national patent rights in several European countries at the time of issue (EPO, 2006). A similar situation exists with respect to the African Regional Intellectual Property Organization (ARIPO, with 19 African member states), the Organisation Africaine de la Propriété Intellectuelle (OAPI, with 17 Francophone African member states) and EAPO (Eurasian Patent Organization, with 9 member states from the former USSR).[7]

The Patent Cooperation Treaty (PCT) came into existence in 1978, and now has 153 countries as contracting signatories. Any resident or national of a contracting state of the PCT may file an international application under the PCT that specifies the office which should conduct the search. The PCT application serves as an application filed in each designated contracting state. However, in order to obtain patent protection in a particular state, a patent needs to be granted by that state to the claimed invention contained in the international application. The advantage of a PCT application is that fewer searches need to be conducted and the process is therefore less expensive. Thus, although application and search are to some extent standardized across offices, grants are not. In fact, 94% of the PCT applications go to one of five patent offices for search: those in Europe (35%), Japan (20%), China (19%), Korea (11%), and the United States (9%) (WIPO 2018). Most of the other systems rely on these offices for the search process and follow them in a number of other areas.

Patents are valuable only if they can be enforced and this fact has a number of implications for their use. First, the ability of the courts to reach the 'correct' verdict with respect to infringement and validity will matter; in situations or jurisdictions where there is a great deal of uncertainty about the outcome, and even if both parties agree as to the merits of the case, it may be worthwhile for one or both of them to pursue the issue further or in some cases, to reach a private financial settlement to avoid a random outcome in the courts.[8] Second, the costs of litigation will matter: parties with deep pockets can threaten those with less access to financial resources, or where the opportunity cost of devoting attention to a patent suit is high, as in small entrepreneurial firms (Lanjouw and Schankerman 2004). On the other hand, smaller parties with little to lose can also hold up firms with large sunk investments at risk (Hall and Ziedonis 2001; Lemley and Shapiro 2007; Shapiro 2010). Finally, the threat of litigation may discourage firms from even entering certain areas, thus providing a disincentive rather than an incentive for R&D. Lerner (1995) documented this phenomenon for biotechnology and Hall, Helmers, and Von Graevenitz (2020) for UK technology firms.

The degree to which these kinds of threats matter depends to a great extent on the costs and extent of litigation, both of which tend to be higher in the United States than in many other countries. However, there are signs that concerns about litigation cost have been increasing elsewhere, notably in Europe, where there has been active debate over the proposals to reduce enforcement costs by creating a supranational patent (the Unitary Patent) and patent court system. This Unified Patent Court was negotiated as an intergovernmental treaty in February 2013 by 25 EU member states, excluding Spain, Poland, and Croatia. At the time of writing, all conditions for its existence have been met, except for ratification by Germany.[9] However, in July 2020 the United Kingdom withdrew its ratification of April 2018, which has increased the uncertainty surrounding the introduction of the Unitary Patent.

3. Some facts

WIPO maintains a number of statistics that allow us to get a broad picture of patenting around the world. They collect the number of applications each year from the participating offices, distinguishing being those filed by residents and by non-residents; the

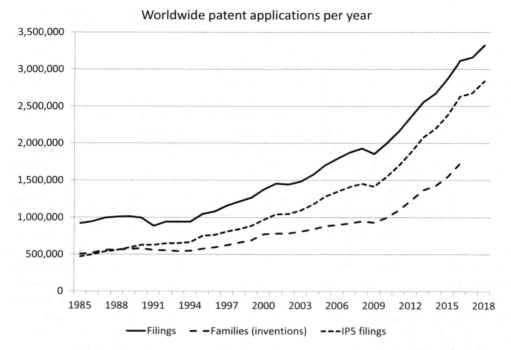

Figure 1. Worldwide patent applications per year. Source: Author's computations from WIPO statistics at http://www.wipo.int/ipstats/en/

latest year of data available is currently 2018. Figure 1 shows the trends during the past 3 decades in total filings, unique invention filings,[10] and filings at the top 5 IP Offices.[11] During this period, filings and invention filings have both more than tripled, while the filings at the top 5 offices have increased over five times.

Figure 2 shows that the primary reason for the large increase in top 5 filings is the growth of applications at SIPO (CNIPA) from a base of essentially zero to 1.6 million applications, although the US applications have also grown by a factor of six. Note that the Japanese data are somewhat noncomparable over time, due to the one claim per patent rule that was changed to allow multiple claims in 1988, leading to a slower growth rate in patenting at that office.

In principle, the separation of application counts into those from residents and non-residents allows an examination of the extent to which a country's patent system benefits local inventors. However, these statistics count an applicant that is a subsidiary of a multinational corporation with a local address as a resident of the country, so they are not really suitable for evaluation of the patenting behavior from local firms. An alternative is to count the filings from inventors resident in the country, but this number is not easily available in aggregate form from the WIPO statistics.

Figure 3 attempts to give some insight into domestic patenting shares around the world, but it also reveals these difficulties in counting local applications. It shows the PPP-adjusted real GDP per capita in 2011 US$ versus the resident share of patent filings in 2017. European countries tend to have high resident shares, reflecting the pattern of US, Japanese, and other multinationals to apply from their European subsidiaries. In

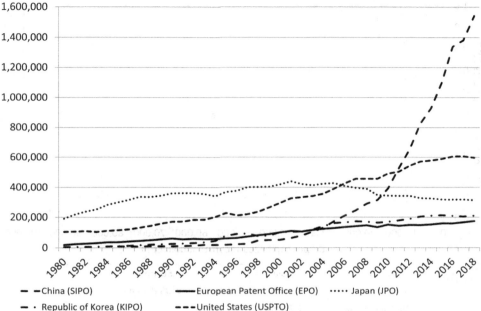

Figure 2. Patent applications at the top 5 IP Offices. Source: Author's computations from WIPO statistics at http://www.wipo.int/ipstats/en/

contrast, the Latin American countries tend to receive many more applications from abroad. Within Europe, Israel and Malta have much lower resident shares, whereas within Asia, China, Japan, and South Korea have much higher resident shares than the other Asian countries. Simple descriptive regressions of the resident share on population and GDP and region dummies show that the variation in resident shares is dominated by regional effects. These regressions also show that controlling for GDP and population, resident shares for all other regions are much lower than those in Europe and that Latin America and Oceania have the lowest resident shares.

A final point about the use of IP around the world is that essentially all IP royalties are received by high-income countries, and most are paid by the same countries. Figure 4, drawn from Neubig and Wunsch-Vincent (2017), shows the shares paid by and received by countries at various levels of development. Note that the middle-income share of payments has increased from 9% to the 16% shown since 1991, due both to their increasing share of worldwide income and the increasing use of multinational patents to secure revenue in those countries.

4. Patents and innovation

A longstanding question in the economics of patents is whether the existence of a patent system is beneficial for innovation. A large body of work has explored this question and a few conclusions have emerged. First, introducing or strengthening a patent system (lengthening the patent term, broadening subject matter coverage or

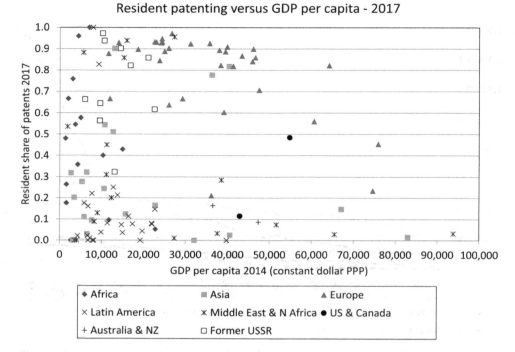

Figure 3. Resident patenting versus GDP per capita - 2017. Source: Author's computations; Penn World Tables9.1 (Feenstra, Inklaar, and Timmer 2015); WIPO statistics

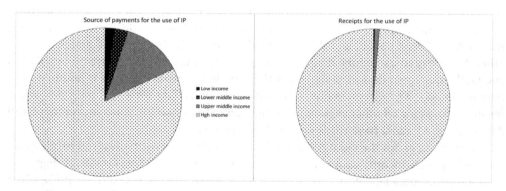

Figure 4. Charges for the use of IP by country income class. Source: Neubig and Wunsch-Vincent (WIPO), based on World Development Indicators, updated 02/01/2017

available scope, improving enforcement) unambiguously results in an increase in patenting and also in the use of patents as a tool of firm strategy (Lerner 2002; Hall and Ziedonis 2001). Second, it is much less clear that these changes result in an increase in innovative activity (Lerner 2002), although they may redirect such activity toward things that are patentable and away from those that can be kept secret within the firm (Moser 2005).

A third finding from the empirical literature is that if there is a beneficial effect on innovation from patents, it is likely to be centered in the pharmaceutical, biotechnology, and medical instrument areas, and possibly specialty chemicals. This conclusion relies mostly on survey evidence from a number of countries which shows rather conclusively that patents are not among the important means to appropriate returns to innovation, except in such industries (Mansfield, 1986; Levin et al., 1987; Cohen, Nelson, and Walsh 2000; Arora et al., 2001). One plausible explanation for this finding is that chemicals naturally lend themselves to clear codification due to the widely accepted system of notation for chemical compounds. This is obviously somewhat an oversimplification, as many patents in these areas do not rely exclusively on a chemical formula, but broadly speaking this fact does make such patents clearer as to their boundaries and somewhat easier to enforce.

Fourth, the relationship between the strength of a domestic patent system and domestic innovation activity may be U-shaped, with domestic innovation falling at first as patent rights are strengthened, and then rising again for developed economies with high levels of the patent rights index.

Fifth and finally, the existence and strength of the patent system affects the organization of industry, by allowing trade in knowledge and technology, which facilitates the vertical disintegration of knowledge-based industries and the entry of new firms that possess only intangible assets (Hall and Ziedonis 2001; Arora and Merges, 2004). The argument is that, by creating a strong property right for the intangible asset, the patent system enables activities that formerly had to be kept within the firm because of secrecy and contracting problems to move out into separate entities. Although limited, research in this area supports this conclusion in the chemical and semiconductor industries.

A separate line of research has noted that patents may also facilitate the suppression of new technology because they can be used by incumbents to prevent the emergence of new technological solutions that threaten the incumbent's profits (Gilbert and Newberry 1982; Gilbert 1987). Such patents are referred to as 'sleeping patents' and may be obtained through acquisition of a new entrant as well as simply taken out by the incumbent firm itself. Several examples of technology suppression are given by Saunders and Levine (2004). Torrisi et al. (2016) documents the importance of strategic reasons in leaving patents unused, finding that this behavior is more prevalent in large firms with large patent portfolios.

5. Patents, innovation, and development

Historically patent systems have developed in response to a perceived need by governments and inventors to protect their creative and inventive endeavors. In the early days they were often a method of patronage that costs the ruler little but benefitted those he or she wished to reward. In other cases, they were designed to attract craftsmen to a particular city or region (Machlup and Penrose 1950; David 1994; Moser 2013). After the French and American revolutions, patent systems democratized – no longer the prerogative of a king or ruler, now anyone with an invention could apply to have the right to exclude others from practicing it.

Nevertheless, the timing of patent system introduction and/or strengthening does seem to have been coincident or even after industrial development rather than preceding it. E.g. in the 18th and 19th century UK, Mokyr (2009) expresses skepticism that patents were essential during the industrial revolution given the costly features of the system and the fact that a number of successful inventors made no use of it. US industrial development during the 19th century does seem to have benefitted from patents, although this development took place prior to the international patent harmonization of the Paris Convention and US inventors probably found the route to a patent easier than foreign inventors. A modern day example is China, which introduced its current patent system seven years after Deng Xiaoping adopted the Open Door Policy in 1978, amended it several times during the next two decades, and then revised it comprehensively as part of the National Intellectual Property Strategy in 2008.[12] This revision recognized the fact that imitation was no longer a viable strategy as China moved to the technology frontier in some areas. Thanks to TRIPS, in many countries the sequencing of development via first imitating and then instituting stronger patent systems is no longer possible, raising again the question of whether the one-size-fits-all approach is ideal for development and innovation in developing countries.

How do developing countries catch up? That is, what are the ways they can learn in order to close the knowledge gap? One channel is clearly the mobility of research and other skilled workers, as well as public resources such as scientific journals, the internet, and international patents. None of this is greatly affected by the presence of a domestic patent system. A second channel is the purchase of investment goods embodying new innovations, imitation and reverse engineering, licensing of patented technologies and technology information from foreign innovators, direct technology transfer by multinational corporations to their subsidiaries, and potential spillovers from those subsidiaries to domestic firms. This latter channel will be sensitive to the presence of a functioning domestic patent system.

Willingness to transfer technology in the form of investment goods, licensing, and knowhow to both domestic firms and multinational subsidiaries is likely to be affected by the protection offered by the local patent system, whereas learning by imitation and the acquisition of technology spillovers by local firms may be inhibited by the use of the patent system by those generating spillovers. This line of reasoning suggests that there are at least two separate but related questions whose answers may be somewhat at odds with each other when considering patent policy. The first is whether stronger patent protection in a host country encourages technology transfer to that country. In particular, how does the presence of patent protection affect the behavior of foreign firms that may potentially invest in the country, sell technology to firms in the country, or form joint ventures with domestic firms? The second question is whether stronger patent protection encourages technology development in the country itself. That is, how does it affect the behavior of domestic firms? The first question has been easier to answer but the second is probably more important for the economic development of the country in question.

With respect to the first question, *a priori* it seems clear that stronger IP protection in the host country should encourage (or at least not discourage) the transfer of technology by foreign firms to their subsidiaries and possibly to domestic firms, either via partnership or simple sale or licensing. Note that this argument presumes that the intellectual property rights are enforceable, which is not an innocuous assumption. Also, note that such transfer may or may not help the local development of innovation skills and human capital. With respect to the second question, it also seems clear that stronger IP protection could encourage the innovative activities of domestic firms, but that such protection could also discourage learning via imitation and therefore inhibit technological catch-up. Thus the impact of IP systems on technological development is ambiguous and requires further investigation.

5.1. Technology transfer and the patent system

International technology transfer typically takes place via trade, foreign direct investment, joint ventures with local partners, or simple technology licensing, although in the latter case, some tacit knowledge probably also needs to be transferred. In all of these cases, foreign firms run the risk that imitation by local firms may erode some of their profits from these activities, so the presence of enforceable IPRs should encourage all these activities. In fact, Edith Penrose goes as far as to argue that for developing countries 'the only economic advantages to be gained from granting foreign patents lies in the possibility that in one way or another such grants will induce the introduction of foreign technology and capital' (Penrose 1973, 770). Obviously, in the cases of more advanced technology, the imitation risk is highest when the host country has the capacity to adopt and develop such technology, which implies that the risk is generally greater in middle-income countries than in low-income countries. This risk is further increased, if technologies require local adaptation in order to fit local needs and regulatory requirements and standards. At the same time, if IPR protection is strong, foreign firms may prefer to license technologies instead of choosing to be a local presence, which could decrease the amount of technology transferred, or cause the transferred technology to be far from the frontier. This decision may also be influenced by the ability of foreign firms to enforce licensing contracts. However, it is also conceivable that stronger IPRs increase the incentives for firms to exploit IPRs themselves instead of licensing out. It is likely that these relationships differ by industry and type of activity, i.e. manufacturing or distribution.

There is some empirical evidence on the trade effects of strengthening IP laws, which suggests that they do indeed have an impact. For example, Maskus and Penubarti (1995) show that increasing patent protection had a positive impact on manufacturing imports into developing countries, an impact that was larger for the larger of these countries. Ivus (2010) used data on exports from developed to developing countries over the period that TRIPS was introduced to show that strengthening patent rights increased high-tech exports to developing countries by about 9%.

In Hall (2014), I reviewed the empirical literature on the relationship between patent systems and technology transfer via trade, foreign direct investment (FDI), and technology licensing.[13] The trade literature suggested that the strength of country's IP system did affect the willingness of developed countries to export manufacturing goods to that country, especially if the country in question had imitative capacity. The FDI literature, which is older and more voluminous, found a positive correlation between FDI and domestic patenting by MNCs as well as a correlation of FDI with the strength of IPR enforcement. See also Braga and Fink 1998, Branstetter et al. (2006), and Yank and Maskus (2009).

Looking specifically at foreign investment in R&D, Thursby and Thursby (2006) surveyed 200 R&D managers from Western European and US multinationals, asking about the factors affecting their choice of location for a new laboratory, distinguishing between location in developed and emerging economies. The most important factor in an emerging economy was its growth potential. However, they found that good IP protection was important in both types of country, ranking only slightly below the factor with the highest importance, the availability of qualified R&D personnel. This result certainly suggests that IPRs will facilitate some technology transfers to middle-income countries.

In summary, the literature indicates a positive correlation between FDI and the level of IPR enforcement. Considering the extensive evidence on FDI serving as a channel for technology transfer, this implies a positive relation between IPR enforcement and technology transfer through the channel of FDI. However, the literature also points to other important factors in attracting FDI, such as country risk and the availability of low-cost high-skilled labor. It also generally emphasizes the importance of absorptive capacity in whether patents will affect technology transfer. That is, if there is no ability to imitate in the destination country, patents will not matter as much to the firm deciding on investment strategies in that country.

5.2. Domestic innovation and the patent system

The results on IP and technology transfer seem sensible and consistent with a priori intuition. However, as suggested earlier, the more important question for policy is the question of the impact of strengthened IPRs on innovation and development within a developing country. Does stronger patent protection help to enable and increase that country's own innovative capacity? This question has been approached empirically by economists in two different ways: looking at the relationship between IP and innovation across countries, as described earlier, and using individual country case studies of changes in patent law. For example, Kim (2003) argues that the Korean case shows that strong IPR protection in earlier stages of industrialization can hinder learning via imitation (see also Lee and Kim 2010). Kumar (2003) reviews the historical relationship between IPRs, technology, and development in East Asia and concludes that 'Japan, Korea, and Taiwan have absorbed substantial amount of technological learning under weak IPR protection regimes during the early phases'. (Kumar 2003: 217).

There is a good-sized literature on patents or IP and economic growth using cross-country regression, pioneered by Ginarte and Park (1997). Gold, Morin, and Shadeed (2017) review the results from this line of research, finding them somewhat inconsistent, especially as concerns the variation in the relationship with the country's income level. As they suggest, some of this inconsistency can be due to the use of different models and data choices, and they construct a new IP index that is sensitive to the many changes induced by TRIPS. They then advance the interesting hypothesis that the IP-growth association is due to a placebo effect: foreign investors believe that IP strength is good for their investment so when they see it increase, they increase their investment even though there is no actual impact of IP strength on the investment success. This hypothesis is supported by their evidence that the impact of IP-intensive imports on growth is many times that of the effect of IP on growth through domestic inventive activity (US patent applications from the country) in lower and upper middle-income countries, controlling for the strength of IP. They also find that the attractiveness of a country as a PCT destination is not related to growth, in the presence of their IP strength index. Although it is not possible to truly test for the placebo effect, the finding that technology transfer rather than domestic invention is more induced by IP strength seems consistent with what other researchers have observed.

6. Recent research on patenting in middle income countries

I now turn to a closer look at what we have learned from recent research on the strengthening of patent systems in middle-income countries, some of which has been TRIPS-induced. Research by my co-authors and myself has looked at the introduction of a broad regional system in the presence of existing national systems, the impact on firm performance from the introduction of a reformed patent system, and finally on the specific impact of patents on pharmaceutical innovation and patenting in developing countries.

6.1. Regional patent systems[14]

Operating a patent system that does full search and examination is an expensive undertaking, and may not be the best use of government spending in many countries. The PCT system described earlier is a partial solution to this problem. In addition, there are a number of regional patent systems that serve more than one country, such as the Organisation Africaine de la Propriété Intellectuelle (OAPI) for French-speaking Africa, the African Regional Intellectual Property Organization (ARIPO) for English-speaking Africa, and the Eurasian Patent Organization (EAPO) for Russia and the former Soviet republics. The most important regional system is undoubtedly the European Patent Convention (EPC), covering about 40 European countries, Do such systems reduce patenting costs for their participants? Do they induce more patentable invention?

Hall and Helmers (2019) explored these questions in a study of accession to the European Patent Convention (EPC) by a number of mostly Eastern European countries during the 2000–2008 period. We looked at changes in patenting behavior around the time of accession by non-residents, residents, and the inventors and firms resident in the country.

The EPC was created in 1977 with 7 countries; it now has 41 contracting states and 6 countries as extension states that allow validation of European patents in their country.[15] The applicant makes a single application to the European Patent Office (EPO), designating the states in which the patent might be validated. After grant, the patent must be validated (and renewal fees paid) in every state for which coverage is desired. Enforcement takes place in national courts.[16] In principle, obtaining a European patent is lower cost than applying at each national office if coverage is desired in more than one or two countries. Other regional systems also use this model.

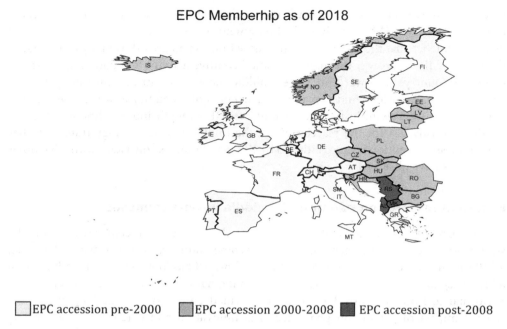

Figure 5. EPC Membership as of 2018

The 14 countries we studied are shown in gray in Figure 5. With the exception of Norway and Iceland, they are classed as middle-income countries, in contrast to most of the other members of the EPC, which are high income. Using patent data at the EPO and at the national offices of the 14 countries, we examined the changes in patent application strategies in these countries and at the EPO around the time of accession to the EPC. We also looked at any changes in FDI in the countries in response to accession.

Our findings were that resident applicants hardly respond to accession, in the sense that they continue to apply to their national office, only occasionally adding an application to the EPO. There was a small response via increased EPO patenting by inventors resident in the countries. In contrast, non-resident applicants respond strongly to accession, as one might have expected, immediately switching their patent applications to the EPO. However, there was little visible change in the willingness of foreign firms to invest in the country, although overall there was growth in FDI before and after accession. We cautioned that the accession of Eastern European countries may be a special case, because many of these countries were in the process of joining the EU at the same time, and investment may have been responding to this fact.

The main conclusion from this study was that non-resident applicants and inventors benefitted from a reduction in the cost of obtaining broader coverage, but that resident inventors were affected very little by the shift. This suggests that they may not have viewed their inventions as valuable or novel enough to justify the expense of dealing with a remote office in a different language.[17] Nevertheless, given the fact that non-resident applicants outnumber residents by approximately threefold, there was a substantial reduction in the costs born by the national offices, as these applicants shifted their applications, which may be by itself a benefit to the country in question.

6.2. Study of Chilean IP use and firm performance[18]

How do firms in a rapidly developing country make use of IP and does it impact their performance? Fink, Hall, and Helmers (2021) looked at this question using a comprehensive panel of Chilean manufacturing firms and their IP holdings. Chile is an interesting case because of its relatively rapid growth after the end of the military dictatorship in 1989, when it transitioned from a middle- to high-income country by the World Bank definitions. Among other changes, this transition to democracy was closely followed by the introduction of a new intellectual property system. In the mid-1980s, 70 countries had a higher real GDP per capita than Chile, whereas by 2014, there were only 57 such countries (see Figure 6). In 2010, Chile became the first South American member of the OECD.

Because Chile introduced a new IP system and joined the Paris convention in 1990/1991, it is useful to study how these changes impacted firms in Chile. Therefore, a joint project of WIPO and INAPI (Chilean National Institute of Industrial Property) was undertaken to construct a dataset combining Chilean patents, trademarks, and design rights between 1991 and 2010, the ENIA manufacturing census 1995–2005, and the Innovacion surveys 1997–1998, 2000–2001, 2003–2010 (Abud Sittler et al. 2013). In Fink, Hall, and Helmers (2021), we used these data to look at whether there was any impact on firm growth or productivity following their first time using the IP system. Because we do not have manufacturing sector data prior to 1991, it is not possible to treat the introduction of the new IP system as a natural experiment, analyzing firm behavior before and after its introduction. In any case, given all the other changes to the macro-economy at

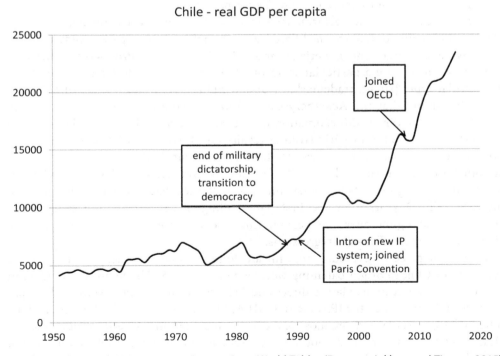

Figure 6. Chilean real GDP per capita. Source: Penn World Tables (Feenstra, Inklaar, and Timmer 2015)

the same time, this would not be a useful procedure. Our approach is to compare firms that use the system for the first time some time post 1991 to those that do not use it during the 1991–2005 period. Obviously, this does not remove all concerns about endogeneity of use, but it still turns out to be somewhat revealing.

The most striking thing in these data from our first look was that most Chilean patents are filed by non-residents (~90% over the 1990–2010 period), whereas the majority of trademarks are filed by local applicants (~70% over the same period). This finding suggests that even in middle-income countries, the first consequence of aligning a patent system to international standards is that it facilitates the extension of patent protection by multinationals, rather than inducing indigenous patentable innovation. In contrast to patents, trademarks in many cases require only distinctness within the country in which they are registered, so may be easier for domestic firms to obtain and will provide some protection against imitation of innovative products that are not eligible for patent protection. Note also that Chile does not have a use requirement for trademarks, which has led to considerable 'squatting' by domestic entities on internationally known trademarks (Fink, Helmers, and Ponce 2018).

We found that the determinants of both patent and trademark use are similar to those in developing countries (Hall et al. 2013 for the UK; Balasubramanian and Sivadasan 2011; Arora, Bei, and Cohen 2016 for the US). Firm size (in terms of employees), market share, whether it exports, and being located in the Santiago metropolitan area were positively associated with both. Controlling for these variables, foreign owned firms were more likely to patent and less likely to trademark than domestic firms, consistent with the aggregate statistics, and publicly (government) owned firms do not trademark much, although they are slightly more likely to file for patents.

We then examined the performance impact of first time IP use during the 1995–2005 period, using difference-in-difference methodology to compare revenue, inputs (employment, capital, and materials), and TFP (Total Factor Productivity) between those who do not use a particular form of IP and those who file for their first IP of a particular type (patent, trademark, or design right). We used a variety of estimates for TFP, finding that the Ackerberg-Caves-Frazier method was preferred, although the results of the diff-in-diff estimation did not depend strongly on the choice of the TFP estimator. We found fairly striking results for all types of IP: the 'treated' firms grew faster both before and after first time IP use, but TFP was unaffected by the adoption of IP. We show the results for patents graphically in Figure 7. There is substantial firm growth before first-time use that then flattens out, with a hint of increased TFP 2 years after the first patent filing. Because patenting samples are small, and changing over the period, this rise did not translate into anything significant in the diff-in-diff regressions.

As a final piece of evidence on Chilean domestic inventive activity, I show the evolution of Chilean origin patenting worldwide in Figure 8. The figure shows Chilean origin patent applications via the direct and PCT route, at all offices worldwide, separately for INAPI (Chile), the IP5 offices (CNIPA, EPO, JPO, KIPO, and USPTO), and the other offices, most of which are those of the higher income Latin American countries. It is clear that Chilean inventors do not file internationally in any appreciable numbers until quite late in our sample, around 2002, 10 years after the country joined the Paris

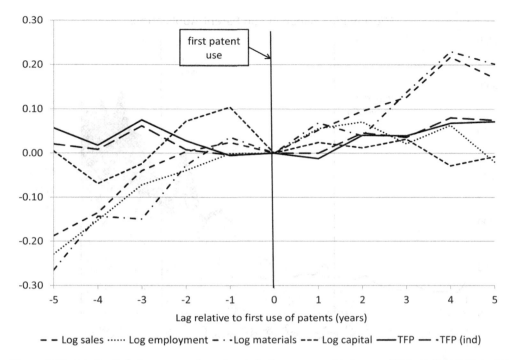

Figure 7. Trends for first-time users of patents (relative to controls). Source: (Fink, Hall, and Helmers 2021).

Convention. This suggests that there can be a considerable lag between the introduction or strengthening of an existing patent system and its effects on domestic invention, which in turn helps to explain why we frequently do not see any impact in short panels.

Our conclusions from this study of IP use by Chilean firms can be divided into two parts: those that represent differences from most developed countries, and those that are the same. The differences from the use of patents in high-income countries are that most patents come from outside the country and that foreign-owned firms are much less likely to do R&D in the country. The similarities to developed countries are that there is heavy trademark use by domestic firms and individuals, and the relationship of R&D and innovation to firm characteristics is very similar, even though the absolute levels are lower (Abud Sittler et al. 2013; Fink, Hall, and Helmers 2018).

6.3. Patents and pharmaceutical innovation in Chile[19]

Much of the debate over the role of patents in developing countries has centered on their use in covering pharmaceutical innovations. The weight of evidence in developed economies suggests that these patents are the most valuable for firms (Hall, Jaffe, and Trajtenberg 2005, Arora, Ceccagnoli, and Cohen 2008) and the most highly valued by managers (Cohen, Nelson, and Walsh 2000). Correspondingly, this technology is often the technology where multinationals choose to extend their patenting activity into developing countries, inhibiting the development of cheaper generic alternatives in

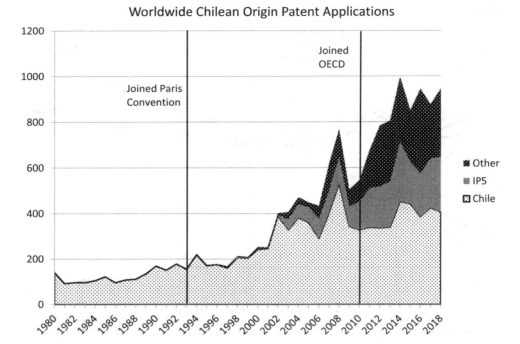

Figure 8. Worldwide Chilean Origin Patent Applications. Source: http://www3.wipo.int/ipstats/

those countries that have the relevant technological capacity (Lanjouw 1997; Scherer and Weisburst 1995). It is also often argued that patent protection in developing countries has the benefit of inducing research into neglected diseases.

The primary justification for the use of patents to protect pharmaceutical product innovations has been the need for firms to recoup the high costs of new pharmaceutical development in the presence of relatively low imitation costs. But many have questioned whether such a system is the best way to ensure that a socially optimal mix of pharmaceuticals is provided. For example, public health considerations may favor vaccine development whereas private incentives may tilt research toward drugs that must be taken over a lifetime, such as blood pressure medication. In addition, patent protection can reduce access to lifesaving drugs by low-income populations, given the quasi-monopolist incentive to restrict output by raising price above marginal cost. For this reason, many economists point to other mechanisms for ensuring access to pharmaceuticals such as patent buyouts or prizes for desirable innovations (Kremer 1998; Stiglitz and Jayadev 2010). Recent highly publicized epidemic diseases (AIDS, Ebola, and Covid-19) have increased the demand for drug and vaccine access and led to a number of policies such as shared patent pools, compulsory licensing, or guaranteed purchase designed to ensure that research is sufficiently funded and that lower income populations have access to treatment and prevention. But for most diseases patents remain the workhorse for eliciting R&D on potential treatments.

Given the often contentious debate around this topic, which affects the health of so many, it is not surprising that a vast amount of research time has been devoted to it. I discuss a few of the recent empirical papers here. The key questions addressed are whether pharmaceutical patent availability increases pharmaceutical innovation, especially for neglected diseases, and whether such availability speeds up the diffusion of drugs to less developed countries from those where they were first introduced. In general, the focus is on pharmaceutical product patents (rather than process patents), because the former were frequently not permitted in a number of countries before TRIPS, whereas the latter were more frequently allowed.

Qian (2007) looks at a broad range of countries over the 1978–2002 period, examining whether R&D or US patenting increases in the country after product pharmaceutical patent introduction. She uses a sample of 26 such countries matched to controls by GDP, population, education level, IPR strength, legal origin, and previous pharmaceutical industry strength. Regardless of whether the country previously allowed process patents, she finds no increase in domestic R&D or US patent filings from product patent introduction except at higher levels of GDP per capita. Kyle and McGahan (2009) exploit the variation in timing of the TRIPS introduction of pharmaceutical product patents, 1990–2006. They associate patents to drugs for particular diseases and find a strong association between the introduction of pharmaceutical patents and R&D effort for diseases that are prevalent in high-income countries, but no association for the 'neglected' diseases prevalent in low-income countries. Thus both these papers are unable to find positive innovation impacts for developing countries from the introduction of pharmaceutical patents.

In contrast, Arora, Branstetter, and Chatterjee (2008) provide one counter example. They find that existing strength in pharmaceutical R&D in local firms that previously produced generic drugs facilitated a positive R&D response to the introduction of product patent via TRIPS in India. This highlights the importance of prior technological competencies in allowing a country to benefit from the introduction of patents.

Turning to the diffusion of drugs that already exist in developed countries, the results are more positive. Cockburn, Lanjouw, and Schankerman (2016) examine 642 new drugs launched in 76 countries during the 1983–2002 period. They find that price regulation delays the launch of such drugs, increasing the diffusion lag by 25% to 80%. Longer and stronger product patents speed up launch, with long patents (those with lifetimes 18 years or longer) reducing the lag by 55%. The results for process patents are more ambiguous – although generally positive for launch, whether the term of process patents increases launch probability depends on the correction for endogeneity of the policy variables. Their results are similar for countries at all income levels.

Kyle and Qian (2014) compare 716 drugs pre – and post – TRIPS compliance in 59 countries in the 2000–2011 period. Like Cockburn et al., they find that patent protection speeds launch, and also that it increases both the price and the quantity of the drug sold. Price discrimination across countries does not depend on whether the drug is covered by a patent, but the price premium for patented drugs declines after compliance with TRIPS. They suggest that policies to mitigate the impact of TRIPS in developing countries, such as price controls, may be responsible for this effect.

Our paper (Abud Sittler, Hall, and Helmers 2015) focuses on a current policy debate in the pharmaceutical patenting area: whether firms are able to extend the patent life of drugs using secondary patents and how this strategy impacts less developed countries. Secondary patents are those on alternate formulations of the drug or on variations in methods of administration. A number of developing contrives have restricted or considered restricting their use.[20] In the unsuccessful negotiations over the Trans Pacific

Partnership a critical issue was patentability of new uses or methods of using a known product and the 'enhanced efficacy of a known product' threshold (Article QQ.E.1). In our paper, we looked at whether foreign pharmaceutical firms use strategic patenting behavior to keep domestic generic producers off the market in Chile. That is, how is entry into the manufacture of drugs for specific therapeutic categories affected by the presence of foreign pharmaceutical patents? Do secondary patents delay entry by Chilean firms into drug production? What is the share of patents held by foreign pharmaceutical companies associated with drugs commercialized on the domestic market?

This debate is encapsulated by the following anonymous quotes by a pharmaceutical company and generic producer in an EU Commission (2009) report on secondary patenting:

"We were recently successful in asserting the crystalline form patent in [name of country], where we obtained an injunction against several generic companies based on these patents by 'trapping' the generics: they either infringe our crystalline form patent, or they infringe our amorphous form process patent when they convert the crystalline form to the amorphous form." *An anonymous pharmaceutical company, EC (2009), p. 189.*

"The entire point of the patenting strategy adopted by many originators is to remove legal certainty. The strategy is to file as many patents as possible on all areas of the drug and create a 'minefield' for the generic to navigate. All generics know that very few patents in that larger group will be valid and infringed by the product they propose to make, but it is impossible to be certain prior to launch that your product will not infringe and you will not be the subject of an interim injunction." *An anonymous generic producer, EC (2009), p. 196.*

There is some prior empirical evidence on secondary patents. The same European Commission study found a primary to secondary patent ratio of 1:7, with a pending patent radio of 1:13, and a granted patent radio of 1:5. There were disproportionately more secondary patents after product launch, suggesting that successful drugs garnered more such patents, not surprisingly. Kapczynski et al. (2012) investigated the type of secondary patents associated with drugs filed at the FDA during the 1991–2005 period: 56% were on formulation, 24% on salt, crystalline or other forms, and 63% methods of use (some of more than one type). Secondary patents were filed after FDA approval and extend exclusivity lifetime by an average of 4 to 5 years, with more secondary patents if the branded drug's sales were higher.

Sampat and Shadlen (2017) compared Brazil, India and Argentina to the US, Europe (EPO patents), and Japan. They found little evidence that secondary patent provisions in the former group of countries have had much effect on limiting them, although grant rates overall tend to be lower in those countries, both for primary and secondary patents.

Our study was based on a match of the complete list of drugs and their active ingredients registered at the Chilean ISP (Institute of Public Health) 1934–2012 with the Chilean patent data.[21] Pharmaceutical patents were not allowed in Chile until the patent reform of 1991, and there has been consistent growth in them since then. The patent law has been amended several times for TRIPS and various free trade agreements, to extend patent life from 15 to 20 years, allow for extension due to delays in grant/registration, and to soften the secondary use restriction.

Our findings were the following: First, only a small fraction of pharmaceutical patents (<2%) are held by Chilean entities, and the largest source countries are the US, Switzerland, and Germany. Second, 113 (22%) of 504 matched patents were primary patents, and primary patents were more likely to have been granted. Third, the top therapeutic classes protected by patents differed depending on the age of the drugs: anti-ulcer, anti-depressants, anti-psychotics are older drugs (pre-1991) and have few primary patents if any, whereas anti-virals (including HIV) and anti-neoplastics (anti-cancer) are newer and had a much higher ratio of primary patents, up to 40% of the total.

The ISP register also contain information on the role of firms registering drugs. Chilean firms were largely engaged in domestic manufacturing, quality control, importing, packaging, and distribution. Only two drugs had a Chilean firm as the source, but no patents (both were generics), while two drugs had secondary patents owned by Chilean firms, and no primary patents: Larmax-D, an anti-histamine compound, and Faronkal, a nasal decongestant compound used for sleep apnea.

Our conclusions from this investigation were that Chilean companies manufacture common drugs with lots of different formulations, but they do not manufacture newer drugs that are patent protected. Almost all pharmaceutical patents are held by foreign firms, and almost no products of domestic companies are protected by patents. Looking across therapeutic classes, we found a negative relationship between the share of drugs patented by foreign companies and the number of drugs manufactured by domestic companies. In addition, we found weak evidence for strategic patenting behavior in pharmaceuticals in the form of extending patent life.

7. Conclusions

I began this survey with a quote from Edith Penrose suggesting that the benefits of international patent systems have been overemphasized relative to the associated costs. The preceding overview of the literature on the role of the patent system in economic development suggests that the benefit–cost ratio may be even less attractive in the case of developing countries, primarily because the benefits are low, while the costs are similar to those in developed countries.

There are a number of reasons to think that having a patent system is not an important ingredient of development policy for low or even middle-income countries. First, there is the historical cross-country evidence of Moser (2005, 2013) and Lerner (2002), mentioned earlier. Mostly based on variation within Europe, both authors use innovation measures that are not contaminated by the local patent system to show that innovation activity is not increased by a stronger system.

Second, the introduction of a regional system with broader patent scope geographically does not increase innovative activity in middle-income countries and only shifts patenting activities marginally. In general, a very small share of firms in those countries uses the system at all. Third, joining the international Paris Convention and increasing patent strength does not lead immediately to more innovation and patenting, although it is true that the few patenting firms in Chile are faster growing, both before and after their first patent. An interesting suggestion from Gold, Morin, and Shadeed (2017) is that the empirically observed feedback or simultaneity in the relationship between IP strength and growth may be partly a placebo effect, where beliefs in the benefits of IP rather than actual use drive growth. This argument may apply to individual firms as well as to the economy as a whole.

From the perspective of a developing country, the most important patents are those taken out by the pharmaceutical sector and to lesser extent, the broader chemical sector. Because these patents are generally the most valuable, they are the most widely used by foreign multinationals, and their enforcement is likely to have the most negative impact on domestic social welfare. In Chile, for example, 60% of patents are in pharmaceutical-chemical technologies, whereas in high-income countries, the share of these technologies is 22%. Similarly, 60% of the non-resident filings in our sample of the countries acceding to the European Patent Convention after 2000 were in the pharmaceutical-chemical technologies before accession. The evidence on the impact of strengthening the patent system via TRIPS on the pharmaceutical sector in developing countries is nuanced: 1) it has had little effect on research directed to 'neglected' diseases; 2) it does speed up the launch of new drugs.; and 3) some of the price impact is mitigated by other domestic policies. With respect to Chile, we found that there was use of secondary patenting by multinationals to extend patent term and little domestic impact on invention or patenting, at least in the short run. According to WIPO statistics, the majority of all Chilean patents (85%) are still held by non-residents in 2017–2018, which is almost the same as in 1980–1981 (86%), even though Chile itself has moved from a middle income to high-income country during the same years and its real GDP per capita has more than tripled.

Overall the investigations surveyed here support Penrose's view in 1951 and 1973 that patent system design should take into account the development level of the economy in question. In addition, they highlight the relative unimportance of patents for domestic entities in these economies, even when a well-administered system exists, and suggest that patenting may not be a key tool in the development policy maker's toolkit.

Notes

1. bhhall@berkeley.edu. This is a revised version of a paper written for the Inaugural Penrose Lectures at SOAS, London, in March 2018. I am grateful to the organizer, Christine Oughton, for giving me the opportunity to present this work, and to an anonymous referee for suggestions that improved the paper.
2. 'International Convention' here refers to the Paris Convention of 1883, which specified national treatment for inventors from all signatory countries (42 countries at the time she wrote) and a period of priority after filing in one of the countries during which filings may be submitted to other countries, along with a number of other provisions. At the present time the number of contracting parties to the Paris Convention is 177. See http://www.wipo.int/treaties/en/ip/paris/
3. See Hall and Harhoff (2012) for a brief survey of the evidence on patent disclosure and Ouellette (2012) for some case studies of disclosure in nanotechnology.
4. This section of the paper is a revised and updated section from Hall and Harhoff (2012).
5. Ladas and Parry (2003). See also the EPO and USPTO websites.
6. For a number of reasons (linguistic differences, variations in the legal system, policies targeted to domestic inventors, etc.), this principle is not always completely achieved (de Rassenfosse et al., 2020).

7. There is also the GCC (Patent Office of the Cooperation Council for the Arab States of the Gulf), but this organization is not a signatory of the Paris Convention nor a member of WIPO. See https://www.wipo.int/export/sites/www/patent_register_portal/en/docs/gcc.pdf
8. See Farrell and Shapiro (2008) for detailed models of this process.
9. See https://www.epo.org/law-practice/unitary/upc/upc-faq.html for further information about the unitary patent and court.
10. Unique invention filings count a family of filings only once, where a family is defined as a set of filings that share a priority patent.
11. These offices are the US Patent and Trademark Office (USPTO), the European Patent Office (EPO), the Japanese Patent Office (JPO), the Korean Intellectual Property Office (KIPO), and the Chinese Intellectual Property Office (SIPO, renamed CNIPA in August 2018).
12. http://www.wipo.int/wipo_magazine/en/2010/06/article_0010.html
13. See also Maskus (2004) and Branstetter (2004) for earlier reviews of this literature.
14. This section is based on joint work with Christian Helmers. See Hall and Helmers (2019) for details.
15. These countries are Bosnia and Herzegovina, Montenegro, Moldovia, Tunisia, Morocco, and Cambodia.
16. The Unitary EU patent (currently for approximately 25 European countries) comes into force in 2018. This patent will have a single set of fees and enforcement will take place at the Unitary Patent Court. Our analysis preceded the introduction of the unitary patent by several years.
17. The official languages at the EPO are English, French, and German. None of the accession countries have these as their 'first' language, although most have a substantial number of speakers of these languages. Applicants to the EPO have two months after the submission of a patent filing to submit a version translated into one of the official languages.
18. This section draws from joint work with Carsten Fink and Christian Helmers (Fink, Hall, and Helmers 2021).
19. This section draws from joint work with Maria Jose Abud Sittler and Christian Helmers (Abud Sittler, Hall, and Helmers 2015).
20. Some examples: India's Glivec decision, 1 April 2013 – imatinib mesylate (beta-crystalline form of an existing anti-cancer drug) rejected by Supreme Court for obviousness. Brazil – Projeto de Lei n° 5.402/2013 (includes provision similar to paragraph 3(d) of India's Patent Act). South Africa – proposed National Policy on IP: '[Legislation] should exclude diagnostic, therapeutic and surgical methods from patentability, including new uses of known products, as is the case under the TRIPS agreement.' See Sampat and Shadlen (2017).
21. This was a complex undertaking; for details on the match and the identification of secondary patents, see Abud Sittler, Hall, and Helmers (2015).

Disclosure statement

No potential conflict of interest was reported by the author(s).

References

Ahn, S., B. H. Hall, and K. Lee, eds. 2014. *Intellectual Property for Economic Development*. KDI Series in Economic Policy and Development. Cheltenham, UK: Edward Elgar and KDI.

Abud Sittler, M. J., B. H. Hall, and C. Helmers. 2015. "An Empirical Analysis of Primary and Secondary Pharmaceutical Patents in Chile." *PLOS ONE*. doi:10.1371/journal.pone.0124257.

Abud Sittler, M. J., C. Fink, B. H. Hall, and C. Helmers (2013). *The Use of Intellectual Property in Chile*. Geneva, Switzerland: WIPO "Economic Research Working paper 11." Available at http://www.wipo.int/publications/en/details.jsp?id=3955&plang=EN

Angeles, L. 2005. "Should Developing Countries Strengthen Their Intellectual Property Rights?" *BE Journal of Macroeconomics* 5 (1): 23. https://doi.org/10.2202/1534-5998.1327

Arora, A., A. Fosfuri, and A. Gambardella (2001). *Markets for Technology*. Cambridge, MA, MIT Press.

Arora, A., L. Branstetter, and C. Chatterjee (2008). "Strong Medicine: Patent Reform and the Emergence of a Research-Driven Pharmaceutical Industry in India." NBER Summer Institute, Cambridge, MA.

Arora, A., M. Ceccagnoli, and W. M. Cohen. 2008. "R&D and the Patent Premium." *International Journal of Industrial Organization* 26: 1153–1179.

Arora, A., and R. P. Merges (2004). "Specialized Supply Firms, Property Rights, and Firm Boundaries." *Industrial and Corporate Change* 13(3): 451–475.

Arora, A., X. Bei, and W. M. Cohen (2016): "Why Firms Trademark (Or Not): Evidence from the US Trademark Data." *Academy of Management Annual Meeting Proceedings* 2016(1): 17249. Available at https://journals.aom.org/doi/10.5465/ambpp.2016.17249abstract

Balasubramanian, N., and J. Sivadasan. 2011. "What Happens When Firms Patent? New Evidence from U.S. Economic Census Data." *The Review of Economics and Statistics* 93 (1): 126–146.

Braga, C. A. O., and C. Fink. 1998. "The Relationship between Intellectual Property Rights and Foreign Direct Investment." *Duke Journal of Comparative and International Law* 9: 163–188.

Branstetter, L. G. 2004. "Do Stronger Patents Induce More Local Innovation?" *Journal of International Economic Law* 7 (2): 359–370.

Branstetter, L.G., R. Fisman, and C.F. Foley. 2006. "Do Stronger Intellectual Property Rights Increase International Technology Transfer? Empirical Evidence from U.S. Firm-Level Panel Data." *Quarterly Journal of Economics* 121 (1): 321–349.

Cockburn, I. M., J. O. Lanjouw, and M. Schankerman. 2016. "Patents and the Global Diffusion of New Drugs." *American Economic Review* 106 (1): 136–164. doi:10.1257/aer.20141482.

Cohen, W. M., R. R. Nelson, and J. P. Walsh (2000). *Protecting Their Intellectual Assets: Appropriability Conditions and Why U.S. Manufacturing Firms Patent (or Not)*. Cambridge, MA: NBER Working Papers 7552.

Comino, S., A. Galasso, and C. Graziano (2017). The Diffusion of New Institutions: Evidence from Renaissance Venice's Patent System. Cambridge: NBER Working Paper No. 24118.

Cimoli, M., G. Dosi, K. E. Maskus, R. L. Okediji, J. H. Reichman, and J. E. Stiglitz, eds. 2014. *Intellectual Property Rights: Legal and Economic Challenges for Development*. Oxford: Oxford University Press.

David, P. A. 1994. "The Evolution of Intellectual Property Institutions." In *Economics in a Changing World*, Vol. 1. *System Transformation: Eastern and Western Assessments*. edited by. A. Aganbegyan, O. Bogomolov, and M. Kaser. London:MacMillan.

de Rassenfosse, G., P. H. Jensen, T. Julius, A. Palangkaraya, and E. Webster. 2020. "Are Foreigners Treated Equally under the Trade-Related Aspects of Intellectual Property Rights Agreement?" *Journal of Law and Economics* 62 (4): 663–685.

European Commission, DG Competition (2009). *Pharmaceutical Sector Inquiry: Final Report*. Available at http://ec.europa.eu/competition/sectors/pharmaceuticals/inquiry/staff_working_paper_part1.pdf

Farrell, J, and C. Shapiro. 2008. "How Strong Are Weak Patents?" *American Economic Review* 98 (4): 1347–1369.

Feenstra, R. P., R. Inklaar, and M. P. Timmer. 2015. "The Next Generation of the Penn World Table." *American Economic Review* 105 (10): 3150–3182. URL. http://www.ggdc.net/pwt/

Fink, C., B. H. Hall, and C. Helmers (2018). "IP Use in Middle Income Countries: The Case of Chile." Earlier version of preceding paper, available at https://eml.berkeley.edu//~bhhall/papers/FinkHallHelmers18_NBERw24348.rev0.pdf

Fink, C., B. H. Hall, and C. Helmers. 2021. "Intellectual Property Use and Firm Performance: The Case of Chile." *Economic Development and Cultural Change* 70 (1): 321–358. forthcoming 2020.

Fink, C., C. Helmers, and C. J. Ponce. 2018. "Trademark Squatters: Theory and Evidence from Chile." *International Journal of Industrial Organization* forthcoming. Available at. doi:10.1016/j.ijindorg.2018.04.004.

Fink, C., and K. E. Maskus. 2005. *Intellectual Property and Development: Lessons from Recent Economic Research*. Washington, D.C: World Bank.

Fink, C., M. Khan, and H. Zhou. 2016. "Exploring the Worldwide Patent Surge." *Economics of Innovation and New Technology* 25 (2): 114–142.

Gilbert, R. J., and D. M. G. Newberry. 1982. "Preemptive Patenting and the Persistence of Monopoly." *American Economic Review* 72 (3): 514–526.

Gilbert, R. J. 1987. "Patents, Sleeping Patents, and Entry Deterrence." *Journal Reprints Antitrust L. & Econ* 17: 205–269.

Ginarte, J. C., and W. G. Park. 1997. "Determinants of Patent Rights: A Cross-national Study." *Research Policy* 26 (3): 283–301.

Gold, E. R., J.-F. Morin, and E. Shadeed. 2017. "Does Intellectual Property Lead to Economic Growth? Insights from a Novel IP Dataset." *Regulation & Governance*. doi:10.1111/rego.12165.

Grossman, G.M., and E.L.-C. Lai. 2004. "International Protection of Intellectual Property." *American Economic Review* 94 (5): 1635–1653.

Hall, B. H., A. Jaffe, and M. Trajtenberg. 2005. "Market Value and Patent Citations." *Rand Journal of Economics* 36: 16–38.

Hall, B. H., and C. Helmers. 2019. "The Impact of International Patent Systems: Evidence from Accession to the European Patent Convention." *Research Policy* 48 (9): 103810. Available at. doi:10.1016/j.respol.2019.103810.

Hall, B. H., C. Helmers, and G. Von Graevenitz (2020). "Technology Entry in the Presence of Patent Thickets." *Oxford Economic Papers*, forthcoming. Available at 10.1093/oep/gpaa034. Cambridge, MA: NBER Working Paper No. 21455.

Hall, B. H., C. Helmers, M. Rogers, and V. Sena. 2013. "The Importance (Or Not) of Patents to UK Firms." *Oxford Economic Papers* 65 (3): 603–629.

Hall, B. H., and D. Harhoff. 2012. "Recent Research on the Economics of Patents." *Annual Review of Economics* 4: 541–566.

Hall, B. H., and R. H. Ziedonis. 2001. "The Determinants of Patenting in the U. S. Semiconductor Industry, 1980-1994." *Rand Journal of Economics* 32: 101–128.

Hall, B. H. 2014. "Does Patent Protection Help or Hinder Technology Transfer?" In *Intellectual Property for Economic Development. KDI Series in Economic Policy and Development*, edited by Ahn S., B. H. Hall, and K. Lee, 11–32. Cheltenham, UK: Edward Elgar and KDI.

Ivus, O. 2010. "Do Stronger Patent Rights Raise High-tech Exports to the Developing World?" *Journal of International Economics* 81 (1): 38–47.

James, T. C. (2007). "Patent Protection in India: Policy Trends." Presentation to the Conference on Intellectual Property Rights, Globalisation and Related Issues. Delhi, India: Delhi School of Economics.

JPO (Japanese Patent Office) (2007). *A history of system of industrial property rights*. Available at http://www.deux.jpo.go.jp/cgi/search.cgi?query=history&lang=en&root=short, accessed 19 December 2006.

Kapczynski, A., C. Park, and B. Sampat. 2012. Polymorphs and Prodrugs and Salts (Oh My!): An Empirical Analysis of "Secondary" Pharmaceutical Patents, 7 PLOS e49470.

Kim, L. (2003), "Technology Transfer and Intellectual Property Rights: The Korean Experience." UNCTAD-ICTSD Issue Paper No. 2, June. Geneva: International Centre for Trade and Sustainable Development.

Kremer, M. 1998. "Patent Buyouts: A Mechanism for Encouraging Innovation." *Quarterly Journal of Economics* 113 (4): 1137–1167.

Kumar, N. 2003. Intellectual Property Rights, Technology and Economic Development: Experiences of Asian Countries. *Economic and Political Weekly* 38 (3): 209–226.

Kyle, M. K., and A. M. McGahan. 2009. "Investments in Pharmaceuticals before and after TRIPS." *Review of Economics and Statistics* 94 (4): 1157–1172.

Kyle, M. K., and Y. Qian (2014). "Intellectual Property Rights and Access to Innovation: Evidence from TRIPS." Cambridge, MA: NBER Working Paper No. 20799.

Lanjouw, J. O., and M. Schankerman. 2004. "Protecting Intellectual Property Rights: Are Small Firms Handicapped?" *Journal of Law and Economics* 47: 45–74.

Lanjouw, J.O. (1997). "The Introduction of Pharmaceutical Product Patents in India: 'Heartless Exploitation of the Poor and Suffering'?" Cambridge, MA: NBER Working Paper No. 6366.

Lee, K., and Y.-K. Kim. 2010. "IPR and Technological Catch-Up in Korea." In *Intellectual Property Rights, Development, and Catch Up: An International Comparative Study. Oxford*, edited by H. A. Goto Odagiri, A. Sunami, and R. R. Nelson, 133–167, Oxford, UK: Oxford University Press.

Lemley, M. A., and C. Shapiro. 2007. "Patent Holdup and Royalty Stacking." *Texas Law Review* 85: 1991–2049.

Lerner, J. 1995. "Patenting in the Shadow of Competitors." *Journal of Law and Economics* 38: 463–495.

Lerner, J. 2002. "Patent Protection and Innovation over 150 Years." *American Economic Review* 92 (2): 221–225.

Levin, R. C., A. K. Klevorick, R. R. Nelson, and S. G. Winter (1987). "Appropriating the Returns from Industrial Research and Development." *Brookings Papers on Economic Activity* 3: 783–832.

Machlup, F., and E. Penrose. 1950. "The Patent Controversy in the Nineteenth Century." *Journal of Economic History* 10 (1): 1–29.

Mansfield, E. (1986). "Patents and Innovation: An Empirical Study." *Management Science* 32 (2): 173–181.

Maskus, K. E. (2004). "Encouraging International Technology Transfer." Geneva, Switzerland: ICTSD and UNCTAD Issue Paper No. 7.

Maskus, K. E., and M. Penubarti. 1995. "How Trade-related are Intellectual Property Rights?" *Journal of International Economics* 39 (3): 227–248.

Mokyr, J. 2009. ""Intellectual Property Rights, the Industrial Revolution, and the Beginnings of Modern Economic Growth". *American Economic Review* 99 (2): 349–355.

Moser, P. 2005. "How Do Patent Laws Influence Innovation? Evidence from Nineteenth-Century World's Fairs." *American Economic Review* 95 (4): 1214–1236.

Moser, P. 2013. "Patents and Innovation: Evidence from Economic History." *Journal of Economic Perspectives* 27 (1): 23–44.

Nelson, R. R., ed. 1993. *National Innovation Systems: A Comparative Analysis.* Oxford, UK: Oxford University Press.

Neubig, T. S., and S. Wunsch-Vincent (2017). "A Missing Link in the Analysis of Global Value Chains: Cross-border Flows of Intangible Assets, Taxation and Related Measurement Implications." Geneva: WIPO Economic Research Paper No. 37.

Ouellette, L. L. 2012. "Do Patents Disclose Useful Information?" *Harvard Journal of Law & Technology* 25: 545–603.

Penrose, E. T. 1951. "The Economics of the International Patent System." In *Johns Hopkins University Studies in Historical and Political Science* . Baltimore: Johns Hopkins Press.

Penrose, E. T. 1973. "International Patenting and the Less-developed Countries." *Economic Journal* 83 (Sept): 768–786.

Prager, F. D. 1946. "Brunelleschi's Patent." *Journal of the Patent Office Society* 28 (2): 109–135.

Qian, Y. 2007. "Do Additional National Patent Laws Stimulate Domestic Innovation in a Global Patenting Environment." *Review of Economics and Statistics* 89 (3): 436–453.

Sampat, B. N., and K. C. Shadlen. 2017. "Secondary Pharmaceutical Patenting: A Global Perspective." *Research Policy* 46: 693–707.

Saunders, K. M., and L. Levine. 2004. "Better, Faster, Cheaper - Later: What Happens When Technologies Are Suppressed." *Mich. Telecomm. & Tech. Law Review* 23: 11–69.

Scherer, F. M., and S. Weisburst. 1995. "Economic Effects of Strengthening Patent Protection in Italy." *International Review of Industrial Property and Copyright Law* 26 (6): 1009–1024.

Scotchmer, S. 2004. "The Political Economy of Intellectual Property Treaties." *Journal of Law, Economics, and Organization* 20 (2): 415–437.

Shapiro, C. 2010. "Injunctions, Hold-Up, and Patent Royalties." *American Law and Economics Review* 12 (2): 280–318.

Stiglitz, J. E., and A. Jayadev. 2010. "Medicine for Tomorrow: Some Alternative Proposals to Promote Socially Benefi Cial Research and Development in Pharmaceuticals." *Journal of Generic Medicines* 7 (3): 217–226.

Thursby, J.G., and M. Thursby. 2006. *Here or There? A Survey of Factors in Multinational R&D Location.* Washington, DC: National Academies Press.

Torrisi, S., A. Gambardella, P. Giuri, D. Harhoff, K. Hoisl, and M. Mariani. 2016. "Used, Blocking and Sleeping Patents: Empirical Evidence from a Large-Scale Inventor Survey." *Research Policy* 45 (7): 1374–1385.

WIPO (World Intellectual Property Organization) (2017). Patent statistics, available at https://www3.wipo.int/ipstats/index.htm?tab=patent, accessed 1 March 2018.

WIPO (World Intellectual Property Organization) (2018). *PCT Yearly Review 2018 – Executive Summary.* Available at https://www.wipo.int/ipstats, accessed 30 August 2018.

Yang, L., and K.E. Maskus. 2009. "Intellectual Property Rights, Technology Transfer and Exports in Developing Countries." *Journal of Development Economics* 90: 231–236.

ê OPEN ACCESS

Collective value creation: A new approach to stakeholder value

Mariana Mazzucato

ABSTRACT
The corporate community has rediscovered an old idea: stakeholder value. The concept's history is rooted in the literature on varieties of capitalism. Within that scholarship it has served to delineate institutional and relational differences between capitalist systems and forms of corporate governance. Today, stakeholder value is being used to argue for the redirection of capitalism to deliver on key goals related to inclusion and sustainability. This paper argues that the concept – and thus the endeavour to change capitalism – will remain weak unless it goes to the centre of how we create value. Moralistic exhortations to business leaders are not enough to bring about a true stakeholder form of capitalism. For this we must have stronger theory and practice on how to restructure finance, production, and public-private partnerships in new ways that recognise the state's market-shaping role and support equitable distribution of value across stakeholders.

1. Introduction: redirecting capitalism

Because the world is facing multiple crises – from climate, health, and biodiversity emergencies to rising inequality and political instability – it is more urgent than ever to collectively revisit the structures and decisions that shape the capitalist systems we live in. Capitalism is not singular and deterministic, with consequences that are either good or bad. The exact form it takes is a result of concrete choices made to structure businesses, government organisations, and transnational institutions – and how they relate to each other. In this sense, the market itself is an outcome, not a set process that imposes inevitable decisions on others. Because capitalism is currently not working for so many, the only way for true transformation is to move beyond a single-minded focus on shareholder value and build a new social contract between businesses, labour, and the state.

Ever since Friedman (1970) famously argued that 'the social responsibility of business is to increase its profits', shareholder value maximization has had a tight grip on global market economies. For decades, Friedman's article promoted the idea that America's economic performance was declining because the principle of profit maximization was being violated. The only way to ensure that managers would not misallocate resources and that companies would run well, was considered to be the maximization of

This is an Open Access article distributed under the terms of the Creative Commons Attribution-NonCommercial-NoDerivatives License (http://creativecommons.org/licenses/by-nc-nd/4.0/), which permits non-commercial re-use, distribution, and reproduction in any medium, provided the original work is properly cited, and is not altered, transformed, or built upon in any way.

shareholder value through a strong market. Importantly, this need to boost shareholder value (Jensen and Meckling 1976) varies across national contexts, depending on institutional rules that shape and govern a particular region (Hall and Soskice 2001). While the literature on the varieties of capitalism highlighted the role of different forms of corporate governance in shaping businesses' response to shareholder pressures, it also created space for the consideration of stakeholders' interests. Put simply, the level of attention given to stakeholder value is associated with the economic and social consequences of different varieties of capitalism.

In recent years the concept of stakeholder capitalism has taken off, no longer an academic concept to describe varieties of capitalism, but a proclamation of change from the business and finance communities. Nevertheless, when companies talk about providing stakeholder value today, they usually frame it as a means to an end – stakeholder engagement as a productive way of increasing shareholder value in the long run. Although there has been much talk about the social goals and responsibilities of businesses, the value they create has not been distributed to all.

For instance, in Larry Fink's 2022 annual address to the CEOs of the companies whose assets his firm manages on behalf of investors, the founding director of BlackRock – the world's largest asset manager – took the opportunity to advocate for a more sustainable, socially-conscious, and forward-looking form of capitalism rooted in stakeholder rather than shareholder value. Yet Fink's vision for stakeholder capitalism – epitomising the conventional view – focuses far too narrowly on intra-organisational corporate governance and fails to see the wider landscape of extra-organisational, institutional relations between different domains and sectors of society. It leaves untouched the traditionally separate identities of stakeholder and shareholder. Stakeholders are to be considered and valued only insofar as their inclusion benefits the ultimate bottom line – the long-term profits of a different set of people, the shareholders, who remain at the top of the pecking order.

However, when value is created collectively, it should be shared collectively. If one does not buy into the first part, with the faulty assumption that wealth creation happens only inside business and the state can, at best, fix market failures along the way, then the second part will continue to prove futile. Accordingly, stakeholder capitalism needs to not only be placed at the centre of corporate governance reform, but at the centre of where value is created in the first place: at the interface between different actors in the economy. Thinking about the redirection of capitalism towards a new social contract and collective value creation requires a stakeholder understanding of capitalism itself. Because businesses can't be successful without the involvement of many groups, civil society, workers, communal organizations, and governments should have the power to influence and benefit from business decisions (Mazzucato 2018a).

The article begins by presenting an alternative view of the state as market shaper, which emphasises the role of public investments in value creation and innovation. Moving towards inclusive and sustainable growth requires a different theory of what government is for. It then develops the notion of mission-oriented policies which can help shift the status quo of market-fixing towards new public-private partnerships (Mazzucato 2021). To do so it's critical to develop institutional capabilities in establishing a new social contract. Indeed, the work of Edith Penrose (1959) on the dynamic capabilities inside our private organizations, can be extended to the kinds of capabilities that need to be developed inside all organizations, including the public ones. The article concludes by developing a notion of stakeholder capitalism which asks how the collective ways in which value is created, can be reflected in how it is distributed. Overall, this article identifies the shortcomings of the current system and outlines a forward-looking vision for stakeholder capitalism guided by dynamic organizational capabilities and collaboration through a mission-oriented approach.

2. The state's role as a market shaper

Over the past half century, many have bought into the ideology that the state's role should be limited to reactively 'fixing' or 'correcting' market failures rather than proactively shaping or creating markets. Orthodox economic discourse disparaged industrial strategies aimed at 'picking winners' and restricted state interventions to levelling the playing field, ensuring only the most competitive would win. The assumption of market failure theory is that markets work well and only when they fail must policymakers and regulators make sure that externalities are properly accounted for. Negative externalities, such as those created by pollution, require public measures that cause the private sector to internalise external costs. Carbon taxes are one example. The aim is to fix failures in carbon-intensive industries – so that negative externalities are fully internalized and priced to truly reflect their social and ecological impacts. Positive externalities arising from public goods will be characterised by underinvestment by the private sector and will therefore require public investment. This is the case for basic research, which has high spillovers that create difficulties in appropriating private returns.

While this market-fixing approach to internalizing externalities is an important departure from the orthodox free market ideology, providing some ground for coordination, it stops short of the radical reinvention required to respond effectively to the massive challenges of climate change, global pandemics, and technological disruption. This is because instead of creating markets, the state is understood to fill gaps, tinker on the edges, and level the playing field. However, to solve the most pressing problems of our time, a mission-oriented approach to economic policy with a clear vision of public value is necessary.

Markets themselves should be viewed as outcomes of the interactions between both public and private actors (as well as actors from the third sector, and from civil society). In his seminal work, *The Great Transformation*, Karl Polanyi describes the role of the state in forcing the so-called free market into existence: 'the road to the free market was opened and kept open by an enormous increase in continuous, centrally organized and controlled interventionism' (Polanyi [1944]2001, 144). Polanyi's perspective debunks the notion of state actions as interventions, rather highlighting the ways in which markets are deeply embedded in social and political institutions (Evans 1995). Indeed, even Adam Smith's notion of the free market is amenable to this interpretation. His free market was not a naturally occurring state of nature, free from government interference. For Smith, the free market meant a market *free from rent*, which indeed requires much policymaking (1776).

Yet what we lack in economic theory are words to refer to how the actions of public institutions (visions, investments, and regulations) *contribute* to value creation. Polanyi's analysis is not only about the way that markets form over the course of economic development. It can also be applied to understanding the most modern form of markets, and in particular those driven by innovation. Some of the most important general-purpose technologies, from mass production, to aerospace, and information and communications technology, trace their early investments to public-sector investments (Ruttan 2006).

Although upstream basic research is the classic public good, market-creating investments are not limited to this sort of activity. Indeed, some of the public investments that led to technological revolutions (information technology, biotech, nanotech) and new general-purpose technologies (such as the Internet) were distributed along the entire innovation chain: basic research through the National Science Foundation (NSF), applied research through the Defense Advanced Research Projects Agency (DARPA) and the National Institutes of Health (NIH), and early-stage financing of companies through agencies such as Small Business Innovation Research (SBIR) (Block and Keller 2011). These kinds of innovation instruments were thus spread through a decentralized network of different agencies across the entire innovation chain. Such agencies might not act together in a planned way, but they are often driven by a vision to create new landscapes, such as in life sciences, rather than only fixing problems in existing landscapes. DARPA, the NIH, and other such agencies have been successful precisely because they led the way, rather than following behind, de-risking the leaders.

It is not just innovation agencies that play a key role here. Globally, public banks have often provided high-risk, early-stage, capital-intensive investment in different sectors. In Israel, the public venture capital fund Yozma was critical for what became Start-Up Nation, and in Germany, the KfW public banks have provided the most patient high-risk finance to green companies. In developing countries, it is often banks like BNDES in Brazil, or the African Development Bank that take on the most risk (Mazzucato and Penna 2015).

Considering the state as a market-maker and shaper provides a different justification for its remit: it is not about correcting but creating objectives that all of society can contribute to. Furthermore, given the collective contributions to economic growth, there must be a collective division of rewards between public and private actors. Both of these areas require rethinking the types of capabilities required in our state structures.

3. Dynamic capabilities of the state: public purpose and mission orientation

Penrose's (1959) work on capabilities contributed to a better understanding of the internal resources and managerial capabilities necessary for a firm's growth. According to her seminal work, the firm should not just position itself competitively, as Michael Porter would later argue, but continuously develop capabilities to promote value creation and innovation. Put simply, the competitiveness of a business depends on its ability to learn; managerial capability serves as the bottleneck on a firm's growth. Penrose's (1959, 48) writes,

> The experience of a firm's managerial group plays a crucial role in the whole process of expansion, for the process by which experience is gained is properly treated as a process creating new productive services available to the firm.

Organisational theorist Teece, Pisano, and Shuen (1997) developed this further into the 'dynamic capabilities' of the firm as the ability to 'integrate, build, and reconfigure internal and external competences to address rapidly changing environments'. The emphasis on internal capabilities meant paying less attention to the external environment of a firm. Instead, a firm's ability to be agile and flexible in navigating its success is considered a key component of building long-term competitive advantage.

Once we accept the role of the state as market shaper, the same question of dynamic capabilities arises for the public sector. To improve the implementation of strategic missions and carry out transformative projects, innovation policy needs to adopt a 'lead-and-learn' approach. In particular, there are three levels of dynamic capabilities to be developed: state capabilities to set ambitious goals and obtain consent, policy capabilities to coordinate and create impact, and administrative capabilities to ensure long-term vision and secure organisational support (Kattel and Mazzucato 2018). Moreover, because outsourcing the delivery of core services and functions undermines the state's capacity of acquiring these capabilities, the state must be embedded in the production of public value (Collington and Mazzucato 2022; Mazzucato and Collington 2023). Only by moving beyond outsourcing can the state respond to ever evolving demands.

The state, when driven by public purpose, should empower all stakeholders and actors in the economy to work together – government agencies, corporations, small businesses, social enterprises, civic institutions, charities, citizen groups and trade unions, in a 'multi-actor perspective' (Avelino and Wittmayer 2016). Collective intelligence can be fostered through the realization of common goals, or missions, with positive spillovers and multipliers fairly distributed between all stakeholders. A mission-oriented approach begins by asking the question 'what is the problem we want to solve?' – framed as a goal to be achieved through investments in sectors and collaborations within individual projects.

Missions are not new. They have been used to inspire and direct action throughout history (Mazzucato 2021). A generation of missions in the 1960s were technological, such as NASA's Apollo mission of putting a man on the Moon by the end of the decade. The moonshot required innovation in many sectors – as diverse as nutrition, textiles, software and aeronautics – and hundreds of projects. NASA would have failed had they not also transformed their own organisation to be more agile and flexible, with horizontal communication between project teams. They also changed their way of doing procurement towards a more challenge led one rather than the old cost-plus one. And given NASA's confidence they made sure to include 'no excess profits' clauses in the contract (Ibid.).

The missions we need today – tackling health crises, climate change, and digital disruptions – are different from NASA's missions in the 1960s. But the lessons of a clear direction from the top, cross-sectoral coordination, bottom-up experimentation and outcomes-oriented budgeting and procurement are vital. Such an approach has already begun to be incorporated within EU innovation policy, for instance, the Horizon program, which has selected five mission areas on the basis of two mission reports I produced (Mazzucato 2018b, 2018c). Those broad mission areas map neatly onto several of the UN Sustainable Development Goals (SDGs), mobilizing those Goals as the navigational stars guiding and illuminating mission maps. But they also break down into specific, concrete missions that can be measured.

Fundamental to delivering a successful modern mission is setting a clear direction, with targeted, measurable, and time-bound goals amenable to reflexive evaluation and continual improvement through experimental trial and error. The mission-led policy model can be summed up as ROAR: setting a Route and direction of change; building a decentralized network of willing Organizations to form mutualistic collaborations; evaluating their impacts through Assessment that can capture dynamic spillovers and feedback loops; and sharing out Risks and rewards fairly between public, private and labour partners through a renewed social contract (Mazzucato, Kattel, and Ryan-Collins 2020).

We need to re-engineer the institutional machinery of the state to gear legal, fiscal and regulatory tools towards stimulating social innovation across the public, private, and third sectors. Only by doing so, can the state's role become the cultivation of supportive financial environments and initiation of dynamic incentive structures for creative experimentation to flourish. It can then marshal resources – human, material, financial, informational – to effectively coordinate multiple dispersed actions to deliver objectives (Mazzucato 2021). This is how we tilt the playing field so market incentives encourage boundary-spanning innovation, and 'winning' entails solving wicked problems (Rittel and Webber 1973). These complex, multi-dimensional, intractable problems are resistant to straightforward scientific resolution, and they require transdisciplinary, multi-sectoral, and trans-scalar solutions directed by missions. So, for example, the creation and growth of new, alternative markets, such as for green energy and circular production, is simultaneously enabled by public investment in research and development, as well as patient capital pipelines for enterprise incubation. If done strategically, this can 'crowd in' private investments into new and nascent markets that create public value, while 'crowding out' old industries that produce little of public value or that contribute to problems such as inequality.

Key here is to use the full range of levers available to governments, from supply-side interventions, with the state acting as an investor of first resort (rather than lender of last resort) and as a funder and regulator with clear direction, to demand-side interventions, with the use of dynamic procurement policy to incentivize innovative solutions in domains ranging from public transport to housing. Governments play a critical role in catalysing and coordinating both public and private investment around common goals, not least transitioning to a green economy. Industrial strategies must not be about subsidizing specific sectors but about catalysing transformation across all sectors in order to meet social goals: climate action requires sectors as diverse as digital, nutrition, transport and construction to innovate and collaborate.

Such a mission-oriented, 'entrepreneurial' state is not engaged in a strategy of 'picking winners' per se but rather one of backing the willing – that is, supporting all those actors and agencies that are capable and committed to finding solutions to wicked problems (Mazzucato 2013). This means moving from seeing government as lender of last resort to investor of first resort. The state is thus engaged in the public support, subsidy, and incubation of innovation ecosystems whose development is essential to meeting a mission – rather than of individual enterprises that appear competitive – for an economy geared towards mission-oriented innovation rather than profit maximization.

Key in all this is the state's relationship to risk. Rather than putting all its eggs in one basket by picking a particular company or technology or sector to support, while foregoing any public stake in their future success, an entrepreneurial state acts more like a venture capitalist to structure its investments as a portfolio, cross subsidizing any losses with gains and reinvesting surpluses in further rounds of innovation (Mazzucato 2013). With greater risk and with higher stakes, comes failure. Failure is an intrinsic part of a more experimental and mission-oriented industrial strategy; the challenge is not to minimize failure per se but rather to minimize its costs and speed up the process of learning from failure, to 'fail faster' (Rodrik 2004).

4. Stakeholder capitalism: sharing both risks and rewards

A mission-oriented approach can be conducive to creating and reinforcing symbiotic public – private partnerships towards addressing societal challenges. Given the state's role as risk-taker and investor of first resort, new thinking is required for the ability of public institutions to share not only risks, but also rewards. This can encourage new thinking on how to achieve growth that is not only 'smart' (innovation-led) but also more inclusive. Mechanisms that find ways to socialize both risks and rewards can have an important effect on inequality as they create a 'pre-distribution' approach.

By allowing the state to retain a share of the rewards created through a process it contributes to, those rewards can be reinvested back into areas that directly create a more inclusive and sustainable economy. This can help states be more strategic and proactive in investments. Without this, government needs to focus most of its energy on *redistribution*, due to the negative consequences on inequality that arise when incomes are skewed, rewarding the few for the activities of the many.

Labour's share of global income is almost at an all-time low. In the US, for instance, the share of gross value added in the nonfarm business sector paid out to workers as wage (or self-employment) income remained stable, between 63% and 65%, for more than a century – but then, around 2000, began to drop to hit a low of 56% in 2013, before recovering slightly to about 58% by 2020 (Grossman and Oberfield 2022). At the same time, and as a consequence, the capital share of global income has risen. Is this because capital has become smarter and more efficient while labour has become less so? No. Even in periods when productivity rose, labour did not reap the rewards. Indeed, the growth of real wages has lagged productivity growth (Jacobs and Mazzucato 2016). This is because the increasing financialization of the economy has meant profits are not reinvested back into the economy, but largely go to shareholders, increasing the divide between those that own capital and those that do not. This, in turn, is a direct consequence of a focus on maximising shareholder value, which simply siphons off rewards for a very small percentage of economic actors. This is a problem across industries, from pharmaceutical research and manufacture (Tulum and Lazonick 2018) through to Big Tech (Strauss et al. 2021).

Corporate taxation has been falling and corporate tax avoidance has been rising globally. Some of the technology companies that have benefitted most from public support, such as Apple and Google, have also been among those accused of using their international operations to avoid paying tax. Perhaps most importantly, while the spillovers that occur from upstream 'basic' investments, such as education and research, should not be thought of as needing to earn a direct return for the state, downstream investments targeted at specific companies and technologies are qualitatively different.

Precisely because some investments in firms and technologies will fail, the state should treat these investments as a portfolio and enable some of the upside success to cover the downside risk.

Considering the ways in which rewards are privatised while risks are socialised, it is key to move from focusing on shareholder value to thinking about a more capacious and collaborative form of stakeholder value (Schwab 2021). An essential part of this transformation is to link the understanding of how value is created collectively to its distribution. Stakeholder capitalism is about recognising and rewarding the contributions that different stakeholders, whether shareholders or not, make to the value creation process (Mazzucato 2018a). Growth is an inherently collective process: value is co-created between producers and consumers, workers and managers, inventors and administrators, regulators, and investors – not just heroic entrepreneurs, venture capitalists and corporate leaders – through the organisational and institutional configurations which enable all to work together. Achieving inclusive growth means that the conditions must be correct in the first place, without over-relying on the taxation system to redistribute problematic forms of wealth creation that create structured inequities. Creation and distribution must be seen as two sides of the same coin. This can happen through both financial and non-financial means. Financial might include equity stakes, while non-financial can include conditionality on how prices are set, as well as the direction of investment making production more sustainable, and workers paid well and treated with dignity.

Historically, the big innovations that have produced value for shareholders of successful companies like Apple and Amazon are more often than not the result of public investment. Most of the innovations driving the IT revolution and the key technologies underpinning the functionality of the smart phone – including GPS and the internet itself – flowed from strategic state investment as opposed to the private entrepreneurialism that free marketeers lead us to believe. Indeed, the smartphone is the classic case of a composition of technologies first invented and developed by the state – the US defence research agency DARPA – and gifted to the world for free (Mazzucato 2013).

The large digital companies, Facebook, Amazon, Apple, Netflix and Google, have received a large share of income produced by a collective value creation process. In 2021, for example, Google's revenue was $185,527 billion while it employed only 139,995 staff. Similarly, while Apple had 147,000 staff members, the company's revenue was $274,515 billion. Both corporations rely largely on the collective value created by their platform's and product's users.[1] Furthermore, given that the underlying algorithms that power Google and Amazon were to a large extent publicly funded (e.g. the NSF funded the Google algorithm, DARPA funded the internet which both companies need, and much of the underlying artificial intelligence is the fruit of collective investment), it is critical to ask how such public investment can incorporate conditions to ensure that the value created is good and not bad (Mazzucato, Gouzoulis and Ryan-Collins 2023). Because, as Zuboff (2019) has so clearly shown, the opposite has happened: algorithms have been constructed to commodify and exploit human feelings and insecurities.

Another example is illustrative: in 2009, the Obama Administration gave two companies – Tesla and Solyndra – a guaranteed loan (Tesla received $465 million and Solyndra received $500 million). Tesla of course went on to become a successful company, while Solyndra failed. The success was seen as a private sector success while bankruptcy a public sector failure, with the usual critique of 'picking winners': the futility of government trying to direct an economy. The irony is that the agreement was that if Tesla did not pay back the loan, the government would get three million shares in Tesla – a bad deal. Instead, had the deal been that the government would get three million shares if the loan was paid back, it would have been a good deal. The money made could have gone back to a public fund, covering both the Solyndra loss and a next investment round. The problem is that by not admitting that the state here acted like a public venture capitalist, it ends up socialising risks but privatising rewards.

There is thus a strong case for arguing that, where technological breakthroughs have occurred as a result of targeted state interventions benefitting specific companies, the state should reap some of the financial rewards over time by retaining ownership of a small proportion of the intellectual property it had a hand in creating. This is not to say that the state should ever have exclusive licence or hold a large enough proportion of the value of an innovation to deter its diffusion (although this is almost never the case). The role of government is not to run commercial enterprises; it is to spark innovation elsewhere. But by owning some of the value it has created, which over time has the potential for significant growth, funds can be generated for reinvestment into new potential innovations.

One tool to engage in more coordinated state investment are conditionalities: funds given or loaned on the condition that the recipient complies with pre-set conditions meant to influence their behaviour, improve outcomes, and increase the chance that the aid will achieve its ultimate intended goal. Ambitious policies with conditionalities attached can help ensure the result is truly inclusive and sustainable. In this context, conditionalities – a typical industrial policy measure – tied to the allocation of public funds – such as on the pricing of final goods and services, knowledge governance, and reinvestment in innovation and local production – can be understood as active attempts to steer benefits directly to society (Mazzucato and Macfarlane 2019).

First, we need to reform intellectual property rights so that the value that's created by public investment in pharmaceutical and other technological inventions is recognized and rewarded. A business model defined by high research costs alongside low production costs, combined with an R&D investment model highly dependent on public funding, creates big incentives for big pharma to extract value by charging astronomically high prices for medicines justified through 'value pricing' (Mazzucato and Roy 2018).

While governments have funded some of the highest risk capital intensive research, private pharmaceutical firms have benefitted from a patent and pricing system that does not take that into account. Patents are often too strong, too wide, and too upstream (Mazzoleni and Nelson 1998). Prices are set by value-based pricing that allows prices to go to whatever the market will bear. However, the system should not be designed in a way that private profit is prioritized over public value. Governments could adopt price-capping regulations instead of relying on market forces to produce equitable prices. Another instrument for ensuring competitive prices is the implementation of competition and antitrust policies, which may be far less tolerant of monopoly prices than has been the case over the past 40 years in the US (Stiglitz 2017).

An unprecedented amount of public funding has been poured into vaccine research, development, and manufacturing. The leading six vaccine candidates have received an estimated $12bn of taxpayer and public money, including $1.7bn for the Oxford/

AstraZeneca jab, $2.48bn for Moderna/Lonza and $2.5bn for the Pfizer/BioNTech candidate (MSF 2020). Governments have used 'advanced market commitments' to guarantee that private companies that successfully produce a COVID-19 vaccine are amply rewarded with huge orders. And yet a large percentage of the world remains unvaccinated. Many lower income countries are unable to afford the necessary doses. Indeed, because of the competition for doses, lack of bargaining power, and opaque licensing agreements, poorer nations are paying significantly more for the same vaccines than rich countries. Even though AstraZeneca agreed to sell its vaccine at cost, different prices are charged in different regions. If we cannot temper the profit motives of big pharma during a global pandemic, in the interests of keeping economies running as well as keeping people alive, what hope is there for a future of intensifying shocks and crises?

To socialize rewards in a non-monetary way we can make sure that the companies receiving public subsidies, guarantees and direct investments operate in a way that serves the public. For example, the extraction of value from the real economy that has been a result of the increasing use of share buybacks (Lazonick 2014) can be reversed through conditionalities that assure that profits being earned from a process of collective wealth creation are reinvested back into the economy. The direction of that investment can also be a condition: for example, making sure that energy companies that receive subsidies transition more to renewables. For example, a recent loan to the German steel industry was conditional on the sector lowering its material composition, which it does through innovations around recycling, repurposing, and reusing material throughout the value chain. The direction of that investment can also be a condition; for example, making sure that energy companies that receive subsidies transition more to renewables, or as occurred in Germany when a recent loan to the steel sector was conditional on steel lowering its material content (Vogl, Åhman, and Nilsson 2021). Most recently, the US CHIPS Act included conditions to protect national security interests and limit stock buybacks. The Act is an opportunity to align private-public partnerships with bold policy goals to ensure that the rewards of investment are shared equitably.

There are also good examples emerging from the ongoing COVID-19 crisis. When negotiating bailouts for industries suffering, such as airlines not flying, some states are seeking concrete societal benefits. To accelerate greening of industrial sectors, Austria has made its airline-industry bailouts conditional on the adoption of climate targets, while France has also introduced five-year targets to lower domestic carbon dioxide emissions. And both Denmark and France are denying state aid to any company domiciled in an EU-designated tax haven and barring large recipients from paying dividends or buying back their own shares until 2021.

Similarly, governing innovation for the public good has been highlighted during the COVID-19 pandemic. To maximize the impact on public health, the innovation ecosystem must be steered to use collective intelligence to accelerate advances. Science and medical innovation thrive and progresses when researchers exchange and share knowledge openly, enabling them to build upon one another's successes and failures in real time. The COVID-19 technology access pool (C-TAP), which is a voluntary pool for health technology-related knowledge, intellectual property and data proposed by Costa Rica and adopted and launched by the World Health Organization on 29 May 2020, has offered a pragmatic solution with game-changing significance (WHO 2020). However, it remains unused to this day.

5. New financial institutions

A political economy based on stakeholder value will require institutional innovations that can ensure the more equitable distribution of value, as well as the sustainability of its creation. State investment banks can provide the much-needed patient capital – whether grants or low-interest loans – to incubate innovation ecosystems, while taking a non-controlling equity stake and distributing dividends for public value. Such institutions invest public finance and crowd-in private investment in new enterprise and innovation that aims to resolve global challenges like the climate crisis – and, importantly, take an equity stake or share in future revenues on behalf of workers and citizens.

Following the Second World War, National Investment Banks' (NIBs) traditional functions were in infrastructure investment and counter-cyclical lending. More recently however, NIBs have become key actors in driving economic growth and innovation. In focusing on tackling modern societal challenges, they play important risk-taking and mission-oriented roles. By placing state investment banks at the centre of industrial strategies and innovation investment processes, countries like Germany and China, as well as the European Union, are steering the path of innovation and value creation towards public goals.

National investment banks can also work alongside public wealth funds to provide public ownership and governance of key assets in land, enterprise, and intellectual property. Public wealth funds can use the revenues generated by state investment banks and other state-capital hybrid institutions to provide a citizen' dividend, public services, and infrastructure to effectively end poverty and dramatically reduce inequalities. Such innovations reimagine value distribution from *redistribution ex post* to *pre*-distribution *ex ante* – moving from an 'income sharing' state to a 'capital sharing' state (Susskind 2020).

Public wealth funds can also be leveraged to enable the state to take a direct stake in the assets of the economy and the revenues generated by capital (Detter, Fölster, and Ryan-Collins 2020). At the national level, a public wealth fund in charge of mature assets would make equity capital injections to larger corporations, when necessary, but could also act as a holding company for assets that governments already own, such as state-owned companies and real estate assets. The long-term argument for public wealth funds is that, by taking equity in risky start-up firms with good long-run potential, the state can help create businesses and an economy that would otherwise never come into being. Importantly, the state shares not only the risks, but also the rewards. The public surpluses generated by this stakeholder approach can be reinvested into further rounds of innovation. This long-term capital sharing approach is particularly important in meeting three objectives where the private sector is unwilling or unable to take the risks: to create new businesses in regions in decline or in a permanently depressed condition; to promote new businesses at the forefront of technology; and to accelerate the response to climate change (Ibid.). Public wealth funds could also be established for regional and urban scales. Regional wealth funds could focus and invest resources in economically disadvantaged communities, where a few small, hard-to-restart businesses are vital to community life and where support may be warranted for both economic and social reasons. Urban wealth funds have been effective funding vehicles in various cities globally to pay for infrastructure investments, including transport, education, and health care, as well as housing, without the use of taxes. Urban wealth funds are also a means by which the public sector can ensure the rise in land values that comes from public investment in infrastructure, in particular transport, is efficiently captured for the public purse (Ryan-Collins, Lloyd, and Macfarlane 2017).

Ultimately, public institutions form the real material basis of a new social contract between the state, capital, and labour. They can reclaim their rightful role as servants of the common good. They must think big and play a full part in the great transformations to come. They must get over their self-fulfilling fear of failure and realize that experimentation and errors are part of the learning process.

6. Conclusion

Despite stakeholder value having gained traction outside the realm of academic conceptualisations, the concept does not go far enough. It undersells the true meaning of stakeholder capitalism. The latter seeks to close the gap between stakeholders and shareholders rather than maintain the distinction. The aim is to empower stakeholders as shareholders – to give workers and citizens, trade unions and community groups, state institutions and NGOs an actual financial as well as political stake in the operation of capitalism.

First, to implement this vision, we need a new social contract. The combined efforts of the public and private sectors are needed to transform technological, economic, and social paradigms and bring better and broader growth. Symbiotic collaborations between government and business that truly serve the public interest are essential for public value creation. This depiction is very different from assuming that the private sector simply needs to be incentivised to invest. Indeed, it is when governments are bold and strategic that the most crowding in has happened.

Second, a mission orientation is necessary to coordinate public and private initiatives and build new networks. Importantly, a mission-oriented framework, which actively co-creates new markets, requires continuous and dynamic monitoring and evaluation throughout the innovation and investment processes. Missions themselves should be co-designed, with different voices at the table – they can help bring public purpose to the heart of policy making. Missions have the ability to be transformative across entire value chains and not be limited to narrow areas where positive and negative externalities exist.

Third, to make a new social contract and a mission-orientation work, we need to build state capabilities to successfully shape and create markets by establishing strong regulations and conditionalities that guide market players towards the achievement of purposeful missions. Without in-house capabilities, governments will resort to outsourcing work and knowledge to third parties such as consulting companies, think tanks, and the private sector. To avoid the hollowing out of government, public institutions need to invest in scientific and technological expertise to nurture their capacity for risk-taking and experimentation.

Fourth, because in many cases public investments have become business giveaways, making individuals and their companies rich but providing little return to the economy or the state, stakeholder capitalism needs to incorporate a fundamentally transformed risk-reward relationship. Acknowledging the collective nature of innovation must result in an increased sharing of the rewards that accrue from the process of innovation.

Lastly, financial institutions themselves can become more capable and mission-oriented by directing public finance towards societal goals. It is crucial to demonstrate ambition and provide patient, long-term finance to organisations willing and able to help steer an economy towards meeting its challenges. The conventional choice between tax rises or public debt to pay for large-scale state investment is a false dichotomy. In countries with monetary sovereignty, money can be generated by the state for public investments.

Note

1. See https://growthrocks.com/blog/big-five-tech-companies-acquisitions/.

Disclosure statement

No potential conflict of interest was reported by the author(s).

References

Avelino, F., and J. M. Wittmayer. 2016. "Shifting Power Relations in Sustainability Transitions: A Multi-Actor Perspective." *Journal of Environmental Policy & Planning* 18 (5): 628–649. doi:10.1080/1523908X.2015.1112259.

Block, F. L., and M. R. Keller. 2011. *State of Innovation: The U.S. Government's Role in Technology Development*. Boulder, CO: Paradigm.

Collington, R., and M. Mazzucato. 2022. "Beyond Outsourcing: Re-Embedding the State in Public Value Production." UCL Institute for Innovation and Public Purpose, Working Paper Series (IIPP WP 2022-14). https://www.ucl.ac.uk/bartlett/public-purpose/wp2022-14.

Detter, D., S. Fölster, and J. Ryan-Collins. 2020. "Public Wealth Funds: Supporting Economic Recovery and Sustainable Growth." *UCL Institute for Innovation and Public Purpose*. Policy Report (IIPP 2020-16). https://www.ucl.ac.uk/bartlett/public-purpose/sites/public-purpose/files/final_pwf_report_detter_folster_ryan-collins_16_nov.pdf

Evans, P. B. 1995. *Embedded Autonomy: States and Industrial Transformation*. Vol. 25. Princeton, NJ: Princeton University Press.

Friedman, M. 1970. "The Social Responsibility of Business is to Increase Profits." *The New York Times*. https://www.nytimes.com/1970/09/13/archives/a-friedman-doctrine-the-social-responsibility-of-business-is-to.html.

Grossman, G., and E. Oberfield. 2022. "Trying to Account for the Decline in the Labour Share." *CEPR.org*. https://cepr.org/voxeu/columns/trying-account-decline-labour-share

Hall, P., and D. Soskice. 2001. *Varieties of Capitalism: The Institutional Foundations of Comparative Advantage*. Oxford: Oxford University Press.

Jacobs, M., and M. Mazzucato, eds. 2016. *Rethinking Capitalism: Economics and Policy for Sustainable and Inclusive Growth*. Oxford, UK: Wiley-Blackwell.

Jensen, M. J., and W.H. Meckling. 1976. "Theory of the Firm: Managerial Behavior, Agency Costs and Ownership Structure." *Journal of Financial Economics* 3 (4): 305–360.

Kattel, R., and M. Mazzucato. 2018. "Mission-Oriented Innovation Policy and Dynamic Capabilities in the Public Sector." UCL Institute for Innovation and Public Purpose, Working Paper Series (IIPP WP 2018-5). http://www.ucl.ac.uk/bartlett/public-purpose/wp2018-05

Lazonick, W. 2014. "Profits Without Prosperity." *Harvard Business Review*. https://hbr.org/2014/09/profits-without-prosperity

Mazzoleni, R., and R. R. Nelson. 1998. "The Benefits and Costs of Strong Patent Protection: A Contribution to the Current Debate." *Research Policy* 27 (3): 273–284. doi:10.1016/S0048-7333(98)00048-1.

Mazzucato, M. 2013. *The Entrepreneurial State: Debunking Public Vs. Private Sector Myths*. London: Anthem Press.

Mazzucato, M. 2018a. *The Value of Everything: Making and Taking in the Global Economy*. London: Allen Lane.

Mazzucato, M. 2018b. "Mission-Oriented Research & Innovation in the European Union: A Problem-Solving Approach to Fuel Innovation-Led Growth." European Commission. https://ec.europa.eu/info/sites/default/files/mazzucato_report_2018.pdf

Mazzucato, M. 2018c. "Governing Missions in the European Union." European Commission. https://ec.europa.eu/info/sites/default/files/research_and_innovation/contact/documents/ec_rtd_mazzucato-report-issue2_072019.pdf

Mazzucato, M. 2021. *Mission Economy: A Moonshot Guide to Changing Capitalism*. London: Allen Lane.

Mazzucato, M., and R. Collington. 2023. *The Big Con: How the Consulting Industry Weakens Our Businesses, Infantilizes Our Governments, and Warps Our Economies*. London: Allen Lane.

Mazzucato, M., G. Gouzoulis, and J. Ryan-Collins. 2023. "The Good, the Bad and the Grey Areas: Mapping Modern Economic Rents." *Cambridge Journal of Economics*.

Mazzucato, M., R. Kattel, and J. Ryan-Collins. 2020. "Challenge-Driven Innovation Policy: Towards a New Policy Toolkit." *Journal of Industry, Competition and Trade* 20 (2): 421–437. doi:10.1007/s10842-019-00329-w.

Mazzucato, M., and L. Macfarlane. 2019. "A Mission-Oriented Framework for the Scottish National Investment Bank." UCL Institute for Innovation and Public Purpose, Policy Paper (IIPP 2019- 02). https://www.ucl.ac.uk/bartlett/publicpurpose/wp2019-02

Mazzucato, M., and C. Penna. 2015. "Beyond Market Failures: The Market Creating and Shaping Roles of State Investment Banks." Levy Economics Institute of Bard College Working Paper No. 831.

Mazzucato, M., and V. Roy. 2018. "Rethinking Value in Health Innovation: From Mystifications Towards Prescriptions." *Journal of Economic Policy Reform* 22 (2): 1–19. doi:10.1080/17487870.2018.1509712.

Medecins san frontiers. 2020. "Governments Must Demand Pharma Make All COVID-19 Vaccine Deals Public." *MSF.org*. https://www.msf.org/governments-must-demand-all-coronavirus-covid-19-vaccine-deals-are-made-public

Penrose, E. 1959. *The Theory of the Growth of the Firm*. Oxford: Basil Blackwell.

Polanyi, K. 19442001. *The Great Transformation: The Political and Economic Origins of Our Time*. 2nd Beacon Paperback ed. Boston, MA: Beacon Press.

Rittel, H., and M. Webber. 1973. "Dilemmas in a General Theory of Planning." *Policy Sciences* 4 (2): 155–169. doi:10.1007/BF01405730.

Rodrik, D. 2004. *Industrial Policy for the Twenty-First Century*. Cambridge, MA: John F. Kennedy School of Government, Harvard University.

Ruttan, V. 2006. *Is War Necessary for Economic Growth? Military Procurement and Technology Development*. Oxford: Oxford Scholarship Online.

Ryan-Collins, J., T. Lloyd, and L. Macfarlane. 2017. "Rethinking the Economics of Land and Housing."

Schwab, K. 2021. *Stakeholder Capitalism: A Global Economy That Works for Progress, People and Planet*. Hoboken, New Jersey: Wiley.

Smith, A. 1776. *The Wealth of Nations*. 1937 ed. New York: Modern Library.

Stiglitz, J. 2017. "America Has a Monopoly Problem – and It's Huge." The Nation, https://www.thenation.com/article/america-has-a-monopoly-problem-and-its-huge

Strauss, I., T. O'Reilly, M. Mazzucato, and J. Ryan-Collins. 2021. "Crouching Tiger, Hidden Dragons: How 10-K Disclosure Rules Help Big Tech Conceal Market Power and Expand Platform Dominance." UCL Institute for Innovation and Public Purpose, IIPP Policy Report No. 2021/04. https://www.ucl.ac.uk/bartlett/public-purpose/2021-04

Susskind, D. 2020. *A World Without Work: Technology, Automation and How We Respond*. London: Allen Lane.

Teece, D., G. S. Pisano, and A. Shuen. 1997. "Dynamic Capabilities and Strategic Management." *Strategic Management Journal* 18 (7): 509–533.

Tulum, Ö., and W. Lazonick. 2018. "Financialized Corporations in a National Innovation System: The U.S. Pharmaceutical Industry." *International Journal of Political Economy* [Online]. 47 (3–4): 281–316.

Vogl, V., M. Åhman, and L. J. Nilsson. 2021. "The Making of Green Steel in the EU: A Policy Evaluation for the Early Commercialization Phase." *Climate Policy* 21: 78–92.

World Health Organization. 2020. "COVID-19 Technology Access Pool." [Online]. https://www.who.int/initiatives/covid-19-technology-access-pool

Zuboff, S. 2019. *The Age of Surveillance Capitalism*. London, England: Profile Books.

Is the most unproductive firm the foundation of the most efficient economy? Penrosian learning confronts the neoclassical fallacy

William Lazonick

ABSTRACT

Edith Penrose's *The Theory of the Growth of the Firm* provides an intellectual foundation for a theory of innovative enterprise, which is essential to any attempt to explain productivity growth, employment opportunity, and income distribution. Penrose's theory of the firm is also an antidote to the absurdity that has been taught by PhD economists to millions of college students for over seven decades: the most unproductive firm is the foundation of the most efficient economy. The dissemination of this 'neoclassical fallacy' to a mass audience began with Paul A. Samuelson's textbook, *Economics: An Introductory Analysis*, first published in 1948. Over the decades, the neoclassical fallacy has persisted through 18 revisions of Samuelson, *Economics* and in its countless 'economics principles' clones. This essay challenges the intellectual hegemony of neoclassical economics by exposing the illogic of its foundational assumptions about how a modern economy operates and performs. To get beyond the neoclassical fallacy, economists must be trained in a 'historical transformation' methodology that integrates history and theory. It is a methodology in which theory serves as both a distillation of what we have learned from the study of history and a guide to what we need to learn about reality as the 'present as history' unfolds.

1. Penrosian learning and innovative enterprise

Edith Penrose's 1959 book, *The Theory of the Growth of the Firm [TGF]*, fits the definition of a 'classic': a work that many cite but few have read.[1] The view that I advance in this essay is that no one should be granted a PhD in economics who has not read *TGF* and understood what this profound economist had to say. Penrose's theory of how a firm grows has transformative implications for comprehending how a modern economy operates and performs. It provides an intellectual foundation for a theory of innovative enterprise, which is essential to any attempt to explain productivity growth, employment opportunity, and income distribution.

Properly understood, Penrose's theory of the firm is also, as I demonstrate in this essay, an antidote to the deception that is foundational to neoclassical economics: The theory, taught by PhD economists to millions upon millions of college students for over seven decades, that the most unproductive firm is the foundation of the most efficient economy. I call this proposition the 'neoclassical fallacy'. Its dissemination to a mass audience of college students began with Paul A. Samuelson's neoclassical textbook, *Economics: An Introductory Analysis*, first published in 1948. Over the decades, the neoclassical fallacy has persisted through 18 revisions of Samuelson's *Economics* and in its countless 'economics principles' clones. This essay challenges the intellectual hegemony of neoclassical economics by exposing the illogic of its foundational assumptions about how a modern economy operates and performs.

The neoclassical fallacy gained popularity in the 1950s, during which decade, as an MIT professor, Samuelson revised *Economics* three times. Meanwhile, Penrose formulated the logic of organizational learning that she lays out in *TGF* from the facts of firm growth, absorbing what was known in the 1950s about the large corporations that had come to dominate the U.S. economy. Also, during that decade, the knowledge base on the growth of firms on which economists could subsequently draw was undergoing an intellectual revolution led by the business historian, Alfred D. Chandler, Jr., who was engaged in the first stage of a career that would span more than a half century. Chandler's contribution documented and analyzed the centrality to U.S economic development of what he would call 'the managerial revolution in American business'.[2]

In *TGF*, Penrose depicts the large industrial corporation as one that grows by investing in organizational learning that endows the firm with unique productive capabilities. Its long-term strategy is to build on its success in developing capabilities in one line of business by redeploying these capabilities to a new, technologically related line of business as the older one matures. As Chandler shows in his seminal book *Strategy and Structure: Chapters in the History of American Industrial Enterprise*, published just three years after *TGF*, from the 1920s through the 1950s U.S. industrial firms implemented the multidivisional structure to enable one company to manage efficiently many different lines of business in its process of growth.[3]

Covering the same subject matter and time period as Penrose, Chandler's *Strategy and Structure* confirmed that her theory of the growth of the firm depicted the type of industrial corporation that had in fact driven the growth of the U.S. economy from the 1920s through the 1950s. Indeed, in 1960, one year after the publication of *TGF*, Penrose made a direct contribution to what would become known as Chandlerian business history with her prize-winning publication in *Business History Review* of a case study of growth through multidivisionalization at Hercules Powder Company, a corporation that she had studied through field research in 1954.[4]

For both Penrose and Chandler, multidivisionalization overcame managerial constraints on the growth of the firm by placing strategic control of the growth process in the hands of salaried executives who, by virtue of being career employees, had deep understanding of the evolving technologies and markets of the industries in which the companies that they led competed. The multidivisional structure could be used to manage multiple lines of business efficiently if these businesses were in industries related by technological capability and/or product markets. The importance of that proviso would become clear when, justified by the ideology that a good manager could manage anything, the conglomerates that expanded through merger and acquisition in unrelated businesses in the 1960s collapsed in the 1970s and 1980s under their own unmanageable weight.[5]

The particular technological and market characteristics of an industry are important to the Penrosian perspective because a firm that can grow successfully is one that engages in organizational learning specific to that industry. In *TGF*, Penrose conceptualizes the modern corporate enterprise as an organization that administers a collection of human and physical resources. People contribute labor services to the firm not merely as individuals but as team members who engage in learning about how to make best use of the firm's productive resources, with senior executives providing entrepreneurial services. This learning is organizational: it cannot be done all alone, and hence it is collective; and it cannot be done all at once, and hence it is cumulative.[6]

At any point in time, this organizational learning endows the firm with experience that gives it productive opportunities unavailable to other firms, even in the same industry, that have not invested in these learning processes and, therefore, have not accumulated the same innovative experience. The accumulation of these unique capabilities enables the firm to overcome the 'managerial limit' that, in the neoclassical theory of the firm, causes the onset of increasing cost and constrains the growth of the firm.[7] The innovating firm can transfer and reshape its existing productive capabilities to take advantage of new business opportunities.

Each strategic move into a new line of business enables the firm to utilize productive capabilities, including human capabilities, accumulated through the process of organizational learning in generating its previous, now mature, products. These unused productive capabilities, along with reinvestment of some of the profits that their previous use has generated, provide foundations for the further growth of the firm, achieved through in-house complementary investments in new productive capabilities or the acquisition and integration of other firms that have already developed these complementary capabilities. For Penrose, the growth of the firm through movement into new lines of business is not a random process but rather entails strategic investments to ensure the utilization, and the further development, of the productive capabilities of the firm's employees over the course of their careers.

In his 1977 book *The Visible Hand*, which covers the historical period for the half century before the 1920s that set the stage for the emergence of the multidivisional structure, Chandler's focus is on managerial coordination of mass production and mass distribution, achieving what he calls 'economies of speed' – or economics of scale per unit of time.[8] This high-speed (or high-throughput) utilization of productive capabilities transforms the high fixed cost of investing in productive capabilities into low unit cost of sold output. Chandler emphasizes that the source of high fixed cost is investment in not only plant and equipment designed for mass production but also distribution channels required to access a large enough extent of the market so that the mass-produced goods can be sold at competitive prices. Assuming that product quality is maintained with scaling of production, the higher the rate of throughput from investment in input to sold output, the lower the unit cost and the greater the profit that can be generated.

This profit is then available to be reinvested in the firm's productive capabilities, which include not only plant and equipment but also training and retaining the employees upon whose skill and effort the profitability of the firm's value-creating processes depends.

Enhanced labor productivity generates the revenues with which employees can be rewarded in the form of rising wages and more stable employment to achieve organizational integration.

Building on an analysis of how cooperation between employers and employees in utilizing effort-saving technology served to generate productivity gains in which both parties could share, as set out in my 1990 book *Competitive Advantage on the Shop Floor*, my contribution to the Chandlerian historical analysis of the relation between managerial coordination and economies of speed has been to show how, in U.S. mass-production workplaces, by the 1920s this 'win-win' outcome was partially achieved, even without unions. With mass layoffs of blue-collar workers by large firms during the 1930s, however, cooperative relations between management and labor broke down in major U.S. industrial enterprises. The consequent rise of mass-production unionism, with its protection of workers' seniority rights, resurrected management-labor cooperation in the immediate post-World War II decades, contributing to more stable and more equitable growth in the U.S. economy as a whole. By the 1970s, however, by virtue of their even more thorough organizational integration of shop-floor workers into the processes of mass production, the Japanese were outcompeting U.S. companies in industries such as automobiles, electronics, and steel – industries in which U.S. companies had previously been the world's leading mass producers.[9]

In *The Visible Hand*, Chandler focuses on the *utilization* of productive capabilities while largely ignoring the *development* of productive capabilities, which is the primary emphasis of Penrose's theory of the growth of the firm. As a result, in his earlier work, Chandler does not explicitly analyze investment in human capabilities as a component of fixed cost. But in his 1990 book *Scale and Scope*, in which he compares 'the dynamics of industrial capitalism' in the United States, Britain, and Germany, Chandler begins to focus on the development of productive capabilities through organizational-learning processes. This business activity is inherent in the concept of *economies of scope*; the spreading of a firm's fixed costs across many lines of business, organized through multi-divisionalization, as Chandler had previously documented and analyzed in *Strategy and Structure*. Recognizing the importance of the development, and not just the utilization, of productive capabilities to the growth of the firm, in 1993 Chandler launched what he called his 'paths of learning' project, researching and writing two books, one on the history of the consumer electronic and computer industries and the other on the evolution of the chemical and pharmaceutical industries.[10]

Historically, the Penrosian and Chandlerian perspectives are rooted in what I have called the 'Old Economy business model', and even in his later 'paths of learning' books, Chandler did not perceive the strategic, organizational, and financial implications for the transformation of industrial innovation and global competition of the rise of the stock-market-oriented 'New Economy business model' in industries such as information-and-communication technology and pharmaceuticals.[11] Nevertheless, in combination, the works of Penrose and Chandler provide intellectual foundations for my own work on the Theory of Innovative Enterprise (TIE) – an endeavor that has enabled me, as an economist, to recognize not only the profound importance of organizational learning for a theory of economic development but also the absurdity of using the neoclassical theory of the firm for understanding the central institution of a modern economy: the business corporation.

In the next section of this essay, building on Penrosian theory and Chandlerian history, I outline the basic assumptions and concepts of TIE. In Section 3, I make use of TIE to demonstrate the neoclassical fallacy: the argument that the most unproductive firm is the foundation of the most efficient economy. Then, in Section 4, I draw out the implications of the neoclassical fallacy for what I call 'the myth of the market economy': the dominance in economic thinking of the view that, ideally even if not actually, a modern economy should rely on markets to allocate resources to their most efficient uses – in effect viewing the existence of the large corporation as a massive 'market imperfection'. In the concluding section of this essay, I summarize the methodological implications of TIE for studying the operation and performance of a modern economy.

2. The theory of innovative enterprise

Through decades of research and teaching, I have constructed TIE to provide an analytical perspective on the microfoundations for achieving stable and equitable economic growth – or what, as a shorthand, I call 'sustainable prosperity'. There is no way in which an economy can attain stable and equitable growth unless its major business enterprises focus on investing in productive capabilities for the sake of generating innovative products. Beginning with a characterization of the innovation process as *uncertain, collective, and cumulative*, TIE articulates three 'social conditions of innovative enterprise' – *strategic control, organizational integration,* and *financial commitment* – that can support the innovation process. Armed with TIE, we can analyze the impacts of the innovation process on employment opportunity, income distribution, and productivity growth. We can ask whether the dominant characteristics of the nation's major business enterprises support or undermine the attainment of stable and equitable growth in the national economy as a whole.

TIE is an analytical framework for understanding how a business enterprise can generate a product that is higher quality and lower cost than products previously available, and thus be a source of productivity growth. As noted above, the innovation process that can generate a higher-quality, lower-cost product is uncertain, collective, and cumulative[12]:

- **Uncertain**: When investments in transforming technologies and accessing markets are made, the product and financial outcomes cannot be known; if they were, the process would not be innovation. Hence the need for *strategy*.
- **Collective**: To generate a higher-quality, lower-cost product, the enterprise must integrate the skills and efforts of large numbers of people with different hierarchical responsibilities and functional specialties into the learning processes that are the essence of innovation. Hence the need for *organization*.
- **Cumulative**: Collective learning today enables collective learning tomorrow, and, to generate a higher-quality, lower-cost product, these organizational-learning processes must be sustained continuously over time until, through the sale of innovative products, financial returns can be generated. Hence the need for *finance*.

Strategic control, organizational integration, and financial commitment enable the firm to manage the uncertain, collective, and cumulative character of the innovation process.

- **Strategic control**: For innovation to occur in the face of technological, market, and competitive uncertainties, executives who control corporate resource allocation must have the *abilities and incentives* to make strategic investments in innovation. Their abilities depend on their knowledge of how strategic investments in new capabilities can enhance the enterprise's existing capabilities. Their incentives depend on alignment of their personal interests and values with the company's purpose of generating innovative products.
- **Organizational integration**: The implementation of an innovation strategy requires integration of people working in a complex division of labor into the *collective and cumulative learning processes* that are the essence of innovation. Work satisfaction, promotion, remuneration, and benefits are instruments in a reward system that motivates and empowers employees to engage in collective learning over a sustained period of time.
- **Financial commitment**: For collective learning to cumulate over time, the sustained commitment of 'patient capital' must keep the learning organization intact. For a startup company, *venture capital* can provide financial commitment. For a going concern, *retained earnings* (leveraged, if need be, by debt issues) are the foundation of financial commitment.

The uncertainty of an innovation strategy is embodied in the fixed-cost investments required to develop the productive capabilities that may, if the strategy is successful, result in a higher-quality product than those available on the market. The higher-quality product, for which those buyers who are less price sensitive will be willing to pay a premium, gives the innovating firm a competitive advantage on the market. Assuming that the firm can maintain this higher quality as it increases output to serve a larger market, it will drive down unit cost as it spreads out its fixed cost over a larger quantity of sold output, which in turn gives the firm greater access to those buyers who are more price sensitive.

By the same token, if the expansion of the firm's output necessitates the utilization of additional variable inputs (purchased at a constant factor price on the particular factor market as required for the firm to expand its output) that turn out to be inferior in quality to those used previously, the rise in average variable cost (AVC) will to some extent offset the decline in average fixed cost (AFC) as the firm expands output. If the rise in AVC more than offsets the decline in AFC, then average total cost (ATC) will rise. Economists call this cost condition 'internal diseconomies of scale', depicted in the textbooks by the U-shaped cost curve, shown on the left-hand side of Figure 1.

The neoclassical theory of the firm assumes that profits are competed away as more identical firms enter an industry. Reflecting the neoclassical fallacy, under conditions of 'perfect competition' – assumed to be the best of all possible economic worlds – the profits that each firm maximizes by equating marginal cost and marginal revenue equal zero. The action of maximizing profit (or, alternatively, minimizing cost) is known as 'optimizing' subject to given technological and market constraints – or 'constrained

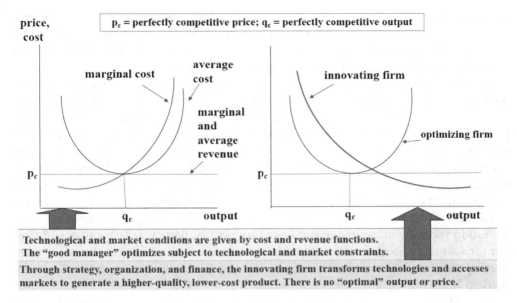

Figure 1. The innovating firm outcompetes the optimizing firm.

optimization' – and hence, as shown on the right-hand side of Figure 1, we can compare the cost structures of the 'innovating firm' of TIE and the 'optimizing firm' of the neoclassical textbooks.

In the neoclassical theory of the firm, the perfectly elastic demand curve shown in Figure 1 indicates that the firm can sell output up to the point at which it can maximize profit (marginal revenue equals marginal cost) without placing discernible downward pressure on the price of the product it is selling. The industry demand curve is typically (and in most cases reasonably) assumed to be downward sloping, but in 'perfect competition' each of the large numbers of identical firms in the industry is so small relative to the size of the industry as a whole that it can sell any level of output needed to maximize profit at the current industry price. If the market price of the product happens to be greater than the minimum price on the average cost curve, neoclassical theory argues, more identical firms will enter the industry, driving down the product price to the point at which all firms maximize profit at a price-output equilibrium at which profits are zero. Neoclassical economists have long called this state of industry affairs 'perfect competition' – a concept to which we shall return when we dissect the neoclassical fallacy in Section 3 of this essay.

Key to TIE is the argument that, through the combination of strategic control, organizational integration, and financial commitment, an innovating firm may be able to differentiate itself from its competitors and generate a higher-quality, lower-cost product that, as shown in Figure 1, gives it a sustained competitive advantage.

Note, however, that an innovation strategy that may eventually enable the firm to generate a higher-quality, lower-cost product may place the innovating firm at a *competitive disadvantage* at low levels of output, as indicated in Figure 1. The reason is that an innovation strategy tends to entail higher fixed cost than the fixed cost incurred under the strategy of optimizing subject to given technological and market constraints. As an essential part of the innovation process, the innovating firm must transform technology and access a sufficient extent of the market for its product to transform high fixed cost into low unit cost (see Figure 1), and, thereby, convert competitive disadvantage at low levels of output into competitive advantage at high levels of output.

The higher fixed cost of the innovating firm derives from both the *size* and the *duration* of the innovative investment strategy. The innovating firm will have a higher fixed cost than the optimizing firm incurs if, as is typically the case, the innovation process requires the *simultaneous development* of productive capabilities across a broader and deeper range of integrated activities than those undertaken by the optimizing firm. Put differently, the innovating firm chooses to 'make' rather than 'buy': Investment in the organizational-learning processes that may be able to generate a higher-quality product means that, strategically, the innovating firm may have to eschew the purchase of certain 'variable cost' inputs on the market that would be needed to expand output, investing instead in vertically integrated operations to supply that particular factor of production. For the sake of developing a higher-quality product, the innovating firm chooses to incur fixed cost rather than avail itself of the option that the existence of one or more factor markets holds out for incurring variable cost.

In addition to the size of the fixed cost of the innovative investment strategy at a given point in time, the firm's fixed cost will increase with the duration that is required to transform technologies and access markets until these processes result in products that are sufficiently high quality and low cost to generate returns through product-market sales. If the size of investments in physical capital tends to increase the fixed cost of an innovation strategy, so too does the duration of the investment required for an organization of people to engage in the collective and cumulative – that is, organizational – learning that innovation requires. As we have seen, organizational learning to transform technologies and access markets is the central characteristic of the innovation process.

The high fixed cost of an innovation strategy creates the need for the firm to attain a high level of *utilization* of the productive capabilities that it has developed and thus to achieve 'economies of scale'. Meanwhile, as already discussed, when it needs an input that is available on a certain factor market in sufficient quality and quantity, the innovating firm can choose to purchase additional quantities of the input as required to expand output, thus incurring the variable cost of using the market as opposed to the fixed cost of investing in the firm. Yet, during the innovation process, the strategic decision-maker's initial assumption that the innovating firm can expand output by accessing an increasing quantity of variable input of the required quality may not be borne out as more output is produced for sale. Given the productive capabilities that it has developed, the innovating firm may experience increasing cost because of the problem of maintaining the quality of a variable input as it employs a larger quantity of this input in the production process.

But rather than, as in the case of the optimizing firm, take increasing cost as a given constraint on the growth of the firm, the innovating firm attempts to transform its access to high-quality productive capabilities at high levels of output. To do so, it invests in the *development* of that productive capability, the *utilization* of which has become the source of increasing variable cost. To overcome the constraint on its innovation strategy posed by reliance on the market to supply it with an input – which is what accessing a variable factor of production entails – the innovating firm integrates the supply of that factor into its internal operations, as depicted in Figure 2. In the process, it transforms a variable cost into a fixed cost, and then seeks to develop the productive capability of that integrated input to justify the augmented fixed-cost investment.

Previously this productive resource was utilized as a variable input that could be purchased incrementally at the going factor price as extra units of the input were needed to expand output. But having found that the expansion of output results in a deterioration in the quality of the variable input, the innovating firm changes its strategy from 'buy' to 'make'.[13] Having, as a result, added to its fixed cost in order to overcome the constraint on enterprise expansion posed by increasing variable cost, the innovating firm is then under even more pressure to generate a higher-quality product so that it can expand its sold output to transform high fixed cost into low unit cost.

In effect, to restate the first principle of economics enunciated by Adam Smith in *The Wealth of Nations*,[14] economies of scale are limited by the extent of the market. The firm's higher-quality product enables it to access a larger extent of the market than its competitors. Indeed, learning about what potential buyers want and convincing them that the firm's product is actually 'higher quality' add to the fixed cost of the innovation strategy. Since its fixed cost results from investments in not only transforming technology but also accessing markets, the innovating firm's increase in fixed cost requires an even larger extent of the market to convert high fixed cost into low unit cost.

When, through the development and utilization of productive capabilities, the innovating firm succeeds in the conversion of high fixed cost into low unit cost, it does not merely 'unbend' the U-shaped cost curve but rather restructures it. By reshaping the cost

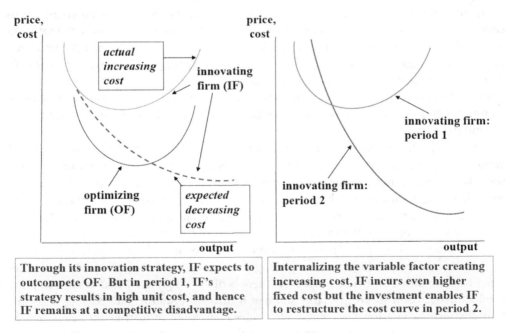

Figure 2. Innovation strategy and the restructuring of the cost curve.

curve in this way, the innovating firm creates the possibility of securing competitive advantage over its 'optimizing' rivals who, as instructed by the economics textbooks, accept increasing diseconomies of scale as a given constraint (see Figure 1 above).

A potent way for an innovating firm to attain a larger extent of the market is to share some of the gains of this cost transformation with its customers in the form of lower prices. If so, the innovating firm may sell a higher quantity of output at a lower price than its 'optimizing' competitors. If the innovating firm continues to expand its market share, it will drive optimizing firms out of the market because they are, relatively, unproductive firms.

The emergence of an innovative enterprise – one that secures a large market share by generating a higher-quality, lower-cost product than was previously available – depends on the social conditions of innovative enterprise. To set innovation in motion, the particular people who occupy positions of strategic control must possess abilities to lead the innovation process and incentives to take up a challenge despite the uncertainty inherent in innovation that creates a distinct possibility of failure. These strategic decision-makers must identify the organizational-learning processes in which to invest in order to generate a higher-quality product. To achieve the collective and cumulative learning that is the essence of innovation, they must put into place incentive systems designed to integrate the work of large numbers of people with different hierarchical responsibilities and functional specialties. The incentive system must include not only pay structures to motivate and reward productive effort but also promotion opportunities through which each employee can build a career in the hope that it will span decades. As Penrose recognizes, organizational integration entails investment in people, who, in effect, represent part of the innovating firm's fixed cost.

Finally, those in positions of strategic control must mobilize financial resources to sustain the innovation process until it can generate the innovative products that yield financial returns. For new ventures, some form of private equity provides this committed finance, with a listing on a public stock market representing an 'exit strategy' through which the private-equity investors can extract returns from their investments in the firm. For established companies that are generating profits, the fundamental source of financial commitment is the cash that a company retains out of profits and reinvests in productive capabilities.

To sum up: In my elaboration of TIE, I use the distinction between fixed cost and variable cost to argue that an innovating firm that experiences rising variable cost as it seeks to expand output will recognize the need to exercise control over the quality of the variable input, the use of which is causing the rise in cost. To do so, the innovating firm will integrate the production of that input into its internal operations, thus transforming the variable cost of using the market into a fixed cost of investing in the enterprise. This strategic move will place the innovating firm at a competitive disadvantage at low levels of output (as shown in Figure 1), increasing the imperative that it attain a large market share to drive down unit cost. Moreover, there is often a high fixed cost of accessing the product market and securing a large share of it through branding, advertising, distribution channels, a salaried sales force, etc. Indeed, in some industries the fixed cost of accessing a large market share is greater than the fixed cost of investing in the transformation of production technologies.

Whether done for the sake of transforming technologies, accessing markets, or both, investment in productive capabilities, including first and foremost those of its labor force, drives innovation and the growth of the firm. To retain and motivate those whom the firm has hired and trained, and who have accumulated productive experience through their work, the innovating firm generally offers these employees higher pay, more employment security, superior benefits, and more interesting work, all of which add to the fixed cost of the productive asset that an employee's labor represents. The innovating firm makes its employees better off, but it can afford, and indeed profit from, the increased labor expense when that labor's productive capability enables the firm to gain a competitive advantage by generating a higher-quality, lower-cost product.

The innovating firm shares the gains of innovation with its employees by making investments in what I have called their 'collective and cumulative careers'.[15] Under such circumstances, increases in labor incomes and increases in labor productivity tend to show a highly positive correlation – an interconnection that, I argue, was prevalent in U.S. business enterprises in the decades after World War II when, for white males at least, the 'career with one company' was the employment norm.[16]

When successful, the innovating firm may come to dominate its industry, with output that is larger and unit cost – and hence, potentially, its product price – that is lower than if a large number of small firms continued to populate the industry. The overall gains from innovation will depend on the relation between the innovating firm's cost structure and the industry's demand structure, while the distribution of those gains among the firm's various 'stakeholders' will depend on their relative power to extract the value that they helped to create.[17] Indeed, as documented in my book with Jang-Sup Shin, *Predatory Value Extraction*,[18] and as will be discussed in the conclusion of this essay, problems of unstable employment, inequitable incomes, and slowing productivity arise when those who have the power to extract the most value from the firm are those who make the smallest – and in many cases negative – contributions to the value-creation process.

There are gains to innovative enterprise that can be shared, and the ways in which these gains are shared determine the extent to which the innovative enterprise contributes to stable and equitable growth in the economy as a whole. In expanding output and lowering cost, it is theoretically possible (although by no means inevitable) for the gains to innovative enterprise to permit, simultaneously, higher pay, more stable employment, and better work conditions for employees; a stronger balance sheet for the firm; more secure paper for creditors; higher dividends and stock prices for shareholders; more tax revenues for governments; and higher-quality products at lower prices for consumers. Innovative enterprise provides a foundation for achieving sustainable prosperity.

3. The neoclassical fallacy

The theory of perfect competition, which is the neoclassical economist's ideal of economic efficiency, views the firm as impotent and the market as omnipotent in allocating the economy's resources. By the neoclassical theory's key assumptions, the firm in perfect competition is, as Paul Samuelson himself revealed – and then, as we shall see, concealed – *an unproductive firm*. Indeed, the more unproductive the firm, the smaller the firm's output as a proportion of industry output, and, hence, the more 'perfect' the competition!

Yet, neoclassical theory posits the firm in perfect competition as the microfoundation of an economy in which the allocation of resources results in the ideal of economic efficiency, even if because of 'market imperfections' that ideal is difficult or impossible to attain.

If neoclassical logic concerning the relation between firm productivity and economic performance sounds absurd, that is because it is. Eighty years ago, Joseph Schumpeter, with his focus on innovation as the fundamental phenomenon of economic development, argued that 'perfect competition is not only impossible but inferior, and has no title to being set up as a model of ideal efficiency'. The reason: Large-scale enterprise is 'the most powerful engine of [economic] progress and in particular of the long-run expansion of total output'.[19]

The neoclassical theory of the firm in perfect competition cannot explain why for well over a century very large firms have dominated the U.S. economy.[20] In the 1950s, when Penrose researched and wrote *TGF*, the large industrial corporation was central to U.S. economic power, and within the United States this power was concentrated in a relatively small number of large corporations. In 1959, 44 of the world's 50 largest corporations in terms of revenues were based in the United States, with the remaining six headquartered in Europe. In that year, U.S. corporations with assets of $100 million or more accounted for one-tenth of one percent of all corporations, but over 55% of all corporate assets, almost 55% of before-tax corporate profits, and 68% of all corporate dividends.[21]

In 2017, 1,100 companies that had 10,000 or more employees in the United States, with an average workforce of 34,308, were only 0.018% of all U.S. businesses. But these 1,100 companies had 10% of all establishments, 29% of employees, 33% of payrolls, and 37% of all revenues. For 2,156 companies with 5,000 or more employees (average, 20,859) in 2017, these shares were 12% of establishments, 35% of employees, 40% of payrolls, and 45% of revenues.[22] The resource-allocation decisions of these large companies have profound implications for employment opportunity, income distribution, and productivity growth in the United States.

Given their adherence to the 'perfect competition' ideal, neoclassical economists view these large firms as 'market imperfections', also known as monopolies or oligopolies. By focusing economic analysis on how the efficiency of the large-scale enterprise falls short of an absurd ideal, the neoclassical perspective precludes an analysis of the productive power of these large firms – and of how they may, or may not, contribute to the achievement of stable and equitable economic growth. In short, neoclassical economics lacks a theory of innovative enterprise. More generally, neoclassical economics avoids the analysis of how, through organizational learning, businesses *develop* productive capabilities as well as the conditions under which innovative investment activities can contribute to stable and equitable growth in the economy as a whole.

If we go back to the basics of the neoclassical theory of the firm, we can perceive what Schumpeter meant when he wrote that 'perfect competition . . . has no title to being set up as a model of ideal efficiency'. As conventionally defined, perfect competition exists when each among a very large number of identical firms in an industry has such a small share of total industry output that any individual firm, acting on its own, can produce its profit-maximizing output without influencing the price of the industry's product. Each of these identical firms is constrained to be very small by the assumption that at a very low level of the firm's output relative to the size of the industry's total output the firm's increasing

AVC overwhelms decreasing AFC, so that the firm faces a U-shaped cost curve in deciding how much output to produce. It follows mathematically that the firm maximizes profit at the output at which marginal revenue equals marginal cost. Thus, we have the theory of the *optimizing firm* that holds center stage – and indeed the only stage – in virtually every introductory economics textbook used worldwide.[23]

With the publication of *Economics: An Introductory Analysis* in 1948, Paul Samuelson created the model for the modern 'principles' textbook. It was reissued in 18 subsequent editions with Samuelson as the sole author through the 11th edition, published in 1980.[24] The large corporation was by no means unknown to Samuelson. In the first edition, in a section entitled 'The Giant Corporation', he observes: 'A list of the 200 largest non-financial corporations reads like an honor roll of American business, almost every name being a familiar household word'.[25] After naming a number of the largest of these companies and referring as well to the 60 largest financial corporations, Samuelson states:

> The tremendous concentration of economic power involved in these giant corporations may be gauged from the following facts: they alone own more than half of the total assets of all nonfinancial corporations, more than a third of all banking assets, and four-fifths of life insurance assets. In manufacturing alone, the 100 most important companies employed more than one-fifth of all manufacturing labor and accounted for one-third of the total value of all manufactured products.[26]

Samuelson recognizes that 'their power did not grow overnight' and that 'large size breeds success, and success breeds further success.'[27] He devotes five pages to 'the evil of monopoly' and 'the pyramiding of holding companies' enabled by the separation of share ownership from managerial control.[28] Samuelson then tells the reader that, 'lest it be thought that the present chapter emphasizes too strongly the defects of the big business,' he is quoting a statement from Joseph Schumpeter's *Capitalism, Socialism, and Democracy* in which 'the world-famous economist' notes the contributions of large corporations to rising standards of living. After assessing the evidence, Schumpeter concludes in the statement Samuelson quotes that 'a shocking suspicion dawns upon us that big business may have had more to do with creating that standard of life than keeping it down.'[29]

According to Samuelson, Schumpeter's perspective 'suggests that the future problem may not be one of choosing between large monopolistic corporations and small-scale competitors, but rather that of devising ways to improve the social and economic performance of large corporate aggregates.'[30] How, then, did these large corporations attain their dominant positions, and why did the top 100 manufacturers achieve high labor productivity relative to all manufacturers? The existence of very large, highly productive firms should have led economists to search for a theory of innovative enterprise as a foundation of economic analysis.[31] Samuelson's scientific papers are virtually all mathematical and devoid of empirical content, while his famous 'principles of economics' textbook in its successive editions promulgates the theory of the unproductive firm in perfect competition as the ideal of economic efficiency.

Perfect competition idealizes the very small firm, its growth constrained by rising AVC as it expands output. But why does AVC rise? And why does it rise to such an extent that it outweighs declining AFC, resulting in the U-shaped cost curve? Current textbooks do not supply an explanation. For example, N. Gregory Mankiw, in his *Principles of Microeconomics*, simply states that the cost curve is U-shaped – representing 'cost curves for a typical firm'[32] – and illustrates this 'principle' with made-up numbers for a hypothetical coffee shop in which AVC increases from $0.30 for an output of one cup of coffee to $12.00 for an output of ten cups, with rising AVC surpassing declining AFC after six cups.[33] Similarly, Paul Krugman and Robin Wells, in their *Essentials of Economics*, argue that a 'realistic marginal cost curve has a "swoosh" shape'[34] and give the example of a salsa maker whose AVC rises from $12.00 for an output of one case of salsa to $120.00 for an output of ten cases, with rising AVC surpassing declining AFC after an output of three cases.[35] Be it Mankiw or Krugman/Wells or a slew of other prominent economists whose textbooks compete in the introductory principles market, the 'explanation' for the U-shaped cost curve *is simply a made-up numerical example!* The authors of these textbooks make no attempt to explain to students what constrains the growth of the firm.

Not so with Samuelson's *Economics*, at least in the first through fifth editions, published between 1948 and 1961.[36] In these editions, Samuelson explains the U-shaped cost curve by assuming that labor is the firm's main variable-cost input and that, with the addition of units of labor as the firm expands output, the average productivity of labor falls because of, in Samuelson's words, 'limitations of plant space and management difficulties'. As the professor puts it (with my emphasis) in the fifth edition of *Economics*, published in 1961 (with wording only slightly different from that in the first edition): 'After the overhead has been spread thin over many units, it can no longer have much influence on Average Cost. Variable items become important, and as *Average Variable Cost begins to rise because of limitations of plant space and management difficulties, Average Cost finally begins to turn up*'.[37]

There it is, the explanation of the most important 'principle' of the neoclassical theory of the firm, and indeed of neoclassical microfoundations of macroeconomic performance, buried away on page 524 of an 853-page textbook. With this explanation of the limits on the growth of the firm, Samuelson argues that the most unproductive firm is the foundation of the most efficient economy. How so?

Note, first, that in Samuelson's explanation quoted above, he states (with my emphasis) that 'Average Cost *finally* begins to turn up'. The word 'finally' betrays Samuelson's methodological bias because if the average cost curve does not turn up – that is, if rising AVC does not outweigh declining AFC as the firm's output increases – then the decision rule of marginal revenue equals marginal cost in determining the firm's optimal output will not come into operation. Yet the general applicability of this principle of constrained optimization is Samuelson's key methodological contribution to economic analysis.[38]

More important, however, is Samuelson's cryptic, yet clear, explanation of why 'Average Cost finally begins to turn up'. When I used the fifth edition of Samuelson's *Economics* in my very first economics course in 1964, my professor told the class (uncritically) that Professor Samuelson was arguing that, as the firm expands output and more workers are added to the workplace as variable inputs, their average productivity falls because of overcrowding that causes them to bump into one another – that is, Samuelson's 'limitations of plant space' – and because the increase in the number of workers to be supervised makes it more difficult for the employer to prevent workers from shirking – that is, Samuelson's 'management difficulties'. The resultant decline in labor productivity as output increases causes AVC to rise. In other words (as I much later came to realize), Samuelson's explanation for rising AVC is that *workers can't work and won't work.* The faster the average productivity of labor declines as the firm expands output, the lower the level of output at which 'Average Cost finally begins to turn up'.

The theory of the optimizing firm does not simply assume that AVC increases as output expands. The cost curve gets its U shape when the rise in AVC is so large that it overwhelms the fall in AFC. With markets and technologies as given constraints, the rising ATC, reflecting declining productivity as the firm expands its output, limits the growth of the firm. It follows that the lower the level of output at which, because of limitations of plant space and management difficulties, the rise in AVC outweighs the decline in AFC, the smaller the firm relative to the size of its industry, and hence the more the fundamental condition for 'perfect competition' prevails.

And since, according to neoclassical economists, perfect competition is the ideal of economic efficiency, it follows from Samuelson's own explanation of the limits to the growth of the firm that the most unproductive firm – one in which, at the lowest level of output, the inability and unwillingness of workers to work cause 'Average Cost [to] finally . . . turn up' – provides the microeconomic foundation for the most efficient possible economy!

Let me repeat this crucial point: The theory of perfect competition idealizes a situation in which the rise of AVC outweighs the decline of AFC at very low levels of firm output relative to total industry output. As a result, there are a very large number of identical competitors in the industry, each of which, by virtue of its small size, can sell its profit-maximizing output without having a discernible impact on the industry's product price (a crucial element of the definition of perfect competition). By Samuelson's own explanation of why 'Average Cost finally begins to turn up', *the firms in perfect competition are very small relative to the size of the industry because they are very unproductive, employing labor whose average productivity falls as the firm's output expands.* Thus, an unproductive firm is the foundation of the neoclassical ideal of economic efficiency known as 'perfect competition'.

'Just a minute', the well-trained neoclassical economist would complain. 'What about the neoclassical theory of monopoly that one can also find in every introductory economics textbook, with its demonstration that, in contrast to the ideal firm in perfect competition, the monopolist, maximizing profit subject to a downward-sloping demand curve, restricts output and raises the product's price? Isn't that proof of perfect competition as the ideal of economic efficiency?'

No, it is not, as Schumpeter recognized some years before Samuelson published the first edition of *Economics*. There is a logical flaw in the neoclassical monopoly model that yields the 'results' – restricted output, higher price – that the neoclassical theory of perfect competition as the ideal of economic efficiency requires. As shown in Figure 3, this model assumes that the monopolist maximizes profit *while subject to the same cost structure* as the perfect competitors. But then how did the monopolist become a monopolist?

In the neoclassical theory of the firm, rather than confront 'limitations of plant space' and 'management difficulties', the employer just optimizes subject to these 'given' constraints. In sharp contrast, the employer in the theory of innovative enterprise could confront 'limitations of plant space' by investing in more spacious plant and 'management difficulties' by creating incentives such as employment security to induce workers to supply higher levels of effort. These investments and incentives would add to the firm's

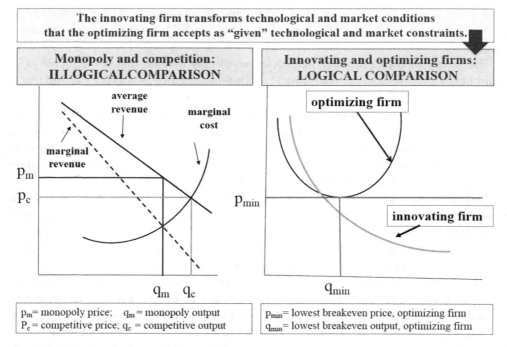

Figure 3. The logical flaw in the neoclassical monopoly model.

fixed cost, but if the innovating firm can increase its productivity sufficiently by making and implementing these expenditures, it may be able to outcompete the optimizing firm, as shown in Figures 1 and 2 above and in the right-hand side of Figure 3.

According to TIE, the firm grows large, and outcompetes perfect competitors, by *transforming the cost structure* – by, for example, investing in more spacious plant to prevent overcrowding, creating positive incentives for employees to expend more work effort, or, in a knowledge-intensive industry, launching an R&D initiative that may yield a higher-quality product. Compared with perfect competitors, who follow the neoclassical directive to optimize subject to given constraints, the innovating firm increases output and, by driving down AFC as it expands output, can lower the product price to consumers while still increasing its profits. For the prosperity of the economy, that's a big plus. For neoclassical theory, however, that's a big minus.

Samuelson's theory requires the firm that is the 'ideal of economic efficiency' to be and to remain small and unproductive. If the economy is dominated by firms in which, to use Samuelson's own words, 'large size breeds success, and success breeds further success', then perfect competition as the 'ideal of economic efficiency' disappears and 'constrained optimization' may not be the management practice that achieves superior economic performance.

As Samuelson writes in the introduction to his textbook, 'the test of a theory's validity is its usefulness in illuminating observed reality'.[39] On that test, the theory of the unproductive firm as the ideal of economic efficiency receives a failing grade. As

Samuelson himself puts it in the concluding sentence of the introduction: 'When a student says, "That's all right in theory but not in practice", he really means, "That's not all right in the relevant theory", or else he is talking nonsense'.[40]

Thank you, Professor Samuelson. In propounding the theory of the unproductive firm as the foundation of the most efficient economy, you were talking nonsense, and your students, broadly construed, have been repeating this drivel ever since. As we have already seen, Samuelson was well aware that the real-world economy can be dominated by large firms that are highly productive. In Chapter 2 ('Central Problems of Every Economic Society') of the fifth edition of *Economics*, Samuelson discusses 'Increasing Costs' and 'The Famous Law of Diminishing Returns' (both subheadings) and provides a table with a numerical example that bears the heading 'Diminishing returns is a fundamental law of economics and technology' and the caption 'Returns of corn when units of labor are added to fixed land'.[41] On the very next page, however, he has the subheading, 'Economies of Scale and Mass Production: A Digression',[42] with the explanation: 'Economies of scale are very important in explaining why so many of the goods we buy are produced by large companies . . . They raise questions to which we shall return again and again in later chapters'.[43]

Samuelson makes his 'honor role of American business' remark, cited above, 100 pages later. But it would be an exaggeration to say that the professor kept his promise to 'return [to this central problem of every economic society] again and again'. After all, for Samuelson the actual importance of economies of scale to the productive economy was just 'a digression' from his obsession with 'the famous law of diminishing returns' as a 'fundamental law of economics and technology'.[44]

Was Paul Samuelson aware of this fundamental flaw in his economic thinking? There is 'smoking-gun' evidence that in the course of revising *Economics* in the early 1960s, Professor Samuelson gave this glaring contradiction between neoclassical ideology and economic reality some deeper thought and came to realize the absurdity of arguing that the unproductive firm is the ideal of economic efficiency. Once the light bulb went off in his brain, he could have then resolved the problem by renouncing the neoclassical theory of the firm and calling for the construction of a theory of innovative enterprise – drawing upon, for example, Edith Penrose's seminal contribution, *The Theory of the Growth of the Firm*, published in 1959, and Alfred Chandler's pioneering historical research documented in his 1962 book *Strategy and Structure*.[45]

But Samuelson simply ignored the work of Penrose and Chandler and the research that they inspired as he rolled out successive editions of *Economics*. Like economies of scale and mass production, the Penrosian and Chandlerian insights were apparently mere digressions. Instead, as part of a significant revision of the material on cost curves in the sixth edition of *Economics*, Samuelson concealed the neoclassical fallacy as articulated in the five previous editions *by excising the sentences quoted above about overhead being spread thin and average cost increasing because of limitations of plant space and management difficulties.*

Beginning with the sixth edition, published in 1964, Samuelson would invoke the 'famous law of diminishing returns' to justify the nonsense that the unproductive firm in perfect competition is the ideal of economic efficiency – with absolutely no explanation of why increasing cost sets in and a rise in variable cost causes the average total cost curve to turn up. And, over the subsequent generations, economists such as N. Gregory Mankiw and Paul Krugman, among other luminaries of the economics profession, have published textbooks that reproduce this nonsense as a principle of economics, taught routinely to students, without examination or explanation.

The problem with perfect competition as the ideal of economic efficiency is not just that millions upon millions of economics students have been, and continue to be, miseducated about the role of the business enterprise in the economy. The much larger problem is that the 'well trained' PhD economists who are supposed to be the educators – including those to whom the Sveriges Riksbank Prize in Economic Sciences in Memory of Alfred Nobel, popularly known as the Nobel Prize in Economics,[46] has been meted out – internalize the inanity that the unproductive firm is the ideal of economic efficiency, and in so doing portray the 'ideal' firm as a powerless entity that does not, and should not, interfere with the market's coordination of the allocation of the economy's resources.

In my own teaching, I have called this view of the world 'sweatshop economics' because the overcrowded and unmotivated firm that Samuelson describes as the micro-foundation of ideal efficiency does, in fact, have the characteristics of a sweatshop. If such firms actually dominated the economy, we would, in a nation such as the United States, all be living in poverty.[47] And, in fact, in many parts of the world where sweatshops prevail, the 'neoclassical' firm and mass poverty go hand in hand.[48]

Meanwhile, the 'well trained' economist views the highly productive firms that grow large, and perhaps even dominate the industries in which they operate, as massive 'market imperfections' that impede the purported efficiency of market resource allocation. In the real economic world, however, the innovative enterprise is a powerful entity that, by transforming technologies and accessing markets, succeeds in generating the higher-quality, lower-cost goods and services that constitute productivity growth. Far from being a market imperfection, the innovative enterprise, properly supported and regulated, can, by confronting and transforming the 'neoclassical constraints' on the growth of the firm, provide the productive foundation for achieving stable and equitable economic growth. If we want economic policies that advance these objectives, then we need a theory of innovative enterprise as a foundation of economic analysis.

The sad irony, however, is that the myth of the market economy that builds on the neoclassical fallacy *actually undermines* the social conditions of innovative enterprise that, if put in place with proper government support and regulation, could enable big business to contribute to stable and equitable economic growth. The next section of this essay explains what I mean by 'the myth of the market economy'. The final section outlines how the neoclassical fallacy provides a theoretical foundation for the destructive ideology that a company should be run to 'maximize shareholder value', while it precludes 'well trained' economists from contemplating, let alone analyzing, the social conditions of innovative enterprise.

4. The myth of the market economy

If PhD economists were to go back to the fifth edition of Samuelson's *Economics*, from which the 'unproductive firm' explanation for the U-shaped cost curve had not yet been excised, their teaching on 'perfect competition' would require them to embrace a theory of the firm that rests on nine assumptions that build on one another, with each assumption more preposterous than the previous one. The nine assumptions that underpin the neoclassical fallacy are:

(1) Assume (as Samuelson states on page 524 of the fifth edition of *Economics*) that the growth of the firm is constrained because of overcrowding of the workplace and loss of control over labor effort as the firm seeks to expand output and more units of labor are added as a variable cost.
(2) Assume that the increase in AVC outweighs the decrease in AFC, causing a rise in ATC that in turn yields a U-shaped cost curve and, hence, a rising marginal cost (i.e. supply) curve.
(3) Assume that the 'entrepreneur' simply optimizes subject to these productivity and cost constraints, opting not to make investments in the firm to deal with overcrowding and control loss.
(4) Assume that ALL FIRMS in the industry are equally constrained by an unwillingness to take risk (e.g. by investing in a more spacious plant) or manage labor (e.g. by offering positive incentives to employees), so that no firm in the industry is able or willing to make any investments to overcome internal diseconomies of scale.
(5) Assume that the level of output at which rising AVC outweighs declining AFC is SO SMALL relative to industry output that each firm can sell its profit-maximizing output without having a discernible impact on the industry's product price (i.e. the industry is in a state of 'perfect competition').
(6) Assume as proof that 'perfect competition' is the ideal of efficiency that a firm that has emerged as dominant in an industry (i.e. a 'monopolist') maximizes profit at an output that is lower and a price that is higher than the industry output and price under 'perfect competition' – and that it does so because it maximizes profit subject to the same cost structure that would characterize the 'perfect competitors' that the monopolist has purportedly displaced.
(7) Assume, therefore, that the existence of large-scale industrial enterprise is a massive 'market imperfection.'
(8) Assume from this illogical monopoly model that a state of 'imperfect' competition represents a deviation from 'perfect' competition that reduces economic efficiency.

And once, on the basis of these eight assumptions, you as a PhD in economics conclude that the most unproductive firm is the foundation of the most efficient economy, the all-important ninth assumption naturally follows:

(9) *Assume you are a well-trained economist.*

You will then, wittingly or not, become an intellectual purveyor of the myth of the market economy. You will assume that, to achieve economic efficiency, market forces must determine economic outcomes, with highly unproductive firms contributing to efficiency by responding to the dictates of supply and demand as they equate marginal revenue and marginal cost to maximize profit. You will then believe that competition in the markets for products, labor, and finance result in the most efficient product prices, wage rates, and interest rates. And, intellectually captive to the myth of the market economy, you will remain impervious to the reality of how an actual economy operates and performs.

Comparative-historical study reveals that markets in products, labor, and finance, as well as in land, are *outcomes*, not causes, of economic development.[49] Product competition assumes the existence of business enterprises that have developed the productive capabilities to generate goods and services of a quality that buyers want or need and that can be sold at prices they are willing or able to pay. Markets in stocks and bonds depend on the existence of business enterprises with the productive capabilities to issue and pay yields on these securities. Employment opportunities that can be accessed via labor markets assume the existence of business enterprises and government agencies that have developed the capabilities to employ labor productively. A market for land exists because households, governments, and businesses have invested in the infrastructure of a particular locality.

For the sake of continued innovation, the organizations on which the economy depends for investments in productive capabilities *need governments to regulate markets* once they have emerged.[50] In the absence of regulation, markets tend to disrupt and undermine the organizational processes that enable investment in productive capabilities. Here are four well-known examples:

- Inadequate minimum wages that result from overcrowded markets for commoditized labor have left many hardworking families in poverty in the United States, even when the heads of households are holding down two full-time jobs.
- The 'free-market' approach to college tuitions and student loans that prevails in the United States has made higher education unaffordable to most working-class households, in a nation that had once been in the forefront of free or low-cost public higher education.
- We need only look back to the financial crisis of 2008–2009 to see the vast devastation visited on American homeowners by government failure to regulate housing markets.
- The physical destruction of communities occurs through 'natural' disasters caused by the failure to regulate industries whose processes and products contribute to climate change.

These outcomes are not 'market failures'; they are regulatory failures. The policy responses of 'well trained' neoclassical economists who are concerned by these adverse economic and environmental outcomes fail because these economists are intellectually captive to the myth of the market economy.

The TIE approach to understanding the operation and performance of the economy stands in stark contrast to the neoclassical focus on market coordination of economic activity. The neoclassical theory of the market economy poses an almost impenetrable intellectual barrier to analyzing and understanding the organizational foundations of economic development. Steeped in the neoclassical fallacy, neoclassical economists assume that an advanced economy is a market economy in which millions of household decisions concerning the allocation of the economy's resources are aggregated into prices for inputs to and outputs from production processes. Any impediments to this process of market aggregation are deemed to be 'market imperfections', and, among neoclassical economists with a liberal social outlook, any undesirable social outcomes from the process are deemed to be 'market failures'.

Markets *are* of utmost importance to our economy and society; they can allow us *as individuals* to choose the work we do, by whom we are employed, where we live, and what we consume. Insofar as we have market choices, however, it is because the economy is wealthy, and it is wealthy because of investments in productive capabilities by business enterprises, supported by investments in physical and human infrastructure by government agencies and investments in the labor force by many tens of millions of household units.

The 'investment triad' of business enterprises, government agencies, and household units must work in concert to develop a nation's productive capabilities.[51] If market processes cannot explain investment in productive capabilities, then the theory of the market economy cannot explain the wealth of nations. Economists who want to devise public policies to shape the processes and influence the outcomes of investment in productive capabilities need to construct an economic theory of 'organizational success'. At its center is a theory of innovative enterprise.

5. Innovative enterprise and sustainable prosperity

Most economists would agree that the purpose of economic policy should be to help the economy achieve stable and equitable growth. Building on the Penrosian insight that the growth of the firm depends on investments in organizational learning, TIE focuses on the social conditions that determine who controls the firm's investment strategy, how the firm integrates the skills and efforts of large numbers of employees into organizational-learning processes, and what sources of finance the firm mobilizes to sustain the innovation process until it can generate competitive products. The growth of the firm through innovation – the generation of higher-quality, lower-cost products than previously existed – provides the microeconomic foundation for macroeconomic growth.

That growth can become a foundation for sustainable prosperity when the corporation shares with employees the gains from innovation, which in a given accounting period manifest themselves as profits, in the form of secure employment, higher wages, superior benefits, promotion opportunities, and satisfying work. Indeed, the history of modern capitalism shows that when a nation's major business corporations share the gains of innovation with employees, a substantial portion of the population experiences upward socioeconomic mobility that results in a strong and growing middle class.[52] The prosperity is *sustainable* because the innovative enterprise rewards employees whose skills and efforts have contributed to the productivity from which higher wages and benefits can be paid. If managed properly, moreover, the ongoing integration of these employees into collective and cumulative learning processes can renew the innovative capabilities, embodied in its labor force, with which the enterprise can compete on product markets.

Hence the importance to U.S. economic development both of Penrose's focus on the firm's redeployment of unused productive capabilities into new lines of business in which it can generate innovative products, and of Chandler's focus on managerial organization in the multidivisional structure to enable the growth of the firm. By the 1950s, when both Penrose and Chandler did their seminal research, employment relations within major

U.S. business corporations had become characterized by the expectation of a career with one company for members of both the blue-collar and white-collar labor forces. Adopting a 'retain-and-reinvest' resource-allocation regime, major U.S. corporations retained a substantial portion of profits and reinvested in the productive capabilities of their employees, sharing with them, in the form of secure employment and rising remuneration, the gains of innovative enterprise that these employees helped to create. As a result, in the U.S. economy as a whole, the growth of real wages tracked the growth of productivity, and there was a tendency toward less income inequality.[53]

Since the late 1970s, however, there has been a growing gap between productivity growth and wage growth, resulting in downward socioeconomic mobility for Americans with only high-school educations. Over these decades U.S. business corporations have transitioned from the 'retain-and-reinvest' resource-allocation regime, characterized by career-with-one-company employment, to a 'downsize-and-distribute' resource-allocation regime. Under the latter, major U.S. corporations downsize their labor forces – at times terminating long-time employees even when the firm is profitable, often in the context of outsourcing and offshoring – and distribute corporate cash to shareholders in the form of cash dividends and stock buybacks.[54] Based on the business practices Penrose observed in the 1950s, she assumed that, through diversification, the business corporation would seek to make use of its 'unused resources', by which she meant first and foremost the labor services of its experienced employees. By the 1990s, however, as the downsize-and-distribute regime became widespread, the assumption that a corporation would seek to make use of its unused labor services could no longer be made.[55]

The rise in the late 1980s of the corporate-governance ideology that a company should be run to 'maximize shareholder value' (MSV) legitimized the replacement of retain-and-reinvest by downsize-and-distribute as the dominant regime of corporate resource allocation in the United States.[56] The leading academic advocate for MSV was Michael C. Jensen, a Chicago-School 'agency theorist', who from 1985 disseminated this ideology as a professor at Harvard Business School. Jensen argued that for the sake of superior economic performance corporations should 'disgorge' their 'free cash flow' so that financial markets would be able to allocate these financial resources to their most efficient uses.[57] The term 'disgorge' implies that the funds that a company retains out of profits are ill-gotten when controlled by the corporation rather than distributed to its shareholders, while the term 'free' could be applied to cash flow made available by laying off employees, including longstanding personnel who had contributed to the growth of the firm and had held the realistic expectation of a career with one company.

Economists who have absorbed the neoclassical fallacy, to which both Chicago-School conservatives (acolytes of Milton Friedman) and Harvard-MIT liberals (acolytes of Samuelson) adhere, do not have a theoretical explanation for why labor, which they view as a variable cost, would actually represent a part of a firm's fixed cost – that is, a productive asset in which the firm invests.[58] For TIE, superior labor productivity derives partly from the development of employees' capabilities through their work experience and partly from the utilization of those capabilities to capture product markets in order to reap economies of scale and scope.[59]

Nor can neoclassical economists comprehend the growth dynamic linking productivity and pay that, occurring within the innovating firm, can raise the living standards of the company's labor force. Rather, they see wage determination by the forces of supply and demand on labor markets as resulting in the most efficient allocation of the economy's resources. More generally, espousing the absurdity that the most unproductive firm is the foundation of the most efficient economy, they lack a theory of how, through the productivity-pay dynamic, the actual efficiency of the economy can change over time as wages increase on a sustainable basis.

Similarly, once one has accepted the validity of the neoclassical fallacy, one assumes, as all neoclassical economists do, that financial markets allocate resources to their 'most efficient uses' – yet they lack a theory of how the most efficient uses come to exist. Nor can the believer in the neoclassical fallacy comprehend theoretically how economic performance can be enhanced when corporate executives retain strategic control over the allocation of some or all of the firm's profits to invest in the firm's productive capabilities rather than 'disgorge the free cash flow', ostensibly to be reallocated to its 'most efficient uses' via financial markets.

The consequences of the colossal intellectual failure of neoclassical economics are not merely academic. Guided by the theory of innovative enterprise, research by my colleagues and me explains how, since the mid-1980s, MSV ideology has functioned to legitimize the implementation of the Chicago-School agenda by means of massive open-market issuer repurchases – aka stock buybacks. The purpose of stock buybacks done as open-market repurchases is to manipulate a company's stock price, concentrating income in the bank accounts of the richest households and making most Americans worse off.[60]

As I have detailed elsewhere,[61] TIE explains the risk-taking roles of households as taxpayers and households as workers in contributing to the value-creation processes that can generate corporate profits. These 'stakeholders' have a claim to a share of those profits if and when they occur. In contrast, *sharesellers*, including senior executives, investment bankers, and hedge-fund managers, reap financial gains by timing their stock trades around buybacks at the expense not only of taxpayers and workers but also of those shareholders who *hold* their shares for the sake of dividend yields. Intellectually captive to the neoclassical fallacy, even 'progressive' neoclassical economists who are deeply concerned with income inequality have failed to mount a critique of the MSV agenda to 'disgorge the free cash flow' as a prime source of the extreme income inequality that prevails in the United States.

The transformation of the U.S. business corporation from retain-and-reinvest to downsize-and-distribute that the MSV agenda legitimizes occurred in the decades after Penrose published *TGF*.[62] Yet the massive value extraction represented by the distribution of the corporation's financial resources, via dividends to shareholders and via buybacks to sharesellers, assumes a prior era of innovative value creation in the history of the particular firm. Understanding the phenomenon that, in our recent book, Jang-Sup Shin and I call 'predatory value extraction' requires a theory of innovative enterprise. As I have argued in this essay, Penrosian learning provides an essential building block for a theory of innovative enterprise, which in turn exposes the neoclassical fallacy.

In *TGF*, however, Penrose herself averts a confrontation with the neoclassical theory of the firm by arguing that its proponents are welcome to go on tending their intellectual garden while she will use her own methods to tend hers. As she puts it in *TGF*:

> Educated laymen as well as economists studying the vagaries of actual business behavior often show an understandable impatience with the 'theory of the firm', for they see in it little that reflects the facts of life as they understand them. It is therefore worth a little trouble, perhaps, to discuss at the very beginning the nature of the 'firm' in the 'theory of the firm', to indicate why it provides an unsuitable framework for a theory of the growth of firms, but at the same time to make clear that we shall not be involved in any quarrel with the theory of the 'firm' as part of the theory of price and production, so long as it cultivates its own garden and we cultivate ours. Much confusion can arise from the careless assumption that when the term 'firm' is used in different contexts it always means the same thing.[63]

Penrose is in effect portraying what I have called the 'optimizing firm' and the 'innovating firm' as two distinct theories of the firm that can be used for different analytical purposes. On this point, Penrose fails to see the profundity of the theory of the firm that she constructed by focusing on its growth – or one might say its 'historical transformation' – over time. As I first pointed out in my contributions in the early 1980s to the debate on Britain's economic decline,[64] what economists call constrained-optimization analysis can be useful for examining how the firm's decision-makers adapt to the technological and market conditions that constrain their price and output choices *at a given point in time*.[65] But as I demonstrated by analyzing the twentieth-century performance of British industry in global competition, the optimizing firm will fail to remain competitive in its industry when confronted by one or more innovating firms that, refusing to take existing technological and market conditions as 'given constraints', instead use strategic control, organizational integration, and financial commitment to transform these conditions so as to generate higher-quality, lower-cost products than had previously existed.

The 'historical transformation' methodology, which is consistent with Penrose's approach to the theory of the firm, focuses on how, in particular historical contexts, the innovating firm transforms technologies and accesses markets – remaking industrial conditions that the optimizing firm takes as 'given constraints' – to generate a higher-quality, lower-cost product.[66] When successful, as we have seen, the innovating firm outcompetes the optimizing firm by virtue of its superior productivity. In view of this analysis of the relation between the two 'theories of the firm', Penrose might have added: Neoclassical economists may prefer to tend their own theoretical garden, but they should recognize that without the nutrients supplied by investment in productive capabilities, the firms that populate their theoretical terrain will wilt and fade away.

In the presence of 'Schumpeterian competition', innovative enterprise vanquishes the optimizing firms that neoclassical economists idealize. In seeking to compete through constrained optimization (as the neoclassical economist would advise), the optimizing firm fails to invest in the productive capabilities that would enable it to respond to the new competition by itself transforming the technological and market conditions that it faces. Economists who ignore the theory of the growth of the firm and the historical transformation of technological and markets conditions that are at its core are left with the argument that firms that engage in constrained optimization are doing the best that can be done in achieving economic efficiency.

The neoclassical fallacy is, then, an extreme version of the neoclassical economist's methodological commitment to the constrained-optimization technique for analyzing the firm's output and price: the more constrained the firm as a productive entity, the more efficient the industry and economy of which these powerless firms are a part.

Hence, as stated previously in this essay, adherence to the neoclassical fallacy enables the neoclassical economist to view the firm as impotent and the market as omnipotent in allocating the economy's resources.

Intellectually captive to constrained-optimization methodology, neoclassical economists fail to recognize the competitive limitations of constrained-optimization decision-making in industries dominated by innovative enterprise. As a prime example of this obeisance to constrained-optimization methodology, in a survey of work in business history, business policy, and organizational behavior published in the *Journal of Economic Literature* in 1980, Richard Caves, a prominent neoclassical industrial-organization economist, concludes that 'the well-trained professional economist could have carried out many of the research projects cited in this paper more proficiently than did their authors, who were less effectively equipped by their own disciplines'.[67] He continues:

> If one accepts the weak postulate that the firm is a purposive organization maximizing some objective function, it follows that its strategic and structural choice represents a constrained-optimization problem. My reading is that students of business organization with disciplinary bases outside of economics would accept that proposition but have lacked the tools to follow its blueprint. Constrained-maximization problems are mother's milk to the well-trained economist.

Caves highlights Chandler's *Strategy and Structure* and *The Visible Hand* as among the works by scholars 'who were less effectively equipped by their own disciplines' to carry out research into, in this case, business history. Caves references Penrose, *The Theory of the Growth of the Firm*, in a footnote as 'an important antecedent' to arguments made by others concerning 'the expansion of the firm holding fixed assets that cannot be costlessly divested in the short run',[68] thus grossly mischaracterizing Penrose as a 'constrained-optimization' economist. As I stated at the outset of this essay, the definition of a 'classic' is a work that many cite but few have read.

Worse is the case of an economist who commented extensively on drafts of *TGF* but then chose not to cite Penrose's book because it did not fit with his constrained-optimization view of the world. I am referring to Fritz Machlup, who was Penrose's faculty advisor at Johns Hopkins University when she was studying for her doctorate from 1947 to 1951 and, subsequently, one of two Johns Hopkins faculty members who supervised Penrose as the researcher on their project on the growth of firms that in 1959 resulted in the publication of *TGF*. Penrose and Machlup remained friends until his death in 1983.[69] Yet Machlup's 1966 American Economic Association presidential address, entitled 'Theories of the Firm: Marginalist, Behavioral, and Managerial', takes up thirty-one pages of text and contains a total of forty-eight bibliographic references, but no mention of Penrose is to be found.[70]

Why? It seems that given the centrality of organizational learning to Penrose's argument, Machlup did not consider *The Theory of the Growth of the Firm* to be 'economic theory' but rather 'organization theory'. As a prelude to the concluding summary of his survey of the three types of theories of the firm, he states:

> I am not happy about the practice of calling any study just because it deals with or employs a concept of the firm "economics" or "microeconomics." But we cannot issue licenses for the use of such terms and, hence, must put up with their rather free use. My own prejudices balk

at designating organization theory as economics – but other people's prejudices are probably different from mine, and we gain little or nothing from arguing about the correct scope of our field.[71]

Earlier in his address, Machlup warns: 'Frankly, I cannot quite see what great difference organizational matters are supposed to make in the firm's price reaction to changes in conditions'.[72] Machlup was the quintessential neoclassical economist, obsessed with 'marginalist' constrained-optimization methodology as the definitive tool of economic analysis. Machlup contends that managerial theories of the firm in which the firm's decision-maker seeks to maximize an objective other than money profits can be subsumed within the constrained-optimization framework through 'expanded marginalist objective functions'[73] without impeding one's understanding of how the economy operates and performs. As he puts it:

> My charge that there is widespread confusion regarding the purposes of the "theory of the firm" as used in traditional price theory refers to this: The model of the firm in that theory is not, as so many writers believe, designed to serve to explain and predict the behavior of real firms; instead, it is designed to explain and predict changes in observed prices (quoted, paid, received) as effects of particular changes in conditions (wage rates, interest rates, import duties, excise taxes, technology, etc.). In this causal connection the firm is only a theoretical link, a mental construct helping to explain how one gets from the cause to the effect. This is altogether different from explaining the behavior of a firm.[74]

As Machlup summed up the 'theories of the firm' surveyed in his presidential address:

> As far as the proponents of managerial theories are concerned, they have never claimed to be anything but marginalists, and the behavior goals they have selected as worthy for incorporation into behavior equations, along with the goal of making profits, were given a differentiable form so that they could become part of marginal analysis. Thus, instead of a heated contest between marginalism and managerialism in the theory of the firm, a marriage between the two has come about.[75]

Machlup does not mention Penrose in his AEA presidential address because it is impossible to interpret her managerial theory of the firm as marginalism. Somehow, she had failed to imbibe the 'mother's milk' of the 'well-trained economist', as Caves would express it some years later. As Penrose put in it in a letter to Machlup in response to his comments on a draft of *TGF*: 'Unlike you, I don't have the answers to all the problems pat from a few simple premises. I don't think the premises are as easy as you do'. Or as she informed her mentor: 'I don't know all the answers before I start as you do'.[76] Notwithstanding his unique position for observing the unfolding of Penrose's work, Machlup's intellectual attachment to constrained-optimization methodology rendered invisible to him her seminal contribution to economic theory, including her treatment of the relation between facts and logic – that is, history and theory.

From my intellectual perspective, Penrose's 'historical transformation' methodology integrates history and theory. At a certain stage of our intellectual development, theory serves both as a distillation of what we have learned from the study of history and a guide to researching what we need to know as 'the present as history' unfolds.[77] As Penrose articulates it in an essay written in the late 1980s that, putting the shoe on the other foot, chastises historians for ignoring theory:

'Theory' is, by definition, a simplification of 'reality' but simplification is necessary in order to comprehend it at all, to make sense of 'history'. If each event, each institution, each fact, were really unique in all aspects, how could we understand, or claim to understand, anything at all about the past, or indeed the present for that matter? If, on the other hand, there are common characteristics, and if such characteristics are significant in the course of events, then it is necessary to analyse both the characteristics and their significance and 'theoretically' to isolate them for that purpose.

Then, applying the boot to 'well trained' economists, Penrose concludes: 'universal truths without reference to time and space are unlikely to characterise economic affairs'.[78] She might have added, a failure to integrate history and theory has led three generations of economists to accept the neoclassical fallacy as a universal truth. The next generation needs new economic thinking. Read Penrose's 'classic' for a start.

Notes

1. Edith T. Penrose, *The Theory of the Growth of the Firm*, Blackwell, 1959
2. Alfred D. Chandler, Jr., *Strategy and Structure: Chapters in the History of the American Industrial Enterprise*, MIT Press, 1962; Alfred. D. Chandler, Jr., *The Visible Hand: The Managerial Revolution in American Business*, Harvard University Press, 1977. Like Samuelson, Chandler was on the faculty of MIT from 1950 to 1963 as he researched and wrote his seminal work on U.S. business history, including his article, highly influential among historians, "The Beginnings of 'Big Business' in American Industry," *Business History Review*, 33, 1, 1959: 1–31. In 1963 Chandler moved to a professorship at Johns Hopkins University, where Penrose had researched *TGF* in the 1950s. By this time, Penrose had a joint appointment to the faculties of the School for Oriental and African Studies (SOAS), University of London and the London School of Economics. Penrose was unaware of Chandler's work when she published *TGF*. Chandler first mentions Penrose in a 1968 comment as one of a number of economists whose work is useful to historians, but goes on to say, 'alas, such writings were too late for my work in investigating the rise of the large corporation [in *Strategy and Structure*].' Alfred D. Chandler, Jr., "Comment [on a paper by Alfred H. Conrad]," *Explorations in Economic History*, second series, 6, 1, 1968, p. 66. To my knowledge, the first time that Penrose and Chandler met was in 1986 at the International Economic History Congress in Berne, Switzerland (I saw them there, chatting). Michael Best proposed that Chandler and Penrose share a plenary session at the Business History Conference at Harvard Business School in 1993. For some reason, the conference organizers did not act on this suggestion, and Penrose and Chandler only appeared together as discussants on a panel of papers in a parallel session. For an illuminating biography of Penrose, see Angela Penrose, *No Ordinary Woman: The Life of Edith Penrose*, Oxford University Press, 2018.
3. Chandler, *Strategy and Structure*.
4. Edith Penrose, "The Growth of the Firm – A Case Study: Hercules Powder Company," *Business History Review*, 34, 1, 1960: 1–23. This article won the Newcomen Prize for best article in *Business History Review* in 1960. Hercules Powder Company became an independent company in 1911 when the Du Pont explosives monopoly was broken up under U.S. antitrust law. Du Pont itself was a key company in Chandler's analysis of the evolution of the multidivisional structure from the 1920s to the 1950s.
5. See Mary A. O'Sullivan, *Contests for Corporate Control: Corporate Governance and Economic Performance in the United States and Germany*, Oxford University Press, 2000, ch. 4; William Lazonick, "Corporate Restructuring," in Stephen Ackroyd, Rose Batt, Paul Thompson, and Pamela Tolbert, eds., The *Oxford Handbook of Work and Organization*, Oxford University Press, 2004: 577–601; William Lazonick, "Alfred Chandler's Managerial

Revolution: Developing and Utilizing Productive Resources," in William Lazonick and David J. Teece, eds., *Management Innovation: Essays in the Spirit of Alfred D. Chandler, Jr*, Oxford University Press, 2012: 89–121.

6. See Michael H. Best, *The New Competition: Institutions of Industrial Restructuring*, Harvard University Press, 1990, p. 125. In contemporary business schools, Penrosian learning is central to the "dynamic capabilities" perspective, developed by David Teece and his colleagues. See David J. Teece, *Dynamic Capabilities and Strategic Management: Organizing for Innovation and Growth*, Oxford University Press, 2009; David J. Teece, *Strategy, Innovation, and the Theory of the Firm*, Edward Elgar Publishing, 2012.

7. On the "managerial limit" in the neoclassical theory of the firm, see William Lazonick, *Business Organization and the Myth of the Market Economy*, Cambridge University Press, 1991, p. 164. The notion was articulated in E. A. G. Robinson, *The Structure of Competitive Industry*, Harcourt, Brace, 1932, ch. 3; and E. A. G. Robinson, "The Problem of Management and the Size of Firms," *Economic Journal*, 44, 174, 1934: 242–257.

8. Chandler, *The Visible Hand*.

9. William Lazonick, *Competitive Advantage on the Shop Floor*, Harvard University Press, 1990; William Lazonick, "Organizational Learning and International Competition," in Jonathan Michie and John Grieve Smith, eds., *Globalization, Growth, and Governance*, Oxford University Press, 1998: 204–238. See also William Lazonick, Philip Moss, and Joshua Weitz, "How the Disappearance of Unionized Jobs Obliterated an Emergent Black Middle Class," Institute for New Economic Thinking Working Paper No. 125, June 15, 2020, https://doi.org/10.36687/inetwp125; William Lazonick, Philip Moss, and Joshua Weitz, "The Unmaking of the Black Blue-Collar Middle Class," Institute for New Economic Thinking Working Paper No. 159, May 20, 2021, at https://www.ineteconomics.org/research/research-papers/the-unmaking-of-the-black-blue-collar-middle-class.

10. Alfred D. Chandler, Jr., *Scale and Scope: The Dynamics of Industrial Capitalism*, Harvard University Press, 1990; Alfred D. Chandler, Jr., *Inventing the Electronic Century: The Epic Story of the Consumer Electronic and Computer Industries*, Harvard University Press, 2001; Alfred D. Chandler, Jr., *Shaping the Industrial Century: The Remarkable Story of the Evolution of the Modern Chemical and Pharmaceutical Industries*, Harvard University Press, 2005.

11. William Lazonick, *Sustainable Prosperity in the New Economy? Business Organization and High-Tech Employment in the United States*, Upjohn Institute for Employment Research, 2009; William Lazonick and Öner Tulum, "US Biopharmaceutical Finance and the Sustainability of the Biotech Business Model," *Research Policy*, 40, 9, 2011: 1170–1187.

12. William Lazonick, "The Theory of Innovative Enterprise: Foundations of Economic Analysis," in Thomas Clarke, Justin O'Brien, and Charles R. T. O'Kelley, eds., *The Oxford Handbook of the Corporation*, Oxford University Press, 2019: 490–514.

13. For the sake of argument, in Figure 2, the innovating firm chooses to 'make' rather than 'buy' the input at a point at which the deterioration in the quality of the input that it previously purchased has gone so far as to create internal diseconomies of scale, as depicted by the innovating firm's U-shaped cost curve. But a much less dramatic increase in AVC (one that does not outweigh the decrease in AFC) may trigger this vertical-integration decision.

14. Adam Smith, *An Inquiry into the Nature and Causes of the Wealth of Nations*, fifth edition (edited by Edwin Cannan), Methuen, 1904, ch. 1 ('On the Division of Labour'); originally published in 1776.

15. William Lazonick, Philip Moss, Hal Salzman, and Öner Tulum, "Skill Development and Sustainable Prosperity: Collective and Cumulative Careers versus Skill-Biased Technical Change," Institute for New Economic Thinking Working Group on the Political Economy of Distribution Working Paper No. 7, December 2014, at https://ineteconomics.org/ideas-papers/research-papers/skill-development-and-sustainable-prosperity-cumulative-and-collective-careers-versus-skill-biased-technical-change; Matt Hopkins and William Lazonick, "Who Invests in the High-Tech Knowledge Base?" Institute for New Economic Thinking

Working Group on the Political Economy of Distribution Working Paper No. 6, September 2014 (revised December 2014), at http://ineteconomics.org/ideas-papers/research-papers/who-invests-in-the-high-tech-knowledge-base.

16. William Lazonick, "Labor in the Twenty-First Century: The Top 0.1% and the Disappearing Middle Class," in Christian E. Weller, ed., *Inequality, Uncertainty, and Opportunity: The Varied and Growing Role of Finance in Labor Relations*, Cornell University Press, 2015: 143–192.

17. Lazonick, *Competitive Advantage on the Shop Floor*; Lazonick, "The Theory of Innovative Enterprise".

18. William Lazonick and Jang-Sup Shin, *Predatory Value Extraction: How the Looting of the Business Corporation Became the U.S. Norm and How Sustainable Prosperity Can Be Restored*, Oxford University Press, 2020.

19. Joseph A. Schumpeter, *Capitalism, Socialism, and Democracy*, Harper, 1950, third edition, p. 106; originally published in 1942.

20. Lazonick, "Alfred Chandler's Managerial Revolution".

21. Carl Kaysen, *The American Corporation Today*, Oxford University Press, 1996, p. 25.

22. United States Census Bureau, "2017 SUSB Annual Data Tables by Establishment Industry," May 2021, at https://www.census.gov/data/tables/2017/econ/susb/2017-susb-annual.html. In 2017, 514 firms with 20,000 or more employees (average, 57,428) in the United States accounted for 8% of establishments. 23% of employees, 25% of payrolls, and 28% of revenues.

23. I would be pleased to be informed of any microeconomics textbook that rejects what I have called the neoclassical fallacy and provides an alternative theory of the firm.

24. "Economics (textbook)," *Wikipedia*, at https://en.wikipedia.org/wiki/Economics_(textbook).

25. Paul A. Samuelson, *Economics; An Introductory Analysis*, first edition, McGraw Hill, 1948, p. 124.

26. Ibid., p. 125.

27. Ibid.

28. Ibid., pp. 126–131.

29. Ibid., p. 132. For the passage that he quotes, Samuelson cites J. A, Schumpeter, "Capitalism, Socialism, and Democracy", Harper & Brothers: New York 1942. (This passage appeared on page 82 of the 1942 edition of *Capitalism, Socialism, and Democracy*.)

30. Samuelson, *Economics*, first edition, p. 132.

31. In the 1940s, economists could have built on Schumpeter's focus on innovation as the fundamental phenomenon of economic development, a proposition put forward in Joseph A. Schumpeter, *The Theory of Economic Development*, Harvard University Press, 1934 (first published in German in 1911). See William Lazonick, "What Happened to the Theory of Economic Development?" in Patrice Higgonet, David S. Landes, and Henry Rosovsky, eds., *Favorites of Fortune: Technology, Growth, and Economic Development since the Industrial Revolution*, Harvard University Press, 1991: 267–296. By the 1960s, as I have indicated in the introduction to this essay, Samuelson could have found powerful explanations, both theoretical and historical, for the growth of the firm in Penrose, *The Theory of the Growth of the Firm*, and Chandler, *Strategy and Structure*. In its 19 editions, spanning 1948 to 2009, Samuelson, *Economics*, never references these scholars or the body of research on the growth of the firm and managerial capitalism that their writings inspired.

32. N. Gregory Mankiw, *Principles of Microeconomics*, Cengage Learning, eighth edition, no date, p. 259.

33. Ibid., p. 254.

34. Paul Krugman and Robin Wells, *Essentials of Economics*, Worth Publishers, fourth edition, 2017, p. 189.

35. Ibid., p. 185.

36. I am grateful to Wynn Tucker for searching through the first edition of Samuelson, *Economics*, to locate the explanation of the U-shaped cost curve.

37. Paul A. Samuelson, *Economics: An Introductory Analysis*, fifth edition, McGraw-Hill, 1961, p. 524.
38. Paul A. Samuelson, *Foundations of Economic Analysis*, Enlarged Edition, Harvard University Press, 1983.
39. Samuelson, *Economics*, 1961, p. 12.
40. Ibid.
41. Ibid., p. 25.
42. Ibid., p. 26.
43. Ibid., p. 27.
44. Note that in the first three editions of *Economics*, the section in Chapter 2 on "The Famous Law of Diminishing Returns" appears just *after* the section on "Economies of Scale: Mass Production and Decreasing Costs" ('Economies of Mass Production and Decreasing Costs' in the first edition). In the fourth edition, however, Samuelson reverses the order of these two sections, placing "The Famous Law of Diminishing Returns" first, while changing the subhead for the section on decreasing costs to "Economies of Scale and Mass Production: A Digression." Samuelson then repeats this formulation in the fifth and sixth editions. A separate paper would be required to document Samuelson's changing portrayal of the large corporation in *Economics*. But these changes made in the fourth edition, and particularly the addition of the term "a digression," appear to be an attempt by Samuelson to diminish the role of big business in his presentation of how a modern economy operates and performs.
45. Penrose, *The Theory of the Growth of the Firm*; Chandler, *Strategy and Structure*.
46. See Avner Offer and Gabriel Söderberg, *The Nobel Factor: The Prize in Economics, Social Democracy, and the Market Turn*, Princeton University Press, 2016.
47. William Lazonick, "Innovative Enterprise or Sweatshop Economics?" In Search of Foundations of Economic Analysis," *Challenge*, 59, 2, 2016: 65-14.
48. See Jason Hickel, "Rethinking Sweatshop Economics," *Foreign Policy in Focus*, 1 July 2011, at https://fpif.org/rethinking_sweatshop_economics/; Christopher Blattman and Stefan Dercon, "Everything we knew about sweatshops was wrong," *New York Times*, 27 April 2017, at https://www.nytimes.com/2017/04/27/opinion/do-sweatshops-lift-workers-out-of-poverty.html?emc=eta1.
49. Lazonick, *Business Organization and the Myth of the Market Economy*; William Lazonick, "The Theory of the Market Economy and the Social Foundations of Innovative Enterprise," *Economic and Industrial Democracy*, 24, 1, 2003: 9-44; William Lazonick, "Varieties of Capitalism and Innovative Enterprise," *Comparative Social Research*, 24, 2007: 21–69.
50. See, for example, Lazonick, *Competitive Advantage on the Shop Floor*; William Lazonick, "The Functions of the Stock Market and the Fallacies of Shareholder Value," in Ciaran Driver and Grahame Thompson, eds., *What Next for Corporate Governance?* Oxford University Press, 2018: 117–151.
51. William Lazonick, "The Investment Triad and Sustainable Prosperity," in Peter Creticos, Larry Bennett, Laura Owen, Costas Spirou, and Maxine Morphis-Riesbeck, eds., *The Many Futures of Work: Rethinking Expectations and Breaking Molds*, Temple University Press, 2021: 120–151.
52. Lazonick, *Competitive Advantage on the Shop Floor*; Lazonick, *Sustainable Prosperity in the New Economy?*; Lazonick, et al., "Skill Development and Sustainable Prosperity"; Lazonick, "Labor in the Twenty-First Century"; Lazonick et al., "How the Disappearance of Unionized Jobs Obliterated an Emergent Black Middle Class."
53. Economic Policy Institute, "The Productivity-Pay Gap," updated August 2021, at https://www.epi.org/productivity-pay-gap/; Lazonick and Shin, *Predatory Value Extraction*, ch. 1.
54. Lazonick et al., "Skill Development and Sustainable Prosperity"; Lazonick "Labor in the 21st Century"; Lazonick et al., "How the Disappearance of Unionized Jobs Obliterated an Emergent Black Middle Class."

55. Lazonick, *Sustainable Prosperity in the New Economy?*; Lazonick "Labor in the Twenty-First Century"; William Lazonick, "Stock Buybacks: From Retain-and-Reinvest to Downsize-and-Distribute," Center for Effective Public Management, Brookings Institution, April 2015, pp. 10–11, at http://www.brookings.edu/research/papers/2015/04/17-stock-buybacks-lazonick;

56. William Lazonick and Mary O'Sullivan, "Maximizing Shareholder Value: A New Ideology for Corporate Governance," *Economy and Society*, 29, 1, 2000: 13–35; Lazonick, "The Investment Triad and Sustainable Prosperity."

57. Michael C. Jensen, "Agency Costs of Free Cash Flow, Corporate Finance, and Takeovers," *American Economic Review*, 76, 2, 1986: 323–329 (the term 'disgorge' is used on pages 323 and 328).

58. These economists fail to recognize the potential productivity benefits of labor as a fixed-cost investment even though, as tenured professors, the very same economists have occupied the most secure career employment positions that exist.

59. For a pioneering exploration of these issues, influenced by the work of Penrose and Chandler, see David J. Teece, "Economies of Scale and Scope of the Enterprise," *Journal of Economic Behavior and Organization*, 1, 3, 1980: 223–247.

60. William Lazonick, "Profits Without Prosperity: Stock Buybacks Manipulate the Market and Leave Most Americans Worse Off," *Harvard Business Review*, September 2014, pp 46–55; Lazonick, "Stock Buybacks: From Retain-and-Reinvest to Downsize-and-Distribute"; Lazonick, "The Investment Triad and Sustainable Prosperity"; Lazonick and Shin, *Predatory Value Extraction*; Ken Jacobson and William Lazonick, "A License to Loot: Alternative Views of Capital Formation and the Adoption of SEC Rule 10b-18," The Academic-Industry Research Network, in progress, January 2022.

61. For a recent statement of my MSV critique, see Lazonick, "The Investment Triad and Sustainable Prosperity."

62. Lazonick and O'Sullivan, "Maximizing Shareholder Value." In the foreword to the third edition of *TGF*, published in 1995, Penrose recognizes the possibility of the financialization of the firm since she originally researched the growth of the firm in the 1950s. See Edith T, Penrose, *The Theory of the Growth of the Firm*, 4th edition, 2009, p. 236. As part of his PhD dissertation at SOAS University of London, Matt Hopkins is completing a study of the financialization of Hercules in the 1990s and 2000s, analyzing the demise of the chemical company that was the subject of Penrose's 1960 *Business History Review* article, "The Growth of the Firm – A Case Study."

63. Penrose, *Theory of the Growth of the Firm*, p. 9.

64. William Lazonick, "Factor Costs and the Diffusion of Ring Spinning in Britain prior to World War I," *Quarterly Journal of Economics*, 96, 1, 1981: 89–109; William Lazonick, "Production Relations, Labor Productivity, and Choice of Technique: British and U.S. Cotton Spinning," *Journal of Economic History*, 41, 3, 1981: 491–516; William Lazonick, "Competition, Specialization, and Industrial Decline," *Journal of Economic History*, 41, 1, 1981: 31–38: William Lazonick, "Industrial Organization and Technological Change: The Decline of the British Cotton Industry," *Business History Review*, 57, 2, 1983: 195–236; Bernard Elbaum and William Lazonick, "The Decline of the British Economy: An Institutional Perspective," *Journal of Economic History*, 44, 2, 1984: 567–583.

65. See William Lazonick, "Innovative Enterprise and Historical Transformation," *Enterprise & Society*, 3, 1, 2002: 35–54.

66. William Lazonick, "The Integration of Theory and History: Methodology and Ideology in Schumpeter's Economics," in Lars Magnusson, ed., *Evolutionary Economics: The Neo-Schumpeterian Challenge*, Kluwer, 1994: 245–263; Lazonick, "Innovative Enterprise and Historical Transformation."

67. Richard Caves, "Industrial Organization, Corporate Strategy and Structure," *Journal of Economic Literature*, 18, 1, 1980, p. 88. Caves was a professor in the Harvard Economics Department from 1962 to 2003, and chair of the PhD in Business Economics, a joint degree of the Harvard Economics Department and Harvard Business School, from 1984 to 1997. "Richard E. Caves," *Wikipedia*, at https://en.wikipedia.org/wiki/Richard_E._Caves.

68. Caves, "Industrial Organization, Corporate Strategy and Structure," p. 66.
69. Penrose, *No Ordinary Woman*, pp. 116–117, 142–146, 172–181.
70. Fritz Machlup, "Theories of the Firm: Marginalist, Behavioral, and Managerial," *American Economic Review*, 57, 1, 1967: 1–33. Nor does he mention Penrose or her work in Fritz Machlup, *The Production and Distribution of Knowledge in the United States*, Princeton University Press, 1962.
71. Machlup, "Theories of the Firm," p. 29.
72. Ibid., p. 13.
73. Ibid., p. 4.
74. Ibid., p. 10.
75. Ibid., p. 29.
76. Penrose, *No Ordinary Woman*, p. 145.
77. Paul M. Sweezy, *The Present as History: Essays and Reviews on Capitalism and Socialism*, Monthly Review Press, 1953. As Sweezy puts it: "Everyone knows that the present will some day be history. I believe that the most important task of the social scientist is to try to comprehend it as history now, while it is still the present and while we still have the power to influence its shape and outcome." Ibid., p. v.
78. Edith Penrose, "History, the Social Sciences and Economic 'Theory,' with Special Reference to Multinational Enterprise," in Alice Teichova, Maurice Lévy-Leboyer, and Helga Nussbaum, eds., *Historical Studies in International Corporate Business*, Cambridge University Press, 1989: 7–14, quoted from p. 11.

Disclosure statement

No potential conflict of interest was reported by the author.

Funding

Funding for the research underpinning this paper was provided by the Institute for New Economic Thinking and the Open Society Foundations. I thank Matt Hopkins and Thomas Ferguson for comments.

The story of flight

John Kay

ABSTRACT

The history of commercial aviation - from the earliest attempts at flight to the modern civil aircraft - is used to illustrate the central role of the evolutionary progress of collective knowledge in what is loosely described as technical progress. No individual knows how to build an airbus - ten thousand people working together do. The emphasis on collective intelligence as a means of solving problems builds on Penrose's insight that the firm is best viewed a s a collection of capabilities to develop a template for the modern corporation that recognises the development of 'capital as a service' and the importance of 'hollow corporations', franchises and platforms in the twenty-first century economy.

The possibility of manned flight has stirred the imagination since ancient times. Icarus fell to earth after he flew too close to the sun, which melted the wax attaching his wings to his arms. Since birds flew by flapping wings, it seemed obvious that flapping wings were the key to flight. But the lesson of Icarus was not just that man could not fly – rather that the attempt to fly was vainglorious. While the great polymath Leonardo da Vinci toyed with possibilities of flight, he was challenging a taboo.

Only with the scientific enlightenment of the seventeenth century did this restriction on thought begin to erode. Robert Hooke is widely credited with the recognition that objects need not fall to earth if they were possessed of sufficient forward thrust – javelins and discs could travel some distance before they returned to the ground. But in the seventeenth century there was no mechanism for achieving that thrust – until the invention of the steam engine, animals were the only practical source of power.

James Watt's condenser (1769) greatly improved the efficiency of Newcomen's (1712) steam engine. Thus, the iconic product of the early years of the industrial revolution – the steam engine – resulted from the addition of Watt's technical breakthrough to existing technology; but the development of Watt's engine required not just the capital but the business acumen of Matthew Boulton. And the continued pre-eminence of the firm of Boulton and Watt owed much to the inventive genius of William Murdoch – who had walked three hundred miles to offer his services to the partnership of Boulton and Watt, and made important incremental improvements to Watt's designs.

Many people experimented with using Newcomen's engine to propel a boat. But until the improvements of Watt and others, steam engines had insufficient power. In

1783 the French Marquis de Jouffroy sailed the first steam-powered boat. The concept was widely imitated; business people in Scotland and the US operated steamboats commercially but with little success.

The idea of mounting a steam engine on wheels is credited to Richard Trevithick (1804). George Stephenson persuaded the promoters of the Stockton and Darlington Railway, built to take coal to the port, to use a steam engine rather than horses to pull freight cars. At the opening in 1825, a carriage labelled *Experiment* carried local dignitaries. The next step was obvious – and revolutionary. Few *people* wanted to travel from mine to dock, but many wanted to travel between Liverpool and Manchester. The line linking the two cities opened for passenger traffic in 1830. Less than half a century later, railroads connected the Atlantic and Pacific coasts of the United States. The nineteenth century saw steady advances in technology and business organisation until by its end steamships were crossing the Atlantic.

But the power-to-weight ratio of early engines was far short of that needed to make aviation a realistic possibility. The development of steam turbines revolutionised seaborne traffic, but the concept of a coal-fired aircraft, which makes us smile today, was within the imagination of visionaries in the nineteenth century. The use of mineral oil as fuel was followed by the development of the internal combustion engine and the first automobiles were built at the end of the nineteenth century. As every schoolboy knows, Wilbur and Orville Wright built the first fixed-wing aircraft to take off under its own power.

But if the Wright brothers had not flown in 1903, someone else would have done something very similar in some other location. Manned flight happened at the beginning of the twentieth century as a result of an accumulation of collective knowledge (by scientists) and its combination into and with collective intelligence (by engineers). Collective knowledge is sometimes described as 'the wisdom of crowds', but the wisdom of crowds lies in the *aggregate of knowledge* rather than the *average of knowledge*.[1] No one knows everything about anything or much about everything.

And even today, while scientists and engineers know how to build planes which remain airborne, there is no comprehensive knowledge of, or complete agreement on, why they do.[2] *Collective intelligence* is more than the aggregate of knowledge; collective intelligence is a *capability*. Collective *intelligence* is at work when the problem-solving capability of the group exceeds the capability of any individual member of that group.

In the century that followed, business people would combine these capabilities with organisational capabilities to develop commercial products. This emphasis on combination and capabilities as definitive of the modern firm was the central insight of Edith Penrose. The business was defined not by the assets it owned, or the contracts it made, but by its capabilities; and its ability to deploy those capabilities in productive services.

This emphasis on combination and capabilities is fundamentally different from the descriptions of firms which dominated – and still do dominate – the economic literature on the firm. Business as capitalist enterprise based on the deployment of essentially homogeneous labour to operate tangible capital was the vision expressed in varied ways by Smith, Marx, Wicksteed, and by Frederick Taylor, the founder of 'management science'. Coase provided an intermediating interlude before the development of a modern legal and economic view of the business as 'nexus of contracts', as in the work of Jensen and Meckling, Williamson, and Grossman and Hart.[3]

THE STORY OF FLIGHT   91

'All the evidence we have indicates that the growth of firms is connected with the attempts of a particular group of people to do something', Penrose wrote.[4] Perhaps that seems obvious. But her emphasis on 'the group' recognises the centrally cooperative and combinatorial nature of business activity, and her identification of purpose – 'to do something' - establishes a focus on solving problems. None of these issues receives emphasis in a world characterised by production functions and the nexus of contracts.

1. The business of flight

It would be half a century between the exploratory flight of the Wright brothers and the availability of commercial aviation at scale. The jet engine was one – but only one – of the many complementary innovations which made flight available to a mass market. Frank Whittle is celebrated in Britain as the inventor of the jet engine, but the German Hans von Ohain was the first to build a functional prototype. The competitive spur provided by World War II energised the British Air Ministry, which had earlier been disdainful of these innovations, and in 1944 both Britain and Germany provided jet fighters to their pilots. (von Ohain was one of more than a thousand German scientists whom the U.S. relocated to work on American military projects after the war; he died in Florida.)

In 1967 the first Boeing 737 entered service with Lufthansa. The 737 is the most successful civil airliner in history with more than 10,000 planes sold. The 747 jumbo jet appeared the following year. The commercial success of these aircraft established Boeing as the world's premier civil aircraft manufacturer, eclipsing its U.S. rivals Lockheed (which left the market in the 1980s) and McDonnell Douglas. By the 1990s only the European Airbus consortium offered effective competition and in 1997 Boeing acquired McDonnell Douglas.

Airbus was conceived in the 1960s as a European project to challenge American supremacy in civil aviation. Airbus was initially supported financially by the British, French and German governments and drew on the resources of the nationalised British Aerospace, the French (nearly) state-owned company Aerospatiale, and the aerospace capabilities of the German engineering industry, particularly those of Daimler, noted for its Mercedes cars. (The victorious Allies had prevented Germany rebuilding its capabilities in military aircraft manufacture until West Germany joined NATO in 1955.)

In 1969 the British government, in a mood of austerity after the previous year's sterling devaluation, pulled out of the project, but the British Aerospace continued to participate since its partners valued its capabilities in the manufacture of wings. In 1972 the Spanish firm CASA joined the consortium, which was structured as a GIE (Groupement d'Intérêt Economique, or economic interest group), a distinctive organisational form available under French law.

In 1987 Airbus launched the A320, which competes directly with Boeing's 737. The A320's forward fuselage is built in Saint-Nazaire, France; the rear fuselage in Getafe, Spain; the wings in Broughton, Wales; and many other parts at other sites across western Europe. A dedicated transport network shifts the parts for assembly in Toulouse. Airbus even has its own specially-designed aircraft for transporting parts from around Europe; the completed plane is then flown to Germany for fitting out in Hamburg.

The A320 was the first entirely 'fly-by-wire'[5] commercial aircraft, and in thirty years 8,000 have been sold – as against 10,500 in the fifty-year history of the 737. In 1999 with a right-wing French government seeking to privatise its industrial interests and what was now Daimler-Chrysler developing global ambitions, EADS (European Aeronautics Defence and Space Company) was formed by a merger of Aerospatiale, the aviation activities of Daimler-Chrysler, and CASA. As the name suggests, the new company has interests and ambitions beyond commercial aviation, but the shares of the merging companies in the Airbus consortium were acquired by EADS. In 2006 the 20% stake in Airbus held by BAE Systems – as the now-privatised British Aerospace had become – was bought by EADS at a knockdown price.

In 2017 EADS renamed itself Airbus, to acknowledge its principal activity. The French and German governments each own 11% of the company and the Spanish government has 4%. Of course, as these corporate restructurings have taken place, engineers in Broughton (North Wales), Hamburg, Toulouse and Toledo have been getting on with their jobs as before.

Airbus has from inception been defined by the assembly of capabilities for a specialist purpose. Airbus was established as a combination of capabilities and remains so. But Airbus illustrates a significant elision of Penrose's idea. There need not be correspondence between the scope of the combination and the legal structure of the firm. In the half century since Penrose wrote, the nature of business organisation would be transformed as the integrated, capital-heavy firms exemplified by the pin factory and General Motors gave way to businesses such as Apple and Amazon whose only function was the assembly of capabilities.

2. Capitalism without capital

Once completed, the A320 enters service with an airline. It is unlikely that the plane you fly in is owned by the airline whose logo is on the fuselage. There are several large aircraft leasing companies – the biggest is the Dublin-based AerCap – but planes may also be owned by partnerships of small investors. The engine is usually owned by yet another business. The airline will typically make a contract for the supply and service of engines from a manufacturer such as Rolls-Royce, which in turn has transferred ownership of the engines to a firm such as GATX, which also owns many railroad cars (including the one which derailed at East Palestine in February 2023).

Apple is the world's most valuable company, with a market capitalisation in excess of $2 trillion. The centrepiece of its operations is the Norman Foster-designed campus at Cupertino, built at an estimated cost of $5 billion.[6] But that deliberately spectacular headquarters is the corporation's principal tangible asset. The company's New York flagship store is in Grand Central Station, owned by a New York real estate developer – not the one who might come to your mind. The European flagship, in London's Regent Street, is jointly owned by the King of England and the sovereign wealth fund of Norway.[7]

Apple expects you (or your credit card provider) to pay promptly. But Apple does not display the same urgency in paying its suppliers, so it has no net working capital. The company has assets of more than $300 billion but two-thirds of these are cash and marketable securities.[8] This extremely profitable company has more money than it knows what to do with. Far from raising new money on stock markets to invest in its business, it is buying back its own existing shares.

Amazon is also one of the world's most valuable companies. But Amazon does not own many of the warehouses which hold its goods, or much of the equipment inside those warehouses. And the goods themselves? Amazon values inventories and accounts receivable at less than the amounts payable to suppliers.[9] Put simply, on average Amazon has sold its goods before it has paid for them. If leased assets and the working capital provided by suppliers are stripped out of the balance sheet, then at Amazon as at Apple only the cash and short-term securities that have accumulated from the company's profits remain.

Prologis is the largest real estate company in the world. Headquartered in San Francisco, its shares are traded on the New York Stock Exchange. However, its market capitalisation is far smaller than that of Amazon, to which it is a principal supplier. Equinix is one of several large data centre companies which provide server space for large corporations, such as Amazon Web Services. AWS, which is derived from the information technology capabilities necessary for the company's logistics, provides cloud computing facilities and Application Programming Interfaces (APIs) – the power behind the apps you use every day – to thousands of corporations. And it is AWS, not the familiar retail juggernaut, which provides most of Amazon's profits. The phone masts which Verizon and Vodafone use to connect you to mobile services are largely owned by specialist companies such as American Tower or (in Europe) Connex.

Neither the harassed Amazon warehouse employee nor the friendly Apple 'genius' knows who owns his or her place of work. And quite possibly their boss does not know either. They don't know because it doesn't matter. They are employees of a corporation. And so are Andy Jassy and Tim Cook (respective CEOs of the two companies). If an Amazon stockholder arrives at a warehouse they will be turned away; if an Apple shareholder attends at 235 Regent Street they will be treated exactly like any other customer.

At the frontier of economic development, in the west in the twenty-first century, we have capitalism without capital. Bezos founded Amazon with some money of his own and the support of his family – less than half a million dollars in total. Subsequently, the business received an $8 million injection from the Silicon Valley venture capital firm Kleiner Perkins, and when it became a public company in 1997 it raised around $50 million from investors.[10] Steve Jobs and Steve Wozniak raised $100,000 from Mike Markkula, who provided 'adult supervision' and helped secure small amounts of further financing from his Silicon Valley friends. Apple finally obtained $100 million from new shareholders at its 1980 IPO.

Neither Amazon nor Apple has raised any money from shareholders since their IPO, and neither is ever likely to in future. Past stockholder investment represents less than .01% of the current value of these businesses. Modern companies are typically cash-generative before they reach a scale at which they become eligible for a listing on a public market. For them, the purpose of the IPO is not to raise capital but to demonstrate to earlier investors and employees that there is value in their shareholdings and enable some to realise that value. The objective is not to put money into the business but to make it possible to take money out of the business. The main requirement for equity capital for industry today is to fund operating losses for start-up businesses before they reach public markets. This is the role that Kleiner Perkins at Amazon and Markkula at Apple played – and played very successfully. Such start-up finance serves a very important function, but the amounts of money at issue are comparatively small, by reference either to the industrial organisation of a century ago, or the total capital stock of a modern economy.

3. As a service

The notion of 'software as a service' came into use in the 1960s to describe a strategy pioneered by IBM. The cost of a mainframe computer was daunting for all but the largest users, so the company shifted focus from selling computers to selling computing. While the vertiginous fall in the price of hardware rendered the original strategy obsolete, the thought behind it took hold. Today, abbreviated to SaaS, 'software as a service' is a major industry.

The concept of 'as a service' is hardly new. Housing 'as a service' has existed for centuries. But even as the rental sector of the housing market declined, new rental contracts became more common in other fields. The Xerox Corporation, whose name was for long synonymous with photocopying, introduced the managed printing service, in which the user paid not for the machine and consumables but for the number of copies printed. The shift from the provision of goods to the provision of services was increasingly widespread, and often gave both buyer and seller greater predictability of costs and revenues.

Modern business buys capital services as it buys water and electricity, accounting, and legal services. All these inputs are essential. But the necessity of buying these means of production does not imply that their provider controls, far less owns, the business that depends on them. If the managers of a modern business do not want to succumb to the demands of their capital supplier, they can buy their capital services somewhere else. In fact, it is generally rather easier for them to exercise that choice than it is to change their water or electricity supplier. The tripartite linkage from personal wealth to tangible assets to control of business – characteristic of businesses from the industrial revolution to the mid-twentieth century hegemony of General Motors – is no longer descriptive of modern corporations.

Modern businesses buy capital as a service; increasingly they also buy labour as a service, especially for routine tasks such as cleaning, security, and catering. The largest companies in this sector are European, perhaps because European businesses can use the practice to circumvent the greater protections which European laws give to direct employees. Compass (British), G4S (British) and ISS (Danish) each have around 500,000 staff.[11] While these businesses specialise in relatively low-paid activities, other firms offer more sophisticated specialisations. IBM, once known for its dominance of the mainframe computer business, is today the largest global consultancy company.[12] Not only does it sell software as a service; it also sells labour as a service.

4. Hollow corporations

The term 'hollow corporation' seems to have been used first by Norman Jonas in an extended article in *BusinessWeek* in 1986.[13] Jonas described how modern firms were outsourcing more and more of their activity to independent, specialist suppliers.[14] But what he described was still only the beginning of a development that would steadily gather pace.

For many, Nike, the largest retailer of sports footwear, is the exemplar of the modern 'hollow corporation'. Gerald Davis has even written of the 'Nikefication' of the American economy.[15] Nike itself manufactures nothing; all the garments and shoes which carry its famous 'swoosh' logo are made in factories in Asia. Davis did not intend 'Nikefication' to be a term of approbation. And there are grounds for real concern over the destruction of communities associated with the demise of large manufacturing plants.

But Apple is an equally striking and much more important exemplar of the hollow corporation. Apple products are designed in California. But that is all. The largest supplier of components for the iPhone is Apple's principal competitor in that market – Samsung. Chips come from Intel, but the latest Apple-specified chips are made by Taiwanese TSMC. Units are assembled in mainland China and prospectively India by Foxconn, subsidiary of another Taiwanese company.

Ray Kroc was a supplier to the hamburger bar of the McDonald brothers, who had developed what they called the Speedee Service System, with a limited menu and an assembly line process. The franchising model Kroc implemented involved a process of rigorous standardisation which gave the customer a predictable product. Today you can enjoy – or at least buy – an almost identical Big Mac in familiar surroundings in thousands of outlets in more than one hundred countries. The formula also enabled inexperienced individuals to establish their own businesses with modest capital and a high probability of success.

That formula was imitated by other fast-food chains and in many service businesses, from print shops to pharmacies to hotels. Common branding would help with marketing and give the collective franchise far more bargaining power with suppliers than any individual franchisee could enjoy. Today, franchising even extends to global accounting firms, with country-specific operations trading under one name worldwide. And both McDonald's and KPMG need to inspect the work of their franchisees to ensure that their brand and reputation are sustained.

The customers of Facebook, Twitter and YouTube are also these companies' suppliers. And much the same is true of eBay and Google. Airbnb and Uber have characteristics of both platforms and franchises. As platforms they link hosts with guests, passengers with drivers; as franchises they must try to monitor the quality of their lodgings and the reliability of their chauffeurs. The 'gig economy' has taken this development a stage further. Uber reports 5 million drivers.[16] Services such as IKEA's TaskRabbit and Amazon's Mechanical Turk connect individuals looking for tasks with consumers requiring services.

But like all the hollow corporations described here, they share the characteristic that the activities undertaken by the business itself have been pared down to the single link in the chain of production at which the corporation holds a distinctive capability and enjoys a competitive advantage. If the assembly line was the defining innovation in business method innovation of twentieth century manufacturing activity, the hollow corporation may be the defining innovation in business method of twenty-first century digital activity.

5. Economics and business strategy

In 1964, Igor Ansoff, often described as the founder of the subject of strategic management, now a course in every business school, explained that he had found little help from economics. 'The so-called microeconomic theory of the firm' he wrote 'sheds relatively little light on decision making processes in a real world firm'.[17]

Ansoff's critique had considerable justification. In 1982, soon after the retirement of Joe Bain from UC Berkeley, the American Economic Association elected him 'distinguished fellow' and described him as 'the undisputed father of modern Industrial Organization Economics'.[18] In his classic 1959 text *Industrial Organisation – a Treatise* Bain had defined the scope of his analysis:

> I am concerned with the environmental setting within which enterprises operate and in how they behave in these settings as producers, sellers and buyers. By contrast, I do not take an internal approach, more appropriate to the field of management science, such as could inquire how enterprises do and should behave in ordering their internal operations and would attempt to instruct them accordingly ... my primary unit for analysis is the industry or competing groups of firms, rather than the individual firm or the economy wide aggregate of enterprises.[19]

Harvard's economics department became the leading centre for industrial organisation, where FM Scherer developed the framework initiated by Bain. Scherer's 1970 *Industrial Market Structure and Economic Performance* succeeded Bain's on the bookshelf of a generation of graduate students. The Structure-Conduct-Performance framework is one in which industry structure determines behaviour which in turn determines performance. The difference of emphasis between Ansoff and Scherer is illustrated by the latter's measures of performance; 'production and allocative efficiency, progress, full employment, and equity'. Each refers to a public benefit from an industry, none to the private benefit to the stockholders of a firm.

In the 1970s, Michael Porter literally and metaphorically crossed the Charles River, which divides the main campus of Harvard University from its Business School, in an attempt to bridge the gap between economics and strategy. Porter's widely discussed 'five forces' framework is effectively a translation of the S-C-P approach into business language.[20] The strategy of the firm is assumed to be determined by the 'five forces' of suppliers, customers, entrants and substitute products, mediated by competitive rivalry. Yet the limitations of that S-C-P/five forces model are immediately apparent. There is no explanation of why different firms, facing the same five forces, perform differently. But the main issue of corporate strategy is how to outperform competitors. Scherer and his colleagues had influence on business through the application of their framework to issues of public policy – antitrust and regulation – not through the use of that framework by people who worked in businesses.

6. The economics of the firm

Much of the foundational literature on corporate governance (Berle and Means 1932), organisational theory (Drucker 1946), business history and corporate strategy (Chandler 1962), business strategy (Ansoff 1965) and the theory of the firm (Coase 1937) was written in the context of a commercial landscape dominated by large manufacturing corporations. As a result, these texts all describe – implicitly or explicitly – General Motors. And General Motors was the epitome of John Kenneth Galbraith's concept of technostructure and the target of Ralph Nader's critique of corporate responsibility. A student could spend several days in a business library without realising that in the twentieth century American business extended beyond a single firm based in Detroit, bordering the freshwater of the Great Lakes.

Although large corporations dominated the economy by the mid-twentieth century, economists for long had little to say about the corporation as an institution. Ronald (Coase's 1937) article (based, he later explained, on ideas conceived five years earlier when he was only twenty-one and formulated after a travelling scholarship had allowed him to visit Detroit) remains seminal.[21] Coase's article initially attracted little attention. It was only after he moved to Chicago, the location of early developments in both the law and economics movement and the theory of financial economics, that his thesis became influential.

In (Coase's 1937) analysis, the boundaries of the firm were defined by the relative costs and efficiency of two methods of coordination. Sometimes markets and the price mechanism were more effective; sometimes central direction and management hierarchies were more appropriate. It was always costly to trade in markets. On the other hand, subordinates might not always carry out the wishes of controllers as diligently or effectively as possible. This became the principal-agent problem and various approaches to it would be developed in the economics literature in subsequent decades.

The choice between markets and hierarchies was also influenced by the need for investment specific to the needs of a commercial relationship, an issue particularly associated with the work of Oliver Williamson.[22] Once such investment had been made, the relative bargaining power of the two parties would be changed – the hold-up problem.

The hold-up problem and the principal-agent problem would occupy the attention of economists for half a century. In 2016 the Nobel Prize in economics was shared between Oliver Hart, for his work on the markets versus hierarchies issue, and Bengt Holstrom, for his work on contract design. (Earlier awards had been made to Coase (1991) and Oliver Williamson (2009) for their contributions to the market versus hierarchy debate and to James Mirrlees (1996) and Eric Maskin (2007) who had considered contract structures.) Yet neither of these approaches to industrial organisation shed light on the central issues of business strategy – how to develop new products and business processes which yield competitive advantage.

7. Entrepreneurship

The claim that George W. Bush told Tony Blair that 'the problem with the French is that they don't have a word for entrepreneur' is, sadly, apocryphal.[23] But the French origin of the word is revealing – from entre, between, and preneur, taker. The original meaning of the term entrepreneur describes a coordinator, someone who brings things together. Modern American usage represents the entrepreneur as a heroic individual who sees what others do not and takes bold risks. While there is some truth in such a description, it misses the essential cooperative and evolutionary character of economic progress. The business founders we identify as legendary modern entrepreneurs – Jeff Bezos, Bill Gates, Steve Jobs – rode the wave of evolving collective intelligence. Online retailing and the personal computer revolution would have happened even if Bezos, Gates and Jobs had never existed. These individuals and their associates piece together relevant capabilities and when they succeed, as Amazon, Microsoft and Apple did but most new firms do not, it is because of the distinctive character of the capabilities of their organisation and the combinations they put together.

Joseph Schumpeter is especially remembered for his discussion of entrepreneurship, and for his vivid coinage of the term 'creative destruction'.[24] For Schumpeter and Opie (1934), the entrepreneur is the person who turns individual or collective knowledge into a product innovation or novel business process. Combination is therefore the crucial element in entrepreneurship. Silicon Valley's most famous and successful business incubator is called Y Combinator – facilitating fresh and productive combinations of capabilities is the essence of what it does. And 'the gale of creative destruction' is the process by which the repeated application of such entrepreneurship leads to economic progress.

For Edith Penrose, less flamboyant than Schumpeter, the firm was defined not by the assets it owned, or the contracts it made, but by its capabilities; and its ability to deploy its capabilities in productive services. Directing attention to capabilities focuses on the fundamentally important question – elided, as I noted above, in the markets and hierarchies and structure-conduct-performance approaches traditionally favoured by economists – of why firms in the same industry, facing the same 'five forces', differ from each other. But Penrose's work made little impact on subsequent theorising in economics – her name is not to be found in the index of standard economics texts such as Milgrom and Roberts[25] *Economics, Organisation and Management* or Tirole's *Theory of Industrial Organization.*[26]

But ideas similar to those of Penrose did have influence in the field of business strategy. The resource-based theory of strategy, as it has become known, was developed by Barney (1991) and Wernerfelt (1984). The task of corporate strategy is to match the capabilities of the firm to its external environment. The boundaries of the firm are defined less by transaction costs than by the appropriate scope of the firm's capabilities. That is why Apple sells music but not groceries but Amazon sells both. Teece (1986) added an emphasis on *dynamic* capabilities. The resource-based view of strategy was widely popularised in the 'core competencies' approach of C. K. Prahalad and Gary Hamel[27] (1990). But that application has been made problematic by the absence of sharp criteria for distinguishing core and other competencies, which allows wishful thinking. Core competencies become pretty much what the senior management of the corporation wanted them to be.

8. Combinations and capabilities

But a more focused view of the capabilities of the firm and its strategic direction emphasises the distinctive nature of the capabilities or the combination of capabilities. The critical resource for a firm lies in combinations of capabilities which cannot easily be replicated. Apple's smartphone offered a pocket computer with an astonishing range of functions. But all of these functions – voice and text messaging, location, navigation, etc.

- were already available. The power and the novelty of the iPhone lay in its combination of these capabilities – and in opening the device up to external developers via the App Store. Without that facility, which enabled app developers to provide constant additions to that range of functions and the capability to repeatedly innovate new, brilliantly designed products, Apple Inc. could only have commanded a fraction of the market capitalisation it has achieved. Distinctive capabilities, such as those of Apple's design team, are those characteristics of a firm that cannot be replicated by competitors, or can only be replicated with great difficulty, even after these competitors realise the benefits which they yield for the originating company.

Business innovation is about process, as well as technology. The low-cost airline provided a product which was already being delivered but in a novel combination, using new distribution channels – at first telephone booking, but subsequently and far more significantly the internet – to bypass the travel agent. The service model increased operating efficiency at the price of a less agreeable customer experience. Airbnb, Uber, Paypal and the retail division of Amazon similarly use new methods to provide familiar services.

Distinctive capabilities can be of many kinds. Government licences, statutory monopolies, or effective patents and copyrights, are particularly stark examples of distinctive capabilities. But equally powerful idiosyncratic characteristics have been built by companies in competitive markets. These include strong brands, patterns of supplier or customer relationships, and specific kinds of collective intelligence – the skills, knowledge and routines which are commonly embedded in teams and which may be specific to technologies, products or markets.

Reproducible or *complementary* capabilities can be bought or created by any firm with reasonable management skills, diligence, and financial resources. Most technical capabilities are of this kind. Few firms derive competitive advantage from their accounting department, although all firms need to have an accounting department and are wise to follow best accounting practice. Complementary capabilities are essential but only *distinctive* capabilities or (often) distinctive combinations of capabilities can be the basis of sustainable competitive advantage.

9. Conclusions

The history of flight – from the impractical fancies of Renaissance thinkers through the six kilometre trajectory of the Wright brothers at Kitty Hawk to the Airbus that can carry 400 passengers non-stop from Europe to Australia – exemplifies what evolutionary anthropologist Joseph Henrich[28] has called 'the secret of our success' - the accumulation of collective knowledge and its translation into collective intelligence. Nikolai Foss correctly characterises Penrose's anticipation of this insight as one about a world 'characterised by...learning, experimentation and change; it is a world in which people adopt or become socialised into cognitive frameworks that allow them to make some sense out of the world, and where the coordination of such actions is dependent upon the sharing of such frameworks'.[29]

There are three key points here. The world is characterised by learning, experimentation, and change – not by equilibrium. People become socialised into cognitive frameworks (cognitive gadgets, to adopt the language of Cecilia Hayes)[30] – collective knowledge and collective intelligence are shared rather than proprietary properties. And coordination is achieved by the sharing of such frameworks – not by the dictates of an organisational hierarchy.

We need these ideas to understand the world of the modern industrial organisation – a world of hollow corporations, of capital as a service, of franchises and platforms. A world Penrose, writing more than sixty years ago, could hardly have imagined. A world in which defining the boundaries of the firm is no longer the central question of economic organisation. And perhaps it never was.

Notes

1. Galton (1907); Surowiecki (2005).
2. Regis (2020).
3. Jensen and Meckling (1976); Williamson (1975); Grossman and Hart (1986).
4. Penrose (1995) p. 2.
5. The pilot communicates all instructions to an electronic console, eliminating the mechanical interface familiar to car drivers and Boeing pilots on planes before the 777.
6. (4 Apr. Burrows 2013).
7. Norges Bank Investment Management (13 Jan. 2011).
8. Apple (2019) p. 31.
9. Amazon (2020) p. 40.
10. (20 Oct. Rosoff 2016).
11. Compass Group (2019), 15; G4S (2019), 2; ISS (2019) p. 8.
12. IBM (2019) p. 64.
13. (3 Mar. Jonas 1986).
14. Jonas (1986)
15. Davis (2016).
16. Uber (6 Feb. 2020) p. 7.
17. Ansoff (1965), 2–3.
18. American Economic Association (1983).
19. Bain (1959) pp. vii – viii.
20. Porter (1979).
21. (9 Dec. Coase 1991).
22. Williamson (1975).
23. (23 Sept. Mikkelson 2007).
24. McCraw (2007)
25. Milgrom and Roberts (1992)
26. Tirole(1988)
27. Prahalad and Hamel(1990)
28. Henrich (2015)
29. Foss (2002) p. 161.
30. Hayes (2018)

Disclosure statement

No potential conflict of interest was reported by the author(s).

References

Amazon. 2020. "2019 Annual Report" Accessed July 27, 2020. https://s2.q4cdn.com/299287126/files/doc_financials/2020/ar/2019-Annual-Report.pdf.

American Economic Association. 1983. "[Photograph]: Joe S. Bain: Distinguished Fellow 1982." *American Economic Review* 73 (3).

Ansoff, H. Igor. 1965. *Corporate Strategy: An Analytic Approach to Business Policy for Growth and Expansion.* New York: McGraw-Hill.

Apple. 2019. "2019 10-K." https://www.sec.gov/Archives/edgar/data/320193/000032019319000119/a10-k20199282019.htm

Bain, J. S. 1959. *Industrial Organization.* New York: Wiley.

Barney, J. 1991. "Firm Resources and Sustained Competitive Advantage." *Journal of Management* 17 (1): 99–120. https://doi.org/10.1177/014920639101700108.

Berle, A., and G. Means. 1932. *The Modern Corporation and Private Property.* New York: Transaction Publishers.

Burrows, P. 2013. "Inside Apple's Plans for Its, Futuristic, \$5 Billion Headquarters." *Bloomberg.* April 4. Accessed October 5, 2021. https://www.bloomberg.com/news/articles/2013-04-04/inside-apples-plans-for-its-futuristic-5-billion-headquarters.

Chandler, A. D. 1962. *Strategy and Structure: Chapters in the History of the Industrial Enterprise.* London: MIT Press.

Coase, R. H. 1937. "The Nature of the Firm." *Economica* 4 (16): 386–405. https://doi.org/10.1111/j.1468-0335.1937.tb00002.x.

Coase, R. H. 1991. "Prize Lecture." *The Nobel Prize.* 9 Dec. Accessed May 3, 2023. https://www.nobelprize.org/prizes/economic-sciences/1991/coase/lecture/.

Compass Group. 2019. *Annual Report 2019.*

Davis, G. F. 2016. *The Vanishing American Corporation.* Oakland, CA: Berrett-Koehler.

Drucker, P. F. 1946. *Concept of the Corporation.* New York: John Day.

Foss, N. J. 2002. "Edith Penrose and Strategic Management." In *The Growth of the Firm*, edited by C. Pitelis, 147–164. Oxford: Oxford University Press.

G4S. 2019. *Integrated Report and Accounts 2019.*

Galton, F. 1907. "Vox Populi." *Nature* 75 (1949): 450–451. https://doi.org/10.1038/075450a0.

Grossman, S. J., and O. D. Hart. 1986. "The Costs and Benefits of Ownership: A Theory of Vertical and Lateral Integration." *Journal of Political Economy* 94 (4): 691–719. https://doi.org/10.1086/261404.

Hayes, C. 2018. *Cognitive Gadgets.* Cambridge, MA: Belknap Press.

Henrich, J. 2015. *The Secret of Our Success.* Princeton, NJ: Princeton University Press.

IBM. 2019. *Annual Report 2019.*

ISS. 2019. *Annual Report 2019.*

Jensen, M. C., and W. H. Meckling. 1976. "Theory of the Firm: Managerial Behavior, Agency Costs and Ownership Structure." *Journal of Financial Economics* 3 (4): 305–360. https://doi.org/10.1016/0304-405X(76)90026-X.

Jonas, N. 1986. "The Hollow Corporation." *BusinessWeek*, Mar 3: 57–59.

McCraw, T. K. 2007. *Prophet of Innovation: Joseph Schumpeter and Creative Destruction.* Cambridge, MA: Belknap Press.

Mikkelson, D. 2007. "Bush and French Word for Entrepreneur." *Snopes.com.* Sept 23. Accessed September 28, 2021. https://www.snopes.com/fact-check/french-lesson/.

Milgrom, P. R., and J. Roberts. 1992. *Economics, Organization and Management.* Englewood Cliffs, NJ: Prentice-Hall.

Norges Bank Investment Management. 2011 "Fund Signs Regent Street Agreement." Jan 13. Accessed May 17, 2023. https://www.nbim.no/en/the-fund/news-list/2011/fund-signs-regent-street-agreement/.

Penrose, E. T. 1995. *The Theory of the Growth of the Firm.* 4th ed. Oxford: OUP. https://doi.org/10.1093/0198289774.001.0001.

Porter, M. E. 1979. "How Competitive Forces Shape Strategy." *Harvard Business Review* 57 (2): 137–145.

Prahalad, C. K., and G. Hamel. 1990. "The Core Competence of the Corporation." *Harvard Business Review* 68 (3): 79–91.

Regis, E. 2020. "No One Can Explain Why Planes Stay in the Air." *Scientific American* 322 (2): 44–51.

Rosoff, M. 2016 "Jeff Bezos Told what Might be the Best Startup Investment Story Ever." *Business Insider*. Oct 20. Accessed October 6, 2021 https://www.businessinsider.com/jeff-bezos-on-early-amazon-investors-2016-10?r=US&IR=T.

Schumpeter, J. A., and R. Opie, translated by 1934. *The Theory of Economic Development.* Cambridge, MA: Harvard University Press.

Surowiecki, J. 2005. *The Wisdom of Crowds.* New York: Anchor Books.

Teece, D. J. 1986. "Transactions Cost Economics and the Multinational Enterprise an Assessment." *Journal of Economic Behavior and Organization* 7 (1): 21–45. https://doi.org/10.1016/0167-2681(86)90020-X.

Tirole, J. 1988. *Theory of Industrial Organization.* Cambridge, MA: MIT Press.

Uber. 2020. *2020 Investor Presentation.* Feb 6

Wernerfelt, B. 1984. "A Resource-Based View of the Firm." *Strategic Management Journal* 5 (2): 171–180. https://doi.org/10.1002/smj.4250050207.

Williamson, O. E. 1975. *Markets and Hierarchies: Analysis and Antitrust Implications.* New York: Free Press.

∂ OPEN ACCESS

Captive markets and climate change: Revisiting Edith Penrose's analysis of the international oil firms in the era of climate change

Damian Tobin

ABSTRACT

Edith Penrose's analysis of the investments of the international oil companies (IOCs) stemmed from her interest in the economics of the large international firm and its implications for developing economies. Her approach highlights the endogenous factors shaping the growth of the large firm and cautions against viewing it as a neutral technocracy where investment automatically responds to price incentives. Drawing on Penrose's concept of a captive market in oil products, this research develops Penrose's ideas around motive, profit, self-financing and the international firm to explain why the IOC's institutional environment still favours investment in fossil fuels. The study collected country and firm level data on investment and production in downstream petrochemical refining. The data show a connection between the captive market and the strategies of the large oil firms in expanding refining capacity as a strategic hedge against regulatory policies to limit climate change. This locks society into a carbon intensive infrastructure, reduces the motivation for investment and adds to global CO_2 emissions. The findings indicate that the oil companies need to take greater risks on green investments with their retained earnings. Governments need to direct this investment towards socially useful purposes using coordinated regulatory pressure.

1. Introduction

'Had we invested massively in renewable energy in the past, we would not be so dramatically at the mercy of the instability of fossil fuel markets .... New funding for fossil fuel exploration and production infrastructure is delusional. It will only further feed the scourge of war, pollution and climate catastrophe'. António Guterres[1]

Investment and the diffusion of new green technologies is central to decarbonisation. Yet increasing evidence indicates that financial markets are not rising to the occasion, oil producers are unwilling to cut output (Jacobsson and Jacobsson 2012; Le Billon and Kristofferson, 2020; Semieniuk et al, 2022) and there has been little substantive progress on decarbonisation at the organisational level (Busch, Bauer, and Orlitzky 2016). One of the main organisation level actors are the large petroleum

---

This is an Open Access article distributed under the terms of the Creative Commons Attribution License (http://creativecommons.org/licenses/by/4.0/), which permits unrestricted use, distribution, and reproduction in any medium, provided the original work is properly cited. The terms on which this article has been published allow the posting of the Accepted Manuscript in a repository by the author(s) or with their consent.

companies (IEA 2018, Christophers 2021). Why have the large petroleum firms continued to invest in downstream capacity that adds to the demand for fossil fuels? Drawing on Edith Penrose's (1968) analysis of the IOCs, this paper focuses on the IOC's strategic decision to go big on plastics and other petrochemicals and its role in increasing the emissions that drive anthropogenic climate change. Although a large body of research has focused on the transition of upstream oil producers (Heede 2014, Blondeel and Bradshaw 2022), much less is known about the strategies and emissions of refiners (Bauer and Fontenit 2021, Jing et al. 2020). Petrochemical refining is responsible for about one-third of future oil demand and along with power generation and cement production accounts for the bulk of stationary CO_2 emissions (IPCC 2018).[2] Increased investments in the petrochemical building blocks for plastics worsens carbon lock-in (Bauer and Fontenit 2021). Penrose's work indicates that the reasons for this expansion are to be found in the relationship between the oil companies long run planning of production and the uneven implementation of climate agreements.

Though often overlooked, Penrose's ideas around state-MNE relations hold enormous potential for influencing policies on sustainable economic development (Pitelis, 2009). In her analysis of the large oil firm, Penrose (1968) highlighted the role of the captive market in reinforcing the power and flexibility that vertical integration gave the IOCs. The basis of Penrose's argument was that the power of the captive market was such that it worsened the policy predicament facing developing economies, forcing them to alternate between a grateful acceptance of the IOCs proprietary technology and distrust of their pricing strategies. Conceptually, as with Penrose's (1959) *The Theory of the Growth of the Firm* (TTGF), this approach differs from viewing the oil market as characterised by Knightian-type uncertainty. Instead, the large oil firm internalises uncertainty by extending its administrative authority across countries, exploiting regulatory gaps and profiting with historical regularity. Climate change introduces a new dimension to this since its impacts on asset owners have been uneven and cooperation on reducing emissions has been limited (e.g. Colgan, Green, and Hale 2021), amplifying the conditions that Penrose (1968) viewed as leading the IOCs to discriminate across countries.

The paper focuses on the interplay between two stylised features of the petrochemical industry. The first is the projected shift in production related emissions from developed OECD economies to developing regions, especially China (IPCC 2018). In the oil sector, this shift has amplified what Penrose (1968) described as a captive market in oil products. Penrose viewed the power of the captive market as evolving from vertical integration. This allowed the IOCs to control access to advanced refining technologies and high value chemicals such as ethylene and propylene. These products have few close substitutes. Investment in refineries is also characterised by large minimum plant sizes and large sunk costs, allowing refineries to operate for extended periods at low average costs (Bauer and Fontenit 2021). Operating at low costs squeezes out the entrance of substitute products, further strengthening the captive market. Penrose (1968) viewed the flexibility and control that underpinned the captive market in oil as being so strong, it could only be broken by government pressure. Today these investments form a significant part of the fossil fuel infrastructure that creates Long Lived Capital Stock, causing societal lock-in to emissions intensive technologies and hindering a low carbon transition (Smith et al, 2019, Fisch-Romito et al. 2021, Kemfert et al. 2022).

This leads to the second feature of the contemporary captive market, namely the role of petroleum firms in ramping up downstream refinery capacity in plastics and other high value petrochemicals as part of a strategic hedge against weakening demand growth for transport fuels (IEA 2020). This increases the non-energy demand for fossil fuels and has a significant impact on emissions. A key driver of non-energy demand are petroleum-derived feedstocks. Feedstocks are key inputs in the production of a range of chemicals, plastics and synthetic rubbers and include naphtha and ethane. Data from the IEA indicate that chemicals produced by refineries account for approximately 90% of the feedstocks for plastics, fertilisers, fuels and resins, and CO_2 emissions from the chemical sector account for 18% of all industrial CO_2 emissions (IEA 2018, 50). Refineries account for around 5.97% of total worldwide CO_2 emissions with 638 plant sources with emissions greater than 0.1 Mt CO_2/year (IPCC 2018, 81). The growth in the production of plastics relative to other high emitting bulk products is driven by the low specific gravity of plastics that gives them weight, cost and fabrication advantages over metals (Freeman, Young, and Fuller 1963). The petrochemical building blocks for plastics also have few close substitutes. Alternatives such as bioplastics, which use bio-based feedstocks and pre-date petrochemicals, account for a low share of total plastics (Altman, 2022). Reducing CO_2 emissions from refining will therefore require either voluntary reductions in capacity or the large-scale investment in and rapid diffusion of low emission technologies such as carbon capture (e.g. IPCC 2018).

The next section draws on Penrose's work to set out the features of the captive market. Section 3 draws on country level data to document the structure of international production, ownership and variations in the technical complexity of refineries across countries. Section 4 analyses the trade dimension of the captive market by focusing on international trade in ethylene. Ethylene is a high value petrochemical derivative and the building block for a wide range of chemicals and plastics. Section 5 focuses on investment and production at the firm level. Given the scarcity of consistent firm level data on petrochemical refiners, a similar approach to other studies on the oil industry is followed (Green et al. 2021, Bauer and Fontenit 2021) where firm-level data on investment and ethylene output is gathered for a sample of large IOCs, NOCs (National Oil Companies) and independent refining companies. The final substantive section looks at the implications for emissions, policy, and theory.

2. The captive market: investment, motive, profits, and uncertainty

This section outlines how Penrose's views on the relationship between the oil price, investment and the large integrated firm differed from those put forward by mainstream economics. It then draws on key theoretical contributions of her work to set out the features that sustain the captive market.

2.1. Misrepresenting oil investment: Penrose vs the mainstream

Taking its lead from the neo-classical preoccupation with equilibrium relationships between prices and investment (e.g. Robinson, 1962), economic analyses of the oil industry tends to use the hypothesised relationship between higher price volatility and lower investment under conditions of uncertainty, reversibility and sunk costs as a starting point (e.g. Bernanke 1983; Henriques and Sadorsky 2011; van Eyden et al, 2019). This frames the oil industry in Knightian terms, facing resource heterogeneity, cognitive limitations, uncertain environments and using experience to profit from uncertainty (Knight 1921, 75). From this perspective, low investment in renewables can be explained by large upfront costs, prices and high risk.

The drawback with this approach is that market power and an oligopolistic structure creates 'a very considerable rent in the international oil price' meaning that while supply and demand influence prices and investment, they do so within a very distorted market (Stevens, 2005, 20). Penrose (1968) argued that the relationship between these variables bore only faint resemblance to that put forward in mainstream theory. Instead, she viewed the large oil firm as characterised by the long run programming of production. This involved searching for certainty, seizing productive or greener opportunities at its boundaries, while also spending time developing existing profitable opportunities (Penrose, 1968, 21). That is not to say that Penrose dismissed the efficacy of the profit motive as a guide to resource allocation. Profit was a core part of *TTGF*. What Penrose questioned was its explanatory function when the market is not permitted and some other authority became the arbiter of the public interest (Penrose, 1968, 22).

That authority was the large integrated oil firm and its role as arbiter of the public interest held significant implications for policy. Like Penrose, Schumpeter (1928) was critical of orthodox approaches for failing to appreciate how the transition from competitive to trustified capitalism resulted in a shift in the source of innovation. Under the latter, innovation is embodied in large existing units and occurred largely independent of individuals. In the oil sector this unit was exemplified by the large oil firm, which operated as a supranational administrative unit of control. This meant that where high profits are generated from a restriction in activity in one product area or country, these can be used to create new markets in another (Penrose, 1968, 21). This occurred without any great level of predictability. In this way the integrated structure acted as an efficient form of professional management (Chandler 2002). It also meant that apart from coming from the same raw material, the prices of oil products bore little connection to that of a barrel of crude, since technological developments determine the mix of products that could be produced (Penrose, 1968, 174).

The analytical challenge this presents is that the source of unpredictability of interest to researchers is often not exogenously determined but is instead to be found in the endogenous deployment of resources within the firm. For Penrose efficiency in producing and distributing oil products, while impressive, was not sufficient to explain the IOCs dominance. In the Penrosian firm, the cohesion of closely interacting and interdependent resources could not be created under a spot market setting (Pitelis and Wahl, 1998). This is illustrated in how the sector has used financial, commercial and political power to address challenges ranging from the oil nationalisation in the Middle East to the emergence of more transparent oil markets. This meant that the control over supply, which had underpinned vertical integration, could easily be replaced by trading divisions (Stevens, 2005). Financial integration became a prerequisite for operational integration, but intermediate oil markets could also substitute for operational integration, allowing the entrance of dedicated refiners (Tordo, 2011).

2.2. The captive market: motive, profit, and international investments

Once we recognise the above, it is possible to unpack the nature of the investment problem by outlining the features of the captive market. Captive markets occur where consumer choice is limited to a small number of producers who operate under monopolistic or oligopolistic market conditions characterised by low price elasticities or captive sources of supply (Hufbauer 1965, Vernon, 1966). For Penrose (1968, 230) the captive market represented 'an insistent attempt on the part of the international companies to maintain their international price structure in those markets where they had a complete monopoly while giving way elsewhere'. This inevitably meant that for many developing economies the price of market entry for the IOCs involved the construction of a refinery as a means of ameliorating the balance of payment pressures associated with importing costly petrochemicals (Hartshorn 1962). Flexibility distinguished the captive market from a cartel, while vertical integration allowed the IOCs to use diversification into petrochemicals as a strategy to upgrade the value of their crude oil (Penrose 1968, 146). These features meant that location of oil refineries and investment had often little to do with market prices. The remainder of this section draws on Penrose's broader work to outline the factors that under-pinned the captive market.

The first is motive. Motive, along with other factors such as technical capabilities and market logic are often assumed to be exogenously determined or constant in studies of the oil sector (Kim 2020). In TTGF, Penrose (1959) argued that it was impossible to have a discussion of the functions of a firm without an understanding of its motivation. Since profits represented a condition for growth and that funds that could be profitably used would be invested in productive opportunities 'growth and profits became equivalent as the criteria for the selection of investment programmes' (Penrose, 1959: 26). Following this logic, whereas energy transitions present firms with productive opportunities, firms will not invest unless there is a clear rational that they meet the criteria of growth and profits.[3] The logic is remarkably like the concept of fossilised capital (Malm 2016, Christophers 2021). Like Penrose, the concept of fossilised capital suggests that there is no simplistic relationship between prices and energy transition and 'if the path to profitability is not clear and compelling, the incentive to invest in renewable energy production will not be nearly substantial enough to drive investment on the scale that is ecologically necessary' (Christophers 2021, 8–9).

A second feature is that because motivation is not a homogenous characteristic of the Penrosean firm, emergent features of capitalism could easily undermine the rational for investment. Penrose's (1952) early work made it clear that she viewed innovation as a purposeful attempt to do something, rather than a chance mutation. In this sense, Penrose's views echoed those of Schumpeter (1942) and Robinson (1962) as competition becomes both 'at once a god and a devil', desirable because it drives innovation and undesirable as it leads to concentrated structures that impede growth (Penrose, 2009: 233). For Schumpeter (1942) trustified capitalism had the potential to undermine the unique characteristics of entrepreneurial innovation. This opened complex questions around whether market power is the price society must pay for rapid technological progress (the Schumpeter Hypothesis), and the type of policy interventions appropriate for productivity growth in concentrated industries (Nelson and Winter 1982).

Concentration could lead to a decline in capital deepening or capacity utilisation caused by changes in the financial sector. Financialization undermines the process of creative destruction in energy by shifting capital from productive to speculative investment (Jacobsson and Jacobsson 2012).

Penrose's analysis captured these points by questioning the extent to which the IOCs could be depended upon to invest in socially useful purposes. For technical progress to occur, the corporate economy requires large firms to invest (Marris and Wood 1971). The challenge this creates was summed up by Kaldor (1957, 595) who wrote that 'a society where technical change and adaptation proceeds slowly, where producers are reluctant to abandon traditional methods ... is necessarily one where the rate of capital accumulation is small'. Penrose located the reluctance to invest in the conservative investment practices of the IOCs and the preference for self-financing as opposed to any lack of financial resources. Firms 'retain as much profit as possible for reinvestment in the firm' instead of taking on external debt (Penrose, 2009: 26). The tendency of the large firm to self-finance reflects a historical feature of the large corporation where corporate retentions, measured as the difference between profits and cash distributions to shareholders, represented the financial foundations for investing in productive assets (Filippi and Zanetti 1971; Lazonick, 2015). Innovation requires firms to take risks with retained earnings (Palladino and Lazonick 2022). Penrose (1968) drew specific attention to the tendency of the IOCs to finance a large proportion of their investment from retained earnings. This provided the IOCs with a considerable financial cushion over debt financed smaller private firms. In the context of current debates around stranded assets (e.g. Semieniuk et al, 2022) and an increasing tendency of large firms to use retained earnings to fund share buybacks (Palladino and Lazonick (2022), Penrose's work implies that the IOCs might better positioned to withstand changes in financial market funding.

The same conservatism also leads oil firms to resist government requests for socially useful investments. Investment outside core business areas accounts for less than 1% of the oil firms' total capital expenditure (IEA 2020). At the same time, there has been a strategic shift towards investment in plastics and other petrochemicals as a means of exploiting the benefits of vertical integration (IEA 2020, 269). Penrose argues that the IOCs conservative financing and investment undermined any claims that unfavourable oil prices and the threat of tax increases would jeopardise future investment (Penrose, 1968, 145). This feature also meant that the IOCs have significant financial resources to invest in petrochemicals. This reflects a broader criticism of policy makers for under-estimating the power of vested interests in protecting current patterns of capital accumulation (Wright and Nyberg, 2015). A key implication from Penrose's work is that states need to understand existing patterns of accumulation and direct innovation activities towards socially beneficial purposes.

A final feature underpinning the captive market and for Penrose, its chief danger as a vehicle for international investment, was the way variations in treatment across countries forced it to discriminate. In this regard, Penrose (1968, 266) was critical of how Berle and Means (1932) viewed the large firm as a 'neutral technocracy' responding to the public interest. Any tendency towards neutrality was obstructed by the international firm's ability to know where to control and where to give way based on a 'very unstable combination of individualist competitive enterprise and co-ordinated planning'

(Penrose, 1968, 150). In the oil industry this inhibited unilateral state policy actions and incentivised the free rider problem (Stevens, 2005). Penrose's analysis draws attention to the relationship between the oil firms' technological advantage and economic policy. Petroleum companies in developed economies could suppress the wider diffusion of new techniques in refining and synthetic chemicals (Mandel, 1968). In earlier work on the patent system, Penrose questioned the social loss associated with suppression of the use of the most efficient processes by all producers (Machlup and Penrose, 1950). Later she showed how this forced developing economies to implement policies incentivising the IOCs to construct refineries as a way of dealing with the balance of payments pressures caused by the large-scale importation of oil products (Penrose: 1968, 224).

Based on the above, what would a green transition for the IOCs look like? Several broad industry approaches to a green transition have emerged including investment in renewables; investment in carbon capture technology; investment in alternative bio-based feedstocks; and the decommissioning of infrastructure such as refineries. Penrose's work suggests that these should be judged on clear evidence that retained earnings are being invested in new technologies, which are diffused in such a way as to ensure their rapid uptake in developing economies. Existing practice points to mixed evidence of progress across these areas. Some IOCs have made voluntary commitments to accelerate investment in and scale up new technologies under the Oil and Gas Climate Initiative. This includes 12 of the largest oil and gas firms accounting for 30% of global production.[4] Green et al. (2021) note that it is telling that the focus is on reducing carbon emissions rather than switching away from fossil fuels. Other IOCs have rebranded as integrated energy companies. Total announced that it would rename itself Total Energies and increase its investments in non-fossil energy sources, but as Bonneuil, Choquet, and Franta (2021) caution, the company has a poor history in this regard. Some European IOCs, such as the Italian firm Eni, have decommissioned oil refineries with the intention of converting these facilities to produce bio-based feedstocks.[5]

3. The evolution of the refining industry

Downstream oil refining has evolved considerably since Penrose's analysis. This section outlines the major changes in location and ownership, with a particular emphasis on how the refining sector has exploited technological developments and market opportunities.

3.1. Geographical trends in refining capacity

One of the defining features of petrochemical refining since the early 1980s has been the closure of European refineries and the shift of refining capacity to the Asia Pacific region (Figure 1). This has seen the closure of large refineries and announcements regarding the planned decommissioning of others and could see many EU countries transition from a surplus to deficit in key petrochemicals. Care must however be taken in how these closures are interpreted, since environmental regulations make it costly to fully close refineries and as result many remain designated as refineries with implications for national capacity data (Stevens, 2005).

A second development has been the re-emergence of the US as a major refiner. Like in Europe, US capacity fell during the 1980s, but began to recover in the early 1990s. By

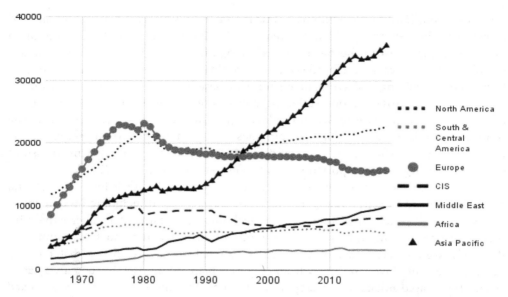

Figure 1. Refining capacities 1965–2019 (Unit: thousand barrels daily). source: adapted from BP (2020).

2019, the US accounted for 18.7% of global refining capacity, making it the county with the largest refining capacity (BP 2020). Recent capacity growth has largely been driven by shale gas discoveries. Technical breakthroughs and cost advantages have made shale oil uniquely responsive to price signals (Kim 2020). This led to an abundance of ethane, a key feedstock for ethane-based ethylene crackers. Ethane crackers yield around 80% ethylene, a key input for plastics, but unlike naphtha-based crackers, this leaves limited scope for other petrochemical products (IEA 2018). Abundant shale oil made the operational and feedstock costs of ethane crackers look extremely competitive relative to other refinery feedstocks in both the US and other regions (Table 1).

The speed at which US refineries were able to ramp up the construction of ethylene refineries in response to the productive opportunity offered by low-cost ethane is remarkable given their general reluctance to invest in lower-emission products. Three new ethylene refineries were constructed in 2017 and a further

Table 1. Feedstock cost by region 2017 (Unit: US$/per tonne of high value chemicals).

	CapEx/OpEx	Feedstock
Ethane - Middle East	176.4	85.4
Ethane - United States	176.4	211.0
Ethane – Europe	176.4	312.2
Methanol-to-Olefins – China	143.7	820.7
Naphtha - United States	244.1	825.5
Naphtha - Middle East	244.1	861.8
Naphtha – China	244.1	872.7
Naphtha – Europe	244.1	880.0

CAPEX refers to Capital Expenditure; OPEX refers to Operation Expenditure.
Source: IEA (2017): Simplified levelized Cost of Petrochemicals for selected feedstocks.

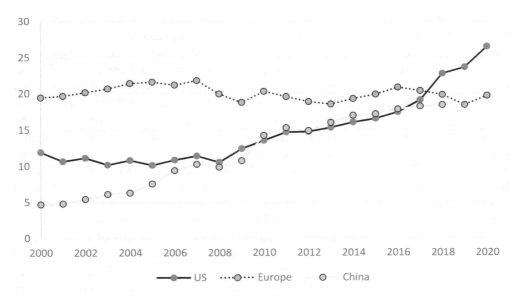

Figure 2. Ethylene output in major producers 2000–2020 (Million tons/year). Source: US data based on figures from US EIA; European data from the European Chemical Industry Council; Chinese data from State Statistical Yearbooks.

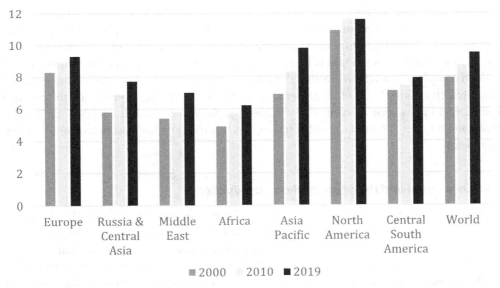

Figure 3. Nelson complexity index by region (2000–2019). Source: ENI (2015; 2020).

six ethylene refineries were penned for completion by the end of 2020.[6] The response saw US ethylene production overtake Chinese production in 2017 and European production after 2018 (Figure 2). This represented an increase in ethylene output from 392,368 thousand barrels daily in 2015 to 628,961 thousand barrels daily by 2020.

A third development has been the growth in refining capacity in Asia and the Middle East. Figure 1 shows that between 2000 and 2019 refining capacity in the Asia Pacific grew by 69% while capacity in the Middle East increased by 50%. Much of the growth in the former has been driven by China, which by 2019 accounted for 16.0% of global capacity, while the latter has been driven by Saudi Arabia, which grew refining capacity from 700,000 barrels per day in 1980 to 2,835,000 barrels per day by 2019 (BP 2020). This has been primarily driven by NOCs seeking to exploit uncertainties in oil markets by replicating the integration advantages of the IOCs by investing in downstream capabilities in large oil consuming countries (Marcel 2006). Countries like Saudi Arabia and Kuwait, which were viewed by Penrose (1968) more as suppliers than competitors to the IOCs, were well suited to this. Saudi Arabia has followed an economic diversification strategy based on capturing more value across the hydrocarbon value chain though vertical integration, exploiting shale oil and leveraging on the region's cost competitiveness (Fattouh 2021). Increasing refining capacity and the complexity of products produced has been a key aspect of this. Middle Eastern ethane enjoys significant cost advantages over the US and European feedstocks as well as over naphtha as feedstock in such regions as China (Table 1). Kuwait has also pursued vertical integration by acquiring overseas refining assets to compensate for any lack of open market refinery demand for its sour crude (Marcel 2006, Tordo, 2011).

The differences between growth in aggregate refining capacity and that in high value-added chemicals such as ethylene illustrate a fourth feature of the market. As such, capacity increases by themselves provide a limited insight into who captures value. Petrochemicals have become more complex reflecting the more sophisticated products demanded by industry. More complex refineries also have higher emissions (Jing et al. 2020). But refinery complexity is unevenly distributed across regions. One measure, the Nelson complexity index, shows that the US (followed closely by Europe) has consistently benefited from more complex refineries (Figure 3). Increasing investment in the Asia Pacific region has seen its complexity increase rapidly over the last decade. The Middle East, which benefits from large oil reserves, has traditionally had lower levels of refining complexity.

3.2. Ownership and the geographies of production

The most significant change to the IOCs since Penrose's account has been the change in control over oil reserves. In the 1970s the IOCs had access to 85% of the world's oil reserves; by 1980 this situation had completely reversed, and the IOCs had full access to 12% and the NOCs had access to some 59% (Diwan, 2007). Further distinctions can be made between the NOCs themselves. Saudi Aramco benefits from a high level of integration between upstream and downstream (Fattouh 2021).[7] While Norwegian, Venezuelan and Mexican NOCs were established to manage large existing reserves, Petrobras was established with the objective of turning Brazil into an oil producer (Priest, 2016). China's NOCs have sought to further national self-sufficiency in production and refining, and have minority listings on international stock markets (Tobin, 2019, Verbeek and Mah, 2020).

There have also been changes in the ownership of refining infrastructure. The share of global capacity accounted for by the IOCs fell, declining from 26% in 2000 to 14% in

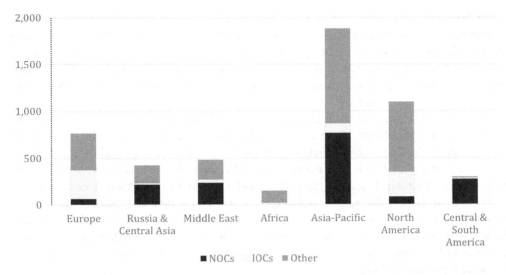

Figure 4. Primary refining capacity by region and type (2019, Unit: million tons). Source: Adapted from ENI (2020)

2019, while the NOCs share increased from 23% to 33% over the same period, with the share of other independent refineries remaining largely stable at around 50% (ENI 2020). These figures vary by region. The IOC's account for a small proportion of refining capacity in the Middle East. Here Saudi Aramco's refining subsidiary Saudi Basic Industries Corporation (SABIC), established in 1976 to develop Saudi Arabia's refining infrastructure, benefits from a lean western-style management structure and has emerged as a globally competitive player (Hertog 2008). In Central and South America, NOCs are responsible for most refining output (Figure 4). The African continent accounts for a small amount of global capacity and lacks established NOCs, with most capacity accounted for by independent refiners. North America accounts for the second largest region in terms of capacity. Here private refiners account for the largest proportion of capacity. Although the IOCs account for a smaller proportion of US capacity, this capacity dwarfs that of other smaller regions. The Asia-Pacific accounts for the largest share of global capacity. Here, the IOCs account for a small proportion of capacity compared to the NOCs and independents.

The above highlights two important factors for further analysis of the captive market. First, in many cases, oil reserves and refining infrastructure are owned by non-publicly traded companies and decisions on their future rest in political hands. In these cases, the risk of stranded assets lies in the hands of governments not market shareholders (Semieniuk et al, 2022). Secondly, the significant role of independent refineries and their control over advanced refining techniques highlights the need to include them in any analysis of the captive market.

4. The captive market, trade and technology

The strength of the Penrose's captive market depends on the ability of refiners to use technical and trade advantages to transform crude oil into a variety of high value-added petrochemicals. It is based on the fact that there is no general relationship between a country's oil reserves, and whether it runs a surplus or deficit in refined oil products. As Penrose (1968) argued, the mix of products that can be refined from a barrel of cure oil continues to depend on a mix of geological characteristics and technical capabilities. This section illustrates this by examining the trade balance in oil products generally and the case of ethylene specifically.

The oil production and product data in Table 2 illustrates this point. The US ran one of the largest deficits in crude oil and oil products in the early 2000s. Technical advancements in shale oil production and more complex refineries allowed the US to turn a large product deficit into a surplus by 2019. Only Russia and the Middle East ran larger oil product surpluses. On the other hand, Central and Southern American countries have run crude oil surpluses but need to import oil products. Similarly, the African continent runs a crude oil surplus and an increasing deficit in oil products. There are also large variations between countries in North and Western Africa, which have larger crude reserves and smaller product deficits and Eastern and Southern Africa, which tend to run crude and product deficits.

Table 2. Oil balance and oil product balances, selected countries and regions.

	2005		2010		2015		2019	
	Product Balance	Crude Balance	Product Balance	Crude Balance	Product Balance	Crude Balance	Product Balance	Crude Balance
United States	−8,964	−10,017	−404	−9,131	2,095	−6,860	2,952	−4,030
South & Central America	671	1,544	−254	2,216	−1,303	3,058	−1,817	2,509
Europe	−9,153	−9,772	−1,252	−8,954	−1,146	−9,597	−1,751	−9,957
Russia & CIS	1,702	5,374	2,057	6,385	3,078	6,219	3,553	7,212
Middle East	2,287	17,124	2,029	16,416	2,178	17,507	3,421	17,730
African Continent	7	6,117	232	6,679	−639	5,427	−1,638	5,853
China	−2,260	−2,418	−638	−4,670	−686	−6,686	−241	−10,177

Source: BP Statistical Review, various years.

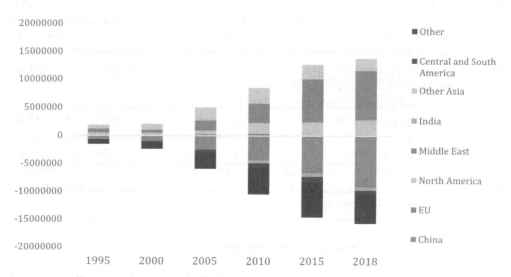

Figure 5. Ethylene polymers trade balance 1995–2018 (Unit: US$ 1,000).
Notes: Trade balances calculated using value of ethylene polymers in primary forms with a specific gravity of more than 0.94 (Product code: 390120) Source: WITS Database

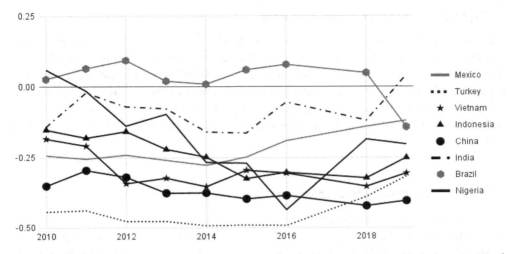

Figure 6. Net imports of ethylene polymers for selected deficit countries (% GDP). Sources: Word Development Indicators; WITS Database

Looking specifically at trade data for ethylene polymers, Figure 5 shows both the growth in the trade of ethylene since the 1990s and how the gap between surplus and deficit countries has seen a consistent widening between exporters and importers. Although China has expanded its ethylene production (Figure 2), this has not been of a sufficient scale to satisfy domestic demand and its trade deficit in ethylene polymers has increased over the period 1995 to 2019. On the other hand, the increased ethylene capacity of US refineries and their ability to export surplus petrochemical products has seen the US emerge as a major exporter of ethylene.

A central concern of Penrose's analysis of the captive market was the impact of these balances on the balance of payment of importing countries. Figure 6 shows ethylene polymer imports as a percentage of GDP. This shows that Nigeria, although benefiting from domestic oil reserves but lacking an advanced refining infrastructure and a state oil company, has seen an increase in its ethylene deficit as a percentage of GDP. In response, Nigeria has sought to expand their existing capacity to mitigate the effect of petrochemical deficits (Ogbuigwe 2018). China, which has the largest ethylene deficit in Figure 5, has sought to grow its capacity rapidly using a combination of NOCs and technology transfer (Tobin, 2019), but has seen its ethylene deficit increase. Turkey and Indonesia continue to run large deficits. Mexico has reduced the size of its deficit since 2014, while Brazil started to run a deficit after 2018. Both countries have used NOCs to develop their domestic oil reserves and refining infrastructures.

The data in Figures 5 and 6 illustrate the increasing import dependence and balance of payments pressures on developing economies. Low-cost ethane benefited countries with technological capabilities in complex refining such as the US but had had a negative impact on the petrochemical deficit countries south of its border. South American countries typically have surplus upstream production (Table 2), but low-cost ethane has locked in the region's dependence on imports from the US and other surplus countries. More generally the data point to a substantial growth in the global trade of emissions intensive petrochemical products.

5. The captive market at the firm level

The value of Penrose's approach is that it reminds us that the data in Figures 5 and 6 reflect endogenous firm-level responses to the institutional environment faced by the large oil firms. This section examines this in greater detail using two metrics: production capacity and the ratio of capital expenditure to retained earnings. This helps assess the validity of Penrose's contention regarding the production and investment strategies of the IOCs and the extent to which these trends are also present in independent refiners and the NOCs.

5.1. The international oil companies

Figure 7(a) provides data for ethylene capacity growth at four of the largest IOCs for which data on ethylene capacity is publicly available. This shows that the IOCs have been quick to ramp up ethylene capacity. Significantly, Figure 7(b) indicates that the ratio of capital expenditure to retained earnings has shown a tendency to decline. Much of the growth in capacity is centred on the IOCs US operations and is geographically clustered around the Texas area. In 2018, Exxon's Corporation Baytown Ethylene Plant (along with Formosa Plastics Corporation Point Comfort Plant) had the largest ethylene capacity in the US with a capacity of 2.3 mtpy (million tonnes per year) followed by Shell's Beaver County Ethylene Plant and Chevron Phillips Chemical's (CPChem) Baytown Ethylene Plant with capacities of 1.5 mtpy. Shell is building an ethylene cracker in Pennsylvania (US) that will process ethane from shale gas to produce 1.6 mtpy of polyethylene. The motivation for the plant is its proximity to the source of low-cost ethane and its customer base for plastics.[8] Other IOCs such as Exxon are taking advantage of the opportunities offered by the growing Asian market. In 2020 it announced the construction of a 1.6 mtpy wholly-owned ethylene facility in Huizhou, China[9].

The long lead times involved supports the view that these investments represent a deliberate and long-term strategic hedge against reduced demand for fuels, rather than resistance to climate action. Exxon Mobil's Baytown ethylene facility was first announced in 2012 and did not come into operation until 2018.[10] The investment was planned with full knowledge of its negative climate impact. Internal planning documents for the project showed that by 2025, the Baytown plant will emit 1.6 million metric tonnes CO_2 equivalent.[11] The same documents revealed that its Huizhou refinery in China is predicted to add some 3.7 million metric tonnes CO_2 equivalent by 2025.

5.2. The independent refiners

Although independent refineries control some of the largest ethylene refining facilities in regions such as North America and Europe, there is less publicly available granular data on their operations. Large chemical refiners such as Dow, Formosa and Nova Chemicals have also made large investments in expanding ethylene capacity in North America. Available data on the ratio of capital expenditure to retained earnings indicate that they also follow a conservative investment approach (Figure 8). Increased production of

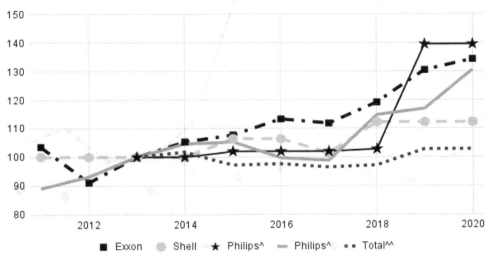

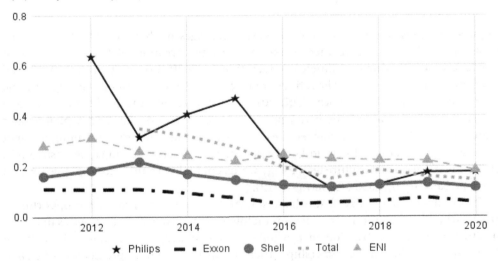

Figure 7. IOCs Ethylene Production Capacity and Capital Investment.
Notes: ^ Data for Philips 66 data based on ethylene capacity at CPChem in which it has a 50% equity share ^^ Total Energy capacity based on Olefins (Ethylene, Propylene and Butadiene) Source: Company Annual Reports and SEC Filings

intermediate chemicals allows the independents reduce their dependence on sourcing these in the market, creating a high value-added integration advantage.

As one of the world's largest producers of ethylene for the plastics industry, Dow provides a useful benchmark for how the independents have responded to the shale oil boom. Dow's announcement in 2015 of a major ethylene investment in its Freeport

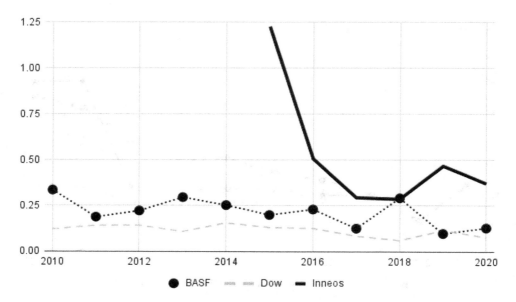

Figure 8. Ratio of CapEx/retained earnings selected independent refiners. Source: Annual Company Reports and SEC filings

refinery in Texas sought to exploit the cost advantages of shale oil. The facility came onstream in 2017 and a further investment saw the creation of the world's largest ethylene cracker, which commenced operation in 2020, bringing the facility's total ethylene capacity to 2 mtpy. The refinery reduced Dow's reliance on purchasing ethylene in the marketplace (Dow, Form 10K, 2015: 14). Illustrating the profitability of these investments, Dow claimed the investment delivered returns on invested capital greater than 15%.[12] In 2021 Dow announced the construction of an additional 1.8-million-ton of ethylene capacity at its refinery in Fort Saskatchewan, Alberta, due to come onstream in 2027. It will use carbon capture technology which could decarbonise 20% of Dow's global ethylene capacity by 2030 (see footnote 12).

Other independents like BASF have sought to exploit the productive opportunity arising from the relaxation of restrictions on full foreign ownership of refineries in China. In 2019 it began construction of a wholly owned refinery in Zhejiang.[13] Part of the justification for the plant's ownership structure was that it would protect what its chief executive described as its 'crown jewels', namely its intellectual property in high value-added chemical refining. There is also evidence of the emergence of new independent refineries in China. One of China's largest ethylene additions to come on stream in the next decade will be the Shandong Yulong Petrochemical Complex, which will have two 1.5 mtpy ethylene crackers.[14] The refinery has a mixed ownership structure involving private owners and a provincial government entity, with the ethylene technology supplied by the US firm Lummus, a global ethylene specialist.

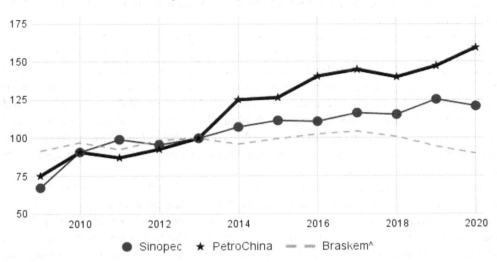

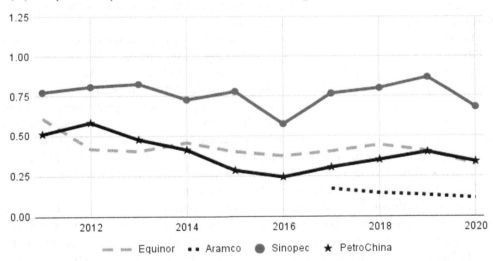

Figure 9. NOCs ethylene production capacity and capital investment.

5.3. *The national oil companies*

For the NOC's there is a clear geographical division between Chinese and Middle Eastern NOCs, who have grown their ethylene capacities, and their South American counterparts. China's NOC's have become significant contributors to the growth in global ethylene capacity (Figure 9). While these growth rates are impressive, they have not reversed China's import demand, suggesting that the IOCs and independents have exercised tight control their intellectual property through ownership of technology or joint ventures (Tobin, 2019).

Saudi Aramco's refining subsidiary SAIBC has significantly expanded its capacity from 12.5 mtpy of basic chemicals including ethylene in 2000 to 35.7 mtpy in 2021 (SABIC, 2000; 2021). This reflects Aramco's strategy of using joint ventures with other NOCs and IOCs to secure a market for its low-cost heavy crude oil. In 2020 it announced a joint venture with Petronas, the Malaysian NOC (SABIC Annual Report, 2020: 63), and in 2021 SABIC announced the commissioning of the world's second largest ethane cracker in Texas as part of a joint venture with Exxon Mobil.[15] These investments appear to be part of a deliberate strategy to position Aramco close to the cost advantages of US ethane and the Asian growth market.

What is remarkable about the investment position of the NOCs is the extent to which it mirrors the that of the IOCs. Only Sinopec, China's largest state-owned refiner runs a ratio of capital expenditure to retained earnings that is noticeably higher than the IOCs. Data from the IEA (2014, 55) for 2002–2012 show that the NOCs financed close to 80% of their investments from retained earnings (IEA 2014, 55). Petrobras, the Brazilian NOC provides a notable exception to this relying on debt financing to fund capital spending in the development of the Lula oilfield (IEA 2014). The use of debt finance represents a big departure from the past where the infusion of social capital was substantial and included tax receipts, the reinvestment of dividends and the favourable pricing of the outputs of Petrobras's refining output (Penrose, 1968, 241).

The data in Figure 9(a) also show that it is difficult to generalise the NOCs. This point is illustrated in the case of Braskem. It has the largest polyethylene refining capacity in Latin America but has struggled to grow capacity Figure 9(a). South American NOCs were severely impacted by the decline in oil prices in the 2010s, with many divesting their downstream refining assets, preferring instead to import cheaper petrochemicals from the US, Middle East and Asia.[16] To diversify its supply of feedstock and take advantage of cheaper US ethane, Braskem has invested in a refining facility in Northern Brazil that will refine ethylene from ethane supplied from the US (Braskem, 2017, Form 20-F: 28). These investments ultimately serve to lock Latin American deficit countries into a captive market, increasing their dependence on cheap US ethane.

Braskem also shows the challenges for NOCs transitioning away from fossil fuel-based refining, even where there are natural resource advantages. Brazil's ample sugarcane supply provides it with a resource advantage in plant-based feedstocks. About 50% of the world's bio-ethylene capacity is in Brazil (IEA 2018, 44). In 2020, Braskem announced a project to expand production capacity for green ethylene, a feedstock made from sugarcane ethanol, which would add 60,000 tonnes/annum capacity by 2022 (Braskem, 2020 20-F: 50). Braskem has a target of increasing its production of green polyethylene to 1 million tonnes/annum by 2030.[17] However, like fossil fuel-based refining, this requires operational integration and scalable technologies. Braskem is dependent on technology provided by US firm Lummus.

Table 3. Forecast refinery expansion by regions (unit: thousand barrels/day).

	2020	2021	2022	2023	2024	2025	2026	Total
OECD Americas	−338	−203	50	250	340			99
OECD Asia Oceania		−466	−120	−109				−694
Europe	−278	−242	−120	0	0	0	0	−640
China	204	266	190	500		400		1,560
Other Asia	14	225	−60	446	100	630	290	1,644
Latin America			33	15			−36	12
Middle East	520	230	610	340	140	−20	60	1,880
Africa		10	650	30	150		100	940
Former Soviet Union		50	30		30			110
Total	121	−129	1,263	1,472	7,60	1,010	414	4,911

Source: Adapted from IEA (2021) Oil 2021 Analysis and forecast to 2026 Table 4. World refinery capacity additions.

6. Policy implications: captive markets, technology and climate

Petrochemical refining represents a growing part of the fossil infrastructure that locks in society to carbon intensive technologies. Each additional unit of refining capacity adds to the demand for fossil fuel inputs. While the analysis here only covers a sample of leading IOCs, NOCs, and independent refiners, its findings are consistent with other research that shows an acceleration of downstream projects, especially in ethylene-based plastics (IEA 2020, Bauer and Fontenit 2021). Forecasts indicate a continued growth in refining capacity, much of which will be in developing economies (Table 3). This section considers the impacts of this for developing economies, climate policy and theory. Its central argument is that reducing the emissions from downstream refining will require recognition of one of Penrose's (1968, 264) key conclusions namely that while 'the administrative controls of international firms are supranational', their strategies impact on individual nations differently, creating a serious distortion of the benefits and costs of their international investments.

Nowhere is this point more apparent than in the relationship between the investment strategies of the large petroleum refiners and their impacts on developing economies. Many developing economies are increasingly dependent on petrochemical imports and the investments of the large firms. In addition, much of new refining capacity to come on stream will come from non-OECD Asia, China and Africa (Table 3). The analysis in this paper indicates that the benefits and costs of this expansion are distorted by the role of the large petroleum firms. The economic benefits of this expansion will largely accrue to a small number of large refining and independent chemical companies, who have the integration advantages and proprietary technology.

While Penrose focused on the balance of payment costs of such investments, climate change has drawn increased attention to their environmental costs. The pollution costs of plastics have been well documented (Altman 2022), but the emissions implications are less well understood. There is a large degree of uncertainty regarding future CO_2 emissions from heavy emitters due to differences in the drivers of their growth and technological progress (IPCC 2018). One study put the carbon impact of refining at 13.9–62.1 kg of CO_2-equivalent per barrel (Jing et al. 2020). The variation in estimates have their origins in Penrose's (1968) point on way technical progress determines the product mix of a barrel of crude. Ethylene units contribute about 258 million tons of CO2 emissions per year globally or 1.08 million tonnes per ethylene cracking unit (IPCC

2018, 81). The EIA (2021) estimates that between 2013 and 2020, the US increased it ethylene capacity from 27 million mtpa to 40 million mtpa. By hedging against a reduction in fuel consumption and focusing on plastics, US refineries have added approximately 14.0 million tonnes of CO2 equivalent.

How do we interpret Penrose's work today and does it help with the policy dilemmas outlined above? One of the implications of Penrose's work is that in the absence of coordinated regulation, the oil companies cannot be depended upon to undertake socially useful investments in green technologies. At the same time, the retreat of states from efforts to shape oil markets, let alone the market for petrochemicals, has allowed the IOCs significant space to shape these markets in their own interests (Hughes 2014). Climate agreements such as the Paris Nationally Determined Contributions and the proposed European Green Deal retain national level flexibility in how targets are met. Klenert et al (2020) argue that in terms of levels of national cooperation, many developed countries have become stage three actors, committing to meet ambitious nationally determined targets, but falling short of meeting what they see as stage four cooperation, which would involve full international cooperation backed by financial resources for lower and middle-income countries.

One of the less explored, but potentially fruitful implications of Penrose's work going forward concerns the regulatory aspects of state-MNE relationships and antitrust policy (e.g. Pitelis, 2009). It is likely that Penrose would have favoured the Harvard approach to antitrust regulation over its Chicago counterpart (Thomson and Wright, 2005). There is empirical evidence to support the positive role for more stringent regulation in the oil industry (Green et al, 2021). Other research has highlighted the dangers and potential contests inherent in an uneven adoption of climate targets and its impacts on large firms holding different forms of climate forcing assets that accelerate damage to the climate such as oil fields and refineries (e.g. Colgan, Green, and Hale 2021). It is increasingly recognised that to be effective, technical solutions such as carbon capture, which tend not to capture all emissions from refineries, will still require a shift towards non-fossil fuel inputs and a regulatory framework that is favourable to a net zero transition (Sunny et al, 2022). Penrose (1968) recognised the tension between firms' supranational coordination and national level policies required coordinated state response that had sufficient power to break the captive market.

7. Conclusion

In drawing attention to question of motive, flexibility and the investments of the large firm, Penrose's (1959, 1968) work highlights the importance of understanding the endogenous and institutional-level incentives underpinning current patterns of accumulation. It cautions against market-based interpretations of the large firm. As supranational administrative units of control, large firms internalise risk and therefore, the relationship between the oil price and investment is distorted by the large firm. Her approach suggests that we need to look closer at the inner workings of oil firms and their external environments to understand why the large oil and chemical firms continue to invest in downstream capacity that adds to the demand for fossil fuels.

The analysis in this paper indicates that the broad institutional environment facing the large oil firm still favours fossil fuel investment. The captive market has enabled the oil firms to hedge against action on climate change by increasing capacity in high value-added chemicals such as ethylene. This adds to global emissions and represents a clear obstacle to a green transition. There is little evidence of decarbonising or a departure from historical trends in accumulation. Instead, the paper shows that the conservative patterns of investment and the tendency to resist government requests for socially useful investments that Penrose identified in her analysis more than fifty years ago still characterise the sector today. These are consistent with the risks that both Schumpeter (1942) and Penrose (1956) associated with a trustified form of capitalism, where monopoly conditions are viewed necessary for continued innovation and progress Penrose (1956, 233–234) was clear that in some cases this condition was plainly not true. In short, the oil firms do not invest or take risks at the scale required for the corporate economy to make a sufficient positive contribution to a green transition. The role of the captive market in slowing a green transition, the potential for global regulatory coordination and business state relations are areas of Penrose's work that deserve further research in this regard.

The international nature of the captive market implies that petrochemical deficit low- and middle-income economies in South America, Asia and Africa continue to face the policy dilemma between becoming locked-in to imports or accepting technological dependence. Climate change adds an additional dimension to this. This highlights a more general point that regardless of whether we talk about alternative or petroleum derived ethylene or the potential of carbon capture technologies, the barrier for many developing economies remains one of access to technology. In this regard further research is needed on the mechanisms that can facilitate faster rates of technical diffusion. In short, addressing the impacts of climate change calls for a better authority as an arbiter of the public interest (Penrose, 1968, 22).

Notes

1. UN Secretary-General's video message to the Sixth Austrian World Summit 14th June, 2022
2. The IEA (2018) predicted oil demand growth of 9.6mb/day from 2017–2030 with petrochemicals accounting for 3.2mb/day.
3. Penrose (2009: 26–27) was clear that in making this assumption 'there is no need to deny that other objectives are often important – power, prestige, public approval, or the mere love of the game – it need only be recognised that the attainment if these ends more often than not is associated directly with the ability to make profits'
4. These include Aramco, BP, Chevron, CNPC, Eni, Equinor, ExxonMobil, Occidental, Petrobras, Repsol, Shell and TotalEnergies. See ocgi.com.
5. In 2021 Eni announced the closure of its Porto Maghera refinery. See 'Italy's petrochems units face uncertain future as Porto Marghera set to close' https://www.icis.com/explore/resources/news/2021/03/24/10621155/italy-s-petchems-units-face-uncertain-future-as-porto-marghera-set-to-close
6. U.S. Energy Information Administration, Short-Term Energy Outlook February 2018.
7. In 2021 Saudi Aramco claimed that 43% of its oil production was consumer by its downstream activities (Annual Report, 2021: 61).
8. See https://www.shell.com/about-us/major-projects/pennsylvania-petrochemicals-complex.html
9. 'Exxon Mobil starts building $10 billion China petrochemical complex: Xinhua' Reuters, 22nd April 2020. https://www.reuters.com/article/us-exxonmobil-china-petrochemical-idUSKCN2241DJ

10. 'ExxonMobil Baytown Cracker Ready to Start' 8th January 2018 https://www.chemanager-online.com/en/news/exxonmobil-baytown-cracker-ready-start
11. 'Exxon knows its carbon future and keeps the data from view', Bloomberg, 23rd December 2020
12. https://investors.dow.com/en/news/news-details/2021/Dow-announces-plan-to-build-worlds-first-net-zero-carbon-emissions-ethylene-and-derivatives-complex/default.aspx
13. BASF breaks ground on $10bn China chemical complex Financial Times 24th November 2019
14. Shandong Yulong lets contract for proposed integrated refining megacomplex Oil and Gas Journal, 8th February, 2022.
15. https://www.chemanalyst.com/NewsAndDeals/NewsDetails/usa-to-have-a-new-ethylene-plant-under-sabic-and-exxonmobil-joint-venture-project-7755
16. Latin America grapples with lack of petrochemical investment, S&P Global Platts Insight 29th June 2016
17. Lummus technology Braskem join forces to accelerate growth green ethylene production. Sustainable Plastics 29th April 2022 https://www.sustainableplastics.com/news/lummus-technology-braskem-join-forces-accelerate-growth-green-ethylene-production

Acknowledgments

The author would like to acknowledge the valuable comments and suggestions of the referees and editor of this journal.

Disclosure statement

No potential conflict of interest was reported by the author.

References

Altman, R. 2022. "How Bad are Plastics for the Environment, Really?" *The Atlantic*,February 1, 2022. https://www.theatlantic.com/science/archive/2022/01/plastic-history-climate-change/621033/

Bauer, F., and G. Fontenit. 2021. "Plastic Dinosaurs – Digging Deep into the Accelerating Carbon Lock-In of Plastics." *Energy Policy* 156:112418. https://doi.org/10.1016/j.enpol.2021.112418.

Berle, A. A., and G. C. Means. 1932. *The Modern Corporation and Private Property*. New York: MacMillan.

Bernanke, B. S. 1983. "Irreversibility, Uncertainty, and Cyclical Investment." *The Quarterly Journal of Economics* 98 (1): 85–106. https://doi.org/10.2307/1885568.

Blondeel, M., and M. Bradshaw. 2022. "International Oil Companies, Decarbonisation and Transition Risks." In *Handbook of International Oil Relations*, edited by R. Danreuther and W. Ostrowski, 372–392. Cheltenham, UK: Edward Elgar.

Bonneuil, C., P.-L. Choquet, and B. Franta. 2021. "Early Warnings and Emerging Accountability: Total's Responses to Global Warming, 1971–2021." *Global Environmental Change* 71:102386. https://doi.org/10.1016/j.gloenvcha.2021.102386.

BP. 2020. *Statistical Review of World Energy*. London: British Petroleum.

Busch, T., R. Bauer, and M. Orlitzky. 2016. "Sustainable Development and Financial Markets – Old Paths and New Avenues." *Business & Society* 55 (3): 303–329. https://doi.org/10.1177/0007650315570701.

Chandler, A. D. 2002. *The Visible Hand: The Managerial Revolution in American Business*. Cambridge, Massachusetts: Harvard University Press.

Christophers, B. 2021. "Fossilised Capital: Price and Profit in the Energy Transition." *New Political Economy* 27 (1): 146–159. https://doi.org/10.1080/13563467.2021.1926957.

Colgan, J. D., J. F. Green, and T. N. Hale. 2021. "Asset Revaluation and the Existential Politics of Climate Change." *International Organization* 75 (2): 586–610. https://doi.org/10.1017/S0020818320000296.

Diwan, R. 2007. "The Current Implications of the World Energy Situation for United States Energy Supplies." Presentation at Federal Trade Commission Conference, Energy Markets in the 21st Century: Competition Policy in Perspective, Washington DC, April 2007.

ENI. 2015. *Fact Book*. Rome: EN S.p.A.

ENI. 2020. *World Oil Review*. Vol. 1. Rome: ENI S.p.A.

Fattouh, B. 2021. Saudi Oil Policy: Continuity and Change in the Era of the Energy Transition. Oxford Institute of Energy Studies. OIES Paper: WPM 81.

Filippi, E., and G. Zanetti. 1971. "Exogenous and Endogenous Factors in the Growth of Firms." In *The Corporate Economy*, 144–171. Palgrave Macmillan UK. https://doi.org/10.1007/978-1-349-01110-0_6.

Fisch-Romito, V., C. Guivarch, F. Creutzig, J. Minx, and M. Callaghan. 2021. "Systematic Map of the Literature on Carbon Lock-In Induced by Long-Lived Capital." *Environmental Research Letters* 16 (5): 053004. https://doi.org/10.1088/1748-9326/aba660.

Freeman, C., A. Young, and J. Fuller. 1963. "The Plastics Industry: A Comparative Study of Research and Innovation." *National Institute Economic Review* 26 (26): 22–62. https://doi.org/10.1177/002795016302600103.

Green, J., J. Hadden, T. Hale, and P. Mahdavi. 2021. "Transition, Hedge, or Resist? Understanding Political and Economic Behavior Toward Decarbonization in the Oil and Gas Industry." *Review of International Political Economy*. https://doi.org/10.2139/ssrn.3694447.

Hartshorn, J. E. 1962. *Oil Companies and Governments: An Account of the International Oil Industry in Its Political Environment*. London: Faber and Faber.

Heede, Richard, 2014. Carbon Majors: Accounting for Carbon and Methane Emissions 1854-2010 Methods & Results Report, Commissioned by Climate Justice Programme & Greenpeace International, Climate Mitigation Services, Snowmass, CO.

Henriques, I., and P. Sadorsky. 2011. "The Effect of Oil Price Volatility on Strategic Investment." *Energy Economics* 33 (1): 79–87. https://doi.org/10.1016/j.eneco.2010.09.001.

Hertog, S. 2008. "Petromin: The Slow Death of Statist Oil Development in Saudi Arabia." *Business History* 50 (5): 645–667. https://doi.org/10.1080/00076790802246087.

Hufbauer, G. C. 1965. *Synthetic Materials and the Theory of International Trade*. London: Gerald Duckworth.

Hughes, L. 2014. *Globalizing Oil: Firms and Oil Market Governance in France, Japan, and the United States*. Cambridge UK: Cambridge University Press.

IEA 2014. World Energy Investment Report. IEA Publications: Paris

IEA. 2018. *The Future of Petrochemicals: Towards More Sustainable Plastics and Fertilisers*. Paris: IEA Publications.

IEA. 2020. *World Energy Outlook*. Paris: IEA Publications.

IPCC. (2018). Special Report on Carbon Dioxide Capture and Storage. https://www.ipcc.ch/site/assets/uploads/2018/03/srccs_wholereport-1.pdf.

Jacobsson, R., and S. Jacobsson. 2012. "The Emerging Funding Gap for the European Energy Sector—Will the Financial Sector Deliver?" *Environmental Innovation and Societal Transitions* 5:49–59. https://doi.org/10.1016/j.eist.2012.10.002.

Jing, L., H. M. El-Houjeiri, J. C. Monfort, A. R. Brandt, M. S. Masnadi, D. Gordon, and J. A. Bergerson. 2020. "Carbon Intensity of Global Crude Oil Refining and Mitigation Potential." *Nature Climate Change* 10 (6): 526–532. (2020). https://doi.org/10.1038/s41558-020-0775-3.

Kaldor, N. 1957. "A Model of Economic Growth." *The Economic Journal* 67 (268, 1): 591–624. https://doi.org/10.2307/2227704.

Kemfert, C., F. Präger, I. Braunger, Hoffart, F. M., and Brauers, H. 2022. "The Expansion of Natural Gas Infrastructure Puts Energy Transitions at Risk." *Nature Energy* 7 (7): 582–587. https://doi.org/10.1038/s41560-022-01060-3.

Kim, I. 2020. "Swinging Shale: Shale Oil, the Global Oil Market, and the Geopolitics of Oil." *International Studies Quarterly* 64 (3): 544–557. https://doi.org/10.1093/isq/sqaa042.

Klenert, D., Funke, F., Mattauch, L., and O'Callaghan, B. 2020. "Five Lessons from COVID☐19 for Advancing Climate Change Mitigation." *Environmental and Resource Economics* 76: 751–778. https://doi.org/10.1007/s10640-020-00453-w.

Knight, F. H. 1921. *Risk, Uncertainty and Profit*. Boston and New York, US: Houghton Mifflin Company.

Lazonick, W. 2015. *Stock Buybacks: From Retain-And-Reinvest to Downsize-And- Distribute*. Washington D.C: Center for Effective Public Management, Brookings Institution.

Le Billon, P., and Kristofferson, B. 2020. "Just cuts for fossil fuels? Supply-side carbon constraints and energy transition." *Environment and Planning A: Economy and Space* 52 (6): 1072–1092.

Machlup, F., and Penrose, E. 1950. "The Patent Controversy in the Nineteenth Century." *The Journal of Economic History* 10 (1): 1–29.

Malm, A. 2016. *Fossil Capital*: The Rise of Steam Power and the Roots of Global Warming. London: Verso Books.

Mandel, E. 1968. *Marxist Economic Theory*. London: Merlin Press.

Marcel, V. 2006. *Oil Titans: National Oil Companies in the Middle East*. Washington: Brookings Institution Press.

Marris, R., and A. Wood. 1971. *The Corporate Economy: Growth, Competition and Innovative Potential*. Cambridge, Mass: Harvard University Press.

Nelson, R. R., and S. G. Winter. 1982. "The Schumpeterian Tradeoff Revisited." *The American Economic Review* 72 (1): 114–132.

Ogbuigwe, A. 2018. "Refining in Nigeria: History, Challenges and Prospects." *Applied Petrochemical Research* 8 (4): 181–192. https://doi.org/10.1007/s13203-018-0211-z.

Palladino, L., and W. Lazonick. 2022. "Regulating Stock Buybacks: The $6.3 Trillion Question." *International Review of Applied Economics* 1–25. https://doi.org/10.1080/02692171.2022. 2123459.

Penrose, E. T. 1956. "Foreign Investment and the Growth of the Firm." *The Economic Journal* 66 (262): 220–235. https://doi.org/10.2307/2227966.

Penrose, E. T. 1959. *The Theory of the Growth of the Firm*. Oxford: Oxford University Press.

Penrose, E. T. 1968. *The Large International Firm in Developing Countries*. Westport, Connecticut: Greenwood Press.

Pitelis, C. N. 2009. *Introduction to* The Theory of the Growth of the Firm. Oxford: Oxford University.

Pitelis, C. N., and M. W. Wahl. 1998. "Edith Penrose: Pioneer of Stakeholder Theory." *Long Range Planning* 31 (2): 252–261. https://doi.org/10.1016/S0024-6301(98)00009-0.

Priest, T. 2016. "Petrobras in the History of Offshore Oil." In *New Order and Progress: Development and Democracy in Brazil*, edited by Schneider B. R. 53–77, New York: Oxford Academic.

Robinson, J. 1962. *Economic Philosophy*. Harmondsworth, Middlesex (UK): Penguin Books.

Schumpeter, J. 1928. "The Instability of Capitalism." *The Economic Journal* 38 (151): 361–386. https://doi.org/10.2307/2224315.

Schumpeter, J. 1942. *Capitalism, Socialism, and Democracy*. New York: Harper.

Semieniuk, G., P. B. Holden, J. F. Mercure, P. Salas, H. Pollitt, K. Jobson, P. Vercoulen, U. Chewpreecha, N. R. Edwards, and J. E. Viñuales. 2022. "Stranded Fossil-Fuel Assets Translate to Major Losses for Investors in Advanced Economies." *Nature Climate Change* 12 (6): 532–538. (2022). https://doi.org/10.1038/s41558-022-01356-y.

Smith, C. J., P. M. Forster, M. Allen, J. Fuglestvedt, R. J. Millar, J. Rogelj, and K. Zickfeld. 2019. "Current Fossil Fuel Infrastructure Does Not Yet Commit Us to 1.5 °C Warming." *Nature Communications* 10 (1): 101. (2019). https://doi.org/10.1038/s41467-018-07999-w.

Stevens, P. 2005. "Oil Markets." *Oxford Review of Economic Policy* 21 (1): 19–42. https://doi.org/10.1093/oxrep/gri002.

Sunny, N., A. Bernardi, D. Danaci, M. Bui, A. Gonzalez-Garay, and B. Chachuat. 2022. "A Pathway Towards Net-Zero Emissions in Oil Refineries." *Froniers in Chemical Engineering* 4:804163. https://doi.org/10.3389/fceng.2022.804163.

Thompson, S., and Wright, M. 2005. "Edith Penrose's contribution to economics and strategy: an overview." *Managerial and Decision Economics* 26 (2): 57–66. https://doi.org/10.1002/mde.1216.

Tobin, D. 2019. "Technical Self-Sufficiency, Pricing Independence: A Penrosean Perspective on China's Emergence as a Major Oil Refiner Since the 1960s." *Business History* 61 (4): 681–702. https://doi.org/10.1080/00076791.2017.1413095.

Tordo, S. 2011 National Oil Companies and Value Creation, Volume I by Silvana Tordo with Brandon Tracy and Noora Arfaa. World Bank Working Paper Series 218, Washington.

US (Energy Information Agency). (2021). U.S. Ethane Production to Grow, Along with Expanding Domestic Consumption and Exports 21st May 2021. www.eia.org.

Van Eyden, R., M. Difeto, R. Gupta, and M. Wohar. 2019. "Oil Price Volatility and Economic Growth: Evidence from Advanced Economies Using More Than a Century's Data." *Applied Energy* 233–234:612–621. https://doi.org/10.1016/j.apenergy.2018.10.049.

Verbeek, T., and A. Mah. 2020. "Integration and Isolation in the Global Petrochemical Industry: A Multiscalar Corporate Network Analysis." *Economic Geography* 96 (4): 363–387. https://doi.org/10.1080/00130095.2020.1794809.

Vernon, R. 1966. "International Investment and International Trade in the Product Cycle." *The Quarterly Journal of Economics* 80 (2): 190–207. https://doi.org/10.2307/1880689.

Wright, C., and Nyberg, D. 2015. *Climate Change, Capitalism, and Corporations: Processes of Creative Self-Destruction.* Cambridge: Cambridge University Press. https://doi.org/10.1017/CBO9781139939676

🔓 OPEN ACCESS

Complementarities between product and process innovation and their effects on employment: A firm-level analysis of manufacturing firms in Colombia

Juana Paola Bustamante Izquierdo 🆔

ABSTRACT

The introduction or adoption of innovations at the firm level has consequences for job creation that may differ across low-middle and high-income countries. Also, the type of innovation that firms introduce, such as process or product innovations, can affect employment through different channels. This paper aims to study the effects of innovation on employment growth at the firm level using a framework that considers the nature of innovation and the relative efficiency of the firms. The study uses a rich panel dataset that combines information from two different surveys in Colombia: the Annual Manufacturing Survey and the Survey on Development and Technological Innovation in the Manufacturing Sector. The article provides empirical evidence supporting the idea that the nature of innovation in the country involves complementarities between process and product innovations. The paper discusses how this result is related to the patterns of innovation in middle income countries, which need not only new technologies but also imitation of processes and products. Another novelty of this analysis is the study of displacement effects of process innovation through improvements in the relative efficiency of the firms. Findings show that some firms reduce employment from process innovations, reflecting high heterogeneity in efficiency among firms.

1. Introduction

Innovation often leads to economic growth, which in turn boosts employment levels in a country. However, it may take time to fully reap the benefits of innovation. In the meantime, the introduction of new products and technologies in firms can impact and modify production systems, which can affect future job creation.

Potential effects of innovation on firm-level employment depend on the nature of the innovation introduced that is 'product innovation' and 'process innovation'. Furthermore, how firms introduce and adopt innovations in low- and middle-income countries may differ from those in high income countries. In low- and middle-income

---

This is an Open Access article distributed under the terms of the Creative Commons Attribution License (http://creativecommons.org/licenses/by/4.0/), which permits unrestricted use, distribution, and reproduction in any medium, provided the original work is properly cited. The terms on which this article has been published allow the posting of the Accepted Manuscript in a repository by the author(s) or with their consent.

countries, firms may passively adopt foreign technologies, but to catch up technologically, they need specific production capabilities that may not currently exist in the country or the firm. These capabilities may include education and business infrastructure. To efficiently utilise the new technology, the firm may need to adapt it to different inputs and take into consideration country-specific tastes, customs, and cultures (Fagerberg, Srholec, and Verspagen 2010).

As a result, in the process of adopting a technology to introduce a new or significantly improved good or service in the country or region, the firm may have to create production capabilities, and in the process of doing so, further innovation may also occur. Moreover, firms in low-middle income countries often improve imported technology which requires a complementary process and product innovation. This pattern is more prevalent in low-middle income countries, while high income economies concentrate more on product innovation. Both ways of developing innovations and introducing them into firms may lead to growth in the economy, yet the effect of innovation on employment in low-middle income countries will have different channels and characteristics. By comprehending these transmission effects, one can design more effective industrial policies.

This article focuses on assessing the effect of innovation on jobs at the firm level. It offers an integrated explanation and detailed empirical analysis of how innovation drives employment creation in Colombia, with a focus on the manufacturing sector. The main novelty is that the analysis can account for both the nature of innovations and the relative efficiency of the firms. The paper provides empirical evidence at the firm level on the role of complementary process and product innovation on job creation in Colombia. Additionally, I introduce an extended empirical framework that allows for differences in relative efficiency among firms.

A shortcoming in previous studies is that panel data on innovation is not often available for low-middle income countries. To address this issue, I have created a unique panel database that covers the years 2008 to 2016 (only even years). This database combines data from two surveys conducted in Colombia: the Annual Manufacturing Survey and the Survey on Development and Technological Innovation in the Manufacturing Sector. Panel data allows for consideration of heterogeneity that cannot be controlled for with cross-sectional data.

The paper obtains empirical evidence on the separate role of process and product innovation after allowing for the potential endogeneity of the innovation decision. To account for endogeneity issues the paper makes use of instrumental variables, particularly, it introduces the role of institutional variables on employment creation through an instrumental variable of a firm's cooperative agreements on innovation. Also, the empirical investigation accounts for the relative efficiency of firms by introducing an estimated variable using stochastic frontier analysis for panel data.

The results show that product innovation increases employment growth. Complementary process and product innovation also have a significant impact on employment growth. Process innovation alone does not have a direct displacement effect. However, more efficient firms compared to less efficient ones are correlated with less new employment at a firm level.

The discussion in this paper is organised as follows. Section 1 presents a literature review of the effects of innovation on employment at the firm level and the hypothesis development. Section 2 explains the panel dataset that was built based on two surveys of manufacturing firms in Colombia. It also presents descriptive statistics on employment and innovation in the country. Section.1 discusses the empirical strategy. Section 1.4.1 presents the econometric estimates and discusses the results. The last section provides concluding remarks and sets out future areas of research.

The supplementary material presents the theoretical model and the stochastic frontier analysis used to estimate the efficiency variable included in the econometric model.

1.1. Literature review and hypothesis development

Penrose's (1959:100) seminal work, The Theory of the Growth of the Firm encapsulated the idea that the survival and growth of firms depend in large part on their ability, 'to anticipate, or at least to match threatening innovations in products, processes and marketing techniques'. Firm growth depends on external and internal causes. Penrose gave particular importance to resources within the firm (internal causes), mainly, managerial resources. The firm's available productive resources need internal coordination and direction to produce goods and services. Firm expansion requires managerial resources (which are not found in the market) to plan, coordinate and make effective use of resources and innovation (Penrose 2009).

Neoclassical analysis is concerned with examining the equilibrium of industries through market-based analysis. It considers the supply and demand functions and factors in the theory of price and output to determine a firm's equilibrium. However, Penrose's ideas are not easily assimilated in neoclassical thinking as they do not assume optimising agents and static equilibria. In this paper, the integration of a Penrosian analysis in a conventional neoclassical analysis can help understand innovation within a firm's growth process (analysing the production function). This way, one can combine the neoclassical perspective of efficient allocation of resources with the Penrosian knowledge creation process in a firm. Instead of assuming that a firm already possesses the required know-how, internally generated knowledge can be utilised to coordinate resource allocation and innovation growth. Here, the internally generated knowledge is useful to coordinate the allocation of resources inside a firm and innovation growth (Pitelis 2009). Furthermore, employment relations in a firm can be explained through productivity gains generated by knowledge growth.

Innovation can create new jobs or displace employment depending on the existing production technology and the type of innovation. Innovation includes both process or product innovations, which can be labour/capital saving, skill-biased, etc (see for instance Acemoglu and Autor (2011) for a study on skill-biased and technical change). Therefore, the overall effect depends on different variables and may differ in the short and long run. Moreover, the link between innovation and employment can be analysed at the firm, sector, or aggregate level.

The effects of innovation on employment at the firm level can be studied through different channels, depending on the type of innovation (product and process innovation). Table 1summarises displacement and compensation effects on employment by type of innovation. The introduction of new or improved goods and services (product innovation) is widely viewed to have a positive effect on employment growth at the firm level due to increased demand (compensation effect) and therefore in

COMPLEMENTARITIES BETWEEN PRODUCT AND PROCESS INNOVATION 131

Table 1. Effects of innovation and efficiency on firm-level employment.

Innovation	Displacement of workers	Compensation effect
Product Innovation	Productivity differences of the new product (- or +). Theory gives no general indication of this.	Demand enlargement (+): The development of new or significantly improved goods has a positive impact on employment. Managerial ability to identify and develop products and organize production activity. Better use of resources can increase a firm's growth (+).
Process Innovations	Productivity effect (-): Productivity increases imply a reduction in unit cost. less labour for a given output However, firms that can survive with low levels of productivity growth may not affect employment[c]	Price effect (+): cost reduction passed on to price (in a competitive market). Lower prices increase demand and therefore output and employment. The extent of the effect will depend on the competitive conditions the firms face.
Complementarity of Product and process innovation		New products increase employment (+)
Production efficiencies	Firms operating beneath the production frontier may increase their output without requiring more input or producing the same level of output using less input (+ neutral or -)	past improvements in efficiency may have a positive effect on future[a] employment[b]
Trend[a]	Productivity effect (-)	

[a]Productivity improvement in the production of existing products due to diffusion of past industry innovations, and learning.
[b]Refers to simultaneous process and product innovation.
[c]Firms that introduce only process innovations may decrease costs for old products or comply with regulations.

output growth. Product innovations can be new to the world, incremental improvements on previous innovations or imitations of goods and services produced in other firms or regions. Usually, new or improved products or services open new markets leading to an increase in production and employment (Pianta 2003). However, there might be productivity differences in the production of new compared to old products since new products that generate new employment may nevertheless come with lower demand for employment (if they are labour-saving innovations) compared to the production of old products. Moreover, it could also be the case of new products replacing old ones.

Concerning process innovation, improvements in the production process affect productivity and unit costs which have a negative and positive effect on employment respectively (see Katsoulacos (1984), Pianta (2003), Vivarelli (2014) and Calvino and Virgillito(2018)) for a discussion on displacement and compensation effects). Process innovation that enhances productivity allows the firm to reduce costs and lower prices. Depending on the elasticity of demand for the good or service, a lower price may increase demand (if demand is sufficiently price responsive) and market share. An increase in demand, if the elasticity is high, will have a positive effect on employment. Similarly, process innovations that increase quality may increase jobs when the demand for the good or service increases (when the elasticity is high).

Alternatively, process innovation may also affect employment through firm efficiency. Specifically, firms that operate beneath the production frontier may move towards the technological frontier by exploiting available knowledge in the innovation process or improvements in organisational methods. To do so, they may increase their output without requiring more inputs or produce the same level of output using fewer inputs

(Coelli et al. 2005, ch 1). Therefore, the overall effect of innovation on the demand for labour depends on the complex balance between labour-creating and saving effects.

Empirically, it is difficult to identify the displacement and compensation effects due to data availability and because firms are often involved in product and process innovation simultaneously (Hall, Lotti, and Mairesse 2008). Measuring the effect of innovation on employment poses the following challenges, including: i) the difficulty of measuring innovation, in particular, investment in innovation and product and process innovation, ii) the identification and measurement of institutional mechanisms such as enforcement of intellectual property rights, and iii) disentangling the final effect of innovation on employment due to other factors such as labour dynamics and macroeconomic cycles (Vivarelli 2014).

Yet, micro econometric studies can look at firm-level variables on product and process innovation and employment growth (Vivarelli 2014). Evidence on the relationship between employment and innovation at the firm level generally indicates that innovation tends to be positively related to employment (Blanchower and Burgess 1998; Pianta 2003; Van Reenen 1997; Vivarelli 2014). However, Greenan and Guellec (2000) using a panel of French manufacturing firms find that innovative firms create more jobs than non-innovative ones but the reverse is true at the sectoral level so the overall effect is negative and only product innovation is job-creating.

Few studies highlight the difference between low-middle income and high income countries, for instance, Raffo et al. (2008) study the relationships between innovation inputs (usually R&D), output (for instance, product innovation), and economic performance (expressed by labour productivity) for three European countries (France, Spain and Switzerland) and three Latin American countries (Argentina, Brazil and Mexico) using firm-level data and the CIS survey and Latin American innovation surveys. The study presents empirical evidence using the Crepon, Duguet and Mairesse's (1998) structural model (CDM model[1]) where R&D intensity affects product innovation. Results indicate innovation has a positive effect on labour productivity in countries studied for Latin America (Brazil and Mexico) except Argentina (however, the result is not robust). The difference in results might reflect the heterogeneity of the countries, for instance, the authors found that in Latin American countries there is a lack of cooperative agreements with Universities and other interactions between academic research and industry.

Empirical literature at the firm level that focuses on the distinction between the effect of process and product innovation on employment presents evidence of the positive impact of product innovation on employment. However, results regarding process innovation are not conclusive since some authors find a negative and significant relation and others find no significant link between process innovation and employment. Hall et al. (2008), Peters (2004) and Harrison et al (2005, 2014), derive an employment growth equation, using the labour demand equations in (4) and a logarithm rate of growth of the old product to derive a linear equation. The equation is derived from an identical separable production function with different Hicks-neutral technological productivity indexed by θ (see Annex 1). In Harrison et al. (2014) the model assumes that the productivity index θ represents the efficiency of the investments in R&D in generating process and product innovation. Hall, Lotti, and Mairesse (2008) interpret productivity as labour productivity rather than total factor productivity in the estimation of the model; since this study did not have data on capital and other materials. Garcia et al., (2004) argue that the productivity index θ, used by Harrison et al. (2005), also gives the degree of efficiency attainable for any firm (independently of its R&D activities) as a result of knowledge spillovers and learning, among others.

Harrison et al. (2014, 2005) use the third wave of the Community Innovation Survey (CIS) from Germany, France, the UK and Spain, finding that process innovation tends to displace employment but the growth of demand for the old products compensates for the effect, while product innovation is basically labour friendly. Overall innovation stimulates employment. Hall, Lotti, and Mairesse (2008) extended this model using combinations of process and product innovation, their results show positive employment effects and no displacement due to process innovation when using a panel of Italian manufacturing firms over the period 1995–2003. Lachenmaier and Rottmann(2011) estimate a dynamic panel GMM system estimation and they find a higher positive result of process innovation on employment as compared to product innovation, with an overall positive effect of innovation on employment. Moreover, Criscuolo (2009) reports estimates on labour productivity in 15 European countries and Brazil, finding a positive relation with product innovation (except for Switzerland). However, the coefficient for process innovation shows a negative or non-significant relation.

Some studies for Latin America have followed previous work by Harrison et al. (2014) with mixed findings. In Chile, Benavente and Lauterbach (2008) used firm-level data from the third survey on innovation in the manufacturing sector (514 manufacturing firms). The authors found a positive and significant effect of product innovation on employment and no effect on process innovation. Alvarez et al (2011) extend the analysis for Chile including additional waves of the innovation survey. The authors find that process innovation does not seem to affect employment growth, but the simultaneous process and product innovation are positively related to employment growth.

Crespi et al. (2019) studied the impact of process and product innovation in Argentina, Chile, Costa Rica, and Uruguay. Their findings indicate product innovation is significantly and positively related in all cases, but process innovation has mixed results. Process innovation was found to have no effect in Argentina and Chile, while it had a significant and negative effect in Uruguay and a positive effect in Costa Rica. Differences in the results might be related to a lack of uniformity in the design of surveys among countries, for instance, the instruments used for the instrumental variables were different for each country since the questionnaire was not the same. Also, the estimates for each country vary in the number of waves and observations.

In most of these studies from Latin America, process innovation is not significantly correlated with employment. Some of the shortcomings are probably due to the assumptions in the model, differences across surveys – including differences in sampling method and coverage – and differences in measurement (innovation such as process only or a combination of process and product innovation). For instance, previous research such as Benavente and Lauterbach (2008) assumes that all technological changes are exogenous, not related to process innovation and identical for all the firms, so the constant term of the production function would represent the average efficiency growth for all firms. Introducing a more flexible assumption can enhance the analysis of the results since process innovation also improves firm efficiency, which, in turn, affects employment.

Yet, these studies do not measure efficiency directly, therefore I included in this paper a measure for relative efficiency in the model proposed.

Management fosters teamwork and cooperation that enables members of the firm to learn and accumulate knowledge on how to use the productive resources of the firm in the best way possible (Fagerberg et al. 2005, ch.2; Penrose 2009, 42–43). For companies to collaborate effectively in innovation, they must have the ability to absorb the latest information and skills. This is refer to as absorptive capacity, which can be defined as firms' ability to assimilate knowledge and ideas from other organisations and apply this external knowledge. Managerial decisions play a crucial part in this process of learning, sharing knowledge and expertise, and applying and adapting relevant information (Michie and Oughton 2016). Management is instrumental in implementing practices that encourage and facilitate knowledge use and sharing through interaction with others. As Penrose suggests, having access to managerial resources is essential for gaining the knowledge required to enter a new field and for a firm's growth. For example, if a company plans to expand by producing multiple products, it will need an appropriate amount of managerial support to achieve this goal.

To introduce an innovation, a firm typically combines various knowledge, skills, capabilities, and resources. Furthermore, as innovation is an ongoing process, the company must engage with its surroundings and other organisations to gain knowledge and learn. According to Freeman (1987), the success of research and development (R&D) in increasing productivity growth relies on how firms interact within an innovation system that includes universities and government. Studies indicate that collaborating on innovation impacts a company's chances of being an innovator and its sales expectations (Becker and Peters 2000; Grazzi et al. 2016). Michie and Oughton (2016) demonstrate that companies that partner with universities have a higher likelihood of innovating.

Moreover, diffusion of innovation, the process of adopting new technologies or replacing an older one with a new one, is a fundamental part of the innovation process and it may involve both process and product innovation. Miravete and Pernias (2006) study the complementarity of process and product innovation in the Spanish ceramic tile industry, finding that innovative process-innovative firms obtain a competitive advantage by reducing costs or applying more efficient processes or technology. Findings show that the complementarities among innovation strategies depend on unobserved heterogeneity, where the characteristics of the firm in terms of managers and organisational forms become crucial elements to coordinate and take advantage of innovation possibilities.

For low-middle income countries, diffusion can be an important part of the process of innovation (Fagerberg, Srholec, and Verspagen 2010; Hall 2004). Hence, process innovation is closely related to product innovation in low-middle income countries since the firm needs to introduce new processes to adopt a new technology. Therefore, one of the approaches I use in this paper is to investigate the simultaneous effects of process and product innovation.

Regarding differences in measurement, innovation surveys in Latin America are not harmonised and this leads to different results. One example concerns the measurement of the percentage of sales of new products as a proportion of total sales, as mentioned by Alvarez et al (2011), while the Chilean survey on innovation reports this variable in intervals (that is, 0, 0–10%, 11–30%, and 71–100%, the Colombian innovation survey reports the value declared by the firm without intervals. Moreover, compared to survey data from other Latin American countries (such as Argentina, Chile, Uruguay, Costa Rica, and Panamá), the Colombian survey is the only one that is a Census and therefore better goodness of fitness in models could be explained by the nature of the survey (Crespi and Zuniga 2012).

To provide a more comprehensive model, the estimations of this paper are done using a five-wave panel database that combines information from the survey of innovation (EDIT survey) with performance indicators from the main survey of manufacturing firms (EAM). Furthermore, this research aims to contribute to the gap in the literature by allowing for differences in efficiency across the firms and investigating the effect of process and product innovation on job creation at the firm level when they happen simultaneously.

The main hypotheses behind the analysis proposed in this research are that:

H1: Product innovation positively affects employment at the firm level.

H2: In Colombia, one of the transmission mechanisms of innovation affecting employment at the firm level is through complementary product and process innovation.

H3: Firms that innovate only in the process (and not in the product) affect employment negatively through efficiency improvements, which are very heterogeneous in middle income countries.

Previous studies have found difficulties in identifying empirically the displacement and compensation effects of innovation on employment due to data availability and measurement issues. Moreover, differences in the introduction of product and process innovations between middle and high income countries may influence the results. This research goes further than the previous literature on innovation and employment by:

- Providing empirical evidence at the firm level on the role of complementary process and product innovation on job creation in Colombia.
- Proposing an extended empirical framework that allows for differences in relative efficiency among firms.
- By accounting for endogeneity issues related to product innovation, the analysis uses instrumental variables I consider the role of institutional variables on employment creation through an instrumental variable of a firm's cooperative agreement on innovation.
- Building a unique panel database, covering the period between 2008 and 2016 (only even years), that combines information from two different surveys in Colombia: the Annual Manufacturing Survey and the Survey on Development and Technological Innovation in the Manufacturing Sector. A shortcoming in previous studies is that panel data on innovation is not often available for low- and middle-income countries. A key advantage of using a panel database is that it allows me to consider heterogeneity that I would not be able to control for using cross-sectional data.

1.2. Data sources and descriptive statistics

A shortcoming in the literature review is the lack of available panel data on innovation in Latin American countries. To address this, I built a comprehensive panel database, which includes details on manufacturing firms and their innovation. This database will help gain insights into the impact of innovation on employment, as well as the role of cooperative agreements and other firm characteristics in promoting innovation. This section provides an overview of the data sources used in the study and the process of constructing the panel dataset, along with relevant summary statistics.

To build the panel dataset I combined two firm-level surveys in the manufacturing sector in Colombia: the Annual Manufacturing Survey (EAM by its acronym in Spanish) and the Survey on Development and Technological Innovation (EDIT by its acronym in Spanish). The Colombian National Administrative Department of Statistics (DANE) conducts the EAM every year and the EDIT every two years (DANE 2017). On one hand, the innovation survey reports data on process and product innovation, innovation expenditures or activities such as R&D expenditures, product design, personnel training, and managerial (Mairesse and Mohnen 2010). On the other hand, the EAM collects specific information on the characteristics of manufacturing firms and their establishments such as age, use of capital, intermediate goods, and region, among others, to study the impact of innovation on employment.

Both the EAM and the EDIT surveys are stratified according to economic sectors and geographical location. The obtained results provide national coverage divided by metropolitan areas and departments of Colombia. Both databases cover the years between 2008 and 2016. The combination of these two databases provides a unique panel dataset that can be used to improve the analysis of manufacturing firms, innovation, and employment issues.

1.2.1. Summary statistics

The complete dataset used for the model estimation is an unbalanced 5-wave panel from 2008 to 2016 (every two years). The database consists of 42,464 observations on manufacturing firms in total, which I classified into innovators and firms that do not innovate. Table 2 shows the number of manufacturing firms for each year between 2008 and 2016, the last column presents the statistics for all five waves together. It shows a summary of descriptive statistics of the percentage of firms, employment growth and average employment by type of firms innovator (non-innovator, process innovator, product innovator and simultaneous process and product innovators).

On average, between 2008 and 2016, 26.7% of manufacturing firms reported innovations while 73% were non-innovators. More manufacturing firms innovated during the years 2008 and 2010, compared to the years 2012, 2014, and 2016. This decreasing trend reflects the lower economic growth after the global financial crisis.

Moreover, information from the EDIT survey allows me to classify firms that innovate into product innovators, process innovators or simultaneous process and product innovators. Most of the firms that innovate reported they do process innovation (11.4% of all manufacturing firms) followed by firms that do both process and product innovation simultaneously (9.4% of all manufacturing firms), while 6% of all firms do product innovation only.

Table 2. Employment growth and innovation.

	2008	2010	2012	2014	2016	All years
Number of firms	7,683	8,643	9,137	9,054	7,947	42,464
Innovators(%)	**37.8%**	**34.4%**	**21.7%**	**19.3%**	**21.7%**	**26.7%**
-Process innovator	9.9%	17.3%	10.0%	9.3%	10.2%	11.4%
-Product innovator	11.8%	5.1%	5.0%	4.4%	4.1%	6.0%
-Process and Product innovator	16.2%	11.9%	6.7%	5.6%	7.3%	9.4%
Non-innovators	**62.2%**	**65.7%**	**78.3%**	**80.7%**	**78.3%**	**73.3%**
Employment growth (%)						
All firms	**5.3%**	**1.9%**	**2.0%**	**1.7%**	**0.8%**	**2.3%**
Innovators(%)	**12.0%**	**5.9%**	**6.5%**	**6.9%**	**5.6%**	**7.7%**
-Process innovator	3.3%	5.2%	5.6%	7.2%	4.5%	5.2%
-Product innovator	27.8%	4.8%	8.0%	5.3%	1.1%	13.2%
-Process and Product innovator	5.8%	7.3%	6.8%	7.6%	9.6%	7.1%
Non-innovators	**1.2%**	**-0.2%**	**0.8%**	**0.5%**	**-0.5%**	**0.3%**
Average employment						
All firms	**90**	**85**	**85**	**90**	**103**	**90**
Innovators	**154**	**151**	**203**	**229**	**233**	**185**
-Process innovator	105	110	146	171	152	134
-Product innovator	128	158	170	203	185	160
-Process and Product innovator	202	209	313	347	374	264
Non-innovators	**52**	**50**	**52**	**56**	**67**	**56**

Analysis of the Colombian data shows that firms that innovate have on average more than three times the number of workers compared to firms that are not innovators. Employment growth decreased drastically after 2008 in line with the fall in GDP growth from 6.8% in 2007 to 1.2% per cent in 2009, related to the decrease in economic growth with the global financial crisis. In 2010 GDP growth started to recover, and the manufacturing sector started to grow again however it did not grow at the same path rate as other sectors such as construction, mining, or services. Interestingly, firms that innovate simultaneously in product and process are the ones that show, on average, higher employment growth for all years.

One way of measuring innovation is to use the percentage of sales derived from new or improved goods and services (Oslo Manual, 2005; Oecd/Eurostat 2018). Table 3 shows the firm yearly average of the share of turnover from new products.

Figure 1 depicts the share of sales of new products and the average employment growth of 22 manufacturing industries in Colombia. Important variability across industries is observed in the graph. These differences are also observed across European industries (see Pianta 2003). Industries such as office and computing machinery (OCM in the graph), Radio, television, and communication equipment (RTE), chemicals (CH), other transport equipment (OTE), electrical machinery (EM) and medical and optical instruments (MOI) have a combination of a higher share of turnover due to new products and better employment performance than other industries (see right-top quadrant). By contrast, basic metals (Met) and refined petroleum (RPe) average negative growth of employment and low innovation as measured by sales from new products. For the case of refined petroleum, one

Table 3. Share of turnover from new products (average).

	2008	2010	2012	2014	2016	All years
Share of turnover from new products	12.8%	8.3%	5.3%	4.0%	5.0%	8.3%

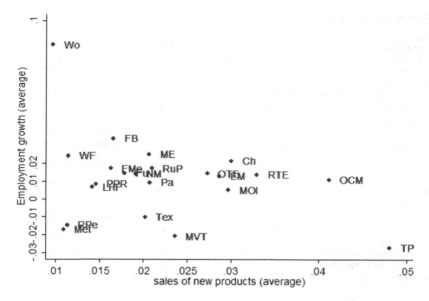

Figure 1. Share of sales of new products and employment growth (average) by industry.

explanation can be a combination of the 2009 financial crisis-induced recession with the low (and volatile) price of oil in the years after the recession. Traditional industries such as textiles (Tex) have an intermediate increase in sales associated with new products and positive job effects. Other industries like wood and products of wood (Wo), food and beverages (FB), wearing apparel and dyeing fur (WF), and fabricated metal products (FMe) have low innovation as measured by sales from new products, with gains in employment.

Regarding the size of the firms survey data indicate that, on average, 39% of enterprises are small (with less or 10 employees) while 61% reported having more than 10 employees.

Human capital is important and firms may have different demands for skills. On average, firms hire 70% of workers with 'up to secondary level', 15% with technical and vocational and 14% with university level education or more. These percentages vary between firms that innovate and do not innovate, with innovators showing a higher proportion of workers from higher education levels compared to non-innovators.

The next section presents the empirical strategy.

1.3. Empirical strategy

In this paper, I propose an analytical framework that allows me to provide empirical evidence on three key areas of firm innovation affecting employment:

(1) The role of complementary process and product innovation on job creation.
(2) Differences in relative efficiency among manufacturing firms as a result of knowledge spillovers, learning, etc. This is important since process innovation can be captured through efficiency improvements. Yet previous studies did not have the

data to make a more flexible assumption to investigate this transmission mechanism.

(3) The role of institutional variables on employment creation through an instrumental variable of the firm's cooperative agreement on innovation. This analysis builds on Edith Penrose's (Penrose 2009) work on the importance of the availability of managerial and planning resources at the firm level, which allows the expansion of the firm and the development of knowledge.

First, I use the empirical framework applied by Hall et al. (2008) and Harrison, Jaumandreu, Mairesse and Peters (2014) to study the effect of displacement and compensation forces of innovation on employment growth at the firm level. The model assumes that: i) a firm is observed in two periods of time, ii) a firm can produce various products (old and new or significantly improved products), and ii) there is an identical separable production function. Using the firm's cost function and assuming cost minimisation the authors estimate the labour demand (Annex 1 Equation 4). Annex 1 discusses the theoretical model in detail. Then, using the labour demand equations and the employment equation one can write the employment growth equation.

Second, I augment the model specification with an efficiency variable to account for the relative efficiency of firms. The model is useful for the analysis since it permits disentangling the effect of innovation on employment at the firm level in product innovation, process innovation and efficiency. This is important to investigate the adoption of innovations in Latin American countries, for instance, these countries might show more complementarities of process and product innovation compared to high-income countries where product innovation alone can be more frequent.

The extended model specification for the employment growth equation augmented by a variable to account for the relative efficiency of firms (f) is the following:

$$l_i - g_{1i} = \alpha_0 + \alpha_1 f + \alpha_2 d_2 + (B_0 + B_1 d_2) g_{2i} + trend + \mu_i (1)$$

i = 1,. . .,N_{firms}

where:

- l_i is the rate of employment growth between the year $t = 1$ and $t = 2$
- g_{1i} is the deflated growth of sales for old products
- $(l_i - g_{1i})$ is the employment growth rate less the rate of growth of deflated sales from old products.
- g_{2i} Increase in sales of new products.
- B_0 is the relative efficiency of the production of old and new products.
- α_0 is the negative of the average efficiency growth in the production of the old products. This indicates that non-process innovators can achieve efficiency gains through learning, and improvements in human capital, among others.
- α_1 is the average efficiency growth for process innovators
- d_2 is a dummy variable that takes the value of 1 if the firm implements simultaneously a process and product innovation

- B_1 is the coefficient measuring the effect of the process and product innovation attributed to the production of new products.
- $d_2 * g_2$ is a variable interacting sales growth for new products with simultaneous process & product innovation
- f is the relative efficiency in production of the firms. I normalised this variable between 0 and 1.
- *trend* is a variable accounting for the trend in sales growth, innovation, and efficiency gains.

Equation 1 can also be interpreted as a measure of labour productivity growth by rewriting equation 5 in the annex 1 as: $y_{2i} + y_{1i} - l_i = -\alpha_0 - \alpha_1 d_1 + (1 - B)y_{2i} - \mu_i$. In this case, the dependent variable is the growth of real output per worker and the analysis could provide an interpretation in terms of productivity growth.

I use stochastic frontier analysis (Aigner, Lovell, and Schmidt 1977; Meeusen and van Den Broeck 1977) to generate the efficiency measure f that accounts for the relative efficiency among firms. Annex 2 presents the econometric model to estimate the stochastic frontier analysis to predict an efficiency measure. Here I assume that not all firms are equally technically efficient (f variable), meaning that there are firms in the manufacturing sector that operate on the frontier, but other firms operate beneath the frontier.

I include a time trend variable (*trend*) to account for trends in sales growth, innovation, and efficiency gains. Productivity improvements in the production of existing products due to past industry innovations or learning can be captured by time trends.[2]

Table 4. Employment, efficiency, and innovation.

$l_i - g_{1i} = a_0 + a_1 f + a_2 d_2 + (B_0 + B_1 d_2)g_{2i} + trend + \mu_i$

	(1) Robust		(2) Bootstrap	
growth_newF(g_2)	2.521+	(1.467)	2.521+	(1.546)
Efficiency (f)	−2.109***	(0.516)	−2.109***	(0.559)
Proc_Product (d_2)	0.114+	(0.0667)	0.114*	(0.0780)
proc_prodXsaleNew ($d_2 * g_2$)	−2.351	(1.581)	−2.351	(1.448)
trend	0.0330*	(0.0136)	0.0330*	(0.0155)
_cons	0.255*	(0.108)	0.255*	(0.121)
N	4551		4551	

Standard errors in parentheses.
$+ p < 0.10$, $*p < 0.05$, $**p < 0.01$, $***p < 0.001$.
Robust specification: (1) Robust standard errors in parentheses.
Bootstrap specification: (2) bootstrap standard errors in parentheses (1000 reps).
L1= employment growth rate less real sales growth.
g_2= rate of sales growth for new products.
f= efficiency variable.
d_2= dummy variable for simultaneously process and product innovation.
d_2*g_2= is a variable interacting sales growth for new products with simultaneous process & product innovation.
Instruments: Cooperative agreements for innovation(iSNCTI).
Increased range of products and Research and Development.

1.4. *Extended model: results*

The results of estimating Equation 1 are reported in Table 4.

1.4.1. *Product innovation*

Starting the production of a new or significantly improved good or service is viewed to have a positive effect on employment. Here product innovation is studied through the coefficient B_0 on real sales growth of production of new goods (g_{2i}) which is positive and significant; implying that innovation that leads to growth of output due to new or significantly improved products (product innovation) increases labour growth, this is the gross effect of product innovation on employment. Moreover, the coefficient B_0 is[3] not significantly different from 1 suggesting that the increase of labour due to the demand of new products is not different compared to the one of old products. In other words, there is no difference in the relative efficiency of production of new products compared to old products. This suggests no displacement of workers from productivity differences between the new and old products.

I instrumented[4] the sales growth due to new products[5] (g_{2i}) using a variable for cooperative agreements on innovation,[6] increased range[7] of products and investment in research and development.

1.4.2. *Process and product innovation*

Preliminary empirical exercise for considering process innovation only suggest no evidence of significant employment displacement effects from process innovation only, the coefficient for the dummy variable was not significant[8] and therefore was not included in the final specification. However, process innovation has a potential impact on employment when firms innovate both in process and product innovation at the same time. Firms that introduce both new process and product innovations (d_2) have a growth of employment of 0.11% higher compared to other firms, so there are no signs of displacement effects. In this case, as suggested by (Peters 2004) process innovations may not necessarily lead to a reduction in labour since firms may want to improve the quality of their products or introduce processes to meet legal requirements. Unfortunately, the survey does not differentiate what share of process innovation goes to new versus old products. Therefore, this effect necessarily captures process innovation related to old products.

To separate the effect of process innovation related to product innovation, I assume that this process innovation is related to new products by including a variable interacting with a process and product indicator with the sales growth due to new products ($d_2 * g_2$). Firms may also introduce new processes to be able to produce a new product and to rationalise in terms of reducing average production costs. The coefficient is negative but is not significant indicating that the effect of improvements in processes related to new products might be reflected in a decrease in prices or quality improvement (compared to similar products in the market), which increases demand and therefore employment. So, in this case, there is no sign of displacement effects on workers (since the coefficient is not significant) due to productivity increases.

This article provides empirical evidence supporting the idea that complementary processes and product innovation do affect employment growth. As suggested by

Bogliacino et al. (2009) low- and middle-income countries differ from high income countries in their patterns of innovation. Innovation in low- and middle-income countries requires the acquisition of new technologies and imitation of processes and products developed in advanced economies, this is, firms need to introduce both process and product innovations. Previous studies focusing on Latin American countries have not found clear results on the role of simultaneous process and product innovation. For instance, Alvarez et al. (2011) found in the case of Chile, that simultaneous process and product innovation is significant and positively related to employment growth, in contrast, Benavente and Lauterbach (2008) found a negative relationship with employment and a small coefficient (the study used one wave of the innovation survey and 514 observations).

1.4.3. Efficiency

Different production efficiencies explain differences in employment growth at the firm level. Least squares econometric production models assume all firms are technically efficient. However, the combination of new technology and process improvements (for instance, organisational improvements and eliminating inefficiencies in the supply chain) increases efficiency and reduces costs. As pointed out by Brynjolfsson and Hitt (2000) some of these savings may improve productivity, increase output quality or introduce variety without increasing the cost. Firms that operate beneath the production frontier may increase their output without requiring more input or produce the same level of output using less input (Chapter 1 Coelli et al. 2005).

One novelty of this article is the study of the displacement effect through the increase in the relative efficiency of the firms using stochastic frontier analysis. Here the intuition is that more efficient firms compared to less efficient ones may be correlated with less new employment at the firm level. The overall efficiency (variable f in Table 4) of the firm does influence employment growth. I normalised the variable between 0 and 1 for interpretation purposes (this allows me to have the same scale for all subjects) and it indicates that more efficient firms, compared to less efficient ones, are correlated with less new employment generation. In particular, the coefficient (-(2.109) related to the variable of efficiency (f) shows that for a 1% increase in efficiency of a firm, compared to other firms, employment decreases by about 2%. Moreover, the coefficient of efficiency is significantly different to one[9] suggesting that innovative firms closer to the technological frontier will increase employment less than proportionally. If the coefficient of efficiency were not significantly different to one, then increases in efficiency would affect employment equally for all firms.

The descriptive results (Annex 2, Figure 2) show that most firms have efficiency values far from 1 (even below or close to 0.5). From a policy perspective one can look at it as an opportunity to innovate while creating jobs at the same time. According to a report by Cornell University (2019), Colombia scores above the regional average in all pillars of innovation inputs, indicating the potential for takeoff in the future. However, the report mentions that the country is lacking in effectively translating innovation investments into innovation outputs.

This could be related to the heterogeneity in efficiency among firms. One interpretation of this heterogeneity is that firms introduce process innovations when they are adopting new technologies, but new frontier technologies do not

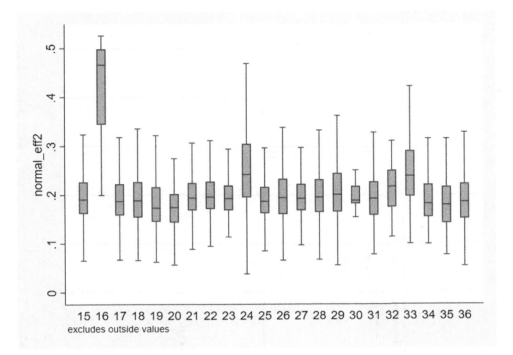

Figure 2. Efficiency by sub-sector of the manufacturing sector. 10 The boxplot shows: the median (middle line inside each box), the 25th and 75th quartiles are represented by the bottom and top of each box, the height of the box is the inter-quartile range, the upper and lower adjacent values depict the spread of the distribution outside the inter-quartile range.

diffuse immediately. Instead, innovative technologies are first adapted to country-specific circumstances and adopted by frontier firms. Then, after technologies are tested, they start to diffuse (Andrews, Criscuolo, and Gal 2015). Another likely explanation is related to knowledge spillovers and the possibility of learning from others since a firm needs to acquire information about the compatibility of new processes or production techniques with the firm's existing capital stock and workers (Davis et al. 1998).

Major differences in efficiency among firms could also reflect the case where firms introduce only process innovations. Firms in middle income countries may introduce new processes to decrease prices and this could be enough to survive in local markets. Studies have observed that in Colombia low productivity firms can stay in business for a long time.[10]

The effects of increasing efficiency are usually perceived over time. Table 5 looks at the dynamics of efficiency by showing the estimates for three cases of my efficiency variable: column 1 refers to the lag of efficiency (*Eff_1*), column 2 presents the efficiency in the current period (*f*) and column 3 shows the results for the case where the efficiency variable is estimated for t + 1 (*Fwd_eff*). The results show that past improvements in efficiency have a positive effect on future employment (*Eff_1*). However, in the period where firms implement these improvements, employment growth is negatively affected by these changes (*f*). The forward efficiency (*Fwd_eff*) can be interpreted as anticipated

Table 5. Dynamics of efficiency: lag, present and forward.

	(Lag_eff) L1		(Eff present) L1		(Fwd_eff) L1	
growth_newF(g_2)	2.223+	(1.176)	2.521+	(1.467)	1.612	(1.313)
eff_1	2.075***	(0.452)				
Proc_Product (d_2)	0.115*	(0.0581)	0.114+	(0.0667)	0.0863	(0.0658)
proc_prodXsaleNew	−1.675	(1.161)	−2.129	(1.465)	−1.181	(1.302)
trend	0.0114	(0.00968)	0.0330*	(0.0136)	0.0229	(0.0177)
Efficiency (f)			−2.109***	(0.516)		
Fwd_eff					2.037**	(0.627)
_cons	−1.575**	(0.139)	−0.255*	(0.108)	−0.586***	(0.194)
N	3983		4551		3343	

Robust standard errors in parentheses.

+ $p < 0.10$, * $p < 0.05$, ** $p < 0.01$, *** $p < 0.001$.

L1= employment growth rate less real sales growth.

g_2= rate of sales growth for new products.

f= efficiency variable.

d_2= dummy variable for simultaneously process and product innovation.

d_2*g_2= is a variable interacting sales growth for new products with simultaneous process & product innovation.

Instruments for growth_newF: Increased range of products(i2r2c1_) Increased market share(i2r4c1_)

R&D(r_d) and Cooperation agreements(iSNCTI)

(1) Lag_eff= model that includes the lag of efficiency

(2) eff= model that includes the efficiency in the current period

(3) Fwd_eff= model that includes the efficiency in t + 1

Lag_eff= model that includes the lag of efficiency

eff= model that includes the efficiency in the current period

Fwd_eff= model that includes the efficiency in t + 1

expectations of the firm's efficiency, and it may be used as a sort of measure for the rationality of the investors.

Finally, the trend variable indicates that efficiency gains across the years are significant and positively related to employment creation. This could be associated with the introduction of new products, and/or if complementarities of new and old products exist, then the positive sign of the trend could also refer to the increase of demand for the old product due to these complementarities.

2. Concluding remarks

This paper finds that in Colombia, innovation often entails a combination of process and product innovation simultaneously. This reflects the dynamics behind the introduction of new technologies into the firm: in the process of putting a new technology into efficient use the firm adapts it and as a consequence not only introduces new or significantly improved products but also new or significantly improved processes.

Results indicate that the sources of employment growth are split between the contribution of growth of sales of new and old products and a simultaneous process and product innovation. Even though there is no evidence of significant employment displacement effects from process innovation only, estimates show robust evidence of displacement effects from differences in the relative efficiency of the manufacturing firms. This reflects process improvements and process innovations. One of the novelties of this analysis is that it allows a more flexible assumption about technological change by assuming that process innovation also improves firm efficiency – which is no longer identical for all firms – and therefore I estimated a variable of relative efficiency, which affects employment. A firm's heterogeneity in middle income countries can be reflected in differences in efficiency or in decisions to introduce innovations into the firm. For example, uncertainty about the development, adoption and regulation of new products, new processes and production techniques affects a firm's decisions to experiment with innovative technologies, which in turn, generates differences in outcomes among firms (Davis et al. 1998). Another likely reason for heterogeneity is differences in managerial ability, including the ability to identify and develop products, adapt to changing circumstances and organise production activity. Edith Penrose (Penrose 2009) conceptualised the importance of the availability of managerial and planning resources at the firm level, which allows the expansion of the firm and the development of knowledge.

Firm heterogeneity is important for explaining the effects of innovation on employment. Firms that have efficiency values close to 1 have higher labour productivity, which is similar to results from high income countries. However, most of the firms show efficiency values far below 1 and, in this case, increases in efficiency do not have such a negative effect on employment creation. This means that Colombia has an opportunity to innovate and create jobs at the same time since a substantial number of firms still need to catch up in terms of efficiency and while doing so, they are not necessarily displacing employment.

In addition, the empirical results show the importance of knowledge for innovation associated with cooperative agreements. This reflects the role of institutional variables, such as cooperative agreements on innovation, in impacting the probability of success of implementing innovations and the expectation in terms of sales growth. That is, cooperative agreements contribute to firm access to extra-industrial technology knowledge. Also, and in line with the literature, this study consistently found evidence of the importance of R&D in shaping innovation outcomes when using the variable as an instrument for product innovation.

The results of this paper do not differentiate by granular type of innovation, for instance, some firms may introduce a new process that is automated, and others introduce a non-automated process but it was not possible to study this difference since the information is not reported in the survey.

Further research should also include whether innovation activities induce a change in the skill structure of employees.

Notes

1. Crepon, Duguet and Mairesse developed a three-step structural model on the relationship between innovation, output and productivity. The first step models the decision of firms to invest in R&D. The second step models the relationship between investment in R&D and the probability to be innovative, using a knowledge production function. The third step is the production function where productivity depends on innovation.
2. As discussed in Coelli et al. (2005, ch 8), if there are observations over time then one should include a time trend to explicitly account for changes in economic relationships, such as production functions, due to technological advances.
3. B_0 can be interpreted as the relative efficiency of the production of old and new products, see Supplementary Material Annex 1 on the Theoretical Model.
4. I test for different specifications and in all cases the Sargan- Hansen test p-value confirms the validity of the instruments, there is no rejection of the null hypothesis.
5. Output growth of new products y_{2i} is not observed but nominal sales. The variable of nominal sales might be correlated with unanticipated shocks because data do not include price changes of sales at the firm level, and both output and prices are affected by movements in demand. This leads to endogeneity of g which could be correlated with the error term since prices changes are in the error term. Due to endogeneity issues applying Ordinary Least Squares (OLS) would result in biased estimates and would underestimate the true effect of product innovation.
6. The variable for cooperative agreements on innovation is a dummy variable indicating if the firm has established these agreements with one of the institutions in the National System of innovation.
7. Takes the value of 0 if the firm reports that the effect of the new or improved products or process (effect of innovation) has been irrelevant for broadening the range of goods and services, and 1 if it has had medium or high importance in the impact on broadening the range of products.
8. One of the reasons for this outcome could be that firms introducing only process innovations may have observed increased sales for old products due to price decreases. So the growth in sales of existing products compensates for possible improvements in labour productivity of old products due to process innovation.
9. $Z_{score} = \frac{\alpha_1 - 1}{\theta}$
10. For instance, Eslava et al. (2019) present evidence suggesting that there is a higher probability that less productive young firms in Colombia survive and continue in business, more commonly as compared to the USA.

Disclosure statement

I wish to acknowledge the Colombian Statistical Agency DANE for allowing me access to the EAM and EDIT surveys and the use of their data, and to their staff for technical support. I am grateful for the beneficial comments provided by the reviewer and the editor. My deepest gratitude to Professor Pasquale Scaramozzino, for his valuable guidance, constructive comments, advice and support through each stage of my research. A special mention goes to Professor Giovanni Trovato, from Tor Vergata University of Rome, who guided me through stochastic frontier analysis and econometric methods. I thank the International J.A. Schumpeter Society" for the Honorary Mention for the paper. Juana Paola Bustamante's affiliation to WHO, where she is a labour economist, is provided for identification purposes only and does not constitute institutional endorsement. Any views and opinions expressed are hers alone and do not represent WHO.

ORCID

Juana Paola Bustamante Izquierdo (iD) http://orcid.org/0000-0002-1665-8486

References

Acemoglu, D., and D. Autor. 2011. "Skills, Tasks and Technologies: Implications for Employment and Earnings." In *Handbook of Labor Economics*, edited by David Card and Orley Ashenfelter, Vol. 4, 1043–1171. New York: Handbook of Labor Economics, Elsevier (printed in Great Britain). https://doi.org/10.1016/S0169-7218(11)02410-5

Aigner, D., C. K. Lovell, and P. Schmidt. 1977. "Formulation and Estimation of Stochastic Frontier Production Function Models." *Journal of Econometrics* 6 (1): 21–37. https://doi.org/10.1016/0304-4076(77)90052-5.

Alvarez, R., J. M. Benavente, R. Campusano, and C. Cuevas. 2011. Employment Generation, Firm Size, and Innovation in Chile. Technical report, Inter-American Development Bank.

Andrews, D., C. Criscuolo, and P. N. Gal. 2015. "Frontier Firms, Technology Diffusion and Public Policy: Micro Evidence from OECD Countries." Technical report, OECD Productivity Working Papers.

Baltagi, B. H. 2015. *The Oxford Handbook of Panel Data*. New York, USA: Oxford University press.

Battese, G. E., and T. J. Coelli. 1992. "Frontier Production Functions, Technical Efficiency and Panel Data: With Application to Paddy Farmers in India." *Journal of Productivity Analysis* 3 (1–2): 153–169. https://doi.org/10.1007/BF00158774.

Becker, W., and J. Peters. 2000. *Technological Opportunities, Absorptive Capacities, and Innovation*. Augsburg: Institut fur Volkswirtschaftslehre der Universitat Augsburg.

Benavente, J. M., and R. Lauterbach. 2008. "Technological Innovation and Employment: Complements or Substitutes?" *The European Journal of Development Research* 20 (2): 318–329. https://doi.org/10.1080/09578810802060744.

Blanchower, D. G., and S. M. Burgess. 1998. "New Technology and Jobs: Comparative Evidence from a Two-Country Study." *Economics of Innovation & New Technology* 5 (2–4): 109–138. https://doi.org/10.1080/10438599800000002.

Bogliacino, F., G. Perani, M. Pianta, and S. Supino. 2009. "Innovation in Developing Countries: The Evidence from Innovation Surveys." In FIRB conference Research and Entrepreneurship in the Knowledge-based Economy Milano: Universita L. Bocconi.

Brynjolfsson, E., and L. M. Hitt. 2000. "Beyond Computation: Information Technology, Organizational Transformation and Business Performance." *Journal of Economic Perspectives* 14 (4): 23–48. https://doi.org/10.1257/jep.14.4.23.

Calvino, F., and M. E. Virgillito. 2018. "The Innovation-Employment Nexus: A Critical Survey of Theory and Empirics." *Journal of Economic Surveys* 32 (1): 83–117. https://doi.org/10.1111/joes.12190.

Coelli, T. J., D. S. P. Rao, C. J. O'Donnell, and G. E. Battese. 2005. *An Introduction to Efficiency and Productivity Analysis*. New York, NY: Springer Science & Business Media.

Cornell University, I. N. S. E. A. D. W. 2019. "The Global Innovation Index 2019: Creating Healthy Lives-The Future of Medical Innovation."

Crépon, B., E. Duguet, and J. Mairesse. 1998. "Research, Innovation and Productivity: An Econometric Analysis at the Firm Level." *Economics of Innovation & New Technology* 7 (2): 115–158.

Crespi, G., E. Tacsir, and M. Pereira. 2019. "Effects of Innovation on Employment in Latin America." *Industrial and Corporate Change* 28 (1): 139–159. https://doi.org/10.1093/icc/dty062.

Crespi, G., and P. Zuniga. 2012. "Innovation and Productivity: Evidence from Six Latin American Countries." *World Development* 40 (2): 273–290. https://doi.org/10.1016/j.worlddev.2011.07.010.

Criscuolo, C. 2009. "Innovation and Productivity: Estimating the Core Model Across 18 Countries." *Innovation in Firms: A Microeconomic Perspective*, 111–138. Paris: OECD Publishing. https://doi.org/10.1787/9789264056213-5-en.

DANE. 2017. *Methodology for the Survey on Development and Technological Innovation in the Manufacturing Sector Edit*. Bogotá, Colombia: Departamento Administrativo Nacional de Estad [istica-DANE].

Davis, S. J., J. C. Haltiwanger, S. Schuh. 1998. *Job Creation and Destruction*, 1. USA: MIT Press Books.

Eslava, M., J. C. Haltiwanger, and A. Pinzon. 2019. *Job Creation in Colombia Vs. the US: "Up or Out dynamics" Meets "The Life Cycle of Plants"*. Massachusetts, USA: National Bureau of Economic Research.

Fagerberg, J., D. C. Mowery, and R. R. Nelson, ed. 2005. *The Oxford Handbook of Innovation*. Oxford university press.

Fagerberg, J., M. Srholec, and B. Verspagen. 2010. "Innovation and economic development." In *Handbook of the Economics of Innovation*, edited by Bronwyn H. Hall and Nathan Rosenberg, Vol. 2, 833–872. North Holland.

Freeman, C. 1987. *Technology Policy and Economic Performance*. London and New York: Pinter Publishers Great Britain.

Garcia, A., J. Jaumandreu, and C. Rodriguez. 2004. Innovation and Jobs: Evidence from Manufacturing Firms. MRPA Paper, (1204).

Grazzi, M., C. Pietrobelli. 2016. *Firm Innovation and Productivity in Latin America and the Caribbean*. Washington DC: Inter-American Development Bank.

Greenan, N., and D. Guellec. 2000. "Technological Innovation and Employment Reallocation." *Labour* 14 (4): 547–590. https://doi.org/10.1111/1467-9914.00146.

Hall, B. H. 2004. Innovation and diffusion. National Bureau of Economic Research, (No. w10212).

Hall, B. H., F. Lotti, and J. Mairesse. 2008. "Employment, Innovation, and Productivity: Evidence from Italian Microdata." *Industrial and Corporate Change* 17 (4): 813–839. https://doi.org/10.1093/icc/dtn022.

Harrison, R., J. Jaumandreu, J. Mairesse, and B. Peters. 2014. *Does Innovation Stimulate Employment? A Firm-Level Analysis Using Comparable Micro-Data from Four European Countries*. International Journal of Industrial Organization Elsevier.

Harrison, Rupert, Jordi Jaumandreu, Jacques Mairesse, and Bettina Peters. 2005. *Does Innovation Stimulate Employment? A Firm-Level Analysis Using Comparable Micro Data from Four European Countries*. Madrid: Mimeo, Department of Economics, University Carlos III.

Katsoulacos, Y. 1984. "Product Innovation and Employment." *European Economic Review* 26 (1–2): 83–108. Journal of Industrial Organization, 35:29-43. https://doi.org/10.1016/0014-2921(84)90023-0.

Lachenmaier, S., and H. Rottmann. 2011. "Effects of Innovation on Employment: A Dynamic Panel Analysis." *International Journal of Industrial Organization* 29 (2): 210–220. https://doi.org/10.1016/j.ijindorg.2010.05.004.

Mairesse, J., and P. Mohnen. 2010. "Using Innovation Surveys for Econometric Analysis." In *Handbook of the Economics of Innovation*, edited by Bronwyn Hall and Nathan Rosenberg, Vol. 2, 1129–1155. North Holland (Printed and bound in the UK).

Meeusen, W., and J. van Den Broeck. 1977. "Efficiency Estimation from Cobb-Douglas Production Functions with Composed Error." *International Economic Review* 18 (2): 435–444. https://doi.org/10.2307/2525757.

Michie, J., and C. Oughton. 2016. "Creating Local Economic Resilience: Co-Operation, Innovation and firms' Absorptive Capacity." In *Global Economic Crisis and Local Economic Development*, edited by J Begley, D Coffey, T Donnelly, and C Thornley, 12–29. Abingdon and New York: Routledge.

Miravete, E. J., and J. C. Pernias. 2006. "Innovation Complementarity and Scale of Production." *The Journal of Industrial Economics* 54 (1): 1–29. https://doi.org/10.1111/j.1467-6451.2006.00273.x.

Oecd/Eurostat, E. C. 2018. Oslo Manual 2018: Guidelines for Collecting, Reporting and Using Data on Innovation. OECD publishing.

Penrose, E. T. 2009. *The Theory of the Growth of the Firm*. United Kingdom: Oxford University Press.

Peters, B. 2004. Employment Effects of Different Innovation Activities: Microeconometric Evidence. ZEW-Centre for European Economic Research Discussion Paper, (04-073).

Pianta, M. 2003. "Innovation and Employment." *The Oxford Handbook of Innovation*.

Pitelis, Christos. 2009. *Edith Penrose's 'The Theory of the Growth of the Firm' Fifty Years Later*. Cambridge, UK: Cambridge University.

Raffo, J., S. Lhuillery, and L. Miotti. 2008. "Northern and Southern Innovativity: A Comparison Across European and Latin American Countries." *The European Journal of Development Research* 20 (2): 219–239. https://doi.org/10.1080/09578810802060777.

Van Reenen, J. 1997. "Employment and Technological Innovation: Evidence from UK Manufacturing Firms." *Journal of Labor Economics* 15 (2): 255–284. https://doi.org/10.1086/209833.

Vivarelli, M. 2014. "Innovation, Employment and Skills in Advanced and Developing Countries: A Survey of Economic Literature." *Journal of Economic Issues* 48 (1): 123–154. https://doi.org/10.2753/JEI0021-3624480106.

Annex 1

Theoretical Model for innovation and employment at the firm level

The assumptions of the theoretical model are the following (Hall et al. (2008), Harrison et al (2014)):

- A firm i is observed at two points in time: t_1 and t_2.
- Firms can produce various products. The firm can produce two types of goods and services: old products (j = 1) in the first period (t1) and, if they innovate, they can also produce new or significantly improved ones (j = 2) in the second period(t2). In this way, I denote outputs at time t as Yjt.
- Each type of product is produced with constant returns to scale in capital (K), labour (L) and intermediate goods (M) (i.e., it is assumed that the model is linear-homogeneous in these inputs).
- There is an identical separable production function with different Hicks-neutral technological productivity indexed by θjt. Here, Harrison et al. (2014) assume that θ represents the efficiency of the investments in research and development (R&D) to generate process and product innovations.

In this paper, I assume a broader definition of efficiency to propose an extended model. That is, θ also gives the degree of efficiency attainable for any firm (independently of its R&D activities) because of knowledge spillovers and learning, among others (Garcia et al., 2004). If I assume that knowledge raises the marginal productivity of inputs then the efficiency in the productive process, both for new and old products, can increase due to learning effects and process innovations (Peters, 2004). Therefore, this research introduces assumptions regarding θ:

  i) Not all firms are technically efficient (θ_{jti}), and
  ii) Process innovation can increase a firm's relative efficiency.

The production function (Y_{jti}) for a product of type j in period t and firm i is represented as follows: In the first period (t_1) the firm produces only the old type of product (j = 1)

$$Y_{1t_1i} = \theta_{1t_1}F(K_{1t_1i}; L_{1t_1i}; M_{1t_1i})e_i^{\eta} \tag{1}$$

In the second period (t_2) the firm produces the old type of product (j = 1) and some firms decide to produce and sell new products (j = 2), hence
Old products:

$$Y_{1t_2i} = \theta_{1t_2}F(K_{1t_2i}; L_{1t_2i}; M_{1t_2i})e^{\eta_i - \mu_i} \tag{2}$$

New products:

$$Y_{2t_2i} = \theta_{2t_2}F(K_{2t_2i}; L_{2t_2i}; M_{2t_2i})e^{\eta_i - \mu_i} \tag{3}$$

where μ_i and v_i are unanticipated productivity shocks.

Using the firm's cost function (see Hall et al. (2008) and Peters (2004)for detailed equations) and assuming cost minimization and applying Shephard's Lemma, labour demand is given by:

$$L_{jti} = c_{wL}\left(w_{jti}\right)\frac{Y_{jti}}{\theta_{jt}e^{\eta_i}} \tag{4}$$

where c_{wL} represents the derivative of the marginal cost to the wage.

The employment equation decomposes the growth of employment into growth due to the production of old and new goods between the two years t=1 and t=2. The assumption is that the prices of inputs are constant in time and equal for both old and new goods.

If efficiency gains related to old products are different between process innovators and non-process innovators, and that firms may implement both[1] process and product innovations- the econometric model can be written as:

---

[1] in which case process innovation can affect the efficiency of old and new products Hall et al. (2008)

COMPLEMENTARITIES BETWEEN PRODUCT AND PROCESS INNOVATION

$$l_i - y_{1i} = \alpha_0 + \alpha_1 d_1 + (B_0 + B_1 d_2)y_{2i} + \mu_i, i = 1, \ldots, N_{firms} \qquad (5)$$

where:

- l_i is the rate of employment growth between the year t = 1 and t = 2
- y_{1i} and y_{2i} are the corresponding rates of output growth for old and new products respectively.
- B_0 is the relative efficiency of the production of old and new products.
- α_0 is the negative of the average efficiency growth in the production of the old products. This indicates that non-process innovators can achieve efficiency gains through learning, and improvements in human capital, among others.
- α_1 is the average efficiency growth for process innovators
- d_1 is a dummy which takes the value of 1 if the firm implements an innovation in a process and it is not associated with product innovation.
- d2 taking the value of 1 if the firm implements simultaneously a process and product innovation.

I proposed an extended model specification augmented by an efficiency variable, to account for the relative efficiency of firms.

$$l_i - y_{1i} = \alpha_0 + \alpha_1 f + \alpha_2 d_1 + (B_0 + B_1 d_2)y_{2i} + trend + \mu_i$$

$$i = 1, \ldots, N_{firms} \qquad (6)$$

where:

- f is the relative efficiency in the production of the firms
- trend is a variable accounting for the trend in the product growth, innovation and efficiency gains.

From the data it is not possible to observe the real growth of sales (y_i) but the nominal increase of total sales). Therefore, instead of using sales of products y_{1i} this article uses the deflated growth of sales g_{1i} (see Hall et al. 2008; Harrison et al. 2014).

Since y_{2i} is not directly observed then the model uses the increase of sales of new products g_{2i}. Therefore, sales in period 2 can be divided into sales growth due to old products) and sales growth due to new products (g_{2i}). Note that from the EDIT survey, it is possible to observe the share of turnover of new products (S_{it}) for firms that innovate. So it is possible to estimate the growth of sales of new products as $g_{2i} = s * (1 + gSales)$ where gSales is the deflated growth of sales of the production of old products.

I include a binary indicator for process innovators only and another one for simultaneous process and product innovators (d_2). However, it is not possible to quantify how much of the process innovation applies to old or new products in the case where the firm innovates both on process and product. Therefore, I performed a preliminary empirical exercise on equation 5 with alternative specifications to consider process[2] innovation and the final preferred equation is the following:

$$L = l_i - g_{1i} = \alpha_0 + \alpha_1 d_2 + (B_0 + B_1 d_2)g_{2i} + \mu_i, i = 1, \ldots, N_{firms} \qquad (7)$$

where the $d_2 y_2$ capture the interaction of simultaneous process and product innovation with the growth of new products. This assumes that the process innovation is related to the introduction of new products and B_1

---

[2] the estimates suggested no evidence of significant employment displacement effects from firms that only introduce process innovation since the coefficient for the dummy variable of process innovation was not statistically significant and therefore I did not include it in the final specification on equation 7

Annex 2 measures the effect.

Annex 2 Stochastic frontier analysis

I estimated the relative efficiency of the firms using Stochastic Frontier Analysis. To study efficiency requires introducing a frontier production process relative to which efficiency can be measured (Baltagi, 2015). Technical efficiency refers to the ability of a firm to obtain the maximum output from given inputs (Coelli et al., 2005). The technical efficiency of a given firm may have different definitions, this paper follows Battese and Coelli (1992) and considers technical efficiency as the ratio of "its mean production (conditional on its levels of factor inputs and firm effects) to the corresponding mean production if the firm utilizes its levels of inputs more efficiently".

In this paper, I use the stochastic frontier analysis to predict efficiency effects by measuring technical efficiency as the ratio of observed output compared to the corresponding stochastic frontier output (Coelli et al., 2005).

This measure of efficiency takes a value between zero and one depending on the distance of the output of the i-th firm relative to the output produced by a fully efficient firm with the same inputs. This estimated variable corresponds to f.

The production function used to estimate the stochastic frontier production for the manufacturing sector in Colombia is a translog production function in which the inefficiency effect is a time-varying decay model. The translog functional form is a second-order log-linear form with all cross terms included, and it is flexible since it allows the data to indicate the curvature of the function. The specification of the stochastic frontier production function for the panel estimated in Table A1 with a time-varying decay model is:

$$lnY_{it} = B_0 + lnY_{t-1} + lnC + lnL + lnIbruta + lnCL + lnCibr + lnLibr + lnL2 + lnC2 + lnIbr2 + v_{it} + u_{it}$$

where Y represents the total value of sales of production ; C includes consumption of intermediate goods, energy and raw materials; L is the number of workers and $Ibruta$ is investment. It also includes the interaction of the variables, the square of the variables and the lag of Y

All the estimated coefficients are statistically significant (Table A1). The parameters in the translog production function do not represent output elasticities, hence I must use a linear combination of frontier parameters to compute elasticities.

The estimate of η in the model shows a negative sign which means that inefficiency increases over time (see Battese and Coelli, 1992).

COMPLEMENTARITIES BETWEEN PRODUCT AND PROCESS INNOVATION

Table A1 Time decay frontier model

Ln y	Coef	Std. Err.
lny_l	0.0179***	0.0014
lnC	-0.3049***	0.0220
lnL	1.1543***	0.0261
lnlbruta	0.0222*	0.0096
lnCL	-0.0889***	0.0024
lnCibr	-0.0028**	0.0009
lnLibr	0.0041**	0.0013
lnL2	0.1017***	0.0045
lnC2	0.0930***	0.0020
lnlbr2	0.0015*	0.0007
_period...2010	0.0300***	0.0053
_period...2012	0.0910***	0.0067
_period...2014	0.1275***	0.0087
_period...2016	0.1852***	0.0111
consta.nt	10.5832***	0.1691
μ	1.5805	0.0966
η	-0.1042	0.0011
$\ln(\sigma_s^2) = \sigma_\mu^2 + \sigma_\upsilon^2$	-2.1097	0.0129
/ilgtgamma	0.4667	0.0262
σ_s^2	0.1212	0.0015
$\gamma = \frac{\sigma_\mu^2}{\sigma_s^2}$	0.6146	0.0062
σ_μ^2	0.07453	0.0015
σ_υ^2	0.0467	0.0005

∂ OPEN ACCESS

Penrose's theory of the firm in an era of globalisation

Chia Huay Lau and Jonathan Michie

ABSTRACT
Penrose analysed why some firms succeed in growing – what the factors are that enable growth, and the ways in which success can breed success, with enhanced capabilities enabling growing market share (or sales), and with increased revenues and profitability enabling those capabilities to be further developed. There is a separate question as to why firms expand their operations internationally. In this paper, we analyse a sector that in Edith Penrose's day operated almost exclusively domestically, namely the 'consulting engineering' sector. We consider why firms in this sector are now increasingly operating internationally. In doing so, we consider whether the factors identified – by Penrose and others – as causing firms to grow are also relevant to the expansion of these firms overseas. Our findings support Penrose's Resource-based Theory, which argues that unique strategic resources that are inimitable and non-substitutable can provide firms with competitive advantages. Internationalisation provides consulting engineering firms with the opportunities to explore and obtain different kinds of expertise and resources from other regions. With a larger pool of expertise to draw from, firms can develop their firm-specific strategic assets and technical advantages.

1. Introduction

What causes firms to grow, and what causes firms to expand their operations overseas? These are important questions, which are related yet distinct. The question as to why firms grow, and what causes this growth, has always been a fundamental question for economists. Central to Adam Smith's discussion of the *Wealth of Nations* was the process by which the growth of the firm created the basis for the increased division of labour which in turn enabled and facilitated productivity growth and hence cost reductions, with the concomitantly lower prices enabling increased sales, in other words increased markets (whether increased market share or an expanded market, or both). This theory linking the division of labour and the extent of the market was conducted implicitly within a national context. Competition between firms was implicitly assumed to be between firms within the locality or region. Similarly with Marshall's analysis of industrial districts: these were implicitly regions within the country.

Penrose's work likewise analysed and described why some firms succeed in growing – what the factors are that enable some firms to succeed, and the ways in which success can

---

This is an Open Access article distributed under the terms of the Creative Commons Attribution-NonCommercial-NoDerivatives License (http://creativecommons.org/licenses/by-nc-nd/4.0/), which permits non-commercial re-use, distribution, and reproduction in any medium, provided the original work is properly cited, and is not altered, transformed, or built upon in any way.

breed success, with enhanced capabilities enabling growing market share (or sales), with increased revenues and profitability enabling those capabilities to be further developed. All the above analyses, from Adam Smith to Edith Penrose, can be pursued within the context of a national economy.

There is then a separate question of why firms expand their operations internationally and globally. In this article, we analyse a sector that in Edith Penrose's day did indeed operate almost exclusively domestically, with none of the companies in the sector operating much overseas, namely the 'consulting engineering' sector. We consider why firms in this sector are now increasingly operating internationally and globally. In doing so, we consider whether the factors identified – by Penrose and others – as causing firms to grow are also relevant to the expansion of those firms overseas and globally.[1]

We also consider the nature of firms' decision-making regarding the *international location* of their activities, and their choice as between *co-operating with other firms* already based in overseas locations, as opposed to *establishing their own overseas subsidiaries*. We analyse these issues using existing data sets, and by analysing data generated through our own questionnaire surveys and follow-up interviews. Williamson (1975) in his Transaction Cost Theory argues that it is likely for firms to internalise the transaction within its own organisation and structure of governance when they are faced with the risk of opportunism by other parties, when there are limited numbers of partners to choose from, and uncertain or complex market condition. Dunning (1989) in his research on the importance of transaction costs in explaining the growth of multinational service activities, finds that foreign direct investment tends to be the preferred entry mode for professional services activities rather than by contractual relationships due to the risk of imitation once competitors have access to the knowledge and geographical diversification which provides advantages to firms. We research the choice of foreign direct investment (FDI), joint venture (JV), and acquisition. Rugman (1979), and Miller and Pras (1980) argue that foreign operations stabilise overall returns due to the fact that different economic conditions tend to be uncorrelated across different international markets; we also study the effect of internationalisation on firm performance.

2. The literature

Penrose (1959) argued in *The Theory of the Growth of the Firm* that while firm size is a by-product of growth, there is no necessary limit to the growth of firms, which will depend rather on 'enterprising managers' and administrative effectiveness, whilst being limited by the extent of the growth of knowledge within the firm. Thus, Penrose argued that the growing experience of management, its knowledge of the resources within the firm, and the potential of using these in different ways, creates opportunities for further expansion of the firm. For Penrose, there is no necessary reason why a firm should limit the prospects of growth and productive opportunities to its existing markets, and from this follows a theory of diversification where firms may expand internationally when the existing market becomes less profitable and the prospect of new markets become more attractive. Hence, *The Theory of the Growth of the Firm* sets out the forces that would lead one to expect firms – including consulting engineering firms – to expand internationally, and what the factors are that both encourage and restrict that process.

Dunning's Eclectic Theory explains the influence of ownership (O), location (L) and institution (I) advantages on the international production of firms, postulating that firms must possess advantages specific to the nature or nationality of their ownership to compete with local firms of the host country, and these advantages must be sufficient to compensate for the cost of setting up and operating in host countries. Dunning (1988) and Kogut (1985) argue that firms carry out international operations if there are transaction gains likely to result from the common governance of activities in different locations, including enhanced arbitrage and leverage opportunities, market hedging, better coordination of financial decisions, multiple-sourcing strategy, the possibility of gains through transfer price manipulation, leads and lags in payments, and so on. There are also long-term factors which will influence whether firms invest in foreign countries such as the size of the domestic market, geographical distance between the home country and its market, psychic distance, and the industrial structure of investment (Dunning 1979). The 'internalisation theory' of Buckley and Casson (2009) posits that firms will internalise the market when the expected benefits of doing so outweigh the expected costs, and that this will be influenced by exogenous factors such as policy changes and technological improvements, which may thus encourage the globalisation of firms.[2]

There are similarities between the Eclectic Theory, the Transaction Cost Theory and the Internalisation Theory in explaining the root cause of the internationalisation of firms, where the focus has been predominantly on lowering transaction costs or achieving cost efficiency and to protect and utilise firm specific advantages. The key motives for consulting engineering firms (CEFs) to internationalise are for market seeking and future growth, and to gain transaction cost benefits and improve cost efficiency via production in lower cost countries. Thus, this paper focuses on both the tangible and intangible benefits which encourage the internationalisation of services firms, such as the desire to develop a global brand, and enhance their international reputation. Firms capitalise on their internationalisation activities to develop further firm-specific advantages, and thus to increase the resilience of their business operations.

The Real Options Theory and Penrose's *The Theory of the Growth of the Firm* argue that internationalisation provides firms with options for future growth due to the increase in market size. Internationalisation may provide firms with opportunities to develop their position in the international market, to capitalise on their global branding, and increase their resilience in the face of different economic cycles in different world regions. The internationalisation of consulting engineering firms has been a strategic response of firms to international market opportunities, not merely a process of optimising transaction costs or protecting firm-specific advantages – rather, it has enabled firms to *augment* their firm-specific advantages and promote future growth.

The 1977 Uppsala Model and Real Options Theory suggest that a foreign direct investment (or organic growth) strategy provides firms with the opportunity for incremental investment and learning when internationalising. Contractor, Kundu, and Hsu (2003), Lu and Beamish (2004) and Abdelzaher (2012) argued that professional services firms are more likely to follow a meore cautious internationalisation process due to the unique features of professional services. However, Buckley and Casson (2009) argued that firms can be born global and do not have to internationalise incrementally, which is relevant for consulting engineering firms since the capital investment involved in FDI for a consulting engineering firm is usually lower than for a manufacturing firm due to the nature of the services offered, enabling them to expand internationally at a more rapid pace. Also, information and communication technologies enable firms to set up a regional office to serve several countries within the same region at once, again leapfrogging the incremental expansion process.

Johanson and Vahlne (2009) in the context of the 2009 Uppsala model, argued that a firm's internationalisation strategy is likely to be influenced by its existing relationships and networks, and that a functioning business relationship could be considered as an asset which can provide advantages to firms involved. This could be relevant to the internationalisation of consulting engineering firms, where firms have decided either to follow their client to invest abroad using the FDI strategy, or to involve a joint venture investment arrangement with their existing business partner to capitalise on the market knowledge or network of their client or partner. Johanson and Vahlne argue, in the context of the 2006 Uppsala Model on commitment and opportunity development, that an acquisition is more likely to be successful following exchanges between the acquirer and acquiree to establish the commitment between the two parties.

Brouthers and Brouthers show that the cost of governing a partner in a joint venture arrangement will have an impact on the survival of foreign subsidiaries. In the context of the entry mode choice of consulting engineering firms, the effect of transaction costs could become significant when firms are involved in international joint ventures (i.e. forming a consortium with other international competitors on large scale projects), or when firms are involved in mergers or acquisitions. The effect of transaction costs in governing an FDI is expected to be less significant for consulting engineering firms due to the nature of the services offered (i.e. there is no requirement to set up manufacturing facilities).

Williamson (1975) postulates that firms will internalise their transactions where there is a risk of opportunism by others. This argument highlights the importance of the level of control in affecting the internationalisation strategy of firms. A higher level of control is required where the investment involves the intellectual properties of firms, and where there is also a high risk of appropriation by others. This is particularly important for consulting engineering firms due to the nature of the services provided and the intellectual properties involved in the process.

Johanson and Vahlne (2009) argue that the lack of knowledge of firms during internationalisation may affect their perception of the cost of internationalisation. The Real Options Theory argues that real options provide firms with the flexibility of whether to undertake any future investment when new information becomes available. The International Diversification Theory postulates that a multinational corporation has a lower systematic risk relative to similar domestic firms. Rugman (1979), and Miller and Pras (1980) propose that foreign operations have the effect of stabilising overall returns of firms, as economic conditions tend to be uncorrelated across different international markets.

3. Research questions and methods

It is clear that when it comes to the theory of the growth of the firm into overseas markets, a key gap in our knowledge arises from a comparative lack of detailed analysis and application of theories of multinational (or transnational) enterprises to *knowledge intensive service sector* industries, as compared with production sectors. This paper therefore considers why firms internationalise, what are the factors affecting their internationalisation strategies, and how internationalisation affects the performance of – and risks faced by – firms, focussing specifically on the 'consulting engineering' sector.

Financial data for UK based consulting engineering firms were obtained from the FAME database. In addition, questionnaires were distributed to the top 50 UK-based consulting engineering firms (ranked by total revenue), with follow up interviews to collect information on factors affecting the firm's internationalisation decision. Questionnaire returns were received from 20 firms (a 40% return). Of these, 70% (fourteen firms) participated in the follow-up interviews.

4. Results: factors driving internationalisation

Globalisation has changed the landscape of the professional services sector. Historically professional services firms were small local organisations where services were delivered locally to consumers. To serve clients who are themselves already global, services firms are building their integrated 'global professional networks' so that they can provide services in countries which their clients operate (Brock 2012).

We analysed the financial data of the top 50 UK based consulting engineering firms, finding 55% received over 50% of their income from overseas activities. We found a positive correlation between internationalisation and firm performance. The question of why they internationalise, and the factors affecting the internationalisation outcomes were then put to the top management of consulting engineering firms via a questionnaire, with follow-up interviews to gather further information and insight. These interviews revealed a series of internal and external factors promoting internationalisation: internal stimuli factors included to provide growth options or opportunities for future growth; increase performance, turnover and profitability; gain or increase international economic and technical advantages through internalisation; gain or increase international competitiveness and market share; develop or enhance international reputation and brand image; reduce risk through achieving greater geographical diversification; and support global clients. External stimuli factors included competition in the domestic market, the home market economic condition, and the economic growth of foreign regions. This is consistent with Barkema and Vermeulen (1998), Hitt, Hoskinson, and Kim (1997), Lu and Beamish (2001), and Vermeulen and Barkema (2001), who suggest firms internationalise to seek revenue growth opportunities, compete against global competitors, increase market power, support global customers, access global knowledge leading to stronger capabilities and innovation, and achieve efficiency in managing value-chain activities through economies of scale and scope.

Firms were asked to rate the importance of having an overseas presence based on the following factors, with 1 being the least significant and 5 being the most significant: turnover, market share, profitability, brand image, reputation, overall performance, and future growth. All had an average score of 3.5 or above, with a median and mode score of 4 or above. Firms perceived internationalisation as a long-term investment strategy that provides opportunities for the future growth of their firms. 'Brand image' and 'reputation' had mean scores of 4.26 and 3.96 respectively. Our questionnaire data were then analysed using the Likert-type Scale Method based on a sample of 25 respondents: the S score is obtained by summation across all the weighted categories; N is the number of

Table 1. Summary of qualitative research analysis.

The importance of having an overseas presence

	Average scores	Likert-scale analysis Z-scores
Turnover	3.92	3.32 (p-value= 0.0005)
Market share	3.50	1.91 (p-value= 0.0281)
Profitability	3.54	2.05 (p-value= 0.0202)
Overall performance	3.92	3.18 (p-value= 0.0007)
Brand image	4.26	4.40 (p-value= 0.00003)
Reputation	3.96	3.46 (p-value= 0.0003)
Future growth	4.58	5.59 (p-value= 0.00003)

respondents; r is the number of equally-spaced categories; V is the variance; and the Z score is calculated as: $Z = (S-(N(r + 1))2)/(\sqrt{N}(r^2-1)/12)$. Table 1 summarises our results:

4.1. Market seeking

The internationalisation of services firms can be reactive (demand-oriented) or proactive (market-seeking) (Majkgard and Sharma 1998; Sharma 1989; as cited in Krull, Smith, and Ge 2012). The reactive strategy is sometimes referred to as the 'client following strategy' where firms follow and customise their services to a key client's requirement to invest overseas. Professional services firms are often dependent on a set of key clients whom they are likely to follow into new markets. Cohen (2007), Inkpen and Ramaswamy (2005) and Abdelzaher (2012) have highlighted the benefits for firms of the 'client following strategy'. Firms were asked in the questionnaires the significance of 'turnover' and 'market share' in their internationalisation decisions. The Z score of 3.32 is significant at .01 level and the value of S = 98 is significantly greater than the expected value of E(S) = 75. So, increasing the turnover of their firms is one of the factors driving their overseas presence. And with a Z score of 1.91 significant at .01 level and the value of S = 88 significantly greater than the expected value of E(S) = 75, increasing 'market share' was a significant motive. Firms reported that internationalisation also increased opportunities in the home country, providing services required by foreign clients in the home country market. The proactive strategy emphasises that firms create competitive advantages by actively seeking new markets and clients (Bagchi-Sen and Kuechler 2000; Erramilli 1990; Erramilli and Rao 1990).

4.2. Efficiency seeking

The interviews indicated a key reason to expand internationally is for efficiency enhancement. Internationalisation provided firms with a higher degree of human asset fluidity and efficiency. Due to the different economic cycles in different world regions, firms with international offices have the flexibility of moving work around different world regions to improve their resource and cost management, providing firms with a higher degree of resilience during economic downturns.

4.3. Strategic asset seeking

Strategic asset seeking foreign direct investment relies on the intellectual capital of firms being located in more than one country, and that it is economically preferable for firms to acquire or create these assets outside, rather than within, their home countries (Dunning and Lundan 2008). According to 'resource-based theory', firms gain competitive advantage by possessing unique strategic resources that are inimitable and non-substitutable. This includes firm-specific resources, capabilities, competencies, and access to markets (Barney 1991; Barney, Wright, and Ketchen 2001; Peng 2001; Teece 2009).

4.4. Ownership advantages

Firms were asked about the importance of internationalisation in enhancing their 'reputation', for which the Z score of 3.46 was significant at .01 level and the value of S = 99 is significantly greater than the expected value of E(S) = 75. Porter (1980, cited in Child, Faulkner, and Tallman 2005) argued that the relative position that firms occupy within their industry's structure determines the generic strategies that are the most viable and profitable for them. Firms were asked in the questionnaires the importance of internationalisation in enhancing the 'brand image' of firms. The analysis indicates the Z score of 4.40 is significant at .01 level and the value of S = 102 is significantly greater than the expected value of E(S) = 72. Our interviews confirmed the importance of being internationally recognised. Working internationally with signature architects and global clients provides firms with international portfolios and brand building opportunities. Aronson (2007), in his research on the upsurge in mergers of services firms, provided a similar argument, rejecting the claim that internationalisation is simply a response to client demand for global service delivery or 'one-stop shopping' – he argues that the difficulty in measuring the quality of services means professional services firms have to compete on the basis of reputation.

Knickerbocker (1973), and Graham (1978, cited in Li and Guisinger 1992) suggest that MNEs often adopt a 'follow the leader' or 'exchange of threats' in their foreign investment strategy to secure competitive advantages over their competitors or as a defence strategy against their competitors. The 'Industry-based view' argued that the right positioning of firms in the industry leads to their competitive advantages (Krull, Smith, and Ge 2012). Internationalisation also provides consulting engineering firms with the access to different types of expertise from other world regions, and it is an effective strategy for firms to gain or secure their international competitiveness. This is consistent with Inkpen and Ramaswamy's (2005) argument that gaining access to knowledge outside the home country is often a strategic necessity for survival in the knowledge-based industry.

4.5. International diversification

Interviews revealed a main reason for cross-border investment is for risk diversification and mitigation. This is consistent with Rugman's Risk Diversification Theory (Rugman 1979), which suggested that MNEs will normally prefer to geographically spread the portfolio of their foreign investments. International investments provide options for firms to deal with unanticipated changes that would otherwise pose risk (Sanchez 1993, 1995). For example, firms with offices in Asia and Australasia were able to bring work back into the UK from countries with stronger growth, such as China and Australia, during the UK recession in 2009. Building on Real Options Theory, networks of international investments of firms provide valuable options for addressing uncertainty in any given market (Allen and Pantzalis 1996; Tang and Tikoo 1999). The multinational investments of MNEs can be viewed as a collection of valuable options that permit the choice of moving activities from one country to another (Kogut and Kulatilaka 1994).

4.6. Growth options and future growth

Internationalisation provides growth opportunities by deploying resources and capabilities in new areas (Canals 1999). Firms were asked about the importance of internationalisation for firm growth, with the Z score of 5.59 significant at .01 level and the value of $S = 114$ significantly greater than the expected value of $E(S) = 75$. Kogut (1983, 1989) stresses the importance of international firms having options to tap into growth opportunities in different countries which firms with only domestic operations do not.

4.7. Optimum size of firm

The literature shows that firm size has a positive impact on the international behaviour of services industries (Terpstra and Yu 1988; cited in Li and Guisinger 1992). Our interviews confirmed that internationalisation provides firms with opportunities such as access to funding, and bigger bases to absorb risks. These factors enable larger firms to make investments in high risk, unexplored markets to gain first-mover advantage – as with Kulatilaka and Perotti's (1998) study of strategic growth options, where under uncertainty and imperfect competition, firms that make early investments in a new market can gain a competitive advantage by pre-empting future growth opportunities.

5. Internationalisation strategy

Entry mode choice is contingent on a range of factors including the level of ownership or control, the level of commitment, firm size, the level of risk, international experience, market size, psychic distance and the nature of local market and competition (Rosenbaum and Madsen 2012; Hsieh, Shen, and Lee 2010; Madhok 1996). Entry modes with a higher degree of control will provide safeguards against opportunism (Oxley 1997, 1999; Williamson 1985). Rosenbaum and Madsen (2012), researching the foreign entry mode choice of professional services firms, find firms prefer high control entry modes when there are uncertainties, such as when partnering with unfamiliar firms and when the services delivered involve a high degree of tacit knowledge. Erramilli and

Rao (1993) observed that firms have a lower tendency to share the control of their foreign operation if it involves high-intensity capital investment. Erramilli (1991) postulates a U-shape relationship between experiential knowledge and the tendency of firms to adopt high control entry modes during internationalisation. Daniels, Ogram, and Radebaugh (1976) and Shetty (1979, cited in Erikson et al. 1997) report a shift toward licensing and joint ventures as the experiential knowledge of firms grew. Davidson and McFetridge (1985) and Hedlund and Kverneland (1985, cited in Erikson et al. 1997) showed a decrease in the reliance on wholly owned subsidiaries as the foreign experience of firms increases. International business scholars such as Contractor, Kundu, and Hsu (2003), Lu and Beamish (2004) and Abdelzaher (2012) argue that professional services firms are more likely to follow a cautious internationalisation process. Our interviews certainly indicated that the entry mode choice and internationalisation strategy of firms are influenced by the nature of the services offered, and the market and the client it is targeting.

Consulting engineering firms were asked in our questionnaire to provide information on the entry mode choice of their international investments, and about the number of acquisitions, joint ventures and foreign direct investments they had been involved with. Foreign direct investment was the most frequently used entry mode (73 in total), followed by acquisition and joint venture (with a total of 69 each). There was no consistent influence of firm size on entry mode choice.

5.1. Internationalisation stages

Based on our interviews, the internationalisation process of firms consists of four stages: exploration, initial implementation, consolidation, and growth. Internationalisation strategy of firms could be either systematic or ad-hoc. The systematic approach includes conducting formal strategic planning and market research, considering different countries and entry modes, and developing risk management strategies for long-term investment. However, there are occasions where consulting engineering firms were required to adopt an ad-hoc internationalisation strategy, such as when the firm has to follow an existing client, or where a firm is faced with competition and ad-hoc investment is required in order to protect the firm's advantages.

5.2. International joint venture (IJV)

Dunning (1993) defined cooperative alliances as cooperative relationships between firms, rather than market or hierarchical relationship. Child, Faulkner, and Tallman (2005) refer to cooperative strategies as attempts by firms to realise their goals through cooperation. Cooperative alliances provide firms with the opportunities to have a pool of complementary strengths and to secure creative synergies between them. The rationale behind the cooperative strategy is that it allows firms the opportunities to seek particular competencies or resources that they lack, by securing the competencies through links with other firms. The cooperative alliance also makes it easier for firms to gain access to new markets, and to acquire opportunities for mutual learning and internalising of knowledge flow without incurring the full set-up costs of a merger (Buckley and Casson 1996). For example, firms may gain access to the partner's advanced technology, or may share the cost of developing new technologies through research and development. Child, Faulkner, and Tallman (2005) argue that cooperation with competitors may enhance a firm's position in the industry – it could be a defensive alliance against dominant firms, or an offensive alliance with stronger competitors. There are also scenarios, for example in some developing countries where partnering with local firms is the only way of entering the market.

For Child, Faulkner, and Tallman (2005) and Kanter (1989), alliances are partnerships between firms which are normally formed as a strategic response to major challenges or opportunities that the partners face. There are three fundamental types of alliances: Multi-company service consortia – normally to create a pool of resources to meet the requirement of large-scale activities; Opportunistic alliances – where each partner supplies the competencies that the other lacks; and Stakeholder alliances – usually between companies at different points of the value chain.

Our interviewees reported the following stimuli factors for IJVs. Firstly, internal: Economic advantages – partnering firms share resources and costs to achieve economies of scale and to lower transaction costs through vertical integration; Risk sharing – notably in terms of capital requirements, and the opportunity to spread financial risk; Complementary alliance and resources dependency – sharing of technical or niche technical resources; Risk mitigation – IJVs were predominantly project-specific, providing firms opportunities for a swift withdrawal from the investment when required; Strategic advantages – to gain access to the partnering firm's specific assets, or to gain complementary skills and technical expertise; Geographical coverage – IJVs provide firms with a wider geographical presence. Secondly, external: IJV reduces the capital investment of partnering firms in comparison to a wholly owned arrangement, therefore reducing the financial risk to firms; and restrictive government policy or other barriers to a foreign market, which an IJV may overcome.

The key findings from our interviews were largely consistent with the existing literature, such as Kogut (1989), Child, Faulkner, and Tallman (2005) and Faulkner (1995), where the basic motivations for a joint venture are to lower transaction costs, gain a strategic position and enhance market power, gain additional resources and acquire organisational learning opportunities, and to spread financial risk. However, interviewees also highlighted the 'country factor', where an IJV was seen as the only option to access the local market due to government policy and investment restrictions applied to foreign firms.

Firms may be able to get a large share of a market early on through an IJV (Child, Faulkner, and Tallman 2005). There are two common motives for IJV arrangement by consulting engineering firms: firstly, joint ventures with similar sized international or local competitors to access a local market or to bid for major international projects; and secondly joint ventures with local firms with good technical skills in lower cost developing countries to achieve cost efficiency in design production. Efficiency-seeking IJVs amongst consulting engineering firms in developing countries are becoming increasingly popular, with medium or small-scale consulting engineering firms using a joint venture with local firms in developing countries to set up production offices. Firms reported that while transaction costs would have an impact on the consideration for entry mode choice, transaction costs on their own is unlikely to be sufficient to determine the entry mode choice, and firms will take into consideration the intangible benefits of joint ventures, such as gaining fast-track access to a certain market, risk sharing, or acquiring resources.

One of the significant factors leading towards a joint venture strategy, as opposed to acquisition or FDI and organic growth, is the requirement of firms to **limit risk**. Child, Faulkner, and Tallman (2005) argue that globalisation and international economic uncertainties are stimuli for alliance formation. There are two main types of risks that consulting engineering firms face when internationalising: financial risks associated with the investment of firms when internationalising, and operational and reputational risks that arise due to insufficient local knowledge and experience when operating in the host country. Our interviews found that one of the main risks faced by firms when internationalising is having insufficient local knowledge and experience of operating in the market, including an insufficient understanding of the local client base, local institutional arrangements, and local design standards. Cross-border collaborations with local firms allow them to develop vital knowledge and capabilities for their operations in foreign markets and to acquire knowledge about international markets. This is consistent with Child's, Faulkner, and Tallman (2005) argument that cross-border collaboration is likely to increase the chances of success of firms in foreign markets – and is directly and positively linked to the internationalisation of knowledge-based services firms.

Our interviewees reported that due to the cyclical nature of the economy across world regions and the inconsistency of the availability of opportunities, consulting engineering firms may require to be a 'hunter' (where firms bid for projects in a country and move on after completing the project), rather than a 'farmer' involving longer-term investment. The key advantages of IJVs is speed to set up, and being carried out on a project-by-project basis. This is consistent with Faulkner's research findings (Faulkner 1995) where he reported that the speed to market is an important factor. Consulting engineering firms also viewed IJVs as a 'transitory arrangement' in a situation where there is a lack of knowledge or understanding of a specific market, the absence of a local network and when it is necessary for firms to cooperate with local firms to start working in the country. In an IJV arrangement, collaboration with local partners provides firms with opportunities to learn about the market and to access the local network of clients.

A joint venture may provide a firm with the opportunities to learn about a technology, product, or market in a way that allows the entrant access to some share of the current revenue stream, and full access to developing knowledge about the putative investment, all for a fraction of the investment of a full acquisition. The capital saved can be used for further investment in the future when uncertainties are reduced or when the investment offers a more positive future outcome. If the joint venture investment fails to perform, the firm has the option of selling the share to a third party or the joint venture can be dissolved. This has, therefore, provided firms with greater flexibility than does either outright ownership or an alternative involving no equity stake (Buckley and Ghauri 2004). Our interviewees saw cooperative alliances as an option for firms to learn more about the market with a relatively small amount of investment and without any major commitment. IJVs with local firms had provided them with opportunities to learn about the foreign market and as a preparatory strategy for setting up their own offices in the future, at a lower level of investment in comparison to greenfield investment or acquisition. IJVs provide firms with access to local networks of clients and the opportunity to understand local institutional arrangements.

5.3. Merger and acquisition

Kogut and Singh (1988) defined acquisition as 'the purchase of stock in an already existing company in an amount sufficient to confer control'. Acquisition can be a strategic option for consolidation and reorganisation, as a vehicle for growth and could also be a form of cooperation strategy with other players in the industry (Faulkner, Teerikangas, and Joseph 2012). Interviewees reported gaining immediate access to a new market or opportunities as the main reason for acquisitions. Despite the increasing popularity of mergers and acquisitions in recent years amongst larger firms, the majority of firms interviewed indicated that acquisition is a less preferred strategy in comparison to the joint venture or foreign direct investment due to the risk of integration failure and the risk of diluting the company's culture post-merger. This is supported by several other research studies of companies post-merger (King et al. 2004; Schoenberg 2006) – that acquiring firms create little or no value from M&A and most of the firms engaging in M&A activity did not achieve the sought-after performance targets. Interviewees reported the main benefits from M&A as being to gain immediate access to new markets, create an immediate boost to the share price of listed firms, acquire new capabilities, enhance the brand and reputation of firms, enhance value creation of firms, and reduce the effect of country-specific factors, such as the psychic distance between the home and host country. Based on the resource-based view, cross-border M&A provides firms entry into foreign countries to acquire local resources (human resources, technology and local business networks) and to gain access to government officials (Barney 1991; Sirmon, Hitt, and Ireland 2007).

5.4. Foreign direct investment (FDI)

87% of interviewees reported FDI as their main internationalisation strategy. FDI is an organic expansion strategy and is perceived by firms as a low risk and low capital investment strategy. The international office is usually set up to follow clients, to work on major international projects. During the project delivery stage, firms could explore the new international market and decide whether there are sufficient opportunities for them to remain in the host country or region, once existing commissions have been completed. One of the key distinguishing features of greenfield FDI investment, when compared to the acquisition or IJV, is that it is established from scratch and does not come with established workers and practices. Our interviews with large UK based international consulting engineering firms revealed that non-listed consulting engineering firms tend to prefer FDI in comparison to acquisition or IJV due to the flexibilities it offers. FDIs can be created to suit the need and culture of the parent company and allow firms to grow at an acceptable pace.

6. Internationalisation and firm performance, economic growth, and firm size

This section investigates the effect of firms' internationationalisation on their performance, and considers the factors affecting the decision by firms to internationalise, such as economic growth and firm size. OLS regressions were used to investigate the correlation between internationalisation and firm performance, UK and world economic growth, and firm size. A sample of 50 top consulting engineering firms from the FAME database, 2000 to 2010 were used for the fixed effect panel estimation. The sample is an unbalanced panel; the database was missing financial data for some firms in some periods, and the firms with too many periods of missing data were dropped. Profit after tax was used as a measure of performance, and overseas revenue was used to measure the firm's international investment. Other explanatory variables were the firm's total assets and liabilities, firm size (measured by number of staff), and UK and world GDP growth, with a dummy variable for the financial crisis (year 2009 with recession = 1; all other years without recession = 0)(Table 2).

6.1. Internationalisation and firm performance

To examine the determinants of internationalisation, we considered:

$$LogPATax_{it} = B_i + B_1LogTORev_{it} + B_2LogTAsset_{it} + B_3LogTLiab_{it} + B_4NoStaff_{it} + B_5UKGDP_{it} + B_6WGDP_{it} + FinCris_t + \varepsilon_{it} \tag{1}$$

A summary of the OLS regression results is presented in Table 3. The OLS analysis indicates that the variables are statistically significant, and the regression model has explanatory power. Firms with higher overseas revenues tend to have higher post-tax profits, even when controlling for their size (measured by assets, liabilities, staff numbers), other trends in the economy (GDP, etc), and factors specific to each firm (eliminated by the fixed effects regression). The highest-performing firms are those most likely to be able to compete internationally; whatever the direction of causation, there's a positive association between firm performance and internationalisation.

6.2. Firm internationalisation, the home country, and world economic growth

$$LogTORev_{it} = B_i + B_1LogTAsset_{it} + B_2LogTLiab_{it} + B_3NoStaff_{it} + B_4UKGDP_{it} + B_5WGDP_{it} + FinCris_t + \varepsilon_{it} \tag{2}$$

Table 2. Table of variables (definition and source).

Variables	Definition and Source of Data
LogPATax	Log of annual profit of firms after tax (1 unit = £1m) (Source: FAME database and firm's annual report)
LogTORev	Log of annual overseas revenue of firms (1 unit = £1m) (Source: FAME database and firm's annual report)
LogTAsset	Log of total asset of firms (1 unit = £1m) (Source: FAME database and firm's annual report)
LogTLiab	Log of total financial liabilities of firms (1 unit = £1m) (Source: FAME database and firm's annual report)
NoStaff	Firm size (measured by number of staff) (Source: firm's annual report)
UKGDP	UK's GDP growth rate (%) (Source: UNCTAD Handbook of Statistics 2017)
WGDP	The world's GDP growth rate (%) (Source: UNCTAD Handbook of Statistics 2017)
FinCris	Financial crisis Year 2009 financial crisis = 1, all other years = 0 with no financial crisis.

Table 3. Summary of OLS regression results.

VARIABLES	Model 1
LogTORev	0.195**
	(0.0822)
LogTAsset	0.857**
	(0.355)
LogTLiab	−0.394
	(0.265)
NoStaff	0.000124***
	(4.65e-05)
UKGDP	−0.225**
	(0.112)
WGDP	0.239***
	(0.0765)
FinCris	−0.454
	(0.525)
Constant	−1.985***
	(0.656)
Observations	239
Number of companies	38
R-squared	0.451

Standard errors in parentheses.
*** $p<0.01$, ** $p<0.05$, * $p<0.1$.

A summary of the OLS regression is presented in Table 4; the variables are statistically significant and the regression model has explanatory power. There is a negative correlation between overseas revenue and UK GDP growth, and a positive correlation between overseas revenue and world GDP growth.

6.3. Internationalisation and firm size

$$LogTORevit = Bi + B1NoStaffit + B2UKGDPit + B3WGDPit + FinCrist + \varepsilon it \quad (3)$$

A summary of the OLS regression is presented in Table 5, with the variables statistically significant and the regression model having explanatory power, indicating a positive correlation between overseas revenue and number of staff. Larger firms may have more capacity to bid for international work, encouraging internationalisation. Conversely, taking on international projects may generate greater profits, allowing the firm to employ more specialists and so raising staff numbers.

6.4. Qualitative analysis

Firms were asked in the questionnaires the importance of internationalisation in influencing the overall performance of their firms(Table 6). The Z score of 3.18 is significant at .01 level and the value of S = 97 is significantly greater than the expected value of E(S) = 75, suggesting overseas presence is correlated with performance.

All those interviewed reported that internationalisation had improved their firm's performance – providing avenues for growth, opportunities to gain firm-specific advantages (economic and technical advantages), and enhanced resilience against external competition and adverse economic conditions. Both the quantitative analysis (of firms' financial data) and the qualitative research (questionnaire analyses and follow-up

Table 4. Summary of the OLS regression.

VARIABLES	Model 1
LogTAsset	0.366
	(0.242)
LogTLiab	0.323*
	(0.187)
NoStaff	2.43e-05
	(3.56e-05)
UKGDP	−0.331***
	(0.0841)
WGDP	0.167***
	(0.0581)
FinCris	−1.076***
	(0.404)
Constant	0.00756
	(0.465)
Observations	279
Number of companies	38
R-squared	0.565

Standard errors in parentheses.
*** $p<0.01$, ** $p<0.05$, * $p<0.1$.

Table 5. Summary of the OLS regression.

VARIABLES	Model 1
NoStaff	0.000151***
	(3.49e-05)
UKGDP	−0.616***
	(0.0796)
WGDP	0.348***
	(0.0578)
FinCris	−1.929***
	(0.413)
Constant	2.208***
	(0.180)
Observations	288
Number of companies	39
R-squared	0.453

Standard errors in parentheses.
*** $p<0.01$, ** $p<0.05$, * $p<0.1$.

interviews) indicated consistent results, that the overall performance of firms is positively correlated to the degree of internationalisation.

Our questionnaire asked whether the 2009 global recession has increased or decreased the degree of internationalisation Table 7. The data were analysed using the Likert-type Scale Method based on a sample of 24 respondents, with the S score obtained by summation across all the weighted categories, N the numbers of respondents, r the numbers of equally-spaced categories, V the variance, and the Z score calculated as $Z = (S- (N(r + 1))2)/(\sqrt{N}(r^2-1)/12)$.

Table 6. Likert-type scale analysis: influence of overall performance on internationalisation.

Overall performance					
Rating	1	2	3	4	5
No. of times this rating was chosen	0	1	8	9	7
Weighted score	0	2	24	36	35
No. of correspondents, $N=$	25				
Summation of all weighted score, $S=$	97				
The expectation of S, $E(S)=$	75				
Variance, Var $(S)=$	50				
z score=	**3.18**	**At 0.01 level, p= 0.0007, <0.05 therefore the Overall Performance factor is significant**			

Table 7. The effect of the 2009 global recession on the degree of internationalisation.

Do you think whether the 2009 recession has increased or decreased the degree of internationalisation of your firm? (1= decreased, 5= increased)					
Rating	1	2	3	4	5
No. of times this rating was chosen	0	3	5	7	9
Weighted score	0	6	15	28	45
No. of correspondents, $N=$	24				
Summation of all weighted score, $S=$	94				
The expectation of S, $E(S)=$	72				
Variance, Var $(S)=$	48				
z score=	**3.25**	**At 0.01 level, p= 0.0007 <0.05 = significant, therefore the 2009 recession has increased the degree of internationalisation**			

The Z score of 3.25 is significant at .01 level and the value of $S = 94$ is significantly greater than the expected value of $E(S) = 72$. The findings are consistent with the quantitative analysis, that the 2009 recession increased internationalisation.

7. Conclusion

We analysed financial data for the top 50 UK based consulting engineering firms to review their internationalisation, and the factors related to this. The question of why they internationalise, and the factors affecting internationalisation outcomes were then put to the top management of consulting engineering firms via both a questionnaire and follow-up interviews. Internal stimuli factors included to provide opportunities for growth; improve the performance, turnover and profitability of firms; gain economic and technical advantages through internalisation; increase international competitiveness and market share; develop international reputation and brand image; reduce risk through greater geographical diversification; and to support global clients. External stimuli factors include the degree of competition in the national market, the home market's economic condition, and the foreign region's economic growth.

These findings support Penrose's theory of the growth of the firm, which argues that unique strategic resources that are inimitable and non-substitutable can provide firms with competitive advantages. Firms can gain sustainable competitive advantages through the accumulation of tangible and intangible resources. Internationalisation was found to provide consulting engineering firms with the opportunities to explore and obtain different kinds of expertise and resources from other regions. With a greater pool of expertise to draw from, firms were able to develop their firm-specific strategic assets and technical advantages in order to ensure the uniqueness of their firms and to distinguish themselves from their competitors.

Our research found that the motives for internationalisation influenced the entry mode choice. Consulting engineering firms viewed FDI as an organic expansion strategy, perceived as a low risk and low capital investment strategy. We found that smaller consulting engineering firms tended to follow their clients to go overseas when internationalising, and to grow their international offices organically in the longer term. We found that larger firms were more likely to adopt acquisition as their internationalisation strategy when entering a new market or region. Acquisitions enable the acquiring firm to obtain immediately a readily available market, framework and skills, and this can be carried out on a large-scale basis. Gaining immediate access to new markets or opportunities was reported by consulting engineering firms as the main reason for their firms pursuing acquisitions. Acquisition of a competing firm with a good track record in both international and local markets may enhance the brand and reputation of the acquiring firm in the host region or country. Our findings in this regard are consistent with the Penrosian resource-based view of the firm.

Notes

1. This paper draws on Chia Huay Lau's DPhil thesis on 'The Global Trading Activities of Consulting Engineering Firms: Managing Risk and Geographical Choice', Kellogg College, University of Oxford, 2019.
2. We take the fact of 'globalisation' as given, but on what that means in practice, see the various authors collected together in Michie (ed.)(2017 and 2019).

Acknowledgment

We are grateful for helpful comments from an anonymous referee and Professor Oughton.

Disclosure statement

No potential conflict of interest was reported by the author(s).

References

Abdelzaher, D. 2012. "The Impact of Professional Services Firms' Challenges on Internationalisation Processes and Performance." *The Service Industries Journal* 32 (10): 1721–1738.

Allen, L., and C. Pantzalis. 1996. "Valuation of the Operating Flexibility of Multinational Corporations." *Journal of International Business Studies* 27 (4): 633–653.

Aronson, B. 2007. "Elite Law Firm Mergers and Reputational Competition: Is Bigger Really Better? An International Comparison." *Vanderbilt Journal of Transnational Law* 40 (3): 763–831.

Bagchi-Sen, S., and L. Kuechler. 2000. "Strategic and Functional Orientation of Small and Medium Sized Enterprises in Professional Services: An Analysis of Public Accountancy." *The Service Industries Journal* 20 (3): 117–146.

Barkema, H., and F. Vermeulen. 1998. "Foreign Entry, Cultural Barriers and Learning." *Strategic Management Journal* 17 (2): 151–166.

Barney, J. B. 1991. "Firm Resources and Sustained Competitive Advantage." *Journal of Management* 17 (1): 99–120. doi:10.1177/014920639101700108.

Barney, J.B., M. Wright, and D.J. Ketchen. 2001. "The Resource-Based View of the Firm: undefined Years After 1991." *Journal of Management* 27 (6): 625–641. doi:10.1177/014920630102700601.

Brock, D. 2012. "Building Global Capabilities: A Study of Globalizing Professional Service Firms." *The Service Industries Journal* 32 (10): 1593–1607.

Buckley, P., and M. Casson. 1996. "An Economic Model of International Joint Venture Strategy." *Journal of International Business Studies* 27 (5): 849–876.

Buckley, P., and M. Casson. 2009. "The Internationalisation Theory of the Multinational Enterprise: A Review of the Progress of a Research Agenda After 30 Years." *Journal of International Business Studies* 40 (9): 1563–1580. doi:10.1057/jibs.2009.49.

Buckley, P., and P. Ghauri. 2004. "Globalisation, Economic Geography and the Strategy of Multinational Enterprises." *Journal of International Business Studies* 35 (2): 81–98.

Canals, J. 1999. *Managing Corporate Growth*. Oxford: Oxford University Press.

Child, J., D. Faulkner, and S. Tallman. 2005. Cooperative Strategy: Managing Alliances, Networks, and Joint Ventures. Oxford: Oxford University Press.

Cohen, S. D. 2007. *Multinational Corporations and Foreign Direct Investment: Avoiding Simplicity, Embracing Complexity*. Oxford: Oxford University Press, Inc.

Contractor, F, S. Kundu, and C Hsu. 2003. "A Three-Stage Theory of International Expansion: The Link Between Multinational and Performance in Service Sector." *Journal of International Business* 34 (1): 5–18.

Daniels, John D., E.W. Ogram, and L.H. Radebaugh. 1976. *International Business: Environments and Operations*. Reading, MA: Addison-Wesley.

Davidson, W., and D. McFetridge. 1985. "Key Characteristics in the Choice of International Technology Transfer Mode." *Journal of International Business Studies* 16 (2): 5–21.

Dunning, J. 1979. "Explaining Changing Patterns of International Production: In Defence of the Eclectic Theory." *Oxford Bulletin of Economics and Statistics* 41 (4): 269–295.

Dunning, J. 1988. "The Eclectic Paradigm of International Production: A Restatement and Some Possible Extensions." *Journal of International Business Studies* 19 (1): 1–31.

Dunning, J. 1989. "Multinational Enterprises and the Growth of Services: Some Conceptual and Theoretical Issues." *The Service Industries Journal* 9 (1): 5–39.

Dunning, J. 1993. "The Theory of Transnational Corporations." *United Nation Library on Transnational Corporations* 1.

Dunning, J., and S. Lundan. 2008. "Institutions and the OLI Paradigm of Multinational Enterprise." *Asia Pacific Journal of Management* 25 (4): 573–593.

Erikson, K., J. Johanson, A. Majkgard, and D. Deo Sharma. 1997. "Experiential Knowledge and Cost in the Internationalisation Process." *Journal of International Business Studies* 28 (2): 337–360.

Erramilli, M.K. 1990. "Entry Mode Choice in Service Industries." *International Marketing Review* 7 (5): 50–62.

Erramilli, M.K. 1991. "The Experience Factor in Foreign Market Entry Behaviour of Service Firms." *Journal of International Business Studies* 22 (3): 479–501.

Erramilli, M.K., and C. Rao. 1990. "Choice of Foreign Market Entry Modes by Services Firms: Role of Market Knowledge." *Management International Review* 30: 135–150.

Erramilli, M.K., and C. Rao. 1993. "Service Firm's International Entry-Mode Choice: A Modifies Transaction- Cost Analysis Approach." *Journal of Marketing* 57: 19–38.

Faulkner, D. 1995. *International Strategic Alliances: Co-Operating to Compete*. Maidenhead: McGraw-Hill.

Faulkner, D., S. Teerikangas, and R. J. Joseph. 2012. *The Handbook of Mergers and Acquisitions*. Oxford: Oxford University Press.

Hedlund, G., and A. Kverneland. 1985. "Are Strategies for Foreign Market Entry Changing? The Case of Swedish Investments in Japan." *International Studies of Management and Organization* 15 (2): 41–59.

Hitt, M., R. Hoskinson, and H. Kim. 1997. "International Diversification: Effects on Innovation and Firm Performance." *Academy of Management Journal* 40: 767–798.

Hsieh, M., C. Shen, and J. Lee. 2010. "Factors Influencing the Foreign Entry Mode of Asian and Latin-American Banks." *The Services Industries Journal* 30 (14): 2351–2365. doi:10.1080/02642060802641567.

Inkpen, A., and K. Ramaswamy. 2005. *Global Strategy: Creating and Sustaining Advantage Across Borders*. Oxford: Oxford University Press.

Johanson, J., and J. Vahlne. 2009. "The Uppsala Internationalisation Process Model Revisited: From Liability of Foreignness to Liability of Outsidership." *Journal of International Business Studies* 40 (9): 1411–1431. doi:10.1057/jibs.2009.24.

Kanter, R. 1989. "The New Managerial Work." *Harvard Business Review* 67 (6): 85–92.

King, D., D. Dalton, C. Daily, and J. Covin. 2004. "Meta-Analyses of Post- Acquisition Performance: Indications of Unidentified Moderators." *Strategic Management Journal* 25 (2): 187–200. doi:10.1002/smj.371.

Knickerbocker, F.T. 1973. *Oligopolistic Reaction and Multinational Enterprise*. Boston: Division of Research, Harvard Business School.

Kogut, B. 1983. *The Multinational Corporation in the 1980s*. Cambridge, MA: MIT Press.

Kogut, B. 1985. "Designing Global Strategies: Corporate and Competitive Value Added Chain." *Sloan Management Review* 25: 15–28.

Kogut, B. 1989. "Research Notes and Communications a Note on Global Strategies." *Strategic Management Journal* 10 (4): 383–389.

Kogut, B., and N. Kulatilaka. 1994. "Operating Flexibility, Global Manufacturing, and the Option Value of a Multinational Network." *Management Science* 40 (1): 123–139.

Kogut, B., and H. Singh. 1988. "The Effect of National Culture on the Choice of Entry Mode." *Journal of International Business Studies* 19 (3): 411–432.

Krull, E., P. Smith, and G. Ge. 2012. "The Internationalization of Engineering Consulting from a Strategy Tripod Perspective." *The Service Industries Journal* 32 (7): 1097–1119.

Kulatilaka, N., and E. Perotti. 1998. "Strategic Growth Options." *Management Science* 44 (8): 1021–1031.

Li, J., and S. Guisinger. 1992. "The Globalization of Service Multinationals in the "Triad" Regions: Japan, Western Europe and North America." *Journal of International Business Studies* 23 (4): 675–696.

Lu, J. W., and P. W. Beamish. 2001. "The Internationalization and Performance of SMEs." *Strategic Management Journal* 22 (6–7): 565–586. doi:10.1002/smj.184.

Lu, J., and P. Beamish. 2004. "International Diversification and Firm Performance: The S-Curve Hypothesis." *Academy of Management Journal* 47 (4): 598–609.

Madhok, A. 1996. "Know-How, Experience and Competition Related Considerations in Foreign Market Entry: An Exploratory Investigation." *International Business Review* 5 (4): 339–366. doi:10.1016/0969-5931(96)00017-0.

Majkgard, A., and D.D. Sharma. 1998. "Client-Following and Market-Seeking Strategies in the Internationalization of Service Firms." *Journal of Business-To-Business Marketing* 4 (3): 1–41.

Michie, J., edited by. 2017. Globalisation and Democracy, *Three Volume Set*. Cheltenham: Edward Elgar.

Michie, J., edited by. 2019. *The Handbook of Globalisation*. 3rd ed. Cheltenham: Edward Elgar.

Miller, J., and B. Pras. 1980. "The Effects of Multinational and Export Diversification on the Profit Stability of Us Corporations." *Southern Economic Journal* 46 (3): 792–805. doi:10.2307/1057148.

Oxley, J. 1997. "Appropriate Hazards and Governance in Strategic Alliance: A Transaction Cost Approach." *Journal of Law, Economics, and Organisation* 13 (2): 387–409. doi:10.1093/oxford journals.jleo.a023389.

Oxley, J.E. 1999. "Institutional Environment and the Mechanisms of Governance: The Impact of Intellectual Property Protection on the Structure of Inter-Firm Alliances." *Journal of Economic Behavior & Organization* 38 (3): 283–309. doi:10.1016/S0167-2681(99)00011-6.

Peng, M.W. 2001. "The Resource-Based View and International Business." *Journal of Management* 27 (6): 803–829. doi:10.1177/014920630102700611.

Penrose, E. 1959, revised edition 2009. *The Theory of the Growth of the Firm*. Oxford: Oxford University Press, University of Oxford.

Porter, M. 1980. *Competitive Strategy*. New York: Free Press.

Rosenbaum, S., and T. Madsen. 2012. "Modes of Foreign Entry for Professional Service Firms in Multi-Partner Projects." *The Service Industries Journal* 32 (10): 1653–1666.

Rugman, A.M. 1979. *International Diversification and Multinational Enterprise*. Lexington, MA: Health.

Sanchez, R. 1993. "Strategic Flexibility, Firm Organization, and Managerial Work in Dynamic Markets." *Advances in Strategic Management* 9: 251–291.

Sanchez, R. 1995. "Strategic Flexibility in Product Competition." *Strategic Management Journal* 16 (Summer special issue): 135–159.

Schoenberg, R. 2006. "Measuring the Performance of Corporate Acquisitions: An Empirical Comparison of Alternative Metrics." *British Journal of Management* 17 (4): 361–370. doi:10. 1111/j.1467-8551.2006.00488.x.

Sharma, D.D. 1989. "Overseas Market Entry Strategy: The Technical Consultancy Firms." *Journal of Global Marketing* 2 (2): 89–110.

Sirmon, D. G., M.A. Hitt, and R.D. Ireland. 2007. "Managing Firm Resources in Dynamic Environments to Create Value: Looking Inside the Black Box." *Academy of Management Review* 32 (1): 273–292. doi:10.5465/amr.2007.23466005.

Tang, C., and S. Tikoo. 1999. "Operational Flexibility and Market Valuation of Earnings." *Strategic Management Journal* 20 (8): 749–761.

Teece, D.J. 2009. *Dynamic Capabilities and Strategic Management*. New York: Oxford University Press.

Terpstra, Vern, and Chwo-Ming Yu. 1988. "Determinants of Foreign Investment of U.S. Advertising Agencies." *Journal of International Business Studies* 19 (1): 33–46. doi:10.1057/ palgrave.jibs.8490373. Spring.

UNCTAD Handbook of Statistics. 2017. "United Nations Conference on Trade and Development."

Vermeulen, F., and H. Barkema. 2001. "Learning Through Acquisitions." *Academy of Management Journal* 44: 457–476.

Williamson, O. 1975. *Markets and Hierarchies, Analysis and Antitrust Implications: A Study in the Economics of Internal Organisation*. New York: The Free Press.

Williamson, O. 1985. *The Economic Institutions of Capitalism*. New York: The Free Press.

Necessary and sufficient conditions for the absorptive capacity of firms that interact with universities

Júlio Eduardo Rohenkohl ⓘ, Andreia Cunha da Rosa, Janaina Ruffoni and Orlando Martinelli

ABSTRACT

A complex concept, absorptive capacity was first introduced by Cohen and Levinthal (1989, 1990) and is connected to the Penrose theory of growth of firms ([1959] 2009) as it is related to a variety of firms' internal resources and external aspects of their environment, such as sources of knowledge. Considering firms that interact with universities in the search for external knowledge, this paper aims to identify the necessary and sufficient conditions of these firms to reach certain levels of absorptive capacity. We conducted a survey of firms that interacted with engineering research groups at universities in the state of Rio Grande do Sul (Brazil). We applied the Fuzzy Sets Comparative Qualitative Analysis. The main results were: (1) the necessary and sufficient conditions for high-level absorptive capacity are a combination of high acquisition and assimilation and medium transformation and exploitation; (2) the necessary and sufficient conditions for medium or non-high absorptive capacity are obtained by medium levels of acquisition, assimilation, transformation and exploitation; and c) that there are a variety of paths to improving the absorptive capacity of firms. These findings are important to formulating more diverse, flexible and less costly public policies aimed towards improving firms' absorptive capacity.

1. Introduction

The creation and exploration of resources and capacities are the basis to a firm's growth and the fundamental pillars of its innovative and competitive advantage in dynamic selective environments. Hence, over time, the formulation of strategies related to the access, combination, and use of knowledge can be crucial to a firm's innovative potential. The concept of absorptive capacity becomes the key to understanding the relationship between a firm's technological, economic and commercial performance and its capacity to access and deploy new knowledge (Flatten et al. 2011).

Edith Penrose's ([1959] 2009) seminal theory of the growth of the firm established that it is a firm's ability to learn and rearrange its resources, including its managerial capacity that enables it to expand the services from these resources in order to effectively renew growth opportunities. A fundamental aspect of Penrose's theory is that the capacity for a firm to grow is shaped by its internal resources and its capacity to create dynamic capabilities. The ability to acquire, assimilate and create knowledge from all sources – external and internal – is a key factor that determines the survival and growth of a firm.

Furthermore, considering the Penrosian perspective of the growth of the firm based on a firm's capacity to create dynamic capabilities and exploring its capacity to absorb knowledge, the emergence of an evolutionary epistemology becomes evident and, therefore, requires us to rethink the methodology to study the firm as an economic agent.

In the seminal works of Cohen and Levinthal (1989), Cohen and Levinthal (1990), absorptive capacity is defined as the firm's ability to recognize the value of new external knowledge, to assimilate it, and to apply it for commercial purposes. More recently, Zahra and George (2002) broadened this definition by associating it with a set of organizational routines and strategic processes by which the firm acquires, assimilates, transforms, and exploits knowledge to create and increase value. The prevalent logic is that firms with higher absorptive capacity levels tend to be more proactive and able to better exploit the existing innovation opportunities in the competitive environment and, thus, become more economically successful. If the firm intends to acquire and deploy external knowledge that is not related to its current knowledge base, deliberate efforts are necessary for that purpose. In this sense, the literature highlights the importance of the interaction between universities and firms (usually referred to university-industry interaction, i.e. UI) as an important mechanism for firms to access new knowledge (Link and Rees 1990; Mansfield 1991; Laursen and Salter 2004).

Despite the considerable number of studies, the literature lacks a consensual methodological framework for the absorptive capacity concept. There is still some ambiguity in the foundation of the construct, both theoretical and epistemological, and even as to empirical validation (Lane, Koka, and Pathak 2006; Camisón and Fóres 2010; Flatten et al. 2011).

Additionally, from an epistemological perspective, the process of absorptive capacity only makes sense if there is some knowledge created that can be somehow absorbed. Therefore, absorptive capacity is indissolubly associated with knowledge and its multiple characteristics, dimensions, and constraints. The abstract and partially tacit nature of knowledge causes absorptive capacity to have an intrinsically intangible, multidetermined, and inaccurate condition, and thus can hardly be measured by well-defined quantifiers.

In this sense, a problematic aspect of several important empirical studies is that they associate absorptive capacity with only a one-dimensional variable. Lane, Koka, and Pathak (2006, 838), when commenting on the exclusive use of R&D as a proxy of absorptive capacity, noted that it reduces absorptive capacity to a static resource. Using relative R&D volume as a proxy for absorptive capacity is a procedure more compatible with: (1) productive and technological environments whose knowledge base is undergoing more intense transformation; and (2) environments in which a firm's learning modes demand more intense financial and cognitive effort.

Other studies have embraced different proxies, such as patents, publications or highly qualified employees (Flatten et al. 2011). These methodological procedures may not be appropriate since, for example in terms of patents, they may bias results depending on a firm's propensity to patent. In terms of R&D and highly qualified employees engaged in absorbing knowledge, it is understandable that dedicated budgets for these investments are more common among larger firms than compared to small and medium-sized firms. Variable-oriented research when using a one-dimensional proxy in a large sample size n produced evidence on 'why' firms obtain relevant absorptive capacity, however, 'how' the proxy is connected to absorptive capacity is only presumed.

There are also studies in which the proxy variable was constructed more broadly on the relationships between various factors that make up absorptive capacity, as presented in Michie and Oughton (2016) and Giuliani and Bell (2005).

The proposal by Zahra and George (2002) contributes to understanding and operationalising the absorptive capacity concept as it categorises absorptive capacity into different dimensions, broadening the concept. The two categories are 'potential' and 'realized' absorptive capacity. 'Potential' is formed by the dimensions of acquisition and assimilation of knowledge; and 'realized' is comprised of the transformation and exploitation of knowledge. Different combinations of these dimensions can be managed to create and sustain absorptive capacity to enhance the innovative performance of firms.

Therefore, considering what has been exposed thus far, the objective of this study is to analyse the absorptive capacity from a broad understanding of the dimensions that represent the firms, considering those that make an effort to obtain external knowledge, captured here by firms that interact with universities. Consequently, our research question aims to define what the possible combinations of absorptive capacity dimensions are that lead firms that interact with universities to reach different levels of absorptive capacity ultimately to identify the necessary and sufficient conditions that cause them to reach different levels of absorptive capacity.

To answer this research question and achieve our main objective, a survey was conducted with firms that interacted with university research groups in the field of mechanical and metallurgical engineering in the state of Rio Grande do Sul (Brazil).

Regarding the empirical aspects of the study, two methodological observations are important. The first is the use of Qualitative Comparative Analysis (QCA). It is a data processing tool designed to define how some categories can be combined to produce a certain result. It is used in a 'diversity-oriented' approach in which categories are constructed based on set theory and processed with Boolean operators (Ragin 1987, 2000). The second observation is the use of Fuzzy Sets (FS) that is a tool for quantifying imprecise propositions or variables, or whose degrees of precision cannot be measured with certainty (Ragin 2000). That is, fuzzy sets (FS) allow us to deal with problems in which imprecision does not result from the random behaviour of the variables, but mainly from the absence of clearly defined criteria of relevance to a given set. The adequacy of QCA to deal with causal diversity is therefore enhanced in cases where categories are built as fuzzy sets. In these cases, a QCA variant, named Fuzzy Set Qualitative Comparative Analysis (fsQCA), is a qualitative research technique suitable to make causal inferences.

This article is organized into five parts, including the Introduction followed by the second section that discusses the antecedent of the absorptive capacity concept based on Edith Penrose's theory of the growth of the firm (Penrose [1959] 2009), the absorptive capacity concept itself and its relationship with University-Industry (UI) interaction; the third section presents the methodological procedures; the fourth section provides an analysis of the data; and lastly, the fifth section, we present our final considerations.

2. Concept of a firm's absorptive capacity and university-industry interaction

2.1. Concept of absorptive capacity and the Penrose theory of the growth of the firm

The influential work of Cohen and Levinthal (1990) defines absorptive capacity as 'the ability of a firm to recognize the value of new external information, assimilate it and apply it to commercial ends' (Cohen and Levinthal 1990, 128). Thus, absorptive capacity refers not only to a firm's acquisition or assimilation of new information but also to a firm's ability to exploit it (Cohen and Levinthal 1990, 131).

To these authors, the power of the firm's absorptive capacity is connected to the functionality of two complementary elements. The first concerns the degree of efficiency of the gatekeeper, i.e. the agent able to both identify new and relevant knowledge and external technologies and to translate them into the firm. The second element regards the ability to operate the firm's previous knowledge base in the sense of using its tangible and intangible resources to assimilate new knowledge internally and use it for commercial purposes. Although the subject matter is more complex, these two elements associated with the conceptual operability of the firm's absorptive capacity are present in Penrose's theory of the growth of the firm (Penrose [1959] 2009). To track this connection, one can start with Penrose's conceptualization of the nature of the firm itself. The author conceptualizes a firm as a bundle of physical and human resources in which productive services are made cohesive by, and thereby specific to, the firm's administrative organiza- tion. This unique collection of resources, particularly the firm's existing human resources, provides both an inducement to expand and a limit to the rate of expansion for the firm (Penrose [1959] 2009; Ghoshal, Hahn, and Moran 1997).

It is worth noting the important conceptual difference between resources and services of resources. Penrose [1959] 2009, 22) notes: 'strictly speaking, it is never the resources themselves that are the "inputs" in the production process, but only the services that the resources can render'. These services refer to how the resources are used or employed. Each firm's resource (productive or not) can offer several potential services and it is these services that matter to its growth.

As firms go along with their productive operations, increased knowledge is generated, also leading to an internal learning process. The results of such learning processes are, first, the expansion of the firm's 'productive opportunity set', that is: 'all of the productive possibilities that its "entrepreneurs" see and can take advantage of' (Penrose [1959] 2009, 28), second, the release of excess managerial resources that can be put to use in other, mostly related, business areas.

In a broader sense, it is possible to understand that for Penrose, a firm's entrepreneur- ism is a very special type of service linked to activities that elaborate expansion plans and actions to introduce and accept new ideas about new products, technologies, markets and organisational forms.

In this sense, the fundamental ingredients for the firm's productive opportunity are those 'inherited' by the firm (e.g. those accumulated throughout the firm's history), as well as those that are available from the firm's external environment which can be incorporated and exploited. However, these new external opportunities for the firm's growth are perceived within the context of the firm's administrative organization (Ghoshal, Hahn, and Moran 1997), i.e. the external opportunities related to all the productive possibilities that its entrepreneurs can 'see' and take advantage of. From a dynamic perspective, they must include the technological and scientific knowledge as internal or external resources that can be exploited by the firm.

Therefore, the firm's ability to identify opportunities depends on the 'quality' of existing entrepreneurial services of each firm. This quality, in turn, depends on the firm itself (e.g. the quality of its organizational structure) and the cognitive dimensions and characteristics of the entrepreneur's activities. This means that the set of opportunities is not something 'fixed' that exists 'out there', but fundamentally depends on the entrepreneur's expectations and perceptions of what the firm can or cannot achieve. In the words of Penrose [1959] 2009, 237): 'The relevant environment, that is the set of opportunities for investment and growth that its entrepreneurs and managers perceive, is different for every firm and depends on its specific collection of human and other resources'.

It is reasonable to argue that the operational logic of the concept of absorptive capacity is implicit in the theory of the Penrosian firm. The role of the Penrosian entrepreneur and its importance for the growth – and competitiveness – of the firm precedes that of the gatekeeper proposed by the further work of Cohen and Levinthal (1989), Cohen and Levinthal (1990). The same can be said for the importance of the firm's conception of a knowledge base that relates to its potential for absorptive capacity. In this line, Penrose already emphasized the importance of the resource base 'inherited' by the firm throughout its history for growth and diversification.

2.2. A firm's absorptive capacity and external knowledge from university-industry interaction

Among the various entrepreneurial initiatives to account for the dynamism and competition in a changeable market, a close relationship between firms and universities stands out. This approach refers to the relationship based on knowledge transfer, in which public and private players cooperate, sharing financial, infrastructure and human resources involved in the venture (Gusmão 2002).

University research rarely generates new technology acting indirectly and enhancing the technological opportunities of firms. Therefore, university-industry interaction becomes fundamental as it enables the application of university research while leading to an increase in a firm's capacity to generate innovation (Nelson 1986).

In Brazil, according to studies conducted by Rapini and Righi (2006, 2011) using data from CNPq's Research Group Directory, the relationship between universities and firms is characterized by 'interaction spots', i.e. the interactions between these two agents cannot be generalized or classified homogeneously; they are concentrated in the engineering and agrarian sciences in the South and Southeast regions of Brazil with a predominance of public universities and large firms. Rapini and Righi (2011) identified

Table 1. Absorptive capacity dimensions.

Component	Dimension	Definition
Potential Absorptive Capability	Acquisition	It is the capability of a firm to locate, identify, evaluate and acquire external knowledge that is important for the development of its operations.
	Assimilation	It is the capability of a firm to understand the knowledge (or information) brought in from outside the organization. It is the ability to analyze, classify, process, interpret, and finally internalize and understand this knowledge.
Realized Absorptive Capability	Transformation	It is the capability of a firm to facilitate the transference and combination of prior knowledge with newly acquired or assimilated knowledge. It consists of adding or eliminating knowledge and interpreting and combining existing knowledge in a new and different way.
	Exploitation	It is the ability of a firm to incorporate acquired, assimilated and transformed knowledge into its operations and routines for the application and use of the firm. This capability will lead to the creation or improvement of new products, systems, processes, forms of organization and skills.

Source: Adapted from Jiménez-Barrionuevo, García-Morales, and Molina (2011).

eighteen spots of interaction nationwide, six being in the areas of materials and metal-lurgical engineering. The state of São Paulo is at the forefront of interaction with 465 research groups. The state of Rio Grande do Sul is second with 265 research groups.

A firm's capacity to absorb knowledge from the external environment (such as that generated by universities) and use it to innovate has become an important issue in industrial economics (Waalkens 2006).

As seen previously, the initial idea of absorptive capacity within firms is anchored in the seminal contribution of Penrose's theory (Penrose [1959] 2009), while the definition of absorptive capacity as developed by Cohen and Levinthal (1989), Cohen and Levinthal (1990) is the main reference for several empirical studies. Subsequently, several re-conceptualisations have arisen in the literature and have been used for empirical work[1]

An important conceptual advance was made by Zahra and George (2002) that defined absorptive capacity as a set of organizational routines and strategic processes by which firms acquire, assimilate, transform and exploit knowledge to create value. These authors, as said before, broaden and split the concept of absorptive capacity into four dimensions divided into two categories: 'potential' and 'realized' absorptive capacity. The 'potential' absorptive capacity allows the organization to be receptive to external knowledge, i.e. to acquire, analyse, interpret and understand this knowledge. The 'realized' absorptive capacity reflects a firm's ability to transform and explore new knowledge, incorporating it into previously existing knowledge in its operations. Table 1 shows the four dimensions of absorptive capacity.

Several works based on Zahra and George (2002) regarding 'potential' and 'realized' absorptive capacity can be cited, such as: Flatten et al. (2011); Jiménez-Barrionuevo, García-Morales, and Molina (2011); Cepeda-Carrion, Cegarra-Navarro, and Jimenez-Jimenez (2012); and Leal-Rodríguez et al. (2014).

In regards to ways of measuring absorptive capacity, Versiani et al. (2010) and Flatten et al. (2011) mention that although a considerable number of empirical studies have been carried out on absorptive capacity, a valid measure incorporating its various dimensions had not yet been developed. The difficulty in defining metrics is a result of a lack of consensus about the dimensions of the concept. Many researchers choose to measure absorptive capacity considering only one dimension, whereas, in general, the attributes of knowledge have been ignored theoretically, empirically and analytically although the importance of technology transference and a firm's knowledge acquisition have been frequently mentioned in the literature (Vega-Jurado, Gutiérrez-Gracia, and Fernández-de-Lucio 2008).

From a somewhat different perspective, there are studies in which the proxy variable for absorptive capacity was constructed more broadly based on relationships between various factors that make up absorptive capacity. Using European Community Innovation Survey (CIS) data for the United Kingdom, Michie and Oughton (2016) proposed five factors to explain cooperative agreements with universities, i.e.: the size of the firm, the proportion of scientists and engineers (at college-level or above) in the workforce, whether advanced management techniques had been introduced, internal R&D expenditure and training expenditure. As these are also absorptive capacity factors, cooperative agreements became a robust proxy to absorptive capacity.

Also aiming for a robust measure, Giuliani and Bell (2005) analysed wine producers in Chile and proposed a measure of absorptive capacity based on three previous variables: (1) the number of technically qualified personnel in the firm and their level of education and training; (2) the experience of professional staff in terms of time in the industry and the number of other firms in which they had been employed, and (3) the intensity and nature of the firm's activities in experimentation. It is important to highlight that the authors mentioned that 'information about expenditure on formal R&D would have been both too narrowly defined and too difficult to obtain systematically' (Giuliani and Bell 2005, 53). In this study, another path is proposed for a multifactorial measure of absorptive capacity that is more oriented towards understanding the absorptive capacity levels of firms that interact with different agents (such as other firms and institutions, for example).

However, Cohen and Levinthal (1990) have conceived that absorptive capacity also stems from the learnings of manufacturing operations. Firms can increase their absorptive capacity with less structured learning. Whereas, when a firm wants to acquire and use knowledge outside of its environment, i.e. knowledge that is not related to its current knowledge base, deliberate efforts along with a new learning structure are necessary for this purpose.

The variety of internal and external sources to stimulate absorptive capacity, along with environments for its exploration, imply other important approaches to measure absorptive capacity. When proposing their re-conceptualisation, Zahra and George (2002) introduced a qualitative and multidetermined measure of knowledge capabilities. They aimed to provide a basis to observe and examine the non-linear ways firms develop their competencies. Therefore, it is necessary to consider that there are complex causality characteristics, as defined by Rihoux and Ragin (2008), and emphasise that it is the combination of conditions that produce an outcome.

Absorptive capacity can be understood as an intangible asset of the firm. As such it can be valued with relevant learning in accelerated proportions facing a change in the industrial-technological frontier or depreciated by obsolescence or by the learning of knowledge irrelevant to the industrial competition. Absorptive capacity is therefore a variable learning process in industries, where it is not possible to determine the reserve of related knowledge. In this sense, more important than identifying whether the firm has absorptive capacity, is knowing its intensity and how (and under what circumstances) it is achieved. When internal and external sources are varied and the magnitude and quality of technological knowledge evolves, an alternative form of evaluating absorptive capacity is to use the perception of individuals involved in the constitution of a firm's absorptive capacity.

To advance these questions, Rosa and Ruffoni (2014) carried out bibliographical research in various databases using the keywords 'Absorptive Capacity', 'Measure' and 'Metrics' for the period between 2000 to 2012. From this review, the authors identified important contributions to address these issues and developed a proposal of an instrument for organizing different indicators that measure the absorptive capacity of firms that interact with universities. The authors' proposal sought to assemble absorptive capacity evaluation items into dimensions of acquisition, assimilation, transformation and exploitation and dividing the four dimensions into two categories: 'potential' and 'realized' absorptive capacity. In the selection of the absorptive capacity measurement items, the authors considered those that are more specific to the profile of firms that seek interaction with universities. This procedure of absorptive capacity measurement was applied in a survey with firms that presented this interaction. The information collected by Rosa and Ruffoni (2014) is empirically based to work out a new methodology, i.e. the use of fsQCA. The new methodological procedures are explained in the following section.

An alternative path to explore absorptive capacity measurement is to establish relations between fuzzy sets that allow the identification of several configurations of the intensity of the potential and realized absorptive capacity and their correspondence with different absorptive capacity levels of firms interacting with universities. This route aggregates a quantitative scale of intensity to qualitative categories conceived by Zahra and George (2002). In doing so, the authors' statements were upheld (Zahra and George 2002, 197) in that 'potential' and 'realized' absorptive capacity explain levels of successful knowledge management. They established a commitment to research and measure absorptive capacity and relate it to multiple results (Zahra and George 2002, 199).

3. Methodological procedures

3.1. Survey data collection

The data analysed were collected through a survey carried out at manufacturing firms located in the state of Rio Grande do Sul (Brazil) that interacted with university research groups as informed by group leaders in the 2010 Census of CNPq's Research Group Directory. A decision was made to focus on firms that interacted with research groups in the fields of mechanical, materials and metallurgical engineering of universities in Rio Grande do Sul since engineering represented an area having the highest number of groups that declared to have relationships with firms. The research population consisted of 71 small, medium and large private firms according to the classification of Brazilian Micro and Small Business Support Service (SEBRAE). Respondents were identified by telephone and were professionals involved in a firm's innovation activities and had already participated in an interactive process with a university.

The instrument prepared for data collection was submitted for evaluation in the pretest stage in which 13 firms were interviewed. A 5-point Likert concordance scale was used to capture absorptive capacity responses, following suggestions from previous studies such as Jiménez-Barrionuevo, García-Morales, and Molina (2011) and Camisón and Fóres (2010). The survey was conducted between January and March 2013. A total of 32 responses were received and validated. This is considered a good rate of return for a survey since 45% of the population answered the questionnaire. It is important to note that this is a survey with a highly specific delimitation of the firm's population and, therefore, with a relatively small number of target respondents (71).[2]

The sample firms were classified according to the National Classification of Economic Activities (CNAE) 2.0 with 84% of them belonging to the manufacturing industry with the highest percentage from the automotive manufacturing sector, accounting for 25% of the total sample.

3.2. Method of data analysis

Charles Ragin (1987) presents two traditional approaches used by social scientists in comparative studies: the 'Variable-Oriented Approach' and the 'Case-Oriented Approach'. The variable-oriented approach aims to test hypotheses derived from theories. The ability to generalize a theoretical idea is more important than understanding a reality in its complexity (Ragin 1987). Simplification strategies in the definition of the problem and the sampling were used to increase the number of observations and validate the testing. The background is to understand 'Why' a result occurs (Ragin 2000), that is, to reach an explanatory purpose.

Case-oriented studies, in turn, deepen and detail the relationships that subsequently encourage the analyst to rethink concepts and hypotheses. Their main objective is to complement historical interpretations and identify causal relationships. The researcher's interest is driven by the explanation of under what circumstances and how a result occurs (Ragin 1987, 2000). In other words, case-oriented studies investigate explanatory causality. Ragin (2000) developed the 'Diversity-Oriented Approach' to combine the complexity of causal relationships established by the tradition of case studies with a greater ability to generalize explanations achieved by the quantitative tradition. The diversity-oriented approach disaggregates populations into categories (or types) and treats cases as configurations of variables.

The methodological challenge is how to delimit social environment complexity to be a workable inference that can be managed by human understanding. The variable-oriented strategy gives the analyst the prerogative to make simplifications and constitute a population of homogeneous observations (comparable by some common attribute), as long as it is justified. The diversity-oriented strategy operationalised with 'Qualitative Comparative Analysis' (QCA) implies that the simplifications result from Boolean logical operators applied to theoretical sets (Ragin 1987, 2000).

QCA is a qualitative research technique that allows for descriptions focused on the diversity between different configurations that will lead to certain results, mainly when the sample basis is not large. The technique uses Boolean Algebra binary logic and enables the interpretation of data qualitatively while simultaneously seeking causal relationships between variables. Cases are treated as configurations, i.e. combinations of characteristics (Ragin 1987).

QCA is an umbrella-term assembled into two main classifications: (1) referring explicitly to the original (Boolean) version of QCA, csQCA notation is used (where 'cs' stands for 'crisp set'); (2) referring explicitly to the fuzzy-set version, fsQCA is used (where 'fs' signifies fuzzy set). This article uses fsQCA set technique as its methodological basis, complemented by the scientific attention to diversity expressed in Ragin (2000). A fuzzy set is mathematically defined by assigning a value that represents the degree of relevance of each individual to the set within the universe studied. This membership degree (μ) represents the similarity of this individual to the significance that gives identity to the whole. The membership functions associated with fuzzy sets depend not only on the concept to be represented but also on the context in which they are used. Functions can have different forms; some properties, such as continuity, may be required. In epistemological and methodological terms, the fsQCA technique follows the subsequent principles (Rihoux and Ragin 2008):

(1) Complex Causality: often assumed to be the combination of conditions that produce a result means the methodology recognizes that every result is caused by a varied combination of conditions that cannot be disassociated or isolated.

(2) Equifinality: presumes that several different combinations of conditions can generate the same result. For example, in one case, event E was generated by the combination of conditions A and B [AB → E], but, in another case, the causes C and D can determine the same result [CD → E].

(3) Context-Sensitive: supposes that depending on the contextual configuration, a given condition may have a different impact on the result. This concept is also called the Principle of Multipurpose, in which certain conditions can create or contribute to generating different results in different contexts or times.

(4) Qualitative Data: data that are associated with the degree of membership of the sets.

A study in this perspective is composed of five methodological steps: the first step defines the sets of linguistic variables (e.g. absorptive capacity), its adjectives (e.g. high, medium and low), and its quantitative scale (e.g. 5-point Likert used as an interval scale); the second, necessarily establishes–from theoretical and empirical references of previous studies–the membership relationships among data from the chosen sets; the third, applies fsQCA techniques to determine the condition settings to obtain the results; the fourth step uses the consistency and coverage criteria to validate (or not) the configurations found; and finally the fifth step is the interpretation of the results.

It is worth mentioning that to construct a robust explanatory force of the regular causal relationships between cases (condition → result), the fsQCA is based on two fundamental epistemological postulates: the necessary condition and the sufficient condition. Conceptually, a condition is 'necessary' for the occurrence of a result [Y] if the condition is always present when [Y] occurs. That is, the result [Y] does not occur in the absence of this condition. A condition is sufficient (but not necessary) if it can produce a result [Y] by itself, but, at the same time, the result [Y] could also occur by reason of other conditions present. Thus, the result [Y] may come not from a single condition, but from a combination of conditions.

Empirically, the data does not always corroborate necessary and sufficient conditions as idealized. There are criteria for establishing acceptance of necessary and sufficient conditions.

The consistency and coverage measures evaluate the adherence of the new empirical data to the theoretical arguments and previous empirical treatments used in the relation of the studied sets.

The consistency measure establishes the relationship between the subset of cases causing the result within the scope of all cases in which the condition existed. In the QCA (crisp sets), this results in proportions. For example, there are ten cases with the AB condition and of these, eight contain the AB → E relationship; the consistency of AB → E on the occurrence of condition AB is

$$Consistency = (8AB \rightarrow E) \div (10AB) = 0.8 \tag{1}$$

When using fsQCA, the consistency measure changes slightly, but the interpretation remains. Considering Xi as the sets or combinations between theoretically antecedent sets for the result Yi, the formula of the consistency of sufficient antecedent sets (Ragin 2006) for a result is:

$$Consistency(Xi \leq Yi) = \frac{\Sigma(min(Xi, Yi))}{\Sigma(Xi)} \tag{2}$$

The fsQCA consistency formula adds up all of the membership degrees to the causal combination,[3] which are equal to or less than the case's membership to the result and thus comprise a subset of the result and divides the sum of these plots by the sum of the membership degrees of each causal combination ($\Sigma(Xi)$). By using the membership degree sum ratio, the method makes it difficult for lower degrees of membership to predominate in establishing consistency.

The coverage measure shows the proportion of cases that contain the condition in the total number of cases in which the result is present. In QCA, coverage measures the importance of a causal combination in view of the total number of cases that presented the same result. For example, if there are sixteen cases in which the E result occurs, and of these, eight result from AB → E, the coverage of the E result is:

$$Coverage = (8AB \rightarrow E) \div (16E) = 0.5 \tag{3}$$

When switching to fsQCA, the variation in the degrees of membership to the sets changes the formula. The sum of the degrees of membership of the intersection between antecedents Xi is compared with the sum of the degrees of membership to the result Yi. The interpretation is very similar to that established in the proportion of the QCA:

$$Coverage(Xi \leq Yi) = \frac{\sum (min(Xi, Yi))}{\sum (Yi)} \tag{4}$$

Consistency and coverage are complementary measures. Primarily, consistency is established, i.e. the number of manifestations of a causal combination that effectively generate a certain result; thereafter, the importance of this causal combination is established in the universe of all the cases that generated the same result.

High values in the consistency measure indicate that the condition is sufficient for the result. The coverage measure is the proportion of cases whose membership degrees of the condition are less than or equal to the result's membership degrees in the total number of cases where its membership degrees are greater than zero. In other words, this measure shows the importance of a cause (or a combination of causes) to obtain a result. If there are several 'paths' to the same result, the coverage measure for any causal relationship must be small.

Considering the previous discussion on absorptive capacity measurement, the method of this research consists of organizing the dimensions of knowledge underlying absorptive capacity as fuzzy sets and processing them through the fsQCA to search for different paths that reach four absorptive capacity levels: High Absorptive Capacity, Medium Absorptive Capacity, Low Absorptive Capacity and Non-High Absorptive Capacity. The latter relationship indicates the combinations of antecedents to be avoided if the firm aims to reach a high absorptive capacity. Comparatively to Zahra and George (2002), the qualitative diversity of possibilities is increased by grading the dimensions into intensity qualifiers (high, medium or low). A quantitative dimension, i.e. a scale ranging from 0 to 1, is also added when measuring the membership of the capabilities to these qualifiers. Finally, the necessary and sufficient conditions for the antecedents to absorptive capacity is empirically organized.

4. Description and analysis of data

Initially, we describe how the necessary and sufficient conditions for a firm to have a high Absorptive Capacity are obtained and tested according to a transcription of the responses to fuzzy sets by the respondents. Procedures for setting Medium Absorptive Capacity, Low Absorptive Capacity and Non-High Absorptive Capacity are analogous. Each theoretical partition of absorptive capacity – acquisition, assimilation, transformation and exploitation capabilities – were investigated through a five-choice Likert-scale questionnaire. For each previous partition (for example, acquisition capability) there were five or six questions used to obtain a mean of the Likert values of each antecedent partition for the different interviewees. Thereafter, each antecedent theoretical partition was

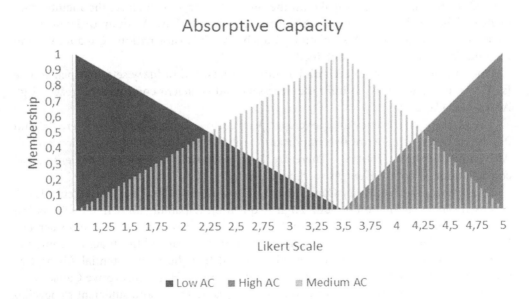

Figure 1. Absorptive capacity fuzzy sets. Source: Authors.

constructed as fuzzy sets. For example, acquisition capability was classified into three sets: Low Acquisition Capability, Medium Acquisition Capability and High Acquisition Capability. The reference points to define the 'high', 'medium' and 'low' intervals on the Likert scale are based on the work of Rosa (2013, 106), which established High Absorptive Capacity in values above 3.6 for the data collected in the survey. In this sense, the value of 3.5 in the Likert scale was designated the membership degree of 0 for the set 'High', whose gradient increases from 0 to the membership degree of 1 to the value of 5 in the Likert scale.[4] According to the superposition-sets principle in fuzzy-set theory, the Likert 3.5 value also referred to the set 'Medium' with a degree of membership 1 and 'Low' with a membership degree 0. All fuzzy sets were proposed as triangular functions as shown in Figure 1.

In Figure 1, the fuzzy sets are represented as triangular fuzzy numbers whose sides are linear membership functions. The membership to High Absorptive Capacity is defined as the upper line of a fuzzy number represented as a triangle; the coordinates defining this line are (3.5; 0) and (5; 1).

The calibration used promotes the superposition of the subsets to capture the ambiguity proper to complex issues. So, Medium Absorptive Capacity is represented by the triangle defined by (1; 0), (3.5; 1) and (5; 0). The area bounded by the coordinates (3.5; 0), (4.25; 0.5), (5; 0) implies that there are points with membership both to High Absorptive Capacity and to Medium Absorptive Capacity.

The coordinates (1; 1) (3.5; 0) present the Low Absorptive Capacity fuzzy subset. The area bounded by the coordinates (1; 0) (2.25; 0.5) (3.5; 0) implies that there are points with membership both to Low Absorptive Capacity and to Medium Absorptive Capacity.

Each firm's average values of responses to the questionnaire of each theoretical partition of Potential Absorptive Capacity (decomposed into Acquisition Capability and Assimilation Capability dimensions) and Realized Absorptive Capacity (decomposed into Transformation Capability and Exploitation Capability dimensions) were applied to the functions that make up the sets in Figure 1. Therefore, the membership degree of the resulting average of each firms' responses to Low, Medium or High sets of Acquisition Capability, Assimilation Capability, Transformation Capability, and Exploitation Capability were obtained.

Once a firm's answers to each dimension are translated to fuzzy sets, an open source fsQCA software was used to infer the necessary and sufficient conditions to reach High Absorptive Capacity.

The levels of consistency and coverage specified to establish sufficiency were 0.8 and 0.5, respectively.[5] There are two important combinations for a firm to develop a High Absorptive Capacity (Table 2). There are four compatible firms with sufficient causal combinations to obtain High Absorptive Capacity.

By activating the Necessary Conditions option of the fsQCA a 0.95 Consistency level[6] was used. The combination of both 'High Acquisition Capability *and* High Assimilation Capability' proved to be consistent and extensive as necessary antecedents to achieve High Absorptive Capacity. Acquisition and Assimilation capabilities together comprise Potential Absorptive Capacity. The results showed that the high Potential Absorptive Capacity is a necessary but insufficient condition to reach High Absorptive Capacity.

Just the combination (A) (expressed in Table 2) is necessary and sufficient to develop High Absorptive Capacity. The combination (B) is sufficient, but not necessary to achieve

Table 2. Conditions to achieve high absorptive capacity.

Necessity	Consistency	Coverage
High Acquisition Capability*High Assimilation Capability ← High Absorptive Capacity	0,978,261	0,615,942
Sufficiency		
High Acquisition Capability*High Assimilation Capability*Medium Transformation Capability*Medium Exploitation Capability → High Absorptive Capacity (A)	0.873333	0.502558
Medium Acquisition Capability*High Assimilation Capability*Medium Transformation Capability*High Exploitation Capability → High Absorptive Capacity (B)	0.875000	0.617647

Source: Authors.

High Absorptive Capacity. The same procedure was adopted to establish necessary and sufficient conditions to obtain Medium Absorptive Capacity, Low Absorptive Capacity and Non-High Absorptive Capacity.

As expressed in Table 3, just one combination is sufficient and necessary to reach Medium Absorptive Capacity: Medium Acquisition Capability *and* Medium Assimilation Capability *and* Medium Transformation Capability *and* Medium Exploitation Capability. There are 23 compatible firms with sufficient causal combinations to obtain Medium Absorptive Capacity.

Concerning the establishment of sufficiency for Low Absorptive Capacity, respondent answers show there is no sufficient way to obtain that level. The low frequency of activation of the output variable Low Absorptive Capacity (by only 6 firms) influences this result.

The Non-High Absorptive Capacity is established by the High Absorptive Capacity complement, i.e.

$$Non - HighAbsorptiveCapacity = (1 - HighAbsorptiveCapacity) \qquad (5)$$

where μ represents membership grade.

The High Absorptive Capacity set complement implies grades of membership for the Medium Absorptive Capacity set or for the Low Absorptive Capacity set (in the case of High Capacity having 0 membership, both Medium or Low can have membership degree 1). As shown in Table 4, for the establishment of the Non-High Absorptive Capacity, the arrangement of Medium Acquisition Capability *and* Medium

Table 3. Conditions to achieve medium absorptive capacity (AC).

Necessity	Consistency	Coverage
Medium Acquisition Capability*Medium Assimilation Capability*Medium Transformation Capability*Medium Exploitation Capability ← Medium AC (A)	0.987687	0.815541
Medium Acquisition Capability*Medium Assimilation Capability*Medium Transformation Capability ← Medium AC (B)	0,977,573	0,847,503
Medium Acquisition Capability*Medium Assimilation Capability*Medium Exploitation Capability ← Medium AC (C)	0,969,657	0,849,384
Medium Acquisition Capability*Medium Transformation Capability*Medium Exploitation Capability ← Medium AC (D)	0,986,807	0,826,215
Medium Assimilation Capability*Medium Transformation Capability*Medium Exploitation Capability ← Medium AC (E)	0,983,289	0,853,435
Medium Assimilation Capability*Medium Transformation Capability ← Medium AC . (F)	0,965,259	0,889,384
Medium Transformation Capability*Medium Exploitation Capability ← Medium AC . (G)	0,976,693	0,867,917
Medium Acquisition Capability*Medium Transformation Capability ← Medium AC . (H)	0,958,663	0,869,219
Medium Acquisition Capability*Medium Exploitation Capability ← Medium AC . (I)	0,952,067	0,862,894
Sufficiency		
Medium Acquisition Capability*Medium Assimilation Capability*Medium Transformation Capability* Medium Exploitation Capability →Medium AC (A)	1,000,000	0,654,353

Source: Authors

Table 4. Conditions to achieve non-high absorptive capacity (AC).

Necessity	Consistency	Coverage
Medium Acquisition Capability*Medium Assimilation Capability*Medium Transformation Capability*Medium Exploitation Capability ← Non-High AC (A)	0.954508	0.838054
Medium Acquisition Capability*Medium Assimilation Capability*Medium Exploitation Capability ← Non-High AC (B)	0,953,681	0,849,043
Sufficiency		
Medium Acquisition Capability*Medium Assimilation Capability*Medium Transformation Capability*Medium Exploitation Capability → Non-High AC (A)	1,000000	0.615385

Source: Authors

Assimilation Capability *and* Medium Transformation Capability *and* Medium Exploitation Capability is a necessary and sufficient condition. There are 22 firms compliant with this causal combination to achieve Non-High Absorptive Capacity.

5. Final considerations

(1) This article assumed that absorptive capacity is a complex concept with multiple dimensions since it is related both to the internal aspects of the firm (e.g. processes of knowledge generation and learning, technological and organizational training), as well as to the specific aspects of the external environment (e.g. limits to public or private knowledge sharing). Considering, in accordance with Penrose, that firms are unique and specific sets of tangible and intangible resources that are exploited based on the tacit knowledge accumulated by the firm's history, the processes of identification, assimilation and exploitation of external knowledge for commercial purposes (Cohen and Levinthal 1989, 1990) should also be understood as specific to each firm and with qualitatively different results. Consequently, measuring absorptive capacity also becomes complex and multidetermined.

To analytically incorporate this complexity, this article applied the fsQCA method to deal with both qualitative and quantitative aspects of the absorptive capacity process. Taking as a reference a quantitative scale of intensity to qualitative absorptive capacity components conceived by Zahra and George (2002), i.e. Potential Absorptive Capacity (decomposed into Acquisition Capability and Assimilation Capability dimensions) and Realized Absorptive Capacity (decomposed into Transformation Capability and Exploitation Capability dimensions), the fsQCA method identified how some possible combinations of a firm's intangible capabilities can result in different levels of absorptive capacity. More specifically, it identified the paths and how the necessary and sufficient conditions would allow a firm to reach four absorptive capacity levels: High Absorptive Capacity, Medium Absorptive Capacity, Low Absorptive Capacity, and Non-High Absorptive Capacity. The latter indicates the combinations of antecedents to be avoided if the firm aims to reach High Absorptive Capacity.

The use of the fsQCA allowed us to model this study with attention to diversity in knowledge capability arrangements and Absorptive Capacity performance. Diversity was increased with intensity qualifiers High, Medium and Low. These intensity qualifiers are translated into quantitative membership of knowledge capabilities. In this sense, the inference combined qualitative and quantitative dimensions to evaluate Absorptive Capacity. A fluid dialogue is established between the evidence provided by the experience of the representatives of the firms and the theoretical contributions on Absorptive Capacity.

The results showed two combinations by which the sampled firms obtained high Absorptive Capacity: (1) a combination of High Acquisition Capability and High Assimilation Capability and Medium Transformation and Medium Exploitation Capability; (2) a combination of Medium Acquisition Capability and High Assimilation Capability and Medium Transformation and High Exploitation Capability.

The high capacity in both dimensions of the Potential Absorptive Capacity is a necessary but insufficient condition to reach a High Absorptive Capacity. The composition with Medium Transformation Capability and Medium Exploitation Capability is what resulted in a necessary causal combination sufficient to obtain the High Absorptive Capacity identified.

The way to reach Medium Absorptive Capacity coincides with the combination of Non-High Absorptive Capacity. The combination of Medium Acquisition Capability and Medium Assimilation Capability and Medium Transformation Capability and Medium Exploitation Capability is both necessary and sufficient to achieve the Medium Absorptive Capacity, likewise for Non-High Absorptive Capacity.

These results signal the importance of knowledge absorptive capacities and the ability of firms to assimilate external knowledge to achieve a high absorptive capacity. Transformation capability (combining and transferring assimilated knowledge) and Exploitation capability (the incorporation of knowledge into routines) do not prove to be so important. It is enough that such firm's capabilities are at a medium level.

Although the conclusions must take into account the particular scope of the information used in this article, that is, a spatial and sectoral cut of the UI interaction in southern Brazil, the evidence shows that it is possible to have several paths to improve the Absorptive Capacity of firms, which is also important in formulating public policy. Especially for non-developed countries, implementing public policies aimed at improving absorptive capacity and the competitiveness of firms could be more diverse, flexible, and less costly. For example, the strategies and public policies to foster innovation through UI interaction in the field of engineering should include first and foremost various stimuli to strengthen the Potential Capacity since it is a necessary condition to reach High Absorptive Capacity. Therefore, efforts aimed at the Realized Absorptive Capacity without the previous or concomitant increment in Potential Capacity would be wasted.

Notes

1. For further details, consult the following publications: (Jansen, Van Den Bosch, and Volberda 2005; Torodova and Durisin 2007; Van Den Bosch, Van Wijk, and Volberda 2003; Versiani et al. 2010; Camisón and Fóres 2010; Mowery and Oxley 1995; Kim 1998; Lane and Lubatikin 1998; Dyer and Singh 1998; Van Den Bosch, Volberda, and De Boer 1999; Zahra and George 2002; Lane, Koka, and Pathak 2006).
2. With this population and sample, the margin of error was slightly high by conventional standards. On the other hand, the outcome of the Cronbach's Alpha test, which assesses the

consistency of the questionnaire, is in the acceptable range (Rosa 2013). The sample average is accepted as representative of the population.

3. This consistency formula is applied to the Fuzzy Truth Table Algorithm of the fsQCA (Ragin 2006) used in processing the combinations sufficient to obtain High Absorptive Capacity, Medium Absorptive Capacity, Low Absorptive Capacity and Non-High Absorptive Capacity. Therefore, the consistency and the respective coverage refer to the sufficiency of the explanatory combinations. The consistency and coverage formulas for the necessary conditions are slightly different. Due to limited space, they are not reproduced here and can be found in Ragin (2006).

4. Likert has characteristics of an ordinal scale. There are arguments in favor of the use of summated scales of the Likert scale as an interval scale for partitions of five points or more and continuous constructs (Curado, Vitorino Teles, and Marôco 2013, 449). The sum of scores and averages of Likert scale scores is adopted on an interval scale.

5. Ragin (2006) points out that for consistency values below 0.75 it is difficult to sustain that there is a relationship between the evaluated sets, i.e. that one is a subset of the other.

6. Schneider and Wagemann (2010) recommend great rigor to establish necessary conditions. In this work the diversity in comparison to the original work was improved considerably (Rosa 2013; Rosa and Ruffoni 2014) by proposing twelve antecedent sets. This resulted in $3^{12}-1 = 531.440$ combinations to be tested. To run the necessary algorithm of the fsQCA, the combinations of sets are chosen manually, thereby considerably increasing the risk of making mistakes. Consequently, we adopted a more 'lax' procedure and ran the necessity test after the sufficiency test, inserting only sets that are included in the sufficient combinations of antecedent categories. This procedure influenced the consistency index in a way that makes it easier to find necessary conditions. With this in mind, we enhanced the consistency level from 0.8 to 0.95.

Acknowledgements

The authors would like to thank the anonymous referees for their helpful comments. We are also grateful for the support received from Luisa Hadres dos Santos and Júlia Driemeier Vieira Rosa, students of UNISINOS. The usual disclaimer applies.

Disclosure statement

No potential conflict of interest was reported by the author(s).

Funding

This work was supported by the Edital Pró-Publicações Internacionais 051/2019, Universidade Federal de Santa Maria (Pro-International Publications Notice 051/2019, Federal University of Santa Maria), registered under the protocol 043/2019.

ORCID

Júlio Eduardo Rohenkohl (iD) http://orcid.org/0000-0003-4969-355X

References

Camisón, C., and B. Fóres. 2010. "Knowledge Absorptive Capacity: New Insights for Its Conceptualization and Measurement." *Journal of Business Research* 63 (7): 707–715. doi:10.1016/j.jbusres.2009.04.022.

Cepeda-Carrion, G., J. G. Cegarra-Navarro, and D. Jimenez-Jimenez. 2012. "The Effect of Absorptive Capacity on Innovativeness: Context and Information Systems Capability as Catalysts." *British Journal of Management* 23 (1): 110–129.

Cohen, W. M., and D. A. Levinthal. 1989. "Innovation and Learning: The Two Faces of R&D." *The Economic Journal* 99: 569–596. doi:10.2307/2233763.

Cohen, W. M., and D.A Levinthal. 1990. "Absorptive-Capacity: A New Perspective on Learning and Innovation." *Administrative Science Quarterly* 35 (1): 128–152. doi:10.2307/2393553.

Curado, M. A., J. M. Vitorino Teles, and J. Marôco. 2013. "Análise Estatística de Escalas Ordinais: aplicações na área de saúde infantil e pediatria [Statistical Analysis of Ordinal Scales: Applications in the Area of Child Health and Pediatrics]." *Enfermaría Global* 30: 446–457.

Dyer, J.H., and H. Singh. 1998. "The Relational View: Cooperative Strategy and Sources of Interorganizational Competitive Advantage." *Academy of Management Review* 23 (4): 660–679. doi:10.5465/amr.1998.1255632.

Flatten, T. C, A. Engelen, S. A. Zahra, and M. Brettel. 2011. "A Measure of Absorptive Capacity: Scale Development and Validation." *European Management Journal* 29 (2): 98–116. doi:10.1016/j.emj.2010.11.002.

Ghoshal, S., M. Hahn, and P. Moran. 1997. "An Integrative Theory of Firm Growth: Implications for Corporate Organization and Management." INSEAD Working Paper, 97/87/SM. Fontainebleau: INSEAD.

Giuliani, E., and M. Bell. 2005. "The Micro-Determinants of Meso-Level Learning and Innovation: Evidence Form a Chilean Wine Cluster." *Research Policy* 34: 47–68. doi:10.1016/j.respol.2004.10.008.

Gusmão, R. 2002. "Práticas e políticas internacionais de colaboração ciência-indústria [Internacional Policies and Practices for Science-industry Collaboration]." *Revista Brasileira de Inovação* 1 (2): 327–360. doi:10.20396/rbi.v1i2.8648863.

Jansen, J. J., F. A. Van Den Bosch, and H. W. Volberda. 2005. "Managing Potential and Realized Absorptive Capacity: How Do Organizational Antecedents Matter?" *Academy of Management Journal* 48 (6): 999–1015. doi:10.5465/amj.2005.19573106.

Jiménez-Barrionuevo, M. M., V. J. García-Morales, and L. M. Molina. 2011. "Validation of an Instrument to Measure Absorptive Capacity." *Technovation* 31 (5–6): 190–202. doi:10.1016/j.technovation.2010.12.002.

Kim, L. 1998. "Crisis Construction and Organizational Learning: Capability Building in Catching-Up at Hyundai Motor." *Organization Science* 9 (4): 506–521. doi:10.1287/orsc.9.4.506.

Lane, P. J., B. R. Koka, and S. Pathak. 2006. "The Reification of Absorptive Capacity: A Critical Review and Rejuvenation of the Construct." *Academy of Management Review* 31 (4): 833–863. doi:10.5465/amr.2006.22527456.

Lane, P. J., and M. Lubatikin. 1998. "Relative Absorptive Capacity and Inter-Organizational Learning." *Strategic Management Journal* 19: 461–477. doi:10.1002/(SICI)1097-0266(199805) 19:5<461::AID-SMJ953>3.0.CO;2-L.

Laursen, K., and A. J. Salter. 2004. "Searching High and Low: What Types of Firms Use Universities as a Source of Innovation?" *Research Policy* 33: 1201–1215.

Leal-Rodríguez, A. L., J. A. Ariza-Montes, J. L. Roldán, and A. G. Leal-Millán. 2014. "Absorptive Capacity, Innovation and Cultural Barriers: A Conditional Mediation Model." *Journal of Business Research* 67 (5): 763–768. doi:10.1016/j.jbusres.2013.11.041.

Link, A. L., and J. Rees. 1990. "Firm Size, University Based Research, and the Returns to R&D." *Small Business Economics* 2: 25–31. doi:10.1007/BF00389891.

Mansfield, E. 1991. "Academic Research and Industrial Innovation." *Research Policy* 20 (1): 1–12. doi:10.1016/0048-7333(91)90080-A.

Michie, J., and C. Oughton. 2016. "Creating Local Economic Resilience: Co-Operation, Innovation and Firms' Absorptive Capacity." In *Global Economic Crisis and Local Economic Development*, edited by J. Begley, D. Coffey, T. Donnelly, and C. Thornley, 12–29. Abingdon: Routledge. (Routledge Series in the Modern World Economy).

Mowery, D. C., and J. E. Oxley. 1995. "Inward Technology Transfer and Competitiveness: The Role of National Innovation Systems." *Cambridge Journal of Economy* 19: 67–93.

Nelson, R. R. 1986. "Institutions Supporting Technical Advance in Industry." *The American Economic Review* 76 (2): 186–189.

Penrose, E. [1959] 2009. *The Theory of the Growth of the Firm*. 4 ed. Oxford: Oxford Press.

Ragin, C. 1987. *The Comparative Method: Moving beyond Qualitative and Quantitative Strategies*. Berkeley: University of California Press.

Ragin, C. 2000. *Fuzzy-Set Social Science*. Chicago: University of Chicago Press.

Ragin, C. 2006. "Set Relations in Social Research: Evaluating Their Consistency and Coverage." *Political Analysis* 14 (3): 290–310. doi:10.1093/pan/mpj019.

Rapini, M. S., and H. M. Righi. 2011. "Metodologia e apresentação da base de dados do censo 2004 do diretório dos grupos de pesquisa do CNPq [Methodology and Presentation of the 2004 Census of the CNPq Research Group Directory]." In *Em Busca da Inovação: Interação Universidade-empresa No Brasil* [In Search of Innovation: University-Firm Interaction in Brazil], edited by W. Suzigan, E. M. Albuquerque, and S. F. Cario orgs, 45–74. Belo Horizonte: Autêntica.

Rapini, M. S., and H. M. Righi. 2006. "O Diretório de Grupos de Pesquisa do Cnpq e a Interação Universidade-Empresa no Brasil em 2004 [The CNPq Research Group Directory and University-Industry Interaction in Brazil in 2004]." *Revista Brasileira De Inovação* 5 (1): 131. doi:10.20396/rbi.v5i1.8648926.

Rihoux, B., and C. C. Ragin. 2008. *Configurational Comparative Methods: Qualitative Comparative Analysis (QCA) and Related Techniques, 51*. Newbury Park: Sage Publications.

Rosa, A. C. 2013. "Capacidade Absortiva de Empresas Que Possuem Interação Com Universidades [Absortive Capacity of Fims that Have Interacion with Universties]." Unpublished master's thesis. São Leopoldo, RS, Brazil: University of Vale do Rio dos Sinos (UNISINOS).

Rosa, A. C., and J. Ruffoni. 2014. "Mensuração da capacidade absortiva de firmas que possuem interação com universidades [Measurement of Absorptive Capacity of Firms that Interact with Universities.]." *Economia e Desenvolvimento* 26 (1). doi:10.5902/1414650912678.

Schneider, C. Q., and C. Wagemann. 2010. "Standards of Good Practice in Qualitative Comparative Analysis (QCA) and Fuzzy-Sets." *Comparative Sociology* 9 (3): 397–418. doi:10.1163/156913210X12493538729793.

Torodova, G., and B. Durisin. 2007. "Absorptive Capacity: Valuing a Reconceptualization." *Academy of Management Review* 32 (3): 774–786. doi:10.5465/amr.2007.25275513.

Van Den Bosch, F. A. J., R. V. Van Wijk, and H. W. Volberda. 2003. "Absorptive Capacity: Antecedents, Models and Outcomes." In *Handbook of Organizational Learning and Knowledge Management*, edited by M. Easterby-Smith and M. A. Lyles, 278–302. Oxford: Blackwell.

Van Den Bosch, F. A. J., H. W. Volberda, and M. De Boer. 1999. "Coevolution of Firm Absorptive Capacity and Knowledge Environment: Organizational Forms and Combinative Capabilities." *Organization Science* 10 (5): 551–568. doi:10.1287/orsc.10.5.551.

Vega-Jurado, J., A. Gutiérrez-Gracia, and I. Fernández-de-Lucio. 2008. "Analyzing the Determinants of Firm's Absorptive Capacity: Beyond R&D." *R&D Management* 18 (4): 392–405. doi:10.1111/j.1467-9310.2008.00525.x.

Versiani, A. F., M. Cruz, M. Ferreira, and L. Guimarães. 2010. "Mensuração da capacidade absortiva: até que ponto a literatura avançou? [Measuring Absorptive Capacity: To What Extent Has Literature Advanced?]." ANPAD 2010. Proceedings of the 26th Encontro da Associação Nacional de Programas de Pós- Graduação em Administração. Rio de Janeiro. ADI2172: 1–17

Waalkens, J. 2006. "Innovation in Medium-Sized Architectural and Engineering Firms." Unpublished doctoral dissertation. The Netherlands: Groningen University.

Zahra, S. A., and G. George. 2002. "Absorptive Capacity: A Review, Reconceptualization and Extension." *Academy of Management Review* 24 (2): 185–203. doi:10.5465/amr.2002.6587995.

ⓐ OPEN ACCESS

Profit rate dynamics in US manufacturing

Michael Joffe ⓘD

ABSTRACT
The attributes and dynamics of the profit rate distribution provide indispensable information on how the economy works. Edith Penrose, in *The theory of the growth of the firm*, took agency, managerial capabilities, heterogeneity and open-endedness as characteristic of the economy. Schumpeter had a similar view. Neoclassical theory, in contrast, envisages convergence to a standard rate of return, invoking inter-industry capital flows and diminishing returns as the main mechanism. I analysed the data on US manufacturing, 1987–2015. There was evidence of convergence, attributable to loss of supra-normal profits in two industries. The features of the distribution confirm Penrose's view. Neoclassical theory fares poorly: the data do not support 'a standard rate of return', and no plausible macro shock exists that could have produced the observed dispersion. The symmetry of the observed distribution indicates that neither market power nor intangible assets play major roles in determining the shape of the profit rate distribution; risk, however, is relevant if reformulated. Intersectoral capital flows were weak, and there was no evidence of diminishing returns. Penrose's conception of heterogeneous managerial capacity refers to a concept of economic power distinct from market power, corresponding to differential ex ante strength; differential profit outcomes represent ex post strength.

1. Introduction

There is no more important proposition in economic theory than that, under competition, the rate of return on investment tends towards equality in all industries. Stigler (1963, 54).

1.1. The research problem

Profitability is one of the most important attributes of a firm, and is a major criterion of its success. The behaviour of the rate of return on investment, or more succinctly the profit rate, is highly informative about economic performance in the aggregate: it can provide evidence about how the economy works. There is, however, little high-quality empirical research on this topic. In particular, the available evidence (such as it is) does not support Stigler's classic assertion. I set out to test Stigler's neoclassical view and its major rivals, the firm-centred approach of Edith Penrose (1959) and Schumpeter's views

---

This is an Open Access article distributed under the terms of the Creative Commons Attribution-NonCommercial-NoDerivatives License (http://creativecommons.org/licenses/by-nc-nd/4.0/), which permits non-commercial re-use, distribution, and reproduction in any medium, provided the original work is properly cited, and is not altered, transformed, or built upon in any way.

on creative destruction (1934, 1943), using a large dataset, nationally representative of US manufacturing, over a period of almost 30 years.

Penrose's contribution is important, because it developed from close and systematic analysis of actual firms. *The theory of the growth of the firm* was a distillation of multiple observations, formed into a causal account of the processes involved when firms expand. In parallel, the business historian Alfred Chandler came to similar conclusions from a detailed examination of the rise of large corporations in the US, as well as comparative studies with the UK and Germany. In addition to strong empirical foundations and a central focus on the firm, their perspectives share the feature that they are fundamentally concerned with change. This dynamic focus is also an attribute of Schumpeter's theory of entrepreneurial profit.

The paper is structured as follows. After some initial methodological observations, I outline the patterns that would be predicted from the dynamic theories of Penrose and Schumpeter. The predictions of neoclassical theory are then presented, together with the main assumptions that, if violated, could lead to deviations from the standard neoclassical model. I then analyse data on US manufacturing at the industry level for 1987–2015: after describing the dataset, I present the observed distribution and its descriptive statistics, plus evidence of a convergent trend. I then examine the differential flow of new capital across sectors. Finally, I analyse the relationship of the profit rate to the capital stock, to test the hypothesis of diminishing returns. I end by discussing the implications of the empirical findings for the various theories.

1.2. Preliminary observations on methodology

Firms assess the potential and the opportunity cost of investments according to their likely profitability, ex ante, often using such measures as the Internal Rate of Return (IRR) or the increase in Net Present Value (NPV). But it is difficult to obtain data that accurately reflect the ex-ante calculations of firms, and economists who have adopted this perspective have had to operationalise it in terms of actual expenditure (e.g. Fisher 1969, 35).

An alternative concept is to examine the achieved rate of return on capital, ex post, using available accounting data on the operating surplus (total revenue minus total costs) and on the cost of investments. Although this may not be identical to firms' ex-ante calculations with complete accuracy, the empirical difference is small (Fritsche and Dugan 1997). And an advantage of the ex post approach is that modern financial reporting, based on the principles of accrual accounting, corresponds closely with managers' concept of the profit rate (Bryer 1993).

In addition, the use of ex post accounting data has the advantage that it reflects the outcome of actual economic events, to the extent that the limitations of data quality allow. For example, it allows account to be taken of macro shocks such as the dot-com boom and crash, China's accession to the WTO and the financial crisis, the effects of which are unknowable to firms ex ante. In contrast, therefore, to the neoclassical view that regards firms' ex ante, subjective calculations as the gold standard, the use of accounting data is 'entirely justified, not as a mere feasible expedient, but as the required method of measuring capitalists' rate of return' (Wells 2007, 22).

Such an analysis can be at the industry or firm level. Each has its advantages and its limitations, so that a comprehensive analysis of the issue needs to include both.

The analysis presented here is at industry level. This is the more appropriate for an initial analysis because a representative sample is obtainable, which is of vital importance when presenting and analysing descriptive statistics. It capitalises on the resource provided by the Bureau of Economic Analysis, that has comprehensive coverage going back as far as the 1980s, with categories that are uniform for the whole period. It has the limitation that only a two-digit industry classification is available, but this is outweighed by the advantages of the BEA dataset for a preliminary study.

The findings at the industry level do not necessarily apply to the firm level, and those at the two-digit level may not be the same as, for example, those at the four-digit level. In particular, a finer classification would tend to generate a distribution with greater dispersion, and one would expect to find less dispersion at the industry level than the firm level because of the within-industry heterogeneity of firms. To that extent, the present analysis has a conservative bias towards underestimating the heterogeneity of profit rates.

However, that would not affect this paper's assessment of neoclassical theory, which would predict a narrow distribution clustered near the standard rate of return at either level, because it states that the tendency towards convergence should be pervasive across the whole economy. A further possible issue is that the reclassification of a single large firm could temporarily distort the observed profit rates of the industries involved (Stigler 1963).

A limitation of firm-level analysis is that firm-level datasets tend to be systematically incomplete: smaller firms' inclusion depends on stock-exchange listing and/or minimum turnover, profit or number of employees. Smaller firms are thus likely to be under-represented, so that the sample is inevitably biased, implying that a representative sample is unobtainable. There are also specific problems associated with very small firms, because they not only have a relatively wide dispersion, but also many extreme and implausible values (Wells 2007, 81; Greenblatt 2013); and they include sole proprietor-ships, for which profit and managerial income are hard to distinguish. In addition, firm-level analyses face the problem of firms' entry and exit, so that it is difficult to assemble a cohesive data series on the profits for each firm; in some cases, survivor bias can also be a serious issue (Cubbin and Geroski 1987).

Some of the causal forces operate at firm level, and in these cases an industry-level analysis is an aggregation of the influence of the actions and fortunes of many firms, which would attenuate the results. A corollary is that it is more difficult to obtain robust findings. Conversely, other causes operate at the industry level, for example a sector that is declining would be expected to lose investment to a more promising up-and-coming one.

The availability of data over this long time period, nationally representative of US manufacturing, is a key advantage of these analyses. It is possible to assess long-term trends in the profit rate and in its dispersion, the trajectories of each industry, patterns of capital flow between industries and the magnitude of diminishing returns, as well as to evaluate the effects of macro shocks. The paper therefore provides important evidence concerning this hitherto-neglected research area.

2. Predictions from theory

2.1. Dynamic theories

2.1.1. Penrose: 'The theory of the growth of the firm'

Penrose's (1959) theory provides a causal account of the process of expansion, for firms that are growing; it does not seek to explain which firms are likely to grow. Profitability plays a role, in that managers are assumed to be primarily motivated by the pursuit of total long-term profit – they deploy the resources available to them, including their own capabilities, to undertake profitable investments that expand the firm itself as well as its profitability. However, Penrose does not focus on the *rate* of profit, or the comparative profitability (the distribution) of different firms or industries. Nevertheless, the key features of her analysis allow a qualitative prediction to be made.

The attributes of Penrose's theory that are relevant to the profit rate distribution and its dynamics are agency, managerial capabilities, heterogeneity and open-endedness. *Agency* is central: managers take initiatives in the light of the resources available to them plus their assessments of potentially profitable opportunities. This is neither optimising – and therefore automatic – behaviour, nor a stimulus-response conception. The quality of initiatives depends on *managerial capabilities*, the degree of ability to make their projects successful, including fund-raising ingenuity (Penrose 1959, 34).

Heterogeneity is emphasised throughout her work: each firm is unique, its strengths depending on its specific resources, which in turn depend in a path-dependent manner on previous actions (e.g. pp. 173–4). In addition, cumulative growth occurs because success breeds further success, amplifying between-firm inequalities. Her theory is *open-ended*, because the future is uncertain; the quality of each ex ante initiative influences but does not determine the ex post consequences, including the degree of profitability.

One would therefore expect a wide distribution of profit rates, both between firms in a given industry, and between industries. There is no inbuilt tendency for this to change over time, except that highly dynamic economies, bristling with multiple initiatives, might be expected to have especially divergent profit rates. Importantly, differential firm size and profitability are not necessarily indications of monopoly power, but rather of 'more able and enterprising managers and entrepreneurs' (p. 164): they result from the unequal ex ante strength of different firms' resources and how they are used, together with the operation of chance. An implication is that a hierarchy of profit rates is not necessarily attributable to market power; a second source of power is superior managerial capabilities. They are not mutually exclusive, because firms that have grown as a result of superior management may then use their position to exercise market power in the conventional sense.[1]

2.1.2. Schumpeter's theory of entrepreneurial profit

According to Schumpeter's *The theory of economic development*, first published in German in 1911, 'Entrepreneurial profit is a surplus over costs', these costs being taken to include rent of the land needed for production, risk, and 'an appropriate wage for labour performed by the entrepreneur' (Schumpeter 1934, 128). Schumpeter contrasts this with circular flow, a static condition in which 'the total receipts of a business – abstracting from monopoly – are just big enough to cover outlays'; 'since the new combinations which are carried out if there is "development" are necessarily more advantageous than the old, total receipts must in this case be greater than total costs' (Schumpeter 1934, 129).

In terms of the implied profit rate distribution, Schumpeter is here proposing a dualistic structure: the static part of the economy that has zero economic rent, in other words equal to the standard rate of return, and the industries that have some degree of supra-normal profit. The implied distribution is therefore semi-continuous, with a spike at the standard rate of return plus a positive distribution. Statistically, this would register as positive skewness rather than symmetric dispersion.

Schumpeter's views on the source of capitalist dynamism changed over time, and he came to see 'the large-scale establishment or unit of control ... [as] the most powerful engine of ... progress and in particular of the long-run expansion of total output' (Schumpeter 1943, 106). In this 'Mark II' version of his theory, he emphasised 'competition which commands a decisive cost or quality advantage and which strikes not at the margins of the profits and the outputs of existing firms but at their very foundations and their very lives' (Schumpeter 1943, 84). Although less explicit about profitability than in the earlier 'Mark I' account, his view remained that creative destruction involved innovation by new firms or industries that were more successful and thus more profitable than the incumbents they replaced. The prediction would therefore again be a positively skewed semi-continuous distribution.

According to Schumpeter's theory, it is not essential that the identity of the industries characterised as 'more advantageous' remain the same. They could vary over time, with specific industries having a static circular-flow nature with zero entrepreneurial profit at certain times, and a positive profit at others. The existence of a group of more dynamic industries at each moment could be regarded as providing a divergent force in the profit rate distribution that counterbalances the prevailing tendency towards convergence.

2.2. Neoclassical theory

2.2.1. The standard account

Neoclassical theory states that under competition, profit rates across industries, and across firms within each industry, tend to converge to a single rate at any given time. There are two possible mechanisms.

The first is that any existing super-normal profit rates, due to market power (see next section), are eroded by new entrants. The situation thereby comes into closer alignment with the assumption of perfect competition. The profit rate distribution becomes more symmetrical as skewness decreases. It is contingent on the arrival of new entrants; were concentration to increase, the opposite tendency would be observed.

The second mechanism is that those with the higher rates of return should attract capital, and those with lower rates fail to attract it. This could be because capital is withdrawn from less profitable sectors and invested in more profitable ones, and/or because over a long period the amount of capital flowing towards failing industries dries up, while thriving sectors attract the available finance. This process ensures the allocation of capital to its most efficient uses across the economy. Diminishing returns then ensures that the copious inflow to dynamic industries brings their profit rate down towards the average for the whole economy and vice versa for struggling industries. Unlike the first mechanism, therefore, the change is not contingent.

Neoclassical theory thus predicts that the economy moves towards an equilibrium with zero dispersion, and zero economic profit (equal to a uniform 'standard' rate of return). At any given moment, however, this may not be observed, because shocks may have caused rates to diverge. These may be economy-wide macro shocks which differentially affect different sectors, such as a financial crisis or a pandemic. In the 2007–09 crisis, for example, the car industry became less profitable, but the food industry prospered (see below).

Alternatively, shocks may be at industry or firm level: innovations that affect profitability, for example via a change in costs or the introduction of a superior product, would be seen as shocks by neoclassical theory. The overall picture is thus of an economy with an endogenous convergent tendency towards a uniform equilibrium profit rate, that is also subject to exogenous shocks that generate divergence away from it.

The tendency towards diminishing returns – which is central to the second mechanism – is generally regarded as axiomatic, and has been assumed in such classic contributions as the standard neoclassical theory of growth (Solow 1956), and modern endogenous growth theory models (Romer 1986; Aghion and Howitt 1998), in which spillovers are just sufficient to overcome diminishing returns. It is also the basis for the Lucas 'puzzle' (Lucas 1990).

2.2.2. Deviations from standard neoclassical theory when its assumptions do not hold

Neoclassical economists allow for the observed behaviour of an economy to deviate from this theoretical account, if its assumptions are not met in practice. These include a perfectly competitive market and the ability of capital to flow freely from a less profitable to a more profitable use, equal risk, identical technology and uniform ability to make it profitable. The assessment of such behaviour may also be distorted by systematic errors in the measurement of capital expenditure and/or of its profitability.

2.2.2.1. Market power. In standard neoclassical theory, all firms in a perfectly competitive market earn zero economic profits. All firms are price takers, and there is free entry and exit, etc.

In practice, however, firms may well have some degree of market power, and therefore economic profit rates above zero. This could be due to barriers to entry and exit, collusion, economies of scale, sunk costs, etc. Market power would lead to a higher rate of return than obtains under perfect competition which corresponds to zero market power. There is no equivalent force acting in the opposite direction, i.e. negative market power leading to a less-than-standard profit rate, so that the distribution of rates of return would have the standard rate of return as its lower bound, and would be positively skewed.

2.2.2.2. Risk. In business as well as in finance, the degree of risk varies: the prospect of getting a return on one's investment is less certain in some sectors than others. In finance, a frequent definition of risk is the probability that an actual return on an investment will be lower than the expected return, possibly due to interest rate risk, exchange rate risk, liquidity risk, etc. A higher expected profit rate would thus be needed to induce the investment. This would imply a baseline of zero risk, plus a variable positive degree of risk, suggesting a profit rate distribution with the standard rate as lower bound, and likely positive skewness. However, other ways of thinking about risk are more symmetric, that may be more realistic (see below).

2.2.2.3. Neglect of intangible assets.

Estimation of the rate of return on capital necessarily depends on the accurate measurement of the capital outlay. In principle, this could be either under- or over-estimated. In practice, the literature is silent on overestimation and focuses entirely on underestimation, specifically on the grounds that firms' expenditure includes items that contribute to future output and/or sales, but which are conventionally listed under current rather than capital spending. Such items are collectively grouped under the heading of intangible assets (Haskel and Westlake 2017), and they include advertising, R&D (Megna and Mueller 1991; Görzig and Gornig 2013), and organisational capital (Görzig and Gornig 2013), as well as software and intellectual property. Neglect of any or all of these understates the true capital expenditure, so the implication is that the *observed* rate of return is higher than the actual one, that is, positively skewed.

A classic study was carried out by Megna and Mueller (1991): they investigated the neglect of R&D and advertising in the US (1967–1988), focusing on pharmaceuticals, distilled beverages, cosmetics and toys at the firm level. Inclusion of advertising and R&D spend in capital did not eliminate the wide dispersion in profit rates. More recently, Görzig and Gornig (2013) have found that the observed (unadjusted) rate of return was reduced by about 20% in Germany 1999–2003, once they allowed for own-account production of ICT, R&D and organisational capital – in other words, after a proportion of specialised labour was reclassified as capital spending.

2.2.2.4. Heterogeneity in managerial capacity or talent.

This is central to Penrose and Schumpeter, but in neoclassical theory identical technology across firms is often assumed. This is taken to imply a common cost structure as well as an exogenously given price, so that the rate of return is uniform. In practice, however, substantial between-firm heterogeneity is observed in growth rates, productivity, productivity growth, efficiency, market performance and the degree of innovativeness, (e.g. Davis, Haltiwanger, and Schuh 1996; Bartelsman and Doms 2000; Foster, Haltiwanger, and Syverson 2008; Dosi et al. 2012; Dosi, Grazzi, and Moschella 2015; Decker et al. 2016; Foster et al. 2017). This literature has not focused on the profit rate, but elsewhere there is some limited evidence on the firm-level profit rate distribution (Wells 2007).

Heterogeneity is present even with the same input prices, and irrespective of the level of industry disaggregation (Dosi, Grazzi, and Moschella 2015). The evidence also supports considerable heterogeneity in participation in export markets (Bernard et al. 2012; Melitz and Trefler 2012). This is clearly in line with the analysis of Penrose's (1959), centred on variations in managerial capacity *between firms*, which also has considerable empirical support (e.g. Bloom, Sadun, and Van Reenen 2012).

It is less certain whether the same explanation applies to profit rate heterogeneity *between industries*. This would occur if there were a systematic tendency for some branches of manufacturing to attract and retain more competent entrepreneurs and managers. There is some evidence to suggest that this may be so, at least to some extent; for example, export propensity is associated with managerial competence (Driver and Temple 2013).

2.2.2.5. Inter-industry differences in monetary or non-monetary rewards. Another possibility is that compensating differentials affect the observed profit rate, either because the work is so unpleasant or hazardous that an additional monetary reward is required, or conversely that the experience of the work is sufficiently pleasant that lower remuneration is needed to attract people into that line of business (Stigler 1963). However, this is probably not relevant in the present context. In manufacturing at least, the profit primarily accrues to firms (employers), whereas it is the workers who would experience any unpleasantness or health risk, or conversely pleasure. Owners of coalmines are unlikely to develop silicosis or to be injured in underground accidents, and it also appears unlikely that the owners or managers of manufacturing firms vary greatly in the degree of pleasure they get from the particular branch of manufacturing that they happen to be in. Furthermore, even if such differences do exist, they are unlikely to vary significantly over time. It is therefore not considered further in this paper.

3. Empirical literature

The analyses presented in this paper primarily relate to two literatures. There are empirical studies of profit rate convergence, and there is a limited empirical literature on diminishing returns to financial capital.

3.1. Convergence

There is a large mainstream literature, primarily within macroeconomics, that investigates the extent to which capital is allocated efficiently across the economy, and the economic impact of misallocation (e.g. Hsieh and Klenow 2009; Eisfeldt and Shi 2018). The starting point is the notion that this capital reallocation is fundamental to the functioning of the economy, because it allows a shift from low to high productivity firms. It is therefore traditionally held to play a major role in growth of productivity and GDP (Stigler 1963). However, leading researchers in this tradition have recently shown that this role is empirically small – what they call 'the reallocation myth' (Hsieh and Klenow 2018).

In line with this re-evaluation of the role of capital reallocation, it is relevant to investigate the prior question, whether such reallocation occurs *at all*. Clearly, if it does not, then its proposed impact on productivity and GDP would not even arise. This would likely require paying attention to changes in production, as Penrose did, rather than to mere reorganisation of existing production – the reallocation notion treats the origin of high-productivity firms as being an external cause, rather than a central element in the growth of firms and economies. At issue here is whether economic dynamism results primarily from the actions of those whose decisions set the direction of the firm, or of those who have the money to pay for new investment when this cannot be financed by retained profits; and whether growth results from innovation in production or from flexibility bringing about a perfect market.

The capital reallocation perspective has hitherto dominated this literature, to the detriment of focusing on innovation in production. It is preferable to empirically investigate the basic features of the economy, making no assumptions about causal processes that may or may not be operating until they have been backed up by evidence.

This direct methodology (such as a 'data-first' approach (Juselius 2011)), that imposes little model structure until it can be empirically justified, could be considered an instance of what has been called 'evidence-based economics' (Joffe 2014; Joffe 2017). In the present context, it involves directly investigating the profit rate at industry level, with a view to assessing what causal processes are compatible with the data.

In the previous empirical literature, much of the historical evidence is at the firm level and applies to the US. In many cases, the samples then available for research constituted a relatively small and probably unrepresentative sample of the economy. In addition, as will be seen, many contributions assume one dominant feature underlying their data, such as concentration, and structure their analysis around that, rather than starting with an open-minded examination of the rates of return.

The earliest analysis of US profit rates was at the industry level, and covered the period 1938–1956 (Stigler 1963, 57–58). Greater dispersion was observed for 1947–56 than for 1938–47, indicating the occurrence of divergence rather than convergence, with a coefficient of variation of 21.9% and 31.5% in the earlier and later periods, respectively; this analysis was restricted to 'unconcentrated' industries, but did not take account of barriers to entry. Stigler's interpretation was that the smaller dispersion in the earlier period could have been due to 'extremely heavy corporate excess-profits taxation', but there is no evidence for this view.

Qualls (1974) investigated the persistence of the gradient of rates across concentration classes, rather than the distribution of rates of return as such, for 1950–65. The aim was specifically to investigate the effect of market power and how it may change. He found that the concentration-related dispersion of the profit rate persisted.

Mueller (1977) found a considerable degree of movement in the ranking of firms' profit rates, using a firm-based sample for 1949–1972. Contrary to expectations, firms that started at the top or the bottom of the rankings were less likely to change position than those in the centre of the distribution. Risk was considered not to explain the persistence of relatively high profit rates. It is unclear whether there was overall convergence or divergence.

A similar analysis was carried out by Connolly and Schwartz (1985) for 1963–1982. They confirmed the finding of persistence of the high rates, but indicated that firms with low profit rates tended to converge towards the average rate.

In a later analysis comparing 1964 and 1980 (Mueller 1990), the degree of persistence of abnormal profit rates was observed to be much lower, although some persisting advantage in the top group (out of six) remained. Convergence had therefore occurred between these two periods. This contrast remained essentially unaltered when the comparison was confined to the 397 firms that were present in both samples, indicating that it was an actual change rather than an artefact of sample selection.

Similarly, convergence was observed at the industry level for 197 industries between 1963, 1967 and 1972 (Levy 1987). The speed of convergence was quite fast when separate industry intercepts were included, but slow in their absence. Jacobsen (1988) also found convergence at the firm level, albeit relatively slow, in 1970–1983.

Thus, the empirical literature suggests a mixed picture, with profit rates moving sometimes in the theoretically expected direction, sometimes in the opposite direction, and at other times appearing not to move at all. Overall, the differences in the findings could be due to the different methods used, or to differences in the details of the particular samples in each study – especially the firm-based analyses, in which the included firms might not be representative of the economy.

Alternatively, the differences may be real. There is a suggestion, albeit tentative given the methodological issues, that in the US there was divergence of profit rates between 1938–47 and 1947–56, relatively little change in the late 1950s and early 1960s, and then convergence starting sometime in the 1960s and continuing into the later period covered by the analyses presented in this paper.

3.2. Diminishing returns

The law of diminishing returns has a venerable history, dating back to Turgot in the eighteenth century and to Ricardo and others in the early nineteenth century (Brue 1993). It has been applied to two very different situations: in production where it has a physical meaning, and in the context of financial capital.

The classical descriptions focused on production, and relied on implicit *physical* properties. They were initially applied to the fertility of land. With a fixed quantity of land, the addition of increasing quantities of inputs, for example of labour and/or capital, was not followed by a proportionate increase in the yield. Many of these pioneering contributions were defined imprecisely and inconsistently, and 'often confused average and marginal returns, homogeneous and heterogeneous inputs, short-run and long-run returns, and more' (Brue 1993). In 1888, John Bates Clark extended this argument beyond agriculture, introducing the now-familiar concept of capital as a fixed factor of production, with labour as the sole variable factor. Subsequently, the concept of diminishing returns in the context of physical production has become accepted as an axiom, even if the theoretical proofs of it have sometimes been unsatisfactory, and the empirical evidence for it is mixed, even in agriculture (Brue 1993).

In the present context, diminishing returns no longer has its roots in a physical relationship, as with the addition of more labour or more fertiliser to an existing plot of land. Rather, the concept of capital here is essentially financial: that the availability of a greater quantity of capital leads to a decrease in its rate of return. Its validity generally tends to be assumed but not tested empirically.

The closest empirical literature I can find to this is in the international context: that the quantity of capital available in a country is inversely related to the profit rate. Most of the literature assumes this to be true. However, Nell and Thirlwall (2017; 2018) have directly estimated the productivity of investment for 84 rich and poor countries over the period 1980–2011, as the ratio of long-run GDP growth to a country's gross investment ratio. They found no significant evidence of diminishing returns.

The assumption that diminishing returns applies in this context is deeply rooted in the mainstream literature. For example, it plays a central role in the canonical Solow neoclassical growth model (as well as new growth theory and the Lucas puzzle, as previously noted), and underlies its prediction that relatively poor countries with low capital endowments are destined to grow faster than rich countries with abundant capital, other things being equal. An implication is that whatever the original level of capital in an economy, it will tend to revert to the equilibrium levels of output and capital indicated by the economy's underlying features. The repeated finding in cross-country growth regressions of a negative coefficient on initial income levels is often taken as conditional convergence, and therefore a confirmation of the Solow model. However, it is equally likely to result from a catch-up effect, for example from the adoption of technology from abroad (Benhabib and Spiegel 1994). The work of Nell and Thirlwall suggests that the latter interpretation may be the correct one.

4. Data

Data were obtained from the Bureau of Economic Analysis (BEA n.d.). Gross operating surplus (GOS) was derived from the table of the components of value added by industry, for 1987–2015. These data do not take account of depreciation, tax, etc. Table 3.3ESI provided the net stock of private fixed assets by industry for 1986–2014, at historical cost. These are year-end estimates of the running total of investments, net of depreciation. Table 3.7ESI provided data on investment in private fixed assets by industry for 1985–2016. These data are classified in 62 sectors; the 19 manufacturing sectors are the focus of the present study and constitute the entire manufacturing sector. See the data Appendix for further details.

The categories used in compiling the data do not necessarily correspond perfectly with theory, which involves theoretical concepts appropriate to its own domain (Stigler 1963). The issues include the deviation of historical and replacement costs; the impact of high inflation on the historic cost of capital, with older assets being less expensive in nominal terms and therefore artificially associated with a higher rate of return; the omission of the 'wages' of the owners of small businesses, in sectors where such firms are predominant; and the omission of noncorporate businesses from the data. Depreciation is likely to have varied between industries and over time. The same is true of taxation. These are likely to have introduced non-differential measurement error. Furthermore, there are controversies over the correct calculation of capital and land, and over the measurement of goodwill and whether it is depreciated. To the extent that these generate non-differential measurement error bias, they would have a diluting effect, making it more difficult to obtain clear-cut findings.

The analysis covered manufacturing only. Additional issues would arise if services were included. For example, inspection of the data revealed that *Legal services* had profit rates in the range 271.6 to 376.0%, far in excess of any manufacturing sector. In such a case, capital in the usual sense probably plays a rather minor role in the cost structure, which is primarily driven by expertise (Biery 2015), undermining the use of fixed assets as the (sole) denominator. In addition, small service firms often rent the capital necessary for production, rather than purchasing capital goods. These expenditures are counted as intermediate consumption in the firm's accounting system (Görzig and Gornig 2013). The inclusion of services would clearly add extra sources of heterogeneity, making interpretation difficult.

5. The range of observations and their implications for theory

The data allow the following types of observation to be made. These can be used to evaluate each of the theoretical propositions outlined above from an empirical viewpoint.

5.1. The profit rate distribution

According to pure neoclassical theory, at equilibrium there should be a single economy-wide rate of return on capital, with minimal dispersion. In practice, however, it is likely that deviations would be observed, due to factors described above. In addition, shocks could lead to further divergence, temporarily at least.

The most informative measures are the standard deviation/variance/coefficient of variation and the skewness of the profit rate distribution. Trends in the variance provide evidence on convergence or divergence, and the degree of skewness favours some of the theoretical propositions over others, as previously noted.

In addition, measurement error can occur giving the false impression of dispersion. If non-differential, the resulting dispersion would be symmetric.

5.2. Industry-specific movements

As part of the examination of heterogeneity, it is possible to observe the trajectories of each industry over time. This could provide some preliminary indication that industry-specific innovations or shocks are present. However, additional information would be needed to illuminate the nature of any such change. This complementary evidence could be quantitative and/or qualitative.

In addition, the pattern of industry-specific movements could provide some information relevant to the possible hypotheses outlined earlier. For example, some of them might be expected to produce differences in profit rates that vary little over time, including Inter-industry differences in monetary or non-monetary rewards.

5.3. Impact of macro shocks

Due to the panel structure of the dataset, the effects of macro-level shocks would be visible as a change in dispersion following a known macroeconomic event, after a suitable lag period. During the period covered by this dataset, the obvious candidates are NAFTA, which came into force in 1995, the dot-com bubble and crash at the turn of the century, China's accession to the WTO in 2001 and the accompanying change in US trade policy (Pierce and Schott 2016), and the financial crisis of 2007-09.

5.4. Convergence

It is possible to test both for σ- and β- convergence using these data, by analogy with the literature on economic growth. Here, σ denotes the standard deviation of the rates of return, and β indicates the regression coefficient when the profit rate is regressed on its lagged value.

5.5. Response of investment to the profit rate

By regressing the quantity of investment on the lagged profit rate, the sensitivity of inter-industry flows to heterogeneous profitability can be assessed. This provides an indication of the degree of fluidity (interchangeability) of capital between sectors.

5.6. Impact of the quantity of capital on its rate of return

Similarly, the rate of return can be regressed on the lagged quantity of capital. This gives information on the presence of diminishing returns.

6. The observed profit rate distribution

The rate of return is calculated as the Gross Operating Surplus for each sector in each year, divided by the Fixed Assets for the previous year, expressed as a percentage. A lag is appropriate because the profit is realised after the investment has been made. The results presented here are for a one-year lag. Sensitivity analyses (not presented) show that the use of other lag structures, for example the average of three or five years, makes little difference. In addition, the use of a one-year lag enables a longer time series to be included.

In order to visualise the distribution of the rates of return, the data for all years, as well as for all sectors, were pooled. With more than 500 observations, a stable distribution was thus obtained, which can be characterised quite precisely.

The mean profit rate was estimated as 38.7%, with a median of 35.9% (Figure 1, panel (a)). This difference suggests right-skewness, which is confirmed by a skewness statistic of 2.2. The standard deviation was 18.9%, and the coefficient of variation was 0.49. The kurtosis was 8.5. The number of observations lying outside the range 25 to 50% was 198 (35.9%).

Inspection of the time course for each of the sectors indicated that one particular sector, *Petroleum and coal products*, was an extreme outlier (see next section). After exclusion of this sector, the distribution appeared more symmetrical (Figure 1, panel (b)): the mean was now estimated as 36.6%, with the median little changed at 35.2%. The skewness was now only 0.9. The standard deviation was 14.5% and the coefficient of variation 0.40. The kurtosis was now down to 1.7. The number of observations lying outside the range 25 to 50% was 178 (34.1%).

7. Profit rate movements over time

7.1. Descriptive statistics

The evolution of the profit rate for all manufacturing sectors is shown in Figure 2(a). The most striking feature is that one sector, *Petroleum and coal products*, is very different from all the other sectors: from early in the twenty-first century, its profits rose sharply to a level quite outside the range of the other sectors, reaching 158.6% in 2005 and staying above 80% for the succeeding ten years. This corresponds to a large rise in the crude oil price at that time.[2]

It is therefore prudent to examine the behaviour of the profit rate after excluding this outlying sector. The sensitivity of the analysis of convergence to such a course of action was assessed by repeating the analysis after sequential removal of each of the next most profitable three sectors (*Apparel and leather and allied products*; *Furniture and related products*; *Food and beverage and tobacco products*). Only the exclusion of *Petroleum and coal products* had a major impact on the findings (details available on request).

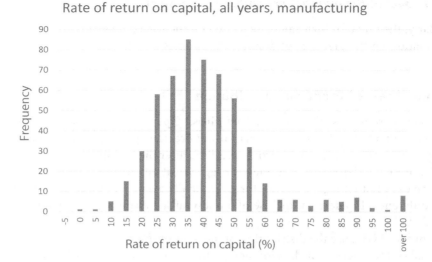

Figure 1. *The observed profit rate distribution in US manufacturing sectors, 1987–2015 (pooled)*, for all manufacturing sectors (panel a), and for all manufacturing sectors, excluding Petroleum and coal products (panel b) (the reason for this is given in the text – see section on Descriptive statistics).

The profit rates for all the remaining sectors are shown in Figure 2(b). Considerable dispersion is visible, especially in the period up to the year 2000. Supra-normal profits are observed in two sectors, *Apparel and leather and allied products* and *Furniture and related products*, during the early part of the period covered. The degree of dispersion and the mean rate of return both diminish over time (evidence available on request).

The position of individual industries is subject to considerable variation. *Apparel and leather and allied products* starts with the highest rate, but declines in the second half of the 1990s and the 2000s, ending with the lowest rate. *Furniture and related products* starts

Figure 2. *The evolution of profit rates by sector, 1987–2015,* for all manufacturing sectors (panel a), and for all manufacturing sectors, excluding Petroleum and coal products (panel b). Note their different vertical axes.

high, plunges to mid-range after 2006, then rises again in the 2010s. At the other end, *Primary metals* starts with the lowest profit rate and stays low, apart from a surge in 2004 through 2008. In general, sharp year-to-year volatility is not a dominant feature; rather, industries tend to maintain their relative position for several years, or even a decade or more, often without any obvious reason for this, for example a technical change or a new product.

The impact of the financial crisis is clearly evident, with a large dispersion in 2009. This is largely due to a fall in profitability of *Motor vehicles, bodies and trailers, and parts*, and a rise for *Food and beverage and tobacco products*, with most industries not showing any obvious effect (Figure 2(b)). The recovery is immediate: by 2010 the degree of dispersion visible is no longer increased. This is statistically confirmed by the variance returning to within the normal range. No other macro shocks are clearly visible, for example of NAFTA, the dot-com boom and crash, or China's accession to the WTO.

7.2. σ-convergence

Figure 3 shows the evolution of the variance over time, together with a linear regression line corresponding to the equation

$$\sigma^2 = \alpha_\sigma + \beta_\sigma t \tag{1}$$

where σ^2 is the variance of the profit rate, t is time, and α_σ and β_σ are parameters to be estimated.

In panel (a), there is a large departure from the previous range of values, starting in 2003. The regression line shows an upward trend. After exclusion of the *Petroleum and coal products* sector (panel (b)), a much lower degree of volatility is observed, and a clearly downward trend over time.

Thus, the impression of convergence from Figure 2(b) is confirmed. Again, the impact of the financial crisis is visible in 2009, and by 2010 the variance of profit rates is down to just below the regression line.

The speed of convergence, while large, was not observed to have brought about a single rate of return on capital across all of manufacturing. At the end of the study period, the rates still varied from 17.0% (*Apparel and leather and allied products*) to 51.6% (*Food and beverage and tobacco products*) – even without the *Petroleum and coal products* sector, which was over 80%.

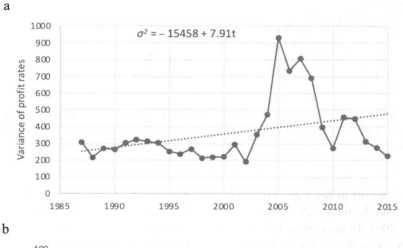

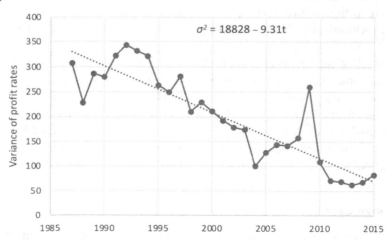

Figure 3. *The variance of the profit rate over time,* for all manufacturing sectors (panel a), and for all manufacturing sectors, excluding Petroleum and coal products (panel b). Note their different vertical axes.

7.3. β-convergence

Beta-convergence implies that the change in profit rate in a particular year is a negative function of the level in the previous year. A relatively high rate will tend to be followed by a fall, and a low rate will be followed by a rise. This can be expressed in the following equation, in which a negative value of β^C indicates convergence.

$$\Delta R = R_{it} - R_{i,t-1} = \alpha^C{}_t + \beta^C{}_t R_{i,t-1} + \gamma^C X_{it} + \in^C{}_{it} \tag{2}$$

where R is the rate of return on capital, and X is a vector of covariates; α^C, β^C and γ^C are parameters to be estimated, and $\in^C$ is the error term.

This can be rearranged as

$$R_{it} = \alpha^C{}_t + \left(1 + \beta^C{}_t\right) R_{i,t-1} + \gamma^C X_{it} + \in^C{}_{it} \tag{3}$$

Convergence could be to a common rate, or to a sector-specific rate. Accordingly, this equation was estimated using both Ordinary Least Squares and Fixed Effects regression. This approach follows the method of panel convergence used in the literature on economic growth. Robust standard errors were used for all regression analyses. The results are shown in Table 1(a) for all sectors, and Table 1(b) after exclusion of *Petroleum and coal products*.

Both tables show highly significant β-convergence. Focusing on Table 1 (b), the rate of convergence is 9.9% (100*(1–0.901)) for OLS, and 15.5% (100*(1–0.845)) for FE. When individual-sector intercepts were included in the FE regression (data not shown), the robust test using Welch's F-statistic was far from significant, with p = 0.80. The time variation was not large, with only 5 out of 27 years being significantly different at the 5% level; addition of the two largest deviations, 2002 and 2009, as dummy variables scarcely altered the main findings. When the average profit rate was added in addition, the estimate of β^C in the OLS regression was 10.9% (95% CI 7.2, 14.6), and that in the FE regression was 18.2% (95% CI 5.3, 31.1). Convergence to the all-manufacturing mean rate was 14.9% (95% CI 2.2, 27.6) for the OLS analysis, and 25.3% (95% CI 10.6, 40.0) for the Fixed Effects analysis.

The results when all sectors were included (Table 1 (a)) were similar: the estimates of β^C were respectively 7.4 and 14.9% for OLS and FE, and Welch's F-statistic gave a value of p = 0.97. With addition of the average profit rate, the estimates of β^C scarcely altered to 7.7 and 15.7%. The estimate of the magnitude of convergence to the all-manufacturing mean rate was similar to that obtained when the *Petroleum and coal products* sector was omitted, but the standard error was far higher, so that in this case it was not significant.

The Schwarz criterion, with *Petroleum and coal products* excluded, was 3189.263 for the pooled OLS regression, 3277.708 for the FE regression, and 3373.589 for the FE regression when time dummies were included. This clearly indicates that the OLS regression is the preferred analysis. It means that the sectors are all converging to a single common rate of return, not a sector-specific rate. Taking column 4 of Table 1 (b) as the definitive analysis, this common rate of return is given by $\alpha^C/(1 - \beta^C) = 3.791/(1-0.898) = 37.2\%$.

8. Response of investment to the profit rate

A standard proposition in economic theory is that investment should flow towards the more profitable sectors (and firms), and away from those that are less profitable. This can

Table 1 (a). The Response of the change in profit rate to the lagged value of the profit rate, all manufacturing sectors.

	OLS (1)	FE (2)	OLS (3)	FE (4)	OLS (5)	FE (6)
Intercept	2.727***	5.609***	2.881***	5.739***	-2.871	-2.214
	(0.446)	(1.279)	(0.472)	(1.220)	(3.414)	(4.256)
R_{t-1} (lagged profit rate)	0.926***	0.851***	0.926***	0.852***	0.923***	0.843***
	(0.015)	(0.033)	(0.016)	(0.031)	(0.020)	(0.034)
2009 dummy			-5.037**	-4.935**	-4.467*	-4.126*
			(1.669)	(1.626)	(1.828)	(1.765)
Average profit rate					0.162	0.229
					(0.102)	(0.122)
Observations	532	532	532	532	532	532

* p < .05.
** p < .01.
*** p < .001

Table 1 (b). The Response of the change in profit rate to the lagged value of the profit rate, excluding the Petroleum and coal products secto.r.

	OLS (1)	FE (2)	OLS (3)	OLS (4)	FE (5)	FE (6)	OLS (7)	FE (8)
Intercept	3.345***	5.406*	3.584***	3.791***	5.716*	5.941*	-1.411	-2.499
	(0.736)	(2.199)	(0.731)	(0.737)	(2.154)	(2.168)	(2.529)	(2.734)
R_{t-1} (lagged profit rate)	0.901***	0.845***	0.899***	0.898***	0.841***	0.840***	0.891***	0.818***
	(0.019)	(0.060)	(0.019)	(0.019)	(0.058)	(0.059)	(0.019)	(0.066)
2009 dummy			-4.643*	-4.833*	-4.799*	-4.991*	-4.291*	-4.100*
			(1.708)	(1.717)	(1.738)	(1.743)	(1.833)	(1.851)
2002 dummy				-5.091***		-5.128***	-4.010**	-3.305*
				(1.314)		(1.268)	(1.278)	(1.254)
Average profit rate							0.149*	0.253**
							(0.065)	(0.075)
Observations	504	504	504	504	504	504	504	504

* p < .05.
** p < .01.
*** p < .001

be expressed in the following equation, in which the proportional change in investment depends on the rate of return in the previous year:

$$\Delta I / I_{i,t-1} = \left(I_{it} - I_{i,t-1} \right) / I_{i,t-1} = \alpha^R{}_t + \beta^R{}_t R_{i,t-1} + \gamma^R X_{it} + \in^R{}_{it} \tag{4}$$

(where I is investment in private fixed assets).

The findings are shown in Table 2. The estimate of the coefficient is 0.0011 for the whole sample. After exclusion of the *Petroleum and coal products* sector, the coefficient is 0.0012 for the whole sample, both with and without the dummies for 2002 and 2009. This means that for a one percentage point change in profit rate, for example from 38.0% to 39.0%, the percentage change in investment is 0.12% (95% Confidence Interval 0.06, 0.18).

Table 2. The proportional change in investment, in response to the lagged profit rate.

	OLS (1)	OLS (2)	OLS (3)
Intercept	−0.000608	−0.00456	0.00302
	(0.00562)	(0.00945)	(0.00994)
R_{t-1} (lagged profit rate)	0.00108***	0.00122***	0.00119***
	(0.00016)	(0.00030)	(0.00030)
2009 dummy			−0.0721*
			(0.031)
2002 dummy			−0.108***
			(0.019)
Petroleum and coal products sector	Yes	No	No
Number of observations	551	522	522

* $p < .05$.
**$p < .01$.
***$p < .001$.

In addition, a more disaggregated set of regression analyses was carried out to show the response of investment to the profit rate in different sectors for each year (Table 3). The findings fluctuate markedly from year to year. The expected positive relationship is seen slightly more often (15) than a negative one (13). Positive coefficients greater than 0.2 are more frequent (8) than negative ones less than −0.2 (2). There is no obvious clustering of years with respect to the direction of flows, nor any obvious impact of major macro events such as NAFTA, the dot-com bubble and crash, China's accession to the WTO, or the financial crisis and ensuing great recession. One can therefore say that investment is attracted to the more profitable sectors, but only in an irregular fashion. Clearly other causes are operating as well.

Table 4 shows the response of investment to the previous year's rate of return, separately for each sector across the whole period of study. Almost all the coefficients are positive, some strongly so. Only four sectors had negative coefficients, with substantially negative values for *Food and beverage and tobacco products*, and for *Printing and related support activities*. Within most sectors, therefore, a higher profit tends to be followed by more investment in the following year.

9. Impact of the quantity of capital on its rate of return

Neoclassical theory proposes that as more capital accumulates, its rate of return will inevitably decrease – the hypothesis of diminishing returns. The magnitude of this effect can be estimated as a regression of the profit rate on the lagged quantity of capital:

Table 3. Percentage investment flow change by year.

Year	1987	1988	1989	1990	1991	1992	1993	1994	1995
β^R	− 0.05	− 0.01	− 0.01	0.08	0.34	0.07	− 0.01	0.29	− 0.05

1996	1997	1998	1999	2000	2001	2002	2003	2004	2005
− 0.14	0.09	0.25	− 0.05	0.15	0.52	0.16	− 0.12	0.26	− 0.02

2006	2007	2008	2009	2010	2011	2012	2013	2014	2015
0.28	0.07	0.17	− 0.09	− 0.42	0.33	0.32	− 0.34	− 0.10	0.00

Table 4. Percentage investment flow change by sector.

Sector	β^R
Wood products	0.76
Nonmetallic mineral products	0.43
Primary metals	0.49
Fabricated metal products	0.06
Machinery	0.40
Computer and electronic products	0.77
Electrical equipment, appliances, and components	0.35
Motor vehicles, bodies and trailers, and parts	− 0.02
Other transportation equipment	− 0.08
Miscellaneous manufacturing	0.20
Textile mills and textile product mills	0.25
Paper products	0.92
Printing and related support activities	− 0.33
Chemical products	0.77
Plastics and rubber products	0.48
Food and beverage and tobacco products	− 0.49
Apparel and leather and allied products	0.09
Petroleum and coal products	0.13

$$R_{it} = \alpha^I_t + \beta^I_t K_{i,t-1} + \gamma^I X_{it} + \in^I_{it} \tag{5}$$

(where K is fixed assets).

The regression coefficient was found to have the expected negative sign, but it was not significant and its magnitude was small (Table 5). Excluding the *Petroleum and coal products* sector, in which the very high profit in the latter part of the period may have diluted the effect, the largest estimate (without the year dummies for 2002 and 2009) was that for each billion dollars invested, the rate of return decreases by 0.0081% (95% CI −0.0400, +0.0239). It is essentially zero.

10. Discussion

10.1. Strengths and limitations

In contrast with some of the early literature on this topic, no assumption was made concerning the predominant causal factor that might explain any observed dispersion or asymmetry in the profit rate distribution, such as market power. Rather, the approach

Table 5. The response of the profit rate to the lagged quantity of capital.

	OLS (1)	OLS (2)	OLS (3)
Intercept	39.14***	37.34***	37.74***
	(3.53)	(3.17)	(3.21)
$K_{i,\,t-1}$ (lagged fixed capital quantity)	−0.00519	−0.00806	−0.00740
	(0.0159)	(0.0163)	(0.0161)
2009 dummy			−7.28*
			(3.28)
2002 dummy			−5.84***
			(1.42)
Petroleum and coal products sector	Yes	No	No
Number of observations	551	522	522

* p < .05.
**p < .01.
***p < .001.

taken here is an exploratory ('data-first') analysis, providing a robust statistical description of the profit rate distribution at industry level. It assumes that multiple causal processes may be operating, and seeks to document what has actually occurred before attempting to attribute the findings to specific causes. As far as I have been able to ascertain, the existing literature does not contain such an analysis. Section 10.2 discusses the theories described in section 2 in the light of these findings.

The dataset allows an analysis that covers the years from 1987 to 2015. This is a sufficiently long period to allay the worry that the findings could be distorted by business-cycle fluctuations. It also covers the implementation of NAFTA, the dot-com bubble/crash and China's accession to the WTO, as well as the financial crisis. Effects of some of these macro shocks were detectable in the econometric analysis, but inclusion of the relevant year dummies did not affect the main findings, and the disturbances attributable to these events were remarkably transient. In fact, the major time-related disturbing factor was the trajectory of the profit rate of the *Petroleum and coal products* sector in the second part of the period covered (which could easily have been missed if the sector-specific time series had not been visualised). This was associated with the more than quadrupling of the global crude oil price at that time. Its exclusion altered the findings on σ-convergence and on skewness, but not on β-convergence, response of investment to the profit rate, or diminishing returns.

The disadvantages of a crude measure such as gross operating surplus (GOS) are well known. It is a measure of the accounting rate of return, rather than the economic concept which focuses on the difference between that and the normal profit rate that prevails at any one time.

Accounting data can certainly be seriously in error when used to assess the return on an individual investment initiative by a particular firm, due to the time patterns in the returns to investment and in the depreciation schedule, and to inflation (Fisher and McGowan 1983). Such problems would tend to even out in the context of the present sector-level analysis and long timespan. In the current context, the main problem with the use of accounting data is that conservative accounting conventions tend to lead to the measured value understating the present value of future profits. Any resulting bias would mean that high (low) measured rates are overvalued (undervalued), so that any observed dispersion would tend to persist (Mueller 1990, 9–10). This implies that the present finding of substantial convergence is, if anything, underestimated.

In addition, non-differential measurement error occurs, e.g. due to year-to-year variation in the relationship between the growth rates of the measured capital stock and of the present value of future profits (Mueller 1990, 9). Such non-differential error would lead to attenuation of the findings on convergence, implying that the clear convergence reported in this paper would have been even more marked if a more accurate measure had been used.

On the other hand, if the measure of GOS used here is subject to unrecognised sources of *systematic* bias, this would be unlikely to explain the observed convergent trend, because that would require a sharp trend *in the sources of bias*. More likely is that the degree of bias in the profit rate estimates is relatively constant, and that the trend corresponds to an actual change in the economy.

10.2. Evaluation of the various theories

10.2.1. Dynamic theories

Penrose's work was not primarily focused on profit rates, and provides less precise predictions than neoclassical theory for this analysis. I therefore extrapolate from her basic perspective, which emphasised agency, managerial capabilities, heterogeneity and open-endedness. It could be argued that *any* firm-centred and empirically-based analysis would inevitably highlight these four features, because they are core features of business in the real world – as would be clear to readers of the economic news.

These attributes predict a broad and persistent profit rate distribution, with no reason to expect a high degree of skewness at firm level. To the extent that industries differ in these respects, the same would apply at industry level. This corresponds well with the findings of this analysis.

The emphasis on agency and heterogeneous managerial/entrepreneurial ability would suggest that a divergent tendency would be more likely in especially dynamic economies. American manufacturing was particularly vibrant during the mid-twentieth century – its Golden Age – and this could explain Stigler's finding of divergence during that period. It would suggest that the relative decline in US manufacturing in the later twentieth century would have been accompanied by an end to the divergent tendency (although Penrose's theory does not predict convergence). This hypothesis is suggested tentatively, and would require further research to provide evidence on it.

One of Penrose's important insights is that relatively large firm size and high profit-ability do not necessarily indicate monopoly power. Her attribution of relative success to 'more able and enterprising managers and entrepreneurs' (p. 164) corresponds to the unequal ex ante strength of different firms' initiatives (investments), which depend on the firm's resources and how well they are used. (Other factors, such as location and access to relevant human and natural resources could also influence this (Tsoul?dis and Tsaliki 2005).) *A relatively high profit rate is therefore not necessarily an indicator of market power in the neoclassical sense; rather, it could result from superior managerial capability which could be seen as a different form of power, in the causal sense of the degree of ability to influence events.*

Schumpeter, like Penrose, emphasised agency and its role in promoting change. In his case, initiatives were taken by entrepreneurial outsiders in Mark I of his theory, and by the innovative parts of established firms on the basis of R&D in Mark II. In both versions, innovation was assumed to be associated with higher profit rates, predicting a positively skewed distribution. In practice, the observed distribution was close to symmetrical.

Similarly, the industries with the highest profit rates at various periods other than *Petroleum and coal products – Apparel and leather and allied products; Furniture and related products; Food and beverage and tobacco products* – would be hard to characterise as 'more advantageous'. Nevertheless, Schumpeter's concept of entrepreneurial profit could readily be reformulated not as an excess over a normal rate, but rather in terms of a varying chance of success, which could well be symmetric.

As with Penrose, Schumpeter's theory of entrepreneurial profit did not necessarily predict a systematic tendency to convergence in profit rates. And again, economies with more successful innovation might be expected to show more divergence, and vice versa.

10.2.2. Neoclassical theory

The neoclassical prediction that all industries (as well as all firms) should have a profit rate close to the standard rate of return was comprehensively refuted by the substantial and persistent profit rate dispersion – despite the conservative bias due to the use of the two-digit industry level, and the likely extent of nondifferential measurement error. *There is no standard rate of return.*

The magnitude of the dispersion at the start of the study period raises the question of the trajectory of profit rates before 1987. If the observed convergence rate were a permanent feature of the US economy, a simple extrapolation backwards in time would be appropriate. This would suggest that the dispersion in, say, the mid-twentieth century was even wider than the more than 7-fold ratio observed in 1987, and still more extreme if one followed the same trend further backwards in time. This is clearly absurd.

The implication is that a divergent force must have been present at some time before 1987. One possibility is that the degree of dispersion could have been brought about by one or more macro shocks. This is highly unlikely, because by far the largest shock since World War II was the 2007–09 financial crisis, and although its effects were clearly evident in the dispersion of profit rates in 2009, they had completely disappeared by 2010. There are no candidates for a macro shock that could have created a *sustained* dispersion.

Alternatively, there could have been a more gradual divergent force operating in the period before 1987, resulting from heterogeneous performances of specific industries and/or firms. In principle, this question could be explored by examining the previous empirical literature. If the studies of earlier periods had used comparable data and methods, a consistent analysis over a much longer timespan would have been possible. Unfortunately, as reviewed above, a number of different approaches were used, apart from the internationally comparable studies reported in Mueller (1990), so that direct comparability is not achievable. As previously argued, the evidence tentatively suggests divergence in the mid twentieth century, a short period of stability, and then convergence starting in the 1960s.

If neoclassical theory cannot explain the persisting dispersion, perhaps it can account for the convergence that did occur? – after all, convergence is the core of the theory. Even in this it is unsuccessful; the empirical analysis presented above indicates that this could not have been brought about by differential capital flows plus diminishing returns. The tendency to differential capital flows was observed to be weak, and in this dataset at least, diminishing returns do not appear to exist. Entrepreneurs apparently stick to the line of business that suits their expertise, even if this means accepting a lower rate of return.

This finding contradicts Stigler's statement that 'Entrepreneurs will seek to leave relatively unprofitable industries and enter relatively profitable industries, and with competition there will be neither public nor private barriers to these movements. ... [without this] the immobility of resources would lead to catastrophic inefficiency' (Stigler 1963, 54). The implication is that neoclassical theory of this kind misinterprets the fundamental nature of capitalist economic success: it does not result from flexibility bringing about a perfect market. Arbitrage between production systems with differing degrees of productivity and profitability may well play little or no role in capitalist dynamism. The important action is in production: a consequence of the investment initiatives of entrepreneurs and firms – dynamic rather than allocative efficiency (Shiozawa 2020).

The finding that diminishing returns did not occur is similar to that of Nell and Thirlwall (2017; 2018) in the context of the impact on GDP of national-level investment. It is remarkable that there is such a small empirical literature on such a fundamental and ubiquitous concept as diminishing returns to financial capital, and that the available evidence is against its occurrence.

This leaves the possibility that supra-normal profits are eroded by new entrants, thus returning the economy to a situation closer to the ideal of a uniform rate of return. This is discussed in the next section.

10.2.3. Deviations from standard neoclassical theory when its assumptions do not hold

The notion of *market power* as a factor that can increase the profit rate above the baseline of the competitive market, but not decrease it, contributes little to the inter-industry variation of profit rates, as shown by the symmetry of the distribution. The extent of churning observed in Figure 2 also suggests that the degree of dispersion is not due to a relatively stable feature such as the extent of market power. It is reminiscent of the churning observed in other contexts (e.g. Foster, Haltiwanger, and Syverson 2008) and 'turbulent' competition (Shaikh 2016). These usually refer to the firm level, but the evidence here is that it occurs also at industry level, possibly as a result of changing competitive conditions, e.g. lower priced imports.

New imports eroding supra-normal profits could explain the observed convergence. *Apparel and leather and allied products* and *Furniture and related products* were relatively profitable specifically in the early part of the study period. Globalisation in the late twentieth century may have forced US firms in these sectors to reduce their prices, and therefore their profits, to compete with less expensive imports. This price undercutting is compatible with neoclassical theory, but it does not require a sophisticated theory to predict that cheaper goods will tend to outsell expensive ones, *ceteris paribus*. Firms with lower unit costs can charge lower prices, without loss of profit margin, and are therefore in a more powerful position.

Neoclassical economists correctly emphasise that profitability must always be seen in relation to *risk*. If interpreted to mean that the baseline level of risk is zero for investments in the least risky industries and positive in the riskier ones, a positive skew would be present, but this is not observed. It is more likely that differential risk is symmetrical, and simply corresponds to the operation of uncertainty ('luck') in the outcome of any initiative.

Neglect of intangible assets is a factor that could possibly distort the observed profit rate in some industries. Again, the symmetry of the distribution argues against this as a major issue. Secondly, it is generally agreed that the importance of intangible capital has increased over time; the quantity of capital would therefore be increasingly underestimated, and the measured profit rate should therefore have increased over time. This is not what is observed. Thirdly, the industries that were found to have periods of relatively high rates of return (apart from *Petroleum and coal products*) were *Apparel and leather and allied products*, *Furniture and related products*, and *Food and beverage and tobacco products.* These industries do not have high levels of intangible assets, apart from advertising.

11. Conclusion

This paper makes the following contributions. It provides an analysis of all 19 US manufacturing sectors for the period 1985–2016 and is nationally representative. It demonstrates that the degree of profit rate dispersion implies that the concept of a standard rate of return has no counterpart in reality.

The symmetry of the distribution implies that the observed departures from neoclassical predictions are not due to market power or the neglect of intangibles, and that theories invoking risk and entrepreneurial profit need to be reformulated. The investigation of inter-industry flows in response to differential profitability is a major contribution to the empirical literature on diminishing returns; it demonstrates that they do not play a major role.

The statistical analysis was designed to impose no causal relations unless they could be empirically justified, to directly investigate what causal processes are compatible with the data. This is in contrast to much of the existing literature where it is often assumed that profit rate equalisation and/or diminishing returns 'must be' fundamental features of the economy.

The context of this analysis is the considerable qualitative research undertaken by Penrose, a large body of rigorous economic history by Chandler (e.g. Chandler 1977), and also Lee's (1999) empirical examination of price setting. Their findings point in the same direction. Together they can be taken as an empirical basis to construct evidence-based causal theory.

The findings correspond closely with the expectations generated from Penrose's perspective. They suggest the following account. Firms take initiatives. Their quality depends on the degree of managerial ability. But their achieved outcome, in terms of the rate of return, is not guaranteed, because the initiative is taken under conditions of risk – or more likely, Knightian uncertainty. In practice, attempts at innovation vary greatly in their degree of success: many fail altogether, and the rate of return even among those that survive can be lower than the prevailing rate as well as above it. There is thus a broad range of possible outcomes in terms of the profitability of the entrepreneurial initiatives.

At the macro level, this manifests as profit rate heterogeneity. It is brought about by uneven success, at both the firm and the industry level, not by shocks, as neoclassical theory requires. It suggests that in an economy with dynamic manufacturing, profit rates will diverge (*ceteris paribus*), and that convergence may indicate relative industrial stagnation.

This interpretation implies that success in business involves the degree of efficacy or relative strength of entrepreneurs, directors and managers – their ability to bring something about. This is one meaning, a specifically *causal* one, of the word 'power', with the implication that market power is not the only type of power that is relevant to the profit rate. Positive profits can occur without 'imperfect competition' or oligopoly, simply as a result of unequal managerial capacity, as is seen every day in the financial news: the existence of a relatively high (low) profit rate tends to reflect a relatively high (low) level of entrepreneurial and/or management ability involved in taking previous investment initiatives; or more accurately, the degree of success in making a profit reflects (albeit imperfectly) the quality of the business plan as manifest in the investments made – its ex ante strength. In addition, achieved profit can be regarded as a source of ex post strength, as it provides the resources that can be used to fund future investment, or for other expenditure that could improve the future position of the firm (Joffe 2015).

The relationship of these two types of power can readily be related to the concept of market power. In any market transaction, monopoly/oligopoly arises when there is only one supplier (or very few), or when the suppliers collude. Monopsony/oligopsony arise when this is true on the demand side. When there are many suppliers, their *inequality* implies a distribution of relative strength, the most powerful one ex ante being the one most successful in competing, e.g. due to ability to produce at lowest unit cost. Similarly, the inequality in profit outcome leads to heterogeneity in ex post strength.

Notes

1. I am grateful to an anonymous reviewer for suggesting that this should be included.
2. The crude oil price rose from $25/barrel in 2002 to over $100/barrel before and after the 2007-09 crisis. This was due to increasing demand from China and other Asian countries, the invasion of Iraq, and possibly speculation in futures markets (Williams n.d.).

Acknowledgements

I would like to thank Ciaran Driver, Andrew Kliman, Tony Thirlwall, Julian Wells, and especially Ron Smith for helpful advice and comments. No funding was received for this work.

Disclosure statement

No potential conflict of interest was reported by the author(s).

Funding

The author(s) reported there is no funding associated with the work featured in this article.

ORCID

Michael Joffe http://orcid.org/0000-0001-6907-6183

References

Aghion, P., and P. Howitt. 1998. *Endogenous Growth Theory*. Cambridge, MA: The MIT Press.
Bartelsman, E. J., and M. E. Doms. 2000. "Understanding Productivity: Lessons from Longitudinal Microdata." *Journal of Economic Literature* 38 (3): 569–594. doi:10.1257/jel.38.3.569.
BEA (Bureau of Economic Analysis). Industry Value Added Tables are Available at https://apps.bea.gov/iTable/iTable.cfm?ReqID=51&step=1. Tables 3.3ESI & 3.7ESI Section 3: Private fixed assets by industry. https://apps.bea.gov/iTable/iTable.cfm?ReqID=10&step=2

Benhabib, J., and M. M. Spiegel. 1994. "The Role of Human Capital in Economic Development: Evidence from Average Cross-Section Data." *Journal of Monetary Economics* 34 (2): 143–173. doi:10.1016/0304-3932(94)90047-7.

Bernard, A. B., J. B. Jensen, S. J. Redding, and P. K. Schott. 2012. "The Empirics of Firm Heterogeneity and International Trade." *Annual Review of Economics* 4 (1): 283–313. doi:10.1146/annurev-economics-080511-110928.

Biery, M. E. 2015. The 10 Highest-Return Industries by ROE. *Forbes Magazine*. https://www.forbes.com/sites/sageworks/2015/02/01/the-10-highest-return-industries-by-roe/#7ec5a22f323c.

Bloom, N., R. Sadun, and J. Van Reenen. 2012. "Does Management Really Work?" *Harvard Business Review* 90 (11): 76–82.

Brue, S. L. 1993. "Retrospectives: The Law of Diminishing Returns." *Journal of Economic Perspectives* 7 (3): 185–192. doi:10.1257/jep.7.3.185.

Bryer, R.A. 1993. "The Late Nineteenth Century Revolution in Financial Reporting: Accounting for the Rise of Investor or Managerial Capitalism?" *Accounting, Organizations and Society* 18 (7/8): 649–690. doi:10.1016/0361-3682(93)90048-B.

Chandler, A. D. Jnr. 1977. *The Visible Hand: The Managerial Revolution in American Business*. Cambridge, MA: The Belnap Press of Harvard University Press.

Connolly, R. A., and S. Schwartz. 1985. "The Intertemporal Behavior of Economic Profits." *International Journal of Industrial Organization* 3 (4): 379–400. doi:10.1016/0167-7187(85)90031-1.

Cubbin, J., and P. Geroski. 1987. "The Convergence of Profits in the Long Run: Inter-Firm and Inter-Industry Comparisons." *The Journal of Industrial Economics* 35 (4): 427–442. doi:10.2307/2098581.

Davis, S. J., J. C. Haltiwanger, and S. Schuh. 1996. *Job Creation and Destruction*. Cambridge, MA: The MIT Press.

Decker, R. A., J. Haltiwanger, R. S. Jarmin, and J. Miranda. 2016. "Where Has All the Skewness Gone? The Decline in High-Growth (Young) Firms in the U.S." *European Economic Review* 86: 4–23. doi:10.1016/j.euroecorev.2015.12.013.

Dosi, G., M. Grazzi, and D. Moschella. 2015. "Technology and Costs in International Competitiveness: From Countries and Sectors to Firms." *Research Policy* 44 (10): 1795–1814. doi:10.1016/j.respol.2015.05.012.

Dosi, G., M. Grazzi, C. Tomasi, and A. Zeli. 2012. "Turbulence Underneath the Big Calm? The Micro-Evidence Behind Italian Productivity Dynamics." *Small Business Economics* 39 (4): 1043–1067. doi:10.1007/s11187-011-9326-7.

Driver, C., and P. Temple. 2013. "Capital Investment: What are the Main Long Term Trends in Relation to UK Manufacturing Businesses, and How Do These Compare Internationally?", Submission to the UK Government's Foresight Future of Manufacturing Project. https://assets.publishing.service.gov.uk/government/uploads/system/uploads/attachment_data/file/283884/ep8-capital-investment-trends-uk-manufacturing.pdf.

Eisfeldt, A. L., and Y. Shi. 2018. *Capital Reallocation*. NBER Working Paper 25085. Cambridge, MA: National Bureau of Economic Research. https://www.nber.org/papers/w25085.

Fisher, I. 1969. "Income and capital." In *Readings in the Concept and Measurement of Income*, edited by R.H. Parker and G. C. Harcourt, 33–53. Cambridge: Cambridge University Press.

Fisher, F. M., and J. J. McGowan. 1983. "On the Misuse of Accounting Rates of Return to Infer Monopoly Profits." *The American Economic Review* 73: 82–97.

Foster, L. S., C. A. Grim, J. Haltiwanger, and Z. Wolf. 2017. "Macro and Micro Dynamics of Productivity: From Devilish Details to Insights." NBER Working Paper 23666, Cambridge, MA: National Bureau of Economic Research. https://www.nber.org/papers/w23666.

Foster, L., J. Haltiwanger, and C. Syverson. 2008. "Reallocation, Firm Turnover, and Efficiency: Selection on Productivity or Profitability?" *The American Economic Review* 98 (1): 394–425. doi:10.1257/aer.98.1.394.

Fritsche, S. R., and M. T. Dugan. 1997. "A Simulation-Based Investigation of Errors in Accounting-Based Surrogates for Internal Rate of Return." *Journal of Business Finance and Accounting* 24 (6): 781–802. doi:10.1111/1468-5957.00133.

Görzig, B., and M. Gornig. 2013. "Intangibles: Can They Explain the Divergence in Return Rates?" *Review of Income and Wealth* 59 (4): 648–664. doi:10.1111/j.1475-4991.2012.00525.x.

Greenblatt, R.E. 2013. "Rates of Profit as Correlated Sums of Random Variables." *Physica A: Statistical Mechanics and Its Applications* 392 (20): 5006–5018. doi:10.1016/j.physa.2013.06.040.

Haskel, J., and S. Westlake. 2017. *Capitalism Without Capital: The Rise of the Intangible Economy.* Princeton, NJ: Princeton University Press.

Hsieh, C.-T., and P. J. Klenow. 2009. "Misallocation and Manufacturing TFP in China and India." *The Quarterly Journal of Economics* 124 (4): 1403–1448. doi:10.1162/qjec.2009.124.4.1403.

Hsieh, C.-T., and P. J. Klenow. 2018. "The Reallocation Myth." *Center for Economic Studies Working Paper* 18–19: 1–25. https://www2.census.gov/ces/wp/2018/CES-WP-18-19.pdf.

Jacobsen, R. 1988. "The Persistence of Abnormal Returns." *Strategic Management Journal* 9 (5): 415–430. doi:10.1002/smj.4250090503.

Joffe, M. 2014. "Can Economics be Evidence Based?" First published in the *Newsletter* of the Royal Economic Society. https://evidence-based-economics.org/articles/short-articles-on-evidence-based-economics/article-4/

Joffe, M. 2015. *The World Created by Capitalist Firms.* Center for Organization Studies (CORS). https://tinyurl.com/je4m2pss.

Joffe, M., and D. Watson. 2017. "Causal Theories, Models and Evidence in Economics—some Reflections from the Natural Sciences." *Cogent Economics & Finance* 5 (1): 1280983. doi:10.1080/23322039.2017.1280983.

Juselius, K. 2011. "Time to Reject the Privileging of Economic Theory Over Empirical Evidence? A Reply to Lawson." *Cambridge Journal of Economics* 35: 423–436.

Lee, F. S. 1999. *Post-Keynesian Price Theory.* Cambridge: Cambridge University Press.

Levy, D. 1987. "The Speed of the Invisible Hand." *International Journal of Industrial Organization* 5 (1): 79–92. doi:10.1016/0167-7187(87)90008-7.

Lucas, R. E. Jnr. 1990. "Why Doesn't Capital Flow from Rich to Poor Countries?" *The American Economic Review* 80 (2): 92–96.

Megna, P., and D. Mueller. 1991. "Profit Rates and Intangible Capital." *The Review of Economics and Statistics* 73 (4): 632–642. doi:10.2307/2109402.

Melitz, M. J., and D. Trefler. 2012. "Gains from Trade When Firms Matter." *Journal of Economic Perspectives* 26 (2): 91–118. doi:10.1257/jep.26.2.91.

Mueller, D. 1977. "The Persistence of Profits Above the Norm." *Economica* 44 (176): 369–380. doi:10.2307/2553570.

Mueller, D., edited by. 1990. *The Dynamics of Company Profits: An International Comparison.* Cambridge: Cambridge University Press.

Nell, K. S., and A. P. Thirlwall. 2017. "Why Does the Productivity of Investment Vary Across Countries?" *PSL Quarterly Review* 70 (282): 213–245. n.

Nell, K. S., and A. P. Thirlwall. 2018. "Explaining Differences in the Productivity of Investment Across Countries in the Context of 'New Growth Theory'." *International Review of Applied Economics* 32 (2): 163–194. doi:https://doi.org/10.1080/02692171.2017.1333089.

Penrose, E. T. 1959. *The Theory of the Growth of the Firm.* Blackwell: Oxford.

Pierce, J. R., and P. K. Schott. 2016. "The Surprisingly Swift Decline of U.S. Manufacturing Employment." *The American Economic Review* 106 (7): 1632–1662. doi:10.1257/aer.20131578.

Qualls, D. 1974. "Stability and Persistence of Economic Profit Margins in Highly Concentrated Industries." *Southern Economic Journal* 40 (4): 604–612. doi:10.2307/1056378.

Romer, P. M. 1986. "Increasing Returns and Long Run Growth." *The Journal of Political Economy* 94 (5): 1002–1037. doi:10.1086/261420.

Schumpeter, J. A. 1934. *The Theory of Economic Development.* New Brunswick & London: Transaction publishers. Originally published in 1911 in German.

Schumpeter, J. A. 1943. *Capitalism, Socialism and Democracy.* London: Routledge.

Shaikh, A. 2016. *Capitalism: Competition, Conflict, Crises.* Oxford: Oxford University Press.

Shiozawa, Y. 2020. "A New Framework for Analyzing Technological Change." *Journal of Evolutionary Economics* 30 (4): 989–1034. doi:10.1007/s00191-020-00704-5.

Solow, R. M. 1956. "A Contribution to the Theory of Economic Growth." *The Quarterly Journal of Economics* 70 (1): 65–94. doi:10.2307/1884513.

Stigler, G. 1963. *Capital and Rates of Return in Manufacturing Industries*. Princeton, NJ: Princeton University Press.

Tsoul?dis, L., and P. Tsaliki. 2005. "Marxian Theory of Competition and the Concept of Regulating Capital: Evidence from Greek Manufacturing." *The Review of Radical Political Economics* 37 (1): 5–22. doi:10.1177/0486613404272324.

Wells, P. J. 2007. *The rate of profit as a random variable*. PhD thesis, The Open University.

Williams, J. L. n.d. *History and Analysis of Crude Oil Prices*. WTRG Economics. London, Arkansas. https://web.archive.org/web/20080102043155/http://www.wtrg.com/prices.htm

Appendix

Data appendix

Gross operating surplus is the amount remaining after the wage bill and taxes on production and imports less subsidies have been deducted from the total revenue. It includes corporate profits and proprietors' income as well as depreciation, net interest, and business transfer payments (Bureau of Economic Analysis 2011). Thus, it is a relatively rough measure of annual profit.

The stocks of fixed assets include estimates of durable equipment, structures and software, using the perpetual inventory method (Bureau of Economic Analysis, 2003). This cumulates past investment flows to indirectly estimate the value of the stock, calculating the net stock in each year as the cumulative value of gross investment through that year less the cumulative value of depreciation through that year. The Bureau of Economic Analysis assumes that most assets have depreciation patterns that decline geometrically over time, an assumption that has strong empirical support, although the actual depreciation rates are of uncertain accuracy.

The data come primarily from the economic censuses conducted every five years by the Bureau of the Census, the Annual Survey of Manufactures, and the Annual Capital Expenditures Survey (e.g. for software). New non-residential structures are derived from the National Income and Product Accounts (NIPA); all the data sources are reconciled with NIPA data (Bureau of Economic Analysis, 2019). Data collected on the historical-cost basis were used in this analysis.

BUREAU OF ECONOMIC ANALYSIS. Fixed Assets and Consumer Durable Goods in the United States, 1925–99. Washington, DC: U.S. Government Printing Office, September, 2003. https://www.bea.gov/system/files/methodologies/Fixed-Assets-1925–97.pdf

BUREAU OF ECONOMIC ANALYSIS. (2011). Measuring the nation's economy: an industry perspective https://www.bea.gov/sites/default/files/methodologies/industry_primer.pdf

BUREAU OF ECONOMIC ANALYSIS. NIPA Handbook 2019, chapter 6 on Private Fixed Investment https://www.bea.gov/system/files/2019-05/Chapter-6.pdf

Sectors covered by the data

Wood products

Nonmetallic mineral products

Primary metals

Fabricated metal products

Machinery

Computer and electronic products

Electrical equipment, appliances, and components

Motor vehicles, bodies and trailers, and parts

Other transportation equipment

Furniture and related products

Miscellaneous manufacturing

Food and beverage and tobacco products

Textile mills and textile product mills

Apparel and leather and allied products

Paper products

Printing and related support activities

Petroleum and coal products

Chemical products

Plastics and rubber products

What is Edith Penrose's legacy for the theory of the firm?

Irene Roele and Sonja Ruehl

ABSTRACT

Prompted by centenary celebrations of the contribution of Edith Penrose to the theory of the firm, the development of resource-based views of the firm (RBV) and knowledge-based perspectives, this article considers the continuing usefulness of Penrose's perspective for strategic management, from the point of view of the practitioner, the management educator and to the development of the academic field of strategic management. As authors, we draw on methods originating with Penrose's pioneering case study methodology by framing illustrative 'vignettes' or case examples for discussion, including that of Tesco, which draws on extensive participant observation as well as theory.

1. Introduction

This article's chief focus is on Penrose's legacy to the field of strategic management, where her seminal ideas led to development of the Resource-Based View of the firm (RBV) and its offshoot, Dynamic Capabilities theory (DC). The effects of her work on the field of strategic management are examined at three different, but interrelated, levels, namely her contribution to:

- the development of the academic field of strategic management
- the application of the field of strategic management to management practice and
- the way that management practice is taught in business schools.

To situate our discussion within that wide field of strategic management, we have selected for emphasis three themes derived from Penrose, which have proved particularly fruitful in working with practitioners to foster a strategic approach to the management issues they face. These themes are

- the emphasis on managers' need to look at the 'internal resources' of the firm as well as its external situation, and the relation between them, in order to build a position of advantage for the firm and to assess what its main locus of competitive advantage is
- associated ideas of a firm as a 'learning organisation', as partly reflecting the embodiment of knowledge in its routines (and in its managerial education

programmes) but as also involving the need to 'unlearn' previous approaches in a changed situation

- the complexity and ambiguity inherent in managerial decision-making and the need to enable managers, particularly middle management and 'spotted talent' who are in the process of being inducted into the organisation, to reflect continually upon the complexity and the relativity of the firm's 'capability', rather than applying set methods or formulae.

Penrose's work has had a profound effect on the way strategy is taught in business schools and one influential aspect of that work is her pioneering use of case study methods in research, the development of theory and in teaching. Penrose's (2009) seminal work on the theory of the firm draws on her case study of the Hercules Powder Company, and she uses the case in developing her theory of the growth of the firm, emphasising the importance of the firm's existing capabilities and the complex interaction of the firm's internal resource organisation and the external environment.

This theoretical framework can be deployed both by academics analysing cases of firms' growth (or lack of it) and by management practitioners facing strategic choices in their own organisations. Thus, Penrose's framework informs both theoretical developments and business practice. Management education is a conduit for transmitting Penrose's concepts to practitioners and, also, management educators together with practitioners are well placed to undertake the 'reflective practice' on strategic issues through casework, which in turn feeds back into developments in concepts and theory of strategic management.

We are, then, as management educators, setting out to explore and celebrate a legacy which is of continuing relevance both theoretically and practically and in a wide field – and in this article, we also use mini case studies or 'vignettes' to focus our deliberations. These case studies are of varying length but one of them, that of Tesco, within our discussion of organisational learning, is based on participant observation.

The paper which follows accordingly begins with an overview of developments in the RBV and DC views of the firm within the strategic management field after Penrose. It then integrates case examples or 'vignettes' into discussion of the three themes above. A fifth section, before we conclude, considers how useful the RBV approach can continue to be in our current circumstances of such rapid change in many sectors including ICT. An environment which includes 'big data' analytics and the possibilities of machine learning and artificial intelligence points up the extreme complexity of the 'capability' a firm now needs, to take advantage of new possibilities or even to survive competitive threats, a capability which needs to be developed not just within the firm (or value chain) but in boundary-spanning processes across an entire 'value web' or configuration of partners, suppliers and customers. Are concepts of 'the firm' now of adequate scope for even contemplating where 'capabilities' lie?

We are following in the footsteps of previous authors in examining Edith Penrose' legacy for the theory of the firm and the way that subject is studied, which includes her use of case study method and much more broadly, development of the discipline of business strategy as a whole. Within strategy studies, we have now had more than 50 years' research on the Resource-Based View of the firm (RBV) to which Penrose contributes seminal ideas, as well as 'dynamic capabilities' theory, an offshoot of RBV (Rugman and Verbeke 2002; Teece, Pisano, and Shuen 1997). Despite this lengthy development, some have even asked the question, 'Do we know much more now?' than we did back in 1994 (Ambrosini and Bowman 2009, 46). Penrose's seminal contribution still shines out (Lockett 2005). Here, in this paper, the authors consider that this perception is partly due to Penrose's approach and style, especially when thinking about the receipt and use of RBV ideas by practicing managers, whose grasp and ability to apply the approach in their own particular business contexts is one key to its continued usefulness.

Before we proceed, we need to record two caveats: one being that we are not the first to explore the legacy of Penrose's contribution from the practicing manager perspective (see, for example, Pitelis 2004). The second is that we are aware that Edith Penrose herself would not have approved of some of the ways that the RBV has subsequently developed, insofar as it has been used to bolster firms' ability to extract 'rents' rather than to create value (Rugman and Verbeke 2002).

To return to the notion that 'the proof of the pudding lies in the eating' – the usefulness of the theory lies in its ability to illuminate aspects of the situation of firms in a complex reality, including to firms' managers facing those situations in practice – we note that this takes us away from the approach to theory in which a theory's usefulness lies in its ability to simplify a complex reality into testable propositions. Sometimes this consequence is explicitly articulated by authors who draw on the RBV or capabilities theory, for example Argyres and Zenger (2012) who consider both the 'dynamic capabilities' and the 'transactions costs' approaches to drawing up firms' boundaries, rejecting the idea that each could satisfactorily just be represented by a separable variable in a testable proposition, since their interaction is part of the complexity that managers face.

Considering Penrose's distinctive contribution, after all, when she comes to consider the question of the growth of the firm – what explains why some firms grow and some do not, and what limits such growth possibilities – Edith Penrose diverges from an economics tradition which conceptualises firm size chiefly in terms of the relationship between inputs and outputs and 'returns to scale' in manufacturing contexts (Wernerfelt 1984). It is part of her legacy that she is able to establish the questions of firm growth and firm size as part of a much wider landscape, one including the outcome of managerial decision-making and choice, and the way managers frame the choices open to them, taking into account the firm's internal resources and strengths in comparison with those of other firms – both rival and complementary – rather than essentially seeing firm size as the outcome of an optimal scale of operation for a given technology. Indeed, such matters are now conceptualised as mere 'operational effectiveness' issues by those (Porter for instance) who have built a discipline of business strategy around the wider themes addressed early on by Penrose.

There may be discussion of the exact origins of some RBV ideas and concepts, for example, in the work of E.A.G. Robinson (Jacobsen 2013) but Penrose's contribution enables work on the sources of growth of firms and on business strategy to be developed by others (Chandler, Kay, Porter, Rumelt, Teece among them) grounded in the close examination of particular firms in context. Her work forms one of the foundations of an approach which opens up the 'black box' of the firm to examine its internal workings in changing situations.

Penrose takes on a microeconomic concept of 'the firm' within a market and shows how its inner workings – including its managers' decision-making – need to be examined and questioned in detail and in interaction with its market situation, before we can explain why some firms grow, why some diversify, or what determines the boundaries of each 'firm' within its market or markets.

Looking 'inside the black box' of each firm highlights the importance of internal management resources and their ability to keep the firm together by issuing authoritative communications about the firm's purpose, values, relations with customers and suppliers, role in community or society, making sure that those working in the firm remain 'on the same page' in their management activities. Penrose saw such management communications as important for coordination, as also establishing routines and detailed instructions. Because authoritative communications may be informal as well as formal ones, the ability to communicate informally among a firm's own managers may even set limits to firms' growth.

Nonetheless, managers facing strategic choices often seem more comfortable looking outside their own firms, rather than looking inwards and questioning the internal resources of their own firms and their internal capabilities, and so it is to that issue of internal resources that we turn in the next section.

2. Turning the lens on internal resources – the main 'locus of competitive advantage'

The RBV approach enables insights to be distilled from the field, that is, distilled from the experience of working with practitioners who are managing a wide range of organisations in the public and semi-public sphere as well as private-sector firms. One of these insights is that managers can easily become too focused on assessing external competition and the external situation of the firm (or other organisation) *within the existing 'rules of the game'*, the status quo – so that one managerial problem is a tendency to exhibit an obsessive focus on immediate competitors and a complete blind-spot to 'rule-breakers', the new entrants coming in from the periphery – such as TESLA in the Auto industry or, more mundanely and locally, the threat posed by Greggs for Tesco a few years back.

Managers seem to be more comfortable looking outwards – at the usual suspects – than looking inwards at the resources of the firm internally so as to further probe them in relation to external challenges and change. In Economics, Baumol (1982) coined the term 'contestable markets' to focus attention on situations where new competitors come into a market deploying a different technology to deliver similar benefits, while resource-based views of the firm enable us to trace how that might play out at the managerial level, within the firm.

It may be the case that firms' 'dominant logic' (Prahalad and Bettis 1986) results in false optimism or even complacency about the continuation of an organisation's superiority and even, at times, misperceptions of infallibility (Collins 2001). Organizations appear to take it for granted that they enjoy a competitive advantage of some kind.

Taking an RBV perspective on the internal resources of the firm, including currently unused or underused resources or the opposite, resources which are currently being pressed too hard, can enable managers to see their organisations in a different light, to see not just what they can do now but what their potential might be and also what the distinctive or even unique 'locus of competitive advantage' of that particular firm actually is. Turning a more specifically Penrosian lens on the firm furthermore fosters a focus on activities and processes within each firm, rather than only on resources *per se*, and it is the services these resources can provide – singly or in combination – which can be a real source of value creation. This means that Penrose's contribution is invaluable, whether working with middle management, senior managers or the very top, because it really helps in thinking about 'the process of value creation and the meaning of strategic advantage' as Prahalad put it (Prahalad 2004). It is a perspective which enables examination of the 'boundary-spanning activities' (Zott and Amit 2010) and the 'orchestration of knowledge' capabilities (McGee 2003) that are crucial now and that we refer to again in section 5.

A Penrosian legacy enables us to start from the assumption and the reality that firms are heterogeneous (Lockett 2005). We note that strategic management perspectives informed the strong advice to Japanese firms, during Japan's 'lost decade' or long stagnation of the 1990s, that they *should become* more consciously heterogeneous, to take a more differentiated look at each firm's specific strengths and capability and focus on that – that is, take a more strategic stance rather than trying to fulfill the needs of all market segments and all customers indiscriminately and imitating the initiatives of rivals as soon as possible. Such a strategy-focused perspective, evident in Porter and Sakakibara (2001) and explored further in Schaede (2008), appears to have borne fruit: in a review of Japan's situation at the end of 2013 (Porter 2013), Porter notes that the business prize that bears his name in Japan has been awarded to 41 firms with distinctive strategies since 2001.

It is striking to note that this advice has been pertinent to Japanese managements even though Japan's best had by the 1980s already become a byword for 'operational effectiveness' and efficiency at the operational level and indeed whose management methods had been imitated around the world such as to become a new global standard. The advice to look inside each firm as well so as to decide what *not* to do, which segments *not* to serve, which products *not* to produce, which potential diversifications or innovations *not* to follow up – such an inward-looking strategic focus has still appeared to need reinforcement even in the context of a management tradition with a fearsome reputation for competition not that long before.

The context now is different, but analogies exist with the here and now and the recent past in the UK. In the aftermath of the 2008 crisis and since, many managers, especially middle managers (but also the very top), are facing a relentless pressure to cut costs, get more from fewer resources, be more efficient and to carry on doing more of the same. In such circumstances, it seems difficult for middle management to 'get off the hamster wheel' in order to do some strategic thinking rather than maintaining a relentless focus on operational efficiencies. More than one recent paper has reinforced this point that an excessive managerial bias towards cost-efficiency can be seriously harmful to corporate performance (Goddard 2014, BCG 2014).

In this context, the RBV can be useful in management education precisely because it does **not** provide all the answers – but rather, because it does prompt managers to think, and allows space to reflect on how to explore new capabilities, not just to exploit existing ones. Even to 'exploit' existing capabilities in fact requires strategic thinking and continuous learning, since just doing more of the same is not enough – 'best practice' is not 'next practice' since there may be newer approaches that haven't been tried yet. As Prahalad expresses it, effective strategy is not about 'extrapolating the past' but rather 'folding the future in' (Prahalad 2004).

3. Complexity, ambiguity, relativity, subjectivity – and the case study method

In what Penrose herself writes about the need for a focus on firm's internal resources, she argues that a firm's productive opportunity is 'determined by the internal resources of the firm: the products the firm can successfully produce, the new areas in which it can set up plants, the innovations it can successfully launch, the very ideas of its executives and the opportunities they see, depend as much on the kind of experience, managerial ability and technological know-how already existing within the firm as they do upon external opportunities open to all' (Penrose 1956, 225). That emphasis upon individual managers' perceptions from within the firm furthermore brings in the importance of interpretation, the need for managers to have time to see their interpretation of the firm's situation as debatable, open to question, often complex and ambiguous, and relative to their own knowledge and experience. Space for acknowledgement of this relativity and subjectivity is useful and so here, we introduce a simple exercise in the relativity of perception, based on an image from a different field, that of colour theory.

This image is based upon an exercise from Josef Albers' 'Interaction of Color' (Plate VI-3. Albers 1975). The point of Albers' exercise is that it demonstrates the relativity of our perceptions of a colour, which depend upon its interaction with other colours, in this case, with background colour. The diagonal lines here are identical and the difference in our perception of them arises from our seeing them against a different background. We offer this as a visual metaphor for the need to allow for relativity in interpreting management situations and their complexity.

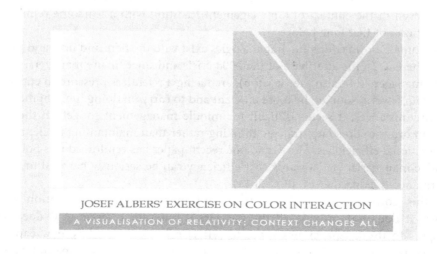

Penrose's innovation of the 'case study' method, which allows us to look at the complexity, ambiguity and relativity of a firm's situation (bringing in the internal resources of the firm, its external situation vis-à-vis competitors and collaborators, and the relation between them, so as to consider the strategic choices which the firm has made or could make in the future – including alternative possibilities), also allows for the importance of subjectivity on the part of the firm's managers. Penrose makes the point that within the organisational boundaries of corporate bureaucracies, entrepreneurs experimentally develop subjective images which enable them to conceive of how productive opportunities might be seized upon, to grow their firms (Penrose 2009: 38: 195). Because a firm's situation is complex, it can be interpreted variously and so construction of a case study should be seen as ambiguous rather than self-evident. Summarising a firm's pathway in a case study needs selectivity, which explains why there can be useful disagreement as to what a given case study demonstrates and what its import actually is. A case study is also 'contestable' or debatable in other words and we suggest that is one of the advantages of the case study method.

To advocate the use of a theoretical perspective and a case study method precisely because they allow for complexity, ambiguity and relativity, and elements of subjectivity, as we do here, may seem perverse. Certainly, it goes against the grain for many managers, who often long for a system of thinking or a set of tools for 'How To Do It'. Examples abound. One would be the approach of the 'Balanced Scorecard' (Kaplan and Norton 1992), a persuasive approach but one which in practice can turn out to be very difficult to implement well (Soderberg et al. 2012).

Managerial decisions are often necessarily taken amid uncertainty and change in a multi-faceted, messily complicated situation such that managers cannot know whether they are 'doing the right thing' until afterwards. In such circumstances, the desire to have a system, a toolkit, a set of 'rules of thumb' is understandable.

Nevertheless, managers generally recognise the thrust of the argument, from an RBV perspective, that they need to focus on and identify what the un(der)used resources of the firm are – or what they were, but no longer are – in relation to defining 'tomorrow's breadwinners'. This is despite the difficulty of translating the RBV into 'prescriptions' for managers to follow. The exploration of complex cases makes it clear that there simply are no easy rules to follow from a resource-based or a 'capabilities' perspective. Even an apparently easy rule over what to integrate, what to outsource, turns out to be deceptive: not even 'make what you make well, buy in what you don't make well' will do as a general guide to capability development because in some cases you might sell a superior capability (which threatens customers) or buy in an inferior capability (and develop it) (Argyres and Zenger 2012).

In fact, an example of the complexity of decisions over what to make, what to outsource, where the boundaries of the firm should remain, and how far a firm should diversify, can be found in Edith Penrose's own case study of the Hercules Powder Company: a business-to-business producer which sometimes did refrain from entering final markets as that would compete with clients. Penrose explains the issue:

"Because of the nature of its market, Hercules stresses 'technical service' to customers; salesmen are for the most part technically trained men. In selling their products the salesmen are expected to take an active interest in the production and market problems of their customers. This permits them to acquire an intimate knowledge of the customers' businesses . . . It is standard practice in the development of new products to get customers to try them out on a 'pilot plant' basis and thus to assist Hercules in the necessary research and experimentation" (Penrose 1960: 54);.

and the consequences for any possible 'vertical integration':

'Forward integration would immediately adversely affect one of the pillars of the sales and market policy of Hercules, for customers would no longer be willing to open their plants, disclose their processes, and discuss their problems with the technical servicemen of Hercules. The technical relationship with customers so carefully cultivated and so important for the creation of new opportunities would be impaired if customers had any reason to fear that Hercules would itself become a competitor'. (Penrose 1960:60)

The firm's technical base, its market, plus the relationship between the two, are all involved in making the decision over what to produce, what to outsource, a complex one in the face of an environment of fluctuating demand.

This example quoted from Penrose incidentally provides an excellent example of 'value co-creation' before the term was coined (Prahalad and Ramaswamy 2004).

Hercules Powder case study was a significant innovation, also discussed by Angela Penrose in her biography of Edith (Penrose 2017). The complexities of Hercules Powder illustrate that what 'case study' methods require include not just simplified accounts of issues facing a firm and the route chosen, but rather, encouragement of debate about what a given rich case study actually shows – what differing interpretations may be possible?

In the face of complexity and ambiguity overall, then, rather than suggesting that managers can see strategy as a 'tame' problem and introducing tools with which to handle it, some recent authors have pressed the issue further, even arguing that strategy is instead inherently 'wicked' (and so not susceptible to routinised, toolkit treatment). 'Strategic problems are inherently wicked – they are essentially unique, highly complex, linked to other problems, can be defined and interpreted in many ways, and have no correct answer, nor a delimited set of possible solutions' (De Wit and Meyer 2014) so that '... this demands that managers behave not as planners but as inventors – searching, experimenting, learning, doubting and avoiding premature lock-in to one course of action' (Beinhocker 2006; see also Stacey 2006).

Compared to the world of the 1950s inhabited by Hercules Powder, where the technical knowledge base and market opportunities are pictured as building upon each other in an evolving and measured way, paying careful attention to important relationships, decisions in the current environment are not only complex but fast-moving and revealing considerable ambiguity and very rapid change over what can be counted as a success or failure. This applies to the possibility of growing firms through acquisitions as much as it does to possibilities of organic growth, since acquisitions also place demands upon the managerial and productive services of the acquiring firm. These costs of acquisition need to be counterposed against those benefits of bringing products and services together 'in-house' so as to take advantage of communications and coordination possibilities that can keep a firm together while it grows.

The early 21st century case of Hewlett Packard provides an illustrative vignette in that last respect. The case illustrates the tensions between the advantages and strains of growth by acquisition, the difficulty of deciding where the boundaries of a firm should remain and how far a firm should diversify.

3.1. Vignette I: Hewlett-Packard

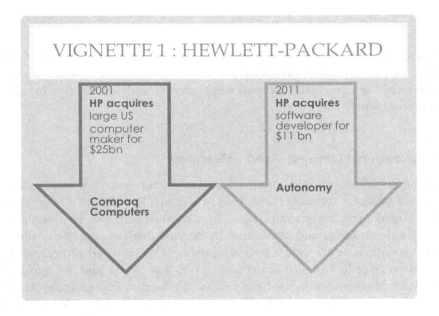

Hewlett-Packard faced the problem that it had become a large conglomerate encompassing both consumer-facing and enterprise-facing businesses. In 2001, the company appeared to have decided to bolster its consumer-facing printer and PC business by buying Compaq Computer in a $25bn acquisition and as late as 2011 that strategy ('better together') was defended by its CEO. However, 3 years later, the same CEO announced a split between the consumer-facing printer and PC making side, to become HP Inc, and the business-facing side comprising hardware, services and software, to become Enterprise (Financial Times 6 October 2014).

VIGNETTE 1: HEWLETT-PACKARD

- **2011 'Better Together'?**

- HP to remain a diversified conglomerate despite views that 'no company can excel at both consumer and enterprise computing'

- **2014 SPLIT !**

HP split announced

HP Inc: Printers, PCs

Enterprise: Hardware Software Services

This case illustrates a dilemma over the size and scope appropriate for the business rather than literally 'what to make, what to outsource' as such but demonstrates the complexity over strategic success and failure in a rapidly changing environment.

4. Organizational learning – and unlearning

One emphasis within the RBV approach and one with Penrosian roots is that firms acquire and build up knowledge and that the acquired knowledge of internal management is bound to be a constraint upon firm growth, whatever possibilities exist of acquiring new resources and capabilities in external markets. Therefore, firms – and other organisations in the public and semi-public sector – need to become 'learning organisations' in order to continue to build on their knowledge base and remain current and relevant. Much attention has been paid to 'the learning organisation' (Senge 1994) and the ability to establish the building of continuous learning and new knowledge acquisition into the ways the organisation operates.

However, there is in practice a tension between such 'new knowledge' acquisition and the transmission of existing knowledge that has been internally acquired within the firm, by its managers, during its development over time. Internally acquired knowledge can be seen as 'embodied' in the routines and in the processes of the firm. This can imply a rigidity which can counteract 'new knowledge' acquisition if it is not continually questioned as well.

This tension exists a fortiori when we consider the codification of existing knowledge within firms' own managerial education programmes which are intended not just to codify such previous learning, but also to make it coherent (with firm values and perceptions of existing core capabilities, probably) and so to transmit it to new generations of incoming managers and 'spotted talent' as being the right way to do things in this firm.

There is an evident danger that such codification into managerial education programmes can become too rigid and prescriptive. This may serve to reinforce existing perceptions that the firm has an unquestionable competitive advantage of some kind or even that the firm has an unassailable position, if only new generations of managers continue to absorb the lessons of experience that have proved successful in the past. Here again, in particular, the 'relentless focus on cost-cutting' only may form part of the problem, as will be illustrated by the next vignette.

In the face of such potential rigidities, a resource-based perspective can usefully counterpose an alternative view: that managers instead need to reflect continually about changing circumstances and the changing position of the firm relative to others' capabilities in a changing context. The learning organisation sometimes needs to 'unlearn' what was previously successful and this can be a painful process for incumbents. The next vignette suggests that UK supermarket Tesco became first of all a prime example of the benefits of becoming 'a learning organisation' but then lost this ability through overly rigid continued application of lessons from the past.

4.1. Vignette 2: Tesco

Firstly, a note on sources and method for this case example of Tesco. This vignette builds upon 'participant observation' (Roele) both as a practitioner in grocery businesses – including as a former manager with Tesco – and as an experienced executive educator now based at Alliance Manchester Business School. Two distinct strands of executive educational experience feed into this analysis, firstly work on strategy-making processes with senior, as well as middle and junior, teams as a facilitator and secondly work with colleagues at AMBS delivering conventional executive education programmes.

Using Penrose's perceptions and the resource-based view of the firm proves invaluable in both settings. In working with senior teams, in situations where they do have the knowledge and the expertise necessary, teams may nevertheless benefit from bringing strategic management concepts to bear in the process of teasing out the implications of that knowledge, to focus their strategies. And whereas senior teams may complain that 'we need our folk to think more strategically', those same folk, their managers, when taking part in executive education programmes, on the other side bemoan the time pressures on them: 'If only we had the time to think', 'We need a plan by the end of the month' – or sometimes, even by the end of the week. One of the best ways to break down that perception that there is no time to think, no time to 'get off the hamster wheel' of constant activity, turns out in practice to be to use the resource-based view of the firm to establish the value, or even the necessity, of strategic thinking.

These experiences, including working as a Tesco manager and later working with Tesco regional and store managers as an educator, all feed into this next vignette which explores the timeline of Tesco's success and its later erosion, in a personal analysis which places the dynamic capabilities of the firm centre-stage.

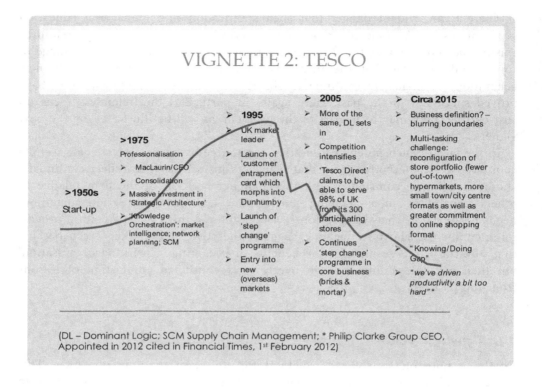

First, we should like to offer a caveat, which is to emphasise that this is simply an illustrative timeline based upon subjective assessment of the rise and fall of Tesco's capability development as a strategic player. As such, it bears a similarity to Larry Greiner's construct 'Evolution and Revolution as Organisations grow' (Greiner 1972). Its shape, as an illustrative curve, also echoes that of Jim Collins' 'From Good to Great- Why some don't make the leap' (Collins 2001). A timeline derived from data such as revenues or profitability, say, would look very different and that is part of the point.

The timeline goes from start-up in the 1950s until around 2015, as an illustrative curve. About 20 years after Tesco's start up, the firm was thoroughly professionalised by Ian McLaurin who came in as CEO, making a massive investment in what one might call Tesco's 'strategic architecture', focused on human capital as much as on technology. This can be viewed as a huge effort to turn Tesco into 'a learning organisation'. For one thing, in the late 1970s and early 1980s a considerable number of PhD graduates were employed at headquarters in Cheshunt, engaged in what would now be called 'knowledge orchestration' which placed them at the forefront of market intelligence. The area of network planning in particular was developed through the employment of geographers. At that time, as is well known, Tesco was opening between 30 and 35 superstores per year, and able to forecast the annual revenues of those stores within a 10% variance.

A key point in the timeline is 1995 when Tesco for the first time surpassed Sainsbury to become market leader among the UK's supermarkets. This was evidence that at that time, Tesco was a firm that was very good at developing dynamic capabilities culminating in reaching that 'market leader' niche. However, in spite of the launch of the customer loyalty (customer entrapment) card at that time, it marked the high point after which the firm's dynamic capabilities in fact started to wane.

This was exemplified by the 'Step Change' programme aimed at store managers and regional managers, which was purely focused on reducing costs and which was incredibly successful in that process – but which, with its exclusive focus on cost reduction, marked the point at which the organisation lost its capacity to learn, meaning that the firm's dynamic capability had actually started to decline. This was not immediately evident, as the firm continued to perform well in revenue and profitability terms for some time even after 2005; the highest turnover and profitability results yet were to come in 2009. Yet, even by 2005, the dominant logic or dominant ideology had set in, such that the firm considered that replicating 'more of the same' cost cutting was all that was needed. A kind of complacency had set in that the firm had discovered 'how to do it' and simply needed to replicate what had been done before, in spite of changing circumstances and new entrants to the competition.

With respect to organisational learning, Tesco had actually reached a point where previous organisational knowledge now needed to be 'unlearnt', but where organisational rigidities prevented that from happening. Even where members of the organisation recognised what they needed to do, there was a gap between 'knowing' this and 'doing' it and the organisation's rigidities made it hard for them to act upon their perceptions. From a 'dynamic capabilities' perspective, the firm had ceased to be a learning organisation capable of reflecting upon such basic issues as: what business is Tesco actually in now? For one thing, the launch of the customer entrapment card had led to a considerable growth of data-gathering and analysis capacity in the wholly owned subsidiary Dunnhumby – a subsidiary at one time valued at around £2 billion – but the strategic direction of Tesco regarding the big new business development of data analysis remained unsettled.

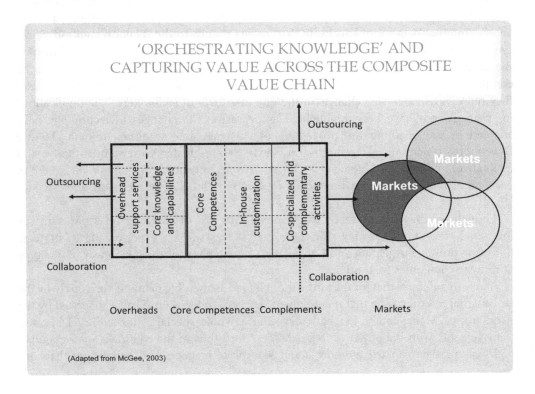

(Adapted from McGee, 2003)

Like many firms, dealing with multiple markets and clusters of competitors across a whole system, Tesco needed to make and to rethink decisions on those key questions, what to outsource and what to keep within the firm, with whom to collaborate both upstream and downstream – including competitors in some instances – and to decide what must be kept in-house in terms of core capabilities or competencies and what might usefully be outsourced or spun off. Those were still key questions facing Tesco from an RBV perspective with the need for the ability to 'orchestrate knowledge' (McGee 2003) remaining a strategic imperative for the firm.

5. The complexity of a firm's 'capability' that is needed now

In asserting the continued relevance of Penrosian and resource-based views of firm growth in practice in the analysis of firms and in management education now, there must be a valid question to be faced about the extent to which the business context – 'the forces at work' – has changed since such views were first mooted. Some sectors that have experienced 'non-linear dynamics' (Burgelman and Grove 2007) and 'disruptive technologies' (Christensen 1995, 2013) are arguably now facing such different challenges that we perhaps need to question even the dominant logic that the firm or the company is still the right unit of analysis when we are looking at 'value creation' (Prahalad 2004). It is not yet clear whether concepts which span the boundaries of the firm, such as 'value webs' or 'value configurations' with their associated ideas of value 'co-creation' will in the end turn out to be clarificatory or the opposite.

It is though clear that the questions already raised by the rapid changes in sectors including ICT and the way that new technologies will be used are huge. Several commentators have noted that currently there are opportunities for some firms to capture and analyse internal data more effectively than others thanks to the digital revolution. Some even see this as the result of a 'technological revolution' that is fundamentally transforming the economy in a so-called 'second machine age', whose effects may turn out to be comparable in magnitude to those of the agricultural and industrial revolutions since they represent such a 'step change' in the rate of growth of technology. The implications for management have been highlighted as pervasive: the changes in technology have enabled or are enabling the processing of vastly greater amounts of data. To use Davenport's mnemonic (Davenport and Harris 2007) : greater Variety (quantitative and qualitative), Volume and Velocity – *'We've become convinced that almost no sphere of business activity will remain untouched by this movement'*. (Brynjolfsson and McAfee 2012).

Though we may not be ready to go along with talk of anything on a par with the industrial revolution, we may still agree that at least we are experiencing a 'strategic inflection point' (Burgelman and Grove 1996), a metaphor for the giving way of one type of industry dynamics to another.

It may therefore be that for the future the ability to analyse 'big data' will turn out to be the key internal resource issue that management will need to focus on. That is suggested by the Academy of Management Journal's devoting a whole special issue to 'Big Data and Management', with the power of 'big data' described thus in the editorial: 'Such granular, high-volume data can tell us more about workplace practices and behaviours than our current data-collection methods allow – and have the potential to transform management theory and practice' (Gerard, Haas, and Pentland 2014).

There are other candidates for transformational technical progress raising new requirements for key resources too, as developments in machine learning, robotics, artificial intelligence and computing move towards the development of machines of various sorts with generalisable capabilities rather than specific ones.

This is enough to remind us that the technological changes currently underway are very significant and that the uncertainties created for management decision-making and hence for managerial education and training are correspondingly so. These are issues well beyond our scope for further discussion by us, here. What we would like to do instead is to illustrate why we think they reinforce the relevance of a Penrosian perspective, as we return to consider how these wide-ranging issues frame a third, small 'vignette' which prompts us to think about the very complexity of the industry situation that managers now face, and ask what capabilities do firms need now and what must they be mindful of?

5.1. Vignette 3: (anonymised) draft job specification for new role/position in an MNE firm operating in the media sector (mainly providing services to the broadcasting sector)

I wonder if any of you can help me?

We are looking to recruit an experienced ICT Strategist to join the Senior Leadership Team. I'm looking for a person or persons who specialise in data analytics and business strategy.

More specifically I need someone, (a 'data architect') who can help us/help the firm to:
- analyse and map our data flows across the whole organisation (specifically between our different systems)
- take a holistic view and incorporate different facets of the business to provide the right solution (planning, cost, strategy)
- understand the industry within which our company operates, and identify what needs to be done with data to stay ahead of the curve
- strategise and identify what and how data will inform our business solutions
- successfully initiate and manage highly technical data projects through to completion

---

This 'tall order' of a job specification surely links to Penrose's general comment that, 'In a sense the final products being produced by a firm at any given time merely represent one of several ways in which the firm could be using its resources' (Penrose, quoted in Augier & Teece (2007)) and that, 'A theory of growth of firms is essentially an examination of the changing productive opportunities of firms'. So, given the fast pace of change in this sector (thanks to disruptive technologies), the capability of identifying how value *creation* and *capture* will evolve is a critical capability and, as the draft job specification illustrates, a very wide-ranging one indeed.

In broadcasting, what has been dubbed the 'TV Ecosystem' is close to imploding, with the market participants taking more control of what they watch and when: customers buying content direct from either content makers [the creators], cable/TV firms (distributors), and other distributors (new entrants) such as Netflix, as well as Internet providers. Changes in technology have essentially enabled this shift to emerge which is markedly resulting in transformations in value capture/appropriation in the sector/ industry. Arguably, the key question for players in this industry now is: Given the changing competitive and market dynamics, which 'few special fields' should players in this sector focus on to maintain some bargaining power or 'defences in depth'? (Pitelis 2005, quoting Penrose). The image of 'Knowledge Orchestration' (McGee 2003) springs to mind: a combination of in-house capabilities (with the focus being on activities, processes, routines and tacit knowledge), outsourcing and co-creation – potentially even with competitors, in a major reshaping of the possibilities, potentials and threats for the firms involved.

6. Conclusion

The business world has changed and will change in specific ways which Edith Penrose could not have foreseen but, nevertheless, her approach continues to be extended and remains applicable.

Of continuing relevance are themes which Penrose explicitly foresees: that enterprises making better use of unused resources will be 'vast', that knowledge generation and organisational learning are key to firm survival and expansion and that ideas, imagination and willingness to experiment on the part of managements are continually required.

We hope to have contributed here to the development of that Penrosian perspective. The RBV leads management educators to stress the need for managers to look continually and critically inside the firm at existing resources and their use, outside the firm at changing environments for competition, cooperation, and co-supply, and at the match between inside and outside environments with an eye to the future, however uncomfortable that comparison may be.

We hope we have also supported the argument for the richness and debatable nature of company strategy 'cases' as pioneered by Penrose in her examination of 'Hercules Powder Company' and other strategic management cases. Other authors have examined how that case study in particular, and the methodology more generally, was developed by Penrose: see, for example, Jago Penrose (Chapter 10, 'The Theory of the Firm', in Penrose 2017, 175–188). We have not presented full 'case studies' here but rather draw on illustrative 'case examples' summarised in brief vignettes.

That of Hewlett-Packard, which was facing the key strategic choice whether to separate consumer-facing and enterprise-facing computing businesses in the early 21st century, shows how rapidly even such a basic strategic choice may be made but then reversed. Strategic choices remain debatable, contestable and changeable over time.

Our second vignette, that of the rise of Tesco as the UK's leading supermarket and the subsequent decline of the firm's 'dynamic capabilities', is based on participant observation. We offer it as a good example of how the growth of a large firm may be rooted in strong initial development of internal management resources – only for that management strength to act as a constraint on further growth and development later, as the lessons learnt are systematised, routinised and eventually stop being questioned, due to the very success they have fostered in the recent past. As Penrose argued, in the RBV, internal management resources are scarce and as the firm struggles to make best use of them, a 'dynamic' interaction occurs between the growth that is fostered, and the limitations on that growth such as internal management resistance to changing a 'winning formula' when that is needed. That internal management strength that Tesco had built up was very much focused on knowledge orchestration and so the rise and fall of Tesco as a 'learning organisation' over time, we suggest, offers a more persuasive picture of what is going on in the firm, than looking only at the hard data of revenue and profitability itself would do.

Our third vignette leads us into the realm of 'big data' and what it will mean for a single firm confronting a new environment. An examination of internal management resources by a media sector firm suggests that it is in urgent need of a senior 'ICT strategist' to join the firm's Senior Leadership Team. A job specification (here, anonymised) is produced as part of that recruitment effort to bolster senior internal management resources.

That is a useful exercise and yet, the articulation of what the firm needs such a senior 'data architect' to do, confronts us with the question of whether such a job is do-able: whether such a senior management specialist within a single firm could possibly meet such a tall order of a job specification now? Further specialisation for the firm, together with more flexible approaches to outsourcing and value co-creation with other players, be they cooperators or even former competitors, might be needed.

The emphasis on knowledge-based perspectives on the theory of firm growth lies firmly in the work of Edith Penrose. However, our third and last 'vignette' shows how we now need to 'push the envelope' of the concept of 'the firm' further, as to whether it can remain the right framework for framing knowledge creation and orchestration in the face of the enormity of the requirements and the possibilities of 'big data' analytics.

Disclosure statement

No potential conflict of interest was reported by the authors.

References

Albers, Josef. 1975. *Interaction of Color*. Westford, Massachusetts: Yale University.

Ambrosini, V., and C. Bowman. 2009. "What are Dynamic Capabilities and are They a Useful Construct in Strategic Management?" *International Journal of Management Reviews* 11 (1): 29–49. https://doi.org/10.1111/j.1468-2370.2008.00251.x.

Argyres, Nicholas S., and Todd R. Zenger. 2012. "Capabilities, Transaction Costs, and Firm Boundaries." *Organization Science* 23 (6): 1643–1657. https://doi.org/10.1287/orsc.1110.0736.

Baumol, William J. 1982. "Contestable Markets: An Uprising in the Theory of Industry Structure." *The American Economic Review* 72 (1): 1–15. American Economic Association.

Augier, M., and D. J. Teece. 2007. Dynamic capabilities and multinational enterprise: Penrosean insights and omissions. MANAGE. INT. REV. 47, 175–192. https://doi.org/10.1007/s11575-007-0010-8

Beinhocker, E. D. 2006. *Origin of Wealth Evolution, Complexity and the Radical Remaking of Economics*. Cambridge, Massachussetts, USA: Harvard Business School.

Boston Consulting Group Inc. 2014. *The Most Innovative Companies 2014: Breaking Through is Hard to Do*. Boston, MA, USA: The Boston Consulting Group, Inc.

Brynjolfsson, E., and A. McAfee. 2012. "Big Data: The Management Revolution." *Harvard Business Review* 90 (10): 60–68.

Burgelman, R. A., and A. S. Grove. 1996. "Strategic Dissonance." *California Management Review* 38 (2): 8–28. Winter 1996. https://doi.org/10.2307/41165830.

Burgelman, R. A., and A. S. Grove. 2007. "Let Chaos Reign, Then Rein in Chaos—Repeatedly: Managing Strategic Dynamics for Corporate Longevity." *Strategic Management Journal* 28 (10): 965–979. https://doi.org/10.1002/smj.625.

Christensen, C. M. 1995. *The Innovator's Dilemma: When New Technologies Cause Great Firms to Fail.* Boston, MA, USA: Harvard Business School Press.

Christensen, C. M. 2013. The Innovator's Dilemma: When New Technologies Cause Great Firms to Fail. Harvard Business Review Press: Reprint Editions.

Collins, Jim. 2001. *"From Good to Great- Why Some Companies Make the Leap and Others Don't".* New York City, NY, USA: Random House Business Books.

Davenport, T. H., and J. G. Harris. 2007. *Competing on Analytics: The New Science of Winning.* Boston, MA, USA: Harvard Business School Press.

De Wit, R., and R. Meyer. 2014. *Strategy: Process, Content, Context.* 4th ed. Boston, Massachussetts, USA: Cengage Publishing.

Gerard, George, Martine R Haas, and Alex Pentland. 2014. "From the Editors: Big Data and Management." *Academy of Management Journal* 57 (2): 321–326. https://doi.org/10.5465/amj. 2014.4002.

Goddard, Jules. 2014."The Fatal Bias."*Business Strategy Review.* London: London Business School. 25 (2): 34–37.

Jacobsen, Lowell. 2013. "On Robinson, Penrose, and the Resource- Based View." *The European Journal of the History of Economic Thought* 20 (1): 125–147. http://dx.doi.org/10.1080/ 09672567.2011.565355.

Kaplan, R. S., and D. P. Norton. 1992. "The Balanced Scorecard: Measures That Drive Performance." *Harvard Business Review* 70, (1 (January–February 1992)): 71–79.

Larry, E. Greiner. 1972. "Evolution and Revolution as Organisations Grow." *Harvard Business Review.* July-August.

Lockett, A. 2005. "Edith Penrose's Legacy to the Resource-Based View." *Managerial and Decision Economics* 26 (2): 83–98. Wiley. https://doi.org/10.1002/mde.1214.

McGee, J. 2003. "Strategy as Orchestrating Knowledge, Chapter 6." In *Images of Strategy,* edited by S Cummings, and D. C Wilson, 136–163. Oxford: Blackwell/Wiley.

Penrose, Angela. 2017. *No Ordinary Woman: The Life of Edith Penrose.* OUP. Oxford. https://doi. org/10.1093/oso/9780198753940.001.0001.

Penrose, Edith. 1956. "Foreign Investment and the Growth of the Firm." *The Economic Journal* 66 (262): 220–235. Royal Economic Society. 1 June 1956. https://doi.org/10.2307/2227966.

Penrose, Edith. 1960. "The Growth of the Firm—A Case Study: The Hercules Powder Company." *Business History Review* XXXIV (1): 1–23. 1. Spring 1960. Harvard. https://doi.org/10.2307/ 3111776.

Penrose, Edith. 2009. *The Theory of the Growth of the Firm.* 4th ed. Oxford: Introduction Chris Pitelis. OUP.

Penrose, Jago. 2017. *The Theory of the Growth of the Firm. Chapter 10, No Ordinary Woman: The Life of Edith Penrose,* 175–188. Oxford: OUP. https://doi.org/10.1093/oso/9780198753940.001. 0001.

Pitelis, Christos. 2005. "Edith Penrose, Organisational Economics and Business Strategy: An Assessment and extension." *Managerial and Decision Economics* 26 (2): 67–82.

Pitelis, Christos N. 2004. "Edith Penrose and the Resource-Based View of (International) Business Strategy." *International Business Review* 13 (4): 523–532. August. Elsevier. https://doi.org/10. 1016/j.ibusrev.2004.04.002.

Porter, M. 2013. *Can Japan Compete? Revisited.* Presentation at the Porter Prize Conference Tokyo, Japan December 5th, 2013.

Porter, M., H. Takeuchi, M. Sakakibara. 2001. *Can Japan Compete?* Macmillan.

Prahalad, C. K. 2004. "The Blinders of Dominant Logic." *Long Range Planning* 37 (2): 171–179. https://doi.org/10.1016/j.lrp.2004.01.010.

Prahalad, C. K., and A. R. Bettis. 1986. "The Dominant Logic: A New Linkage Between Diversity and Performance." *Strategic Management Journal* 7 (6): 485–501. https://doi.org/10.1002/smj. 4250070602.

Prahalad, C. K., and V. Ramaswamy. 2004. *The Future of Competition: Co-Creating Unique Value with Customers*. Boston, Ma, USA: Harvard Business School Press.

Rugman, Alan M., and Alain Verbeke. 2002. "Edith Penrose's Contribution to the Resource-Based View of Strategic Management." *Strategic Management Journal* 23 (8): 769–780. https://doi.org/10.1002/smj.240. August 2002.

Schaede, U. 2008. *Choose and Focus: Japanese Business Strategies for the 21st Century*. Ithaca, New York, USA: Cornell University Press.

Senge, P. M. 1994. *The Fifth Discipline: The Art and Practice of the Learning Organization*. New York City, NY, USA: Doubleday Press.

Soderberg, M., S. Kalagnanam, N. T. Sheehan, and Vaidyanathan. 2012. "When is a Balanced Scorecard a Balanced Scorecard?" *International Journal of Productivity & Performance Management* 60 (7): 688–708. https://doi.org/10.1108/17410401111167780.

Stacey, Ralph. 2006. *Strategic Management and Organisational Dynamics: The Challenge of Complexity (To Ways of Thinking About Organisations)*. 6th ed. Harlow, Essex, UK: FT Prentice Hall.

Teece, D. J., G. Pisano, and A. Shuen. 1997. "Dynamic Capabilities and Strategic Management." *Strategic Management Journal* 18 (7): 509–533. Wiley. https://doi.org/10.1002/(SICI)1097-0266 (199708)18:7<509:AID-SMJ882>3.0.CO;2-Z.

Wernerfelt, B. 1984. "A Resource-Based View of the Firm." *Strategic Management Journal* 5 (2): 171–178. Wiley. https://doi.org/10.1002/smj.4250050207.

Zott, C., and R. Amit. 2010. *Business Model Design: An Activity System Perspective, Long Range Planning*, 216–226. Amsterdam, Netherlands.: Elsevier.

Regulating stock buybacks: The $6.3 trillion question

Lenore Palladino and William Lazonick

ABSTRACT
Corporate resource allocation decisions shape business investment, income distribution, and productivity growth. Stock buybacks—a term denoting when a corporation repurchases its own shares on the open market—manipulate stock prices and enrich senior corporate executives and hedge fund managers. We argue that the growing distribution of corporate funds to share-sellers via stock buybacks is a source of productivity fragility in the US economy. This article presents new data on the use of stock buybacks by US corporations in 2010–2019. We show the widespread and growing use of stock buybacks across industries and sectors and describe policies that will curb the excessive use of corporate funds on stock buybacks.

1. Introduction

Corporate resource allocations shape investment, accumulation, income distribution, and productivity growth. Stock buybacks—when corporations repurchase their own shares on the open market— divert profits from retention and productive reinvestment, manipulate stock prices, and enrich senior corporate executives and hedge fund managers (Lazonick 2014; Lazonick and O"Sullivan 2000; Palladino 2020; Shilon 2021). The growing allocation of corporate funds to share-sellers via stock buybacks raises fragility and diminishes productivity growth in the US economy. This article presents new data on the use of stock buybacks by US corporations in 2010–2019, the decade preceding the COVID-19 pandemic. We show the widespread and growing use of stock buybacks across industries and sectors and describe policies that will curb the excessive use of corporate funds on stock buybacks.

By dint of their size, longevity, managerial function, and capacity for pooling and bearing risk, corporations have high potential to innovate – to produce higher-quality products at lower unit costs over time. To innovate, corporations must take risks with retained earnings derived from profits that require sustained financial commitment. The distributions of corporate cash to stock-market traders via essentially unregulated stock buybacks has negatively impacted innovation. Stock buybacks have become a predominant use of corporate funds: over the past decade stock buybacks plus cash dividends averaged 100% of nonfinancial corporations' corporate profits,[1] supplanting the deployment of profits as a dynamic resource for future spending. Analysis of SEC public filings shows that over 2010–2019, total spending by all publicly traded companies on stock buybacks totaled $6.3 trillion.[2] Stock buybacks are widespread throughout all sectors of the economy.

Stock buybacks divert enterprises from innovation. When executives prioritize using corporate funds for stock buybacks, they reduce funds available for investment that yields future productivity gains (Bhargava 2013; Davis and McCormack 2021; Gutiérrez and Philippon 2016). When buybacks are financed with substantial corporate debt, firms become financially fragile (Joan, Michaely, and Schmalz 2021). Stock buybacks manipulate the market price of corporate stock and incentivize corporate insiders to personally benefit from selling their own shareholdings after stock buybacks have boosted share prices (Bonaimé and Ryngaert 2013; Bonaimé et al. 2020; Cziraki, Lyandres, and Michaely 2021; Fried 2005; Palladino 2020; Shilon 2021).

In this article we outline the theory of innovative enterprises and describe the harms that stock buybacks (as distinct from corporate dividends)[3] pose to innovation, followed by evidence of the growing importance of stock buybacks in corporate resource allocation in the decade of 2010–2019. In Section 3 we describe the history of U.S. regulatory policies meant to limit the potential for market manipulation from excessive buybacks, as well as the effects of the permissive Securities and Exchange Commission Rule 10b-18 regulation that went into effect in 1982. We then outline several options for regulatory policy moving forward. Regulation that restricts buybacks may favorably shock management, putting the onus on executives to engage in product innovation rather than in financial manipulation. Section 4 concludes.

2. Innovative enterprises and the potential impacts of restricting stock buybacks

In this section we conceptualize the harms of stock buybacks by contrasting the theory of the innovative enterprise with the dominant corporate governance framework of shareholder primacy. We then describe the effects of stock buybacks on stock prices and the incentives for corporate insiders to misuse stock buybacks for personal gain. We review the benefits that would result from limiting stock buybacks: reduced incentives to direct corporate profits to shareholder payments; reduced potential for market manipulation; and reduced ability of corporate insiders to personally benefit from their ability to direct corporate funds to be used for stock buybacks.

2.1. Innovation and sustainable prosperity: the theory of the innovative enterprise

Shareholder primacy as a theory of corporate governance is embedded in the neoclassical model of the firm, which lacks a theory of how corporations innovate over time (Chandler 1992; Lazonick and Shin 2020; Lazonick 2020; Penrose 1959). The 'theory of the innovative enterprise' provides a framework for analyzing what allows firms to produce higher-quality products at lower unit costs over time – to innovate – resulting in increased productivity that, in a given accounting period, appear as profits (Lazonick 2019a; O'Sullivan 2000). These profits can be shared among contributors to corporate value creation, including the firm's employees, and invested in new rounds of innovation. The theory posits that because innovation is uncertain, collective, and cumulative, it requires managers to be strategic, employees to be integrated into organizational learning processes, and management to have access to financial resources that can sustain the innovation process over an uncertain timeline. The structure of corporate governance in large US companies today and the focus on value extraction at the expense of value creation are harmful to innovation. Stock buybacks play a leading role in diverting executives from a strategic focus on innovation, undermining organizational learning processes, and reducing financial resources available for the risky but crucial innovation process that generates higher-quality, lower-cost products.

How do stock buybacks impact innovation at the company level? An innovation strategy requires a firm to 'retain and reinvest' (Lazonick 2015a). Retained profits can be used to expand the capital stock, to embed technological innovations, and to enhance employees' productive capabilities. In contrast, a financialized firm-one that is focused on its stock market price – tends instead to downsize and distribute. The financialized firm lays off workers and depresses wages, outsources production, and sells off assets while using its cash flow to increase distributions to shareholders. Its employees are deprived of the opportunity to engage in collective and cumulative learning, and the company is deprived of the innovative products that organizational learning can generate. If a firm has secured a dominant position in a product market, it may avoid downsizing while still disproportionately distributing profits to shareholders, but the dominate-and-distribute resource-allocation regime can rapidly decay into downsize-and-distribute should the dominant market position disappear.

Senior corporate executives embraced shareholder-value ideology fully starting in the 1980s. Outside 'activist' shareholders, such as hedge funds, campaigned aggressively for value extraction with stakes no larger than one percent in a company's outstanding shares permitting them to exert pressure on corporate executives to increase distributions to shareholders. Institutional shareholders, once envisioned as responsible longer-term managers of capital, have instead enabled value extraction, operating under the proxy-voting rules that empower fund managers to vote the shares in the portfolio of assets that they manage (Coffee and Palia 2016; Lazonick and Shin 2020). All three actors, corporate insiders, activist shareholders, and fund managers have abetted the rise of stock buy-backs, with single-minded dedication to raising share prices – at cost of productive innovation.

2.2. Market manipulation

When announcing stock buyback programs, corporate executives explicitly state the goal of increasing the price of outstanding corporate equity. While the legal definition of market manipulation is complex and lacks clear bright lines that would determine a threshold for manipulation, the volume at which stock buybacks are currently conducted should be considered stock-price market manipulation, a violation of Section 9(a)(2) of the Exchange Act (Allen and Gale 1992; Fox, Glosten, and Rauterberg 2018). Besides enabling a corporation to inflate its market capitalization, the price-shock from buybacks enables companies to hit promised quarterly earnings per share (EPS) targets. Companies that are at risk of missing quarterly EPS forecasts show a sharp increase in the probability of share repurchases (Almeida, Fos, and Kronlund 2016).

In the 1970s, the Securities and Exchange Commission discussed regulatory options that would have permitted companies to conduct some limited buybacks without fear of liability for market manipulation (see Section 3 for further discussion of the regulatory proposals put forward in the 1970s). The draft regulation laid out bright-line conditions that were explicitly meant to keep the volume and timing of stock buybacks from manipulating market prices. Financial markets in most other advanced economies have regulations in place to limit the manipulative effects of stock buybacks (Jaemin, Schremper, and Varaiya 2004). However, stock buyback regulation in the United States enables companies to manipulate the market price of their stock without fear of prosecution.

2.3. Incentives for personal gain by corporate insiders and professional traders

Stock buybacks enable corporate insiders and professional traders to realize gains by timing the sale of their personal shares during the price elevation following buybacks (Bonaimé and Ryngaert 2013; Bonaimé et al. 2020; Chan et al. 2012; Kim and Varaiya 2008; Lazonick 2019b; Palladino 2020; Ramsay 2018; Shilon 2021[4]). Corporate executive compensation is largely tied to stock prices, as executives are paid in stock and bonuses are tied to stock-price-related metrics (Shilon 2021). Figure 1 details the average total pay and percentage shares of pay components for the 500 highest-paid US executives. Even in the depressed stock market of 2009 stock-based pay was 60% of the $15.9 million average remuneration, and in the booming stock market of 2015, stock-based pay was 83% of

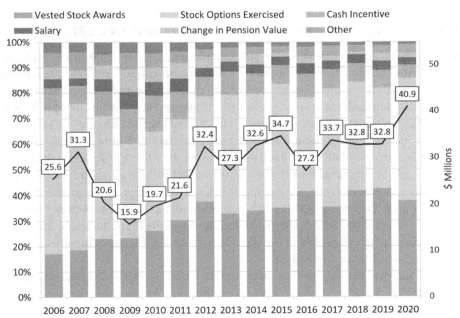

Figure 1. Components of executive pay for top 500 highest-paid CEOs, 2006–2020. Source: S&P Execucomp Database, accessed through Wharton Research Data Services

Table 1. Cash dividends and Stock buybacks as percentages of net income, 1981–2019.

	1981–1984	1985–1989	1990–1994	1995–1999	2000–2004	2005–2009	2010–2014	2015–2019
DV/NI%	48.3	50.3	53.9	37.0	40.5	40.7	35.7	50.5
BB/NI%	8.6	29.5	20.5	40.7	38.0	54.8	44.3	61.7
(DV+BB)/NI%	56.9	79.8	74.4	77.7	78.4	95.5	80.0	112.2

Source: Cash dividends (DV) and stock buybacks (BB) as percentages of net income (NI), 1981–2019, for the 216 business corporations in the S&P 500 Index as of January 2020 that were publicly listed for all 39 years. S&P Compustat database and company 10-K filings, compiled by Mustafa Erdem Sakinç and Emre Gömeç of the Academic-Industry Research Network.

$34.6 million average remuneration. The shift to stock-based pay rewards senior executives for 'making decisions that foment speculation and manipulate stock prices' (Lazonick 2019a).

While insiders face strict requirements to report their personal transactions of corporate stock, the reporting requirements for stock buybacks do not identify the day of the transaction. Hence, insider share sales and stock buybacks cannot be matched closely enough to establish insider trading. Even with limited disclosure, research has established that corporate insiders who are using corporate funds to conduct stock buybacks are personally benefiting. Palladino (2020) finds that net insider personal sales of over $100,000 are nearly twice as common in quarters when meaningful stock buyback transactions take place than they are in other quarters, and a 10% change in insider share selling is associated with a 0.5% change in stock buyback transactions, and a $4.2 million increase in stock buybacks is associated with a $900,000 increase in quarterly insider share sales. Former SEC Commissioner Robert Jackson Jr. found a similar link between stock buyback announcements––which also tend to increase share prices, even before actual repurchases take place––and corporate insider share selling (Jackson 2018).

2.4. Evidence for the growing importance of stock buybacks: 2010–2019

Company spending on open-market stock repurchases is available from required SEC 10-K and 10-Q public filings by all publicly traded companies.[5] In 1981–1983, dividends were 49.7% of the combined net income of all reporting companies, buybacks were only 4.4%, and the remainder was largely retained for investment. The SEC adopted Rule 10b-18 in 1982, providing companies with a 'safe harbor' against charges of manipulation when they conduct large-scale open-market repurchases. Figure 2 shows the rise of buybacks and dividends for the 216 companies in the S&P 500 Index in January 2020 that had been publicly traded for the period from 1981 to 2019. Stock buybacks have risen sharply since the mid-1980s, surpassing dividends as a form of distribution to shareholders for the first time in 1997. In 2017–2019, dividends were 49.6% of net income, but buybacks now absorbed 62.2%. Buybacks are more volatile than dividends, and they tend to be executed when stock prices are already high and rising, as companies compete to show strong stock-price performance.

Table 1 displays the data on buybacks and dividends in Figure 2 as percentages of net income for the 216 companies for 1981–1984, and then for five-year periods from 1985–1989 through 2015–2019. The proportions for 2005–2009 and 2015–2019 capture the surges in buybacks during years (except for 2008 and 2009) in which profits were high and the stock market was booming. From 2003 to 2007, the value of buybacks done by

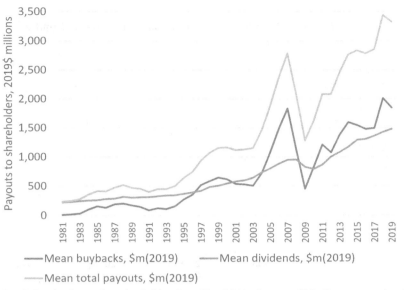

Figure 2. Stock buybacks and cash dividends, 1981–2019. Source: S&P Compustat database and company 10-K filings, compiled by Mustafa Erdem Sakinç and Emre Gömeç of the Academic-Industry Research Network. Data presented in 2019$billions, for the 216 business corporations in the S&P 500 Index in January 2020, publicly listed for the entire period

companies in the S&P 500 Index quadrupled. In general, these publicly listed companies have done buybacks when stock prices have been high and rising, as they have competed with one another to give manipulative boosts to their stock prices. These data also show that even as buybacks have absorbed a large proportion of net income, these companies have paid ample dividends. The half-decade 2015–2019 is particularly noteworthy for the extent of distributions to shareholders in the years preceding the onset of the Covid-19 pandemic.

These distributions to shareholders come at the expense of rewards to employees in the form of higher pay, superior benefits, and more secure jobs as well as corporate investment in the new products and processes that can sustain a firm as an innovative enterprise in the future. These distributions are a prime cause of the concentration of income among the richest households and the erosion of middle-class employment opportunities (Lazonick and Shin 2020).

In the 2010s all US publicly listed companies spent $6.3 trillion in aggregate on open-market share repurchases. To put this figure in context, total US GDP for the decade was approximately $172 trillion; spending on open-market share repurchases alone was equivalent to 4% of US spending on goods and services. Aggregate buyback spending grew steadily through the decade after the Great Recession, peaking in the fourth quarter of 2018 at $270.6 billion and then accelerating again. In the first quarter of 2020 alone, immediately preceding the pandemic, the average corporation engaged in buybacks spent nearly $90 million. Figure 3 shows the growth of aggregate spending on stock buybacks by quarter for the sample period.

Buybacks are concentrated among large companies. In the 2010s, the 500 companies included in the S&P 500 Index executed a combined $5.2 trillion in stock buybacks,

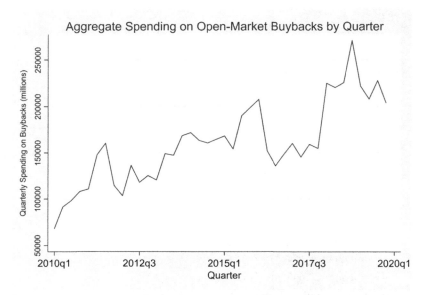

Figure 3. Aggregate spending on open-market share repurchases by quarter. Source: S&P Compustat

representing 53% of their net income, while also distributing $3.8 trillion in dividends, another 39% of net income. Among these companies, the 25 largest repurchasers among US non-financial companies spent $1.8 trillion on buybacks, equal to 34% of the total for the S&P 500 and 29% of all buybacks done by all publicly listed companies in the United States.

Of the 466 companies that were consistently in the S&P 500 from 2010–2019, the 50 largest repurchasers conducted 51% of all buybacks. Figure 4 shows average spending on buybacks by firm revenue quartile for the decade, normalized by firm revenue. Market dominance, stemming from both innovation and market power, can lead to enormous profits, supporting elevated shareholder payments (Gutiérrez and Philippon 2018). In contrast, smaller and less profitable firms do not attract the same pressures, nor do they have the same funds available to engage in mass buyback activity (though there are exceptions).

Companies often do buybacks to boost their stock prices. The decisions about the timing and magnitude of buybacks for each company are made by corporate insiders in conjunction with other influential shareholders. Stock buybacks as a share of corporate net income shows how buybacks drain retained earnings, which could otherwise compensate employees for contributions to corporate profits and provide capital for investment in the next generation of innovative products (Lazonick 2014; Lazonick and Shin 2020). Corporate net income spent stock buybacks displaces the use of retained profits for future innovation. Figure 5 shows the ratio of buyback spending to net income (profit/loss) for all firms. Spending by corporations on stock buybacks as a percentage of net income remained high for the entire decade, with some fluctuation mainly due to dips in profit.

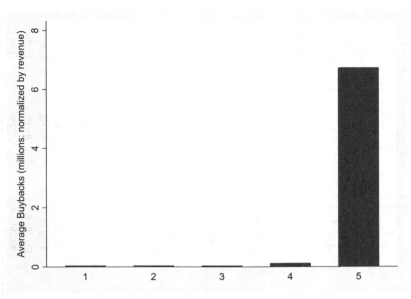

Figure 4. Average buybacks by firm revenue quartile. Source: S&P Compustat. Data is normalized by firm revenue.

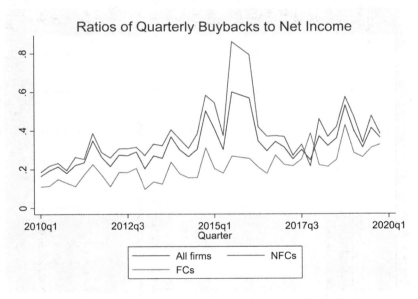

Figure 5. Ratios of quarterly stock buybacks to net income by sector, 2010–2019.

2.4.1. Industry and sectoral buyback activity

A sectoral analysis of buybacks can give insight into how retained earnings for innovation and the conditions of financial commitment depend on the technological, market, and competitive characteristics of an industry. Table 2 presents data on aggregate spending

Table 2. Stock Buybacks Spending at the Sectoral Level, 2010–2019.

NAICS Code	Sector	Aggregate Buybacks (in billions)	Aggregate Revenue (in billions)	% of Total Buybacks	% of Total Sector Revenue
11	Agriculture, Forestry, Fishing and Hunting	$12.21	$294.83	0.20%	0.11%
21	Mining, Quarrying, and Oil and Gas Extraction	$147.99	$9,025.57	2.38%	3.40%
22	Utilities	$26.42	$14,400.00	0.43%	5.43%
23	Construction	$25.07	$1,702.74	0.40%	0.64%
31-33	Manufacturing	$2,489.52	$109,200.00	40.11%	41.16%
42	Wholesale Trade	$80.72	$12,000.00	1.30%	4.52%
44-45	Retail Trade	$473.55	$28,100.00	7.63%	10.59%
48-49	Transportation and Warehousing	$191.35	$11,210.59	3.08%	4.23%
51	Information	$986.70	$26,100.00	15.90%	9.84%
52	Finance and Insurance	$1,229.23	$31,600.00	19.81%	11.91%
53	Real Estate and Rental and Leasing	$66.95	$2,771.82	1.08%	1.04%
54	Professional, Scientific, and Technical Services	$114.91	$4,184.61	1.85%	1.58%
56	Administrative and Support and Waste Management and Remediation Services	$50.60	$1,670.86	0.82%	0.63%
61	Educational Services	$9.62	$229.74	0.16%	0.09%
62	Health Care and Social Assistance	$74.47	$3,843.77	1.20%	1.45%
71	Arts, Entertainment, and Recreation	$7.30	$373.33	0.12%	0.14%
72	Accommodation and Food Services	$154.35	$2,516.89	2.49%	0.95%
81	Other Services (except Public Administration)	$8.27	$189.48	0.13%	0.07%
99		$57.40	$5,876.98	0.92%	2.22%
Total		$6,206.62	$265,291.18	100%	100%

Source: Authors' Calculations of Form 10-K data, provided by S&P Compustat.

on buybacks by industry, along with aggregate revenue, organized by two-digit North American Industry Classification System (NAICS) codes. Spending on stock buybacks varies by sector and by company; in many sectors, buybacks represent 1–2% of revenue, but some sectors stand out, including Information (9.8% of revenue); Finance, Insurance and Real Estate (11.9% of revenue); and Retail (10.6% of revenue). Table 2 presents additional data on the percentage of total buybacks and total revenue for each sector, showing that in some cases, such as Manufacturing, the sector comprises roughly the same percentage of buybacks and revenue for all companies, whereas for some sectors, like FIRE, their share of buybacks far outpaces their share of revenue.

Even sectors that are not commonly thought of as financialized and with substantial receipt of public funds – such as the health, social services, and arts and recreation – are also spending significant funds on stock buybacks. These sectors may follow a distinct path from manufacturing's transition from retain-and-reinvest to downsize-and-distribute. Given the amount of public funds flowing into these sectors (for example, Medicaid and Medicare spending on hospitals and nursing homes, and public funding for education) and recurring concerns about underfunding (especially in the pandemic era), stock buyback activity shows that service sectors are not immune to pressure for increased shareholder payments.

A closer investigation of buybacks in human services, that is, the health care and education sectors, may be illustrative. Buybacks in the Ambulatory Health Care Services sector (NAICS 621) exceeded $9 billion in 2017 and was almost $60 billion for the decade. Buybacks in Nursing Care and Residential Care Facilities, a sector largely funded by Medicare and Medicaid, peaked at nearly $70.8 million for 2011. Buybacks by Hospitals, often structured as non-profits, peaked at $3 billion for 2016. Even industries thought of as largely public, such as the NAICS three-digit sectoral category 611 of Educational Service Firms, has consistently engaged in stock buybacks. The sector's spending peaked in late 2014, when companies spent nearly $80 million collectively on stock buybacks. The highest corporate spenders for each of these sub-sectors is presented in Table A1 in the Appendix.

The focus on maximizing shareholder value had specific harmful effects on product markets that became critical in the Covid-19 pandemic: ventilator and personal protective equipment (PPE) production. Lazonick and Hopkins (2020) document in detail the history of the development, production, and delivery of ventilators to the Strategic National Stockpile, showing that 'the weakness of the [government-business collaborations engaged in production] appeared when these innovative manufacturers fell under the control of business corporations committed to the ideology of "maximizing shareholder value",' (Lazonick and Hopkins 2020, 1). In each of the two government contracts meant to produce ventilators for the national stockpile, the innovative ventilator companies (Newport Medical and Respironics) that retained profits and reinvested in productive capabilities were acquired by larger financialized companies (Covidien and Philips). This focus undermined the development and delivery of ventilators while prioritizing value extraction, in particular through the use of stock buybacks.[6]

2.4.2. The largest corporate repurchasers

Table 3 ranks U.S. industrial corporations by the value of stock buybacks executed in the decade 2010–2019. It is noteworthy that SEC Rule 10b-18 states that a company will not

Table 3. Twenty largest stock repurchasers, 2010–2019, among U.S. industrial corporations, their subsequent repurchases to the last 10-Q or 10-K filing on or before 31 December 2021, and their SEC Rule 10b-18 safe-harbor average daily trading volume (ADTV) limits for repurchases on 19 October 2019 and 23 June 2021.

		2010–2019			ADTV Amount	
COMPANY	$BB RANK	BB, $b.	BB/NI%	(BB+DV)/NI%	21 October 2019, $m.	23 June 2021, $m.
APPLE	1	305.0	73	94	1,597	2,526
ORACLE	2	113.7	121	145	183	261
MICROSOFT	3	101.1	48	92	754	1,522
EXXON MOBIL	4	92.4	35	80	166	410
IBM	5	88.2	71	107	125	144
CISCO SYSTEMS	6	81.5	100	144	226	254
PFIZER	7	76.7	60	116	146	235
WALMART	8	70.2	50	91	141	259
INTEL	9	66.8	51	87	219	318
HOME DEPOT	10	64.4	93	137	188	299
JOHNSON & JOHNSON	11	62.1	49	110	267	280
PROCTER & GAMBLE	12	54.9	52	117	186	319
AMGEN	13	51.2	92	129	97	164
GENERAL ELECTRIC	14	50.3	135	314	94	197
QUALCOMM	15	49.4	119	178	116	241
DISNEY	16	47.8	61	85	231	341
MERCK	17	45.8	81	172	144	265
MCDONALD'S	18	45.8	87	145	159	149
BOEING	19	43.4	87	137	292	708
GILEAD SCIENCES	20	39.6	56	75	93	122

BB=stock buybacks; DV=cash dividends; NI=net income; ADTV=average daily trading volume limit to secure the safe harbor against stock-price manipulation charges under SEC Rule 10b-18.
Sources: Data have been collected by the authors from company 10-K and 10-Q filings with the SEC; Yahoo Finance daily historical stock prices.

be charged with manipulation if the trading volume of its buybacks on any single day are no more than 25% of the previous four weeks' average daily trading volume (ADTV), and there is no presumption of manipulation even if the corporation's repurchases exceed the stated limit. Under Rule 10b-18, many large publicly listed companies can do hundreds of millions of dollars of open-market repurchases per day.

Of the twenty largest stock repurchasing companies, thirteen distributed more than 100% of net income to shareholders over the decade while the remaining seven distributed 75% or more of net income. Coming into the pandemic, twelve companies in the list, Apple, Oracle, Microsoft, Cisco, Walmart, Intel, Home Depot, Johnson & Johnson, Amgen, Qualcomm, Disney, and Gilead, enjoyed significant market dominance and could use profits from their still-dominant market positions to support their stock price without a substantial squeeze on corporate investment or employment. The remaining eight companies, Exxon Mobil, IBM, Pfizer, Procter & Gamble, General Electric, Merck, McDonald's, and Boeing, were in 'downsize-and-distribute' mode, distributing corporate cash to shareholders as they simultaneously downsized their labor forces (Lazonick and Hopkins 2021).

Lazonick (2022, 25) has analyzed the financial behavior of the 20 company in Table 3 during the pandemic through September 2021. Despite macroeconomic upheaval, Apple, Oracle, Microsoft, Walmart, Intel, Home Depot, Procter & Gamble, Qualcomm, and Amgen spent 42% or more of net income on buybacks. These nine companies benefited from very strong demand for their products and high profits during the pandemic. Pfizer benefitted during the pandemic from its involvement with Germany-based BioNTech by manufacturing and delivering the COVID-119 vaccines. But through September 2021, the financial condition of ExxonMobil, IBM, General Electric, Disney, Merck, McDonald's, and Boeing – deteriorated.

The relation between innovation and financialization must be analyzed at both the aggregate and company level: analyses done at the aggregate or industrial sector level can be misleading because of variation among companies within a sector. In semiconductors, for example, while Intel has been among the largest repurchasers in the United States since the late 1990s, its rival AMD has never paid a dividend and prior to 2020 had only done $77 million in buybacks in 2001 after its board authorized a $300 million repurchase program. In 2020, AMD did $78 billion in buybacks to cover employee withholding taxes on vesting of employee equity grants. On 19 May 2021, however, with its profits during the pandemic at about seven times its profits in 2018 and 2019 (which were good years for the company), AMD announced a $4 billion repurchase program (AMS 2021). In fact, AMD did $256 million billion in buybacks in the second quarter of 2021 and another $748 million in the third quarter.

3. Policy reforms to limit stock buybacks and promote innovation

The current regulatory regime for buybacks dates to the 1982 issuance of Rule 10b-18 by the Securities and Exchange Commission (SEC), and there has been no significant update to the rules that govern stock buyback activity in the forty years since.[7] In this section we describe the history of stock buybacks regulation and propose several options for policies to reduce the negative impacts of stock buybacks on corporate innovation and financial markets.

Rule 10b-18 provides a company with a 'safe harbor', or presumption of innocence, against charges of stock-price manipulation if its buybacks conform to certain volume, broker, and timing conditions. The safe harbor provision applies if the buybacks that a company executes on any single trading day do not exceed 25% of the stock's average daily trading volume (ADTV) over the previous four weeks. For large companies with high trading volume and high stock prices, the daily limit may permit hundreds of millions of dollars of buybacks, and the company may conduct additional daily buybacks up to this limit trading day after trading day. SEC reporting rules have never required that companies disclose the specific trading days on which buybacks are carried out, and therefore, as the SEC itself admits, it is impossible to monitor whether corporate buyback activity remains within the safe-harbor limit (Dayen 2015). Even if companies violate the 'safe harbor' limits, there is no presumption of wrongdoing.

3.1. Overview of the history of policies regarding stock buybacks

Prior to the adoption of Rule 10b-18 in 1982, companies executing open-market share repurchases could be held liable for market manipulation under Section 9(a)(2) and 10(b) of the Securities Exchange Act of 1934 .[8] The Williams Act of 1968, which enabled the SEC to adopt regulations governing share repurchases, stated that it is unlawful for issuers to repurchase their own securities if the purchase 'is in contravention of such rules and regulations as the Commission . . . may adopt (A) to define acts and practices which are fraudulent, deceptive, or manipulative, and (B) to prescribe means reasonably designed to prevent such acts and practices'.[9] Not all companies engaging in repurchases were doing so for purposes of increasing stock prices by reducing outstanding common stock, however; some bought back stock to fulfill their obligations under stock-based employee compensation plans (Lazonick and Jacobson 2022).

The SEC debated the rules and regulations to adopt regarding stock buybacks without the presumption of liability for manipulation throughout the 1970s, at the outset proposing far more restrictions than it ultimately adopted under President Reagan in 1982. Proposed Rule 13e-2 would have made open-market stock buybacks subject to bright-line volume limits and would have required disclosure by corporate insiders who might be considering buying or selling securities for their personal account at the same time that the company was engaging in share repurchases on the open market.[10] In 1980, the commissioners clearly stated that their intent behind the proposed rule was to 'prevent the issuer from leading or dominating the market through its repurchase program. In fashioning those limitations, the Commission has balanced the need to curb the opportunity to engage in manipulative conduct against the need to avoid excessively burdensome restrictions'.[11]

By the close of 1982, in what was termed a 'regulatory about-face' by SEC staff, the Reagan Administration SEC had replaced proposed Rule 13e-2 with the new Rule 10b-18, which provided corporate repurchasers a safe harbor from liability for manipulation under certain conditions, while not automatically regarding buybacks executed outside the safe harbor as prohibited (Feller and Chamberlin 1984; Hudson 1982). This shift was part of the larger transition of the SEC from a financial-regulatory agency that sought to limit stock-price manipulation without being overly intrusive to a financial-promotion agency that authorized stock issuers to engage in large-scale stock-price manipulation with impunity (Lazonick and Shin 2020; Seligman 1995). Based on a systematic misunderstanding of the role of secondary-market trading in capital formation, the SEC proceeded to conduct its rulemaking based on the view that trading on the secondary markets was the key to corporate investment and innovation in the nonfinancial economy, even though secondary-market trading does not send new funds to corporate coffers. Some secondary-market trading, such as buyback spending undertaken to push up share prices, can drain retained earnings and reduce funds available to firms for productive investment.

Under Rule 10b-18, disclosure that might discourage companies from straying beyond the bounds of the safe harbor is not required, nor does exceeding the conditions of the safe harbor trigger a presumption that manipulation is taking place. Specifically, companies are limited to limiting their volume of stock buybacks to one-quarter of their daily volume of trading, averaged over the previous four weeks (§240.10b-18(13iv(B1)).[12] When Rule 10b-18 was adopted in 1982, one of the SEC commissioners, John Evans, warned that some manipulation of the market would now go unprosecuted (Hudson 1982). Lazonick and Jacobson (2022) show that there was no sound empirical basis for setting the average daily trading volume (ADTV) limit at 15%, as had been the case under proposed Rule 13e-2, let alone the much more expansive 25% in Rule 10b-18 (Lazonick and Jacobson 2022). Given the increase in trading volume generally, including both block trading and high-frequency trading in particular, this trading-volume limit is based on a denominator that now permits far more 'safe harbor' market manipulation than it did four decades ago.

In addition to the lack of presumed liability for exceeding the safe harbor, corporations do not have to report metrics such that the SEC can determine whether they are within the safe harbor. Because stock buyback activity must only be reported on a monthly basis, not daily, it is impossible for even regulators to tell if there has been a violation of the 'safe harbor', showing that the Rule has no practical impact on corporate decision-making. Companies may circumvent the safe harbor limit by doing 'accelerated share repurchases' with no apparent response from the SEC (Kurt 2018). In Table 2, we present calculations of the ADTV limits of the nation's largest industrial repurchasers in October 2019, prior to the pandemic, and June 2021, when the pandemic had become normalized. For all companies (with the exception of McDonald's) the ADTV limit was higher, and in most cases substantially higher, in June 2021, reflecting a general increase in stock-market speculation and manipulation, with some innovation, during the pandemic. Whether prior to the pandemic or in its midst, it is clear from these calculations that the Rule's stipulations do not in fact serve to curb large transactions that affect the market price of a company's stock.

3.2. Summary of policy reform proposals

In the absence of a suite of countervailing institutions to limit pressure for shareholder payments and encourage innovative corporate investment, limiting stock buybacks may not be a silver bullet, but it is a necessary component of a broader reform agenda that would move US corporations away from shareholder value maximization and in the direction of innovation and sustainable prosperity.

First, Rule 10b-18 should be repealed and replaced by regulations that will limit buybacks and encourage the redirection of US corporations toward innovation. The most effective policy reform to curb the harms of stock buybacks would be for Congress to prohibit open-market share repurchases under the Securities and Exchange Act Sec. 9 (a)(2). The act governs trading of equities in the secondary markets and regulates fraud and manipulative activity. Congress could limit open-market share repurchases altogether or place bright-line limits on buybacks (Palladino 2019). Congress has a range of options for reforming the practice of stock buybacks. Congress can ban open-market repurchases of an issuing company's own stock while leaving options available for private repurchase transactions,[13] which are not currently regulated under Rule 10b-18.[14] This prohibition would recognize that open-market share repurchases allow a company to manipulate the market price of its stock and would ban them on those grounds. This is the most straightforward proposal for reducing market manipulation and creating conditions for innovation in the United States.

Short of an outright ban, legislated bright-line limits on buyback activity and the removal of the safe harbor provision could reduce harms from buybacks (Palladino 2019). This would be justified under the same argument––that open-market stock buybacks are a tool for stock market manipulation––and would be in line with the regulations in place in many advanced financial markets (Jaemin, Schremper, and Varaiya 2004). A bright-line limit should not simply adopt the current limits contained in Rule 10b-18; the choice of 25% of the average daily trading volume was based on no evidence that this ratio forestalls manipulation (Lazonick and Jacobson 2022). Further study should be required to define an exact set of bright-line limits, but it is clear that given the speed and volume of trading in the 21st century, there is no a priori reason to accept the twenty-five percent of trading volume metric.

Several recent Congressional proposals would make a company's authorization to conduct stock buybacks contingent on improved corporate behavior. For example, buybacks would be forbidden to companies with underfunded pension obligations; with recent layoffs; with excessive wage dispersion; or with executive compensation above a certain absolute limit or ratio relative to median worker pay. These proposals, though useful from a narrative perspective in tying together the issues of stock buybacks and economic inequality as experienced by workers, would nonetheless leave substantial opportunities for corporate executives to manipulate data to permit buybacks. Such proposals might thus create more openings for buybacks than intended and should be avoided.

Any reform of open-market share repurchases must remove the incentives for corporate insiders to benefit personally from stock buyback transactions. Corporate insiders should be forbidden from selling their personal shareholdings in conjunction with buybacks that they authorize. Congress should also require immediate disclosure and determination concerning the permissibility of buybacks (Palladino 2020; Fried 2000). Yet disclosure mandates without reform of Rule 10b-18 could make matters worse by encouraging speculative use of the disclosure data to time the buying and selling of shares (Lazonick 2015b). Much of the incentive problem derives from the fact that the vast majority of senior corporate executives are paid at least partly––and often predominantly––in financial instruments whose values are tied to the price of their company's stock. These executives are in a position to gain significantly when a stock price rise spurred by buybacks coincides with their exercise of stock options or the vesting of their stock awards (Hopkins and Lazonick 2016; Shilon 2021). Structuring executive compensation in this manner presents a clear threat to management's focus on corporate innovation and broader reforms of the rules governing executive compensation are crucial.

The SEC is already authorized to issue rules[15] regulating stock buybacks, including: bright-line limits; the ability of corporate insiders to benefit from buyback transactions; and real-time disclosure requirements to alert the public of stock buyback activity as it takes place. Section 2(e)(1) of the Williams Act Amendment to the Exchange Act of 1968 explicitly states that it is unlawful for companies to engage in an open-market share repurchase if that purchase 'is in contravention of such rules and regulations as the Commission ... may adopt (A) to define acts and practices which are fraudulent, deceptive, or manipulative, and (B) to prescribe means reasonably designed to prevent such acts and practices'. Thus, even without congressional action, the commission can take affirmative steps to reduce the ability of companies to manipulate the market price of their own stock, require a comprehensive disclosure regime, and end the ability of corporate insiders to benefit from stock buyback execution concurrent with their personal share-selling.

To begin, the SEC must repeal Rule 10b-18 and issue new rulemaking that puts companies on notice that they may be found liable for open-market share repurchases that constitute potential market manipulation. Then, the SEC should place bright-line limits on stock buybacks rather than offering repurchasers a safe harbor bounded by the current limits on volume, timing, and purchaser. As with the congressional policy approach, the SEC must undertake an empirical analysis to determine the correct bright-line limits for repurchase volumes rather than rely on the 25% of average daily trading volume (ADTV) or even the 15% of ADTV proposed over 40 years ago. The commission must also focus on the personal incentives that stock buyback activity creates for executives. Corporate insiders could be prohibited from trading their personal holdings during a quarter in which buybacks have been executed, or at minimum required to disclose in real time when they are doing so. Most other advanced financial markets – including those of the United Kingdom, Japan, France, Hong Kong, Canada, and the Netherlands – explicitly restrict trading by insiders during periods of stock buyback activity (Jaemin, Schremper, and Varaiya 2004).

Finally, even if substantial reforms take more time, under Rule 10b-18 regulators should at minimum immediately require disclosure of stock buyback activity on a daily basis to ensure that companies are complying with the limited requirements that constitute the safe harbor. To be clear, the ability of companies to spend 25% of ADTV is still manipulative, but disclosure is a bare minimum and should have been required all along (Lazonick 2015b). Without such disclosure, the 'safe harbor' idea is meaningless, as the SEC does not even collect the data necessary to determine whether companies are staying within the safe harbor's limits (Dayen 2015).

4. Conclusion

The nation's recovery from the COVID-19 pandemic offers an opportunity for reform of the four-decade old value-extractive corporate model. The ideology of shareholder primacy in corporate governance contributed to the country's widening income and wealth inequality by directing corporate funds to the wealthiest 10% of households (largely white) who now own 88.7% of corporate stock, while workers experienced four decades of wage stagnation (Distributional Financial Accounts 2021). As the negative experience following 1982 demonstrates, policymakers have remarkable power to redirect the nation's corporate resources. Restricting the extractive practice of stock buybacks, which was unleashed in 1982, can initiate a recovery towards innovation and sustainable prosperity. Policy design is critical, and both Congress and the Securities and Exchange Commission have excellent options for reform.

Notes

1. Profits, or net income, are defined in corporate SEC 10-K statements as Total Revenue less (costs of goods sold + operating expenses + other gains or losses + other expenses + depreciation + interest expense + taxes).
2. Since 2004, SEC disclosure regulations have required corporations to report the repurchasing of their shares on their Form 10-Q quarterly reports by stating the number of shares repurchased and the average purchase price per share. Companies are not required to disaggregate shares purchased on the open market that are (nominally) regulated by Rule 10b-18 and in other repurchase transactions. More details on data availability are found in Appendix B.
3. It is important to differentiate between two types of distributions made to shareholders: dividends and stock buybacks (we use the term "distributions" rather than "returns to shareholders", as the vast majority of shareholders today purchase shares on the secondary markets, and thus have never contributed financial assets to the company in the first place). Although the *volume* of funds spent on dividends and stock buybacks can be similar, stock buybacks create harms that dividends do not. Dividends do not directly bid up the stock price, and they do not encourage insiders to strategically time the sale of their own shares. While dividends have historically risen steadily, boards do not want to create expectations of perennially unsustainable dividend levels. Dividend increases accrue to all shareholders (with the same class of stock), while stock buybacks directly benefit only shareholders who sell strategically around the buyback.
4. A letter to the SEC from an executive at Investors Exchange LCC stated: "As the global head of trading at a large asset manager put it: *When it comes to handling the corporate buyback, what's painfully obvious to us is that the corporate buyback is probably the most gameable order in the marketplace. If you pursue liquidity in a corporate buyback algorithm, other participants can easily sense how the algorithm is going to react and try to trade in front of it*". (Ramsay 2018).
5. We use S&P Compustat, a data vendor available through Wharton Research Data Services, to aggregate individual corporate 10-Q and 10-K filings.
6. Lazonick and Hopkins (2020) detail the complete history of the shift in prioritization from innovation toward shareholder value maximization in the companies responsible for producing ventilators for the US national stockpile.
7. The SEC issued Proposed Rule SR for public comment on December 15, 2021. As of this writing, the public comment period is still open. The proposal does include some of the recommendations made herein. See "Share Repurchase Disclosure Modernization", Release Nos. 34–93783, https://www.sec.gov/rules/proposed/2021/34–93783.pdf.
8. Under the Securities and Exchange Act of 1934, which governs secondary trading in the financial markets, companies are subject to anti-fraud and anti-manipulation rules in their trading activity. Capital is a stock, not a flow, and secondary trading relates to financial flows, not investment in an asset (i.e. a stock).

REGULATING STOCK BUYBACKS: THE $6.3 TRILLION QUESTION 259

9. Williams Act, Pub. L. No. 90–439, 82 Stat. 455 (1968).
10. The initial proposal to limit buybacks to 15% of average daily trading volume was based on a single article published in 1965, based on share repurchases conducted by large companies in that year for the purposes of employee compensation, not stock-price manipulation (Guthart 1965; Lazonick and Jacobson 2022).
11. Purchases of Certain Equity Securities by the Issuer and Others, 45 Fed. Reg. at 70891.
12. Specifically, the Rule reads: "*(1)* The total volume of Rule 10b-18 purchases effected on any single day does not exceed the lesser of 25% of the security's four-week ADTV or the issuer's average daily Rule 10b-18 purchases during the three full calendar months preceding the date of the announcement of such transaction".
13. Private repurchase transactions and "tender offers" are direct offers to shareholders made publicly by companies to repurchase their shares at a particular price, and do not involve the same potential for market manipulation because they are disclosed in advance and do not take place in the open market. Also see footnote 3, above.
14. This was first proposed by Senator Tammy Baldwin (D-WI) in the "Reward Work Act".
15. In the United States, Congress passes legislation, which independent regulatory agencies, like the Securities and Exchange Commission, carry out through promulgating rules, which must be within the scope of what has been passed legislatively. In this case, only Congress could ban stock buybacks substantively, but the SEC has the authority to revise rules of corporate conduct (subject to the Administrative Procedures Act.) For a theoretical treatment of the difference between legislation and regulation, see (Kosti, Levi-Faur, and Mor 2020).
16. Phillip Brzenk and Aye M. Soe, "Digging Deeper into the U.S. Preferred Market", *S&P Dow Jones Indices*, October 2015, https://www.spglobal.com/spdji/en/documents/research/research-digging-deeper-into-the-us-preferred-market.pdf.
17. See Matt Hopkins and William Lazonick, "The Mismeasure of Mammon: Uses and Abuses of Executive Pay Data", *Institute for New Economic Thinking Working Paper* No. 49, August 29, 2016, https://www.ineteconomics.org/research/research-papers/the-mismeasure-of-mammon-uses-and-abuses-of-executive-pay-data.

Acknowledgements

The authors would like to thank Chirag Lala and Ken Jacobson for excellent research assistance and feedback.

Disclosure statement

No potential conflict of interest was reported by the author(s).

Funding

William Lazonick acknowledges funding for his research on stock buybacks from the Institute for New Thinking.

ORCID

Lenore Palladino ⓘ http://orcid.org/0000-0001-9225-2843

References

Allen, Franklin, and Douglas Gale. 1992. "Stock-Price Manipulation." *The Review of Financial Studies* 5 (3): 503–529. doi:10.1093/rfs/5.3.503.

Almeida, Heitor, Vyacheslav Fos, and Mathias Kronlund. 2016. "The Real Effects of Share Repurchases." *Journal of Financial Economics* 119 (1, January): 168–185. doi:10.1016/j.jfineco.2015.08.008.

Bhargava, Alok. 2013. "Executive Compensation, Share Repurchases and Investment Expenditures: Econometric Evidence from Us Firms." *Review of Quantitative Finance and Accounting* 40 (3): 403–422. doi:10.1007/s11156-011-0260-1.

Bonaimé, Alice a, M Kathleen, Kahle, David Moore, and Alok Nemani. 2020. "Employee Compensation Still Impacts Payout Policy." Available at SSRN: https://papers.ssrn.com/sol3/papers.cfm?abstract_id=3180292

Bonaimé, Alice a, and Michael D Ryngaert. 2013. "Insider Trading and Share Repurchases: Do Insiders and Firms Trade in the Same Direction?" *Journal of Corporate Finance* 22: 35–53. doi:10.1016/j.jcorpfin.2013.03.003.

Chandler, Alfred. 1992. "What is a Firm? A Historical Perspective." *European Economic Review* 36 (2–3): 483–492. doi:10.1016/0014-2921(92)90106-7.

Chan, Konan, David L Ikenberry, Inmoo Lee, and Yanzhi (Andrew) Wang. 2012. "Informed Traders: Linking Legal Insider Trading and Share Repurchases." *Financial Analysts Journal* 68 (1): 60–73. doi:10.2469/faj.v68.n1.3.

Coffee, John C, and Darius Palia. 2016. "The Wolf at the Door: The Impact of Hedge Fund Activism on Corporate Governance." *Journal of Corporate Law* 545: 1–94.

Cziraki, Peter, Evgeny Lyandres, and Roni Michaely. 2021. "What Do Insiders Know? Evidence from Insider Trading Around Share Repurchases and Seos." *Journal of Corporate Finance* 66: 168–185. doi:10.1016/j.jcorpfin.2019.101544.

Davis, Leila, and Shane McCormack. 2021. "Industrial Stagnation and the Financialization of Nonfinancial Corporations." *Review of Evolutionary Political Economy* 30 (1): 1–27.

Dayen, David. 2015. "SEC Admits It's Not Monitoring Stock Buybacks to Prevent Market Manipulation." *The Intercept*, August 13, 2015. https://theintercept.com/2015/08/13/sec-admits-monitoring-stock-buybacks-prevent-market-manipulation/

Distributional Financial Accounts. 2021. Federal Reserve. https://www.federalreserve.gov/releases/z1/dataviz/dfa/index.html

Feller, Lloyd, and Mary Chamberlin. 1984. "Issuer Repurchases." *The Review of Securities Regulation* 993-998.

Fox, Merritt B., Lawrence R. Glosten, and Gabriel V. Rauterberg. 2018. "Stock Market Manipulation and Its Regulation." *Yale Journal on Regulation* 35 (1). https://digitalcommons.law.yale.edu/yjreg/vol35/iss1/2/.

Fried, Jesse M. 2000. "Insider Signaling and Insider Trading with Repurchase Tender Offers." *The University of Chicago Law Review.* 67 (2): 421. Spring 2000 doi:10.2307/1600492.

Fried, Jesse. 2005. "Informed Trading and False Signaling with Open Market Repurchases." *California Law Review* 93 (5): 1323–1386.

Guthart, Leo A. 1965. "More Companies are Buying Back Their Stock." *Harvard Business Review* 23 (2): 40–54, March-April.

Gutiérrez, Germán, and Thomas Philippon. 2016. "Investment-Less Growth: An Empirical Investigation." NBER Working Paper 22897. doi:10.3386/w22897

Gutiérrez, Germán, and Thomas Philippon. 2018. "Ownership, Concentration, and Investment." *AEA Papers and Proceedings* 108: 432–437.

Hopkins, Matt, and William Lazonick. 2016. "The Mismeasure of Mammon: Uses and Abuses of Executive Pay Data." Working Paper no. 49. Institute for New Economic Thinking Working Paper Series. New York: INET. https://www.ineteconomics.org/uploads/papers/WP_49-Hopkins-Lazonick-Updated.pdf

Hudson, Richard. 1982. "SEC Eases Way for Repurchase of Firms' Stock." *Wall Street Journal,* November 10, 1982.

Jackson, Robert J. 2018. "Stock Buybacks and Corporate Cashouts." US Securities and Exchange Commission, June 11, 2018. https://www.sec.gov/news/speech/speech-jackson-061118

Jaemin, Kim, Ralf Schremper, and Nikhil P. Varaiya. 2004. "Open Market Repurchase Regulations: A Cross-Country Examination." *Corporate Finance Review* 9: 29–38. https://papers.ssrn.com/sol3/papers.cfm?abstract_id=496003.

Joan, Farre-Mensa, Roni Michaely, and Martin C. Schmalz. 2021. "Financing Payouts." Ross School of Business Paper No. 1263, Available at SSRN: Available at SSRN: https://ssrn.com/abstract=2535675

Kim, Jaemin, and Nikhil Varaiya. 2008. "Insiders' Timing Ability and Disclosure on Corporate Share Buyback Trading." *Review of Accounting and Finance* 7 (1): 69–82. doi:10.1108/14757700810853851.

Kurt, Ahmet C. 2018. "Managing EPS and Signaling Undervaluation as a Motivation for Repurchases: The Case of Accelerated Share Repurchases." *Review of Accounting and Finance* 17 (4, November): 453–481. doi:10.1108/RAF-05-2017-0102/full/html.

Lazonick, William. 2014. "Profits Without Prosperity." *Harvard Business Review*, September. https://hbr.org/2014/09/profits-without-prosperity

Lazonick, William. 2015a. *"Stock Buybacks: From Retain-And-Reinvest to Downsize-And-Distribute".* April. Washington, D.C.: Center for Effective Public Management, Brookings Institution.

Lazonick, William. 2015b. "Clinton's Proposals on Stock Buybacks Don't Go Far Enough." *Harvard Business Review*, August 11, 2015b. https://hbr.org/2015/08/clintons-proposals-on-stock-buybacks-dont-go-far-enough

Lazonick, William. 2019a. "The Value-Extracting CEO: How Executive Stock-Based Pay Undermines Investment in Productive Capabilities." *Structural Change and Economic Dynamics* 48 (January): 53–68. doi:10.1016/j.strueco.2017.11.006.

Lazonick, William. 2019b. "The Theory of Innovative Enterprise: Foundations of Economic Analysis." In *The Oxford Handbook of the Corporation*, edited by Thomas Clarke, Justin O'Brien, and Charles R. T. O'Kelley. Oxford: Oxford University Press. doi:10.1093/oxfordhb/9780198737063.013.12.

Lazonick, William. 2020. "Corporate Governance, Employment Relations, and Investment Finance: What Can the United States Learn from Germany?" Presentation for Academic-Industry Research Network Conference Workshop on German Codetermination, February 26, 2021.

Lazonick, William. 2022. "Investment in Innovation: A Policy Framework for Attaining Sustainable Prosperity in the United States," Institute for New Economic Thinking Working Paper No. 182. https://www.ineteconomics.org/research/research-papers/investing-in-innovation-a-policy-framework-for-attaining-sustainable-prosperity-in-the-united-states

Lazonick, William, and Matt Hopkins. 2020. "How 'Maximizing Shareholder Value' Minimized the Strategic National Stockpile: The $5.3 Trillion Question for Pandemic Preparedness Raised by the Ventilator Fiasco." Working Paper no. 127. Institute for New Economic Thinking Working Paper Series. New York: INET. https://papers.ssrn.com/sol3/papers.cfm?abstract_id=3671025

Lazonick, William, and Matt Hopkins. 2021. "Why the Chips are Down; Stock Buybacks and Subsidies in the US Semiconductor Industry, Institute for New Economic Thinking Working Paper No. 165, September 27, 2021. doi:10.36687/inetwp165.

Lazonick, William, and Ken Jacobson. 2022. "A License to Loot: Opposing Views of Capital Formation and the Adoption of Rule 10b-18." (Forthcoming).

Lazonick, William, and Mary O'Sullivan. 2000. "Maximizing Shareholder Value: A New Ideology for Corporate Governance." *Economy and Society* 29 (1): 13–35. doi:10.1080/030851400360541.

Lazonick, William, and Jang-Sup Shin. 2020. *Predatory Value Extraction.* Oxford: Oxford University Press.

O'Sullivan, Mary. 2000. "The Innovative Enterprise and Corporate Governance." *Cambridge Journal of Economics* 24 (4): 393–416. doi:10.1093/cje/24.4.393.

Palladino, Lenore. 2019. "The $1 Trillion Question: New Approaches to Regulating Stock Buybacks." *Yale Journal on Regulation Bulletin* 36: 89–106.

Palladino, Lenore. 2020. "Do Corporate Insiders Use Stock Buybacks for Personal Gain?" *International Review of Applied Economics* 34 (2, January): 152–174. doi:10.1080/02692171.2019.1707787?journalCode=cira20.

Penrose, Edith. 1959. *The Theory of the Growth of the Firm.* New York: Wiley.

Ramsay, John. 2018. Investors Exchange LLC, Letter to Brent J. Fields, Securities Exchange Commission, March 27, 2018, at https://www.sec.gov/rules/petitions/2018/petn4-722.pdf

Seligman, Joel. 1995. *The Transformation of Wall Street: A History of the Securities and Exchange Commission and Modern Corporate Finance.* 3rd ed. Aspen Publishers.

Shilon, Nitzan. 2021. "Stock Buyback Ability to Enhance CEO Compensation: Theory, Evidence, and Policy Implications." *Lewis & Clark Law Review* 25 (1): 303–359.

Appendices

Appendix A

Table A1. Top Corporate Spenders by NAICS.

Ambulatory Health Care Services

NAICS	Sector	Aggregate Buybacks (2019) in Millions
621	Davita Inc.	$2,402.53
621	Humana Inc.	$870.04
621	Fresenius Medical Care AG&Co.	$581.39
621	Laboratory CP of Amer Holdings	**$464.41**
621	Quest Diagnostics Inc.	$365.68
621	Mednaxinc.	**$145.30**
621	Chemed Corp.	$92.63
621	Amedisys Inc.	**$9.40**
621	LHC Group Inc.	$9.29
621	Apollo Medical Holding Inc.	$7.31

Hospitals

NAICS	Sector	Aggregate Buybacks (2019) in Millions
622	HCA Healthcare Inc.	$1,030.96
622	Encompass Health Corp.	$62.54
622	Select Medical Holdings Corp	$38.52
622	Community Health Systems Inc.	$3.60
622	Acadia Healthcare Co. Inc.	$2.27
622	Quorum Health Corp.	$0.13
622	Amedisys Inc.	$9.40
622	LHC Group Inc.	$9.29
622	Apollo Medical Holding Inc.	$7.31

Education Services

NAICS	Sector	Aggregate Buybacks (2019) in Millions
611	Laureate Education Inc.	$270.87
611	Adtalem Global Education Inc.	$242.41
611	Grand Canyon Education Inc.	$43.93
611	American Public Education	$40.50
611	Bright Scholar Edu -Adr	$39.12
611	Perdoceo Education Corp.	$6.63
611	Sunlands Tech Group -Adr	$4.54
611	Graham Holdings Co.	$1.86
611	Rise Edn Cyn Ltd -ADS	$1.58
611	Laix Inc. -ADR	$1.53

Nursing and Residential Care Facilities

NAICS	Sector	Aggregate Buybacks (2019) in Millions
623	Brookdale Senior Living Inc.	$23.02
623	Ensign Group Inc.	$13.71
623	National Healthcare Corp.	$0.84
623	Five Star Senior Living Inc.	$0.03

Social Care

NAICS	Sector	Aggregate Buybacks (2019) in Millions
624	Bright Horizons Family Solutions	$34.78

Source: Authors' Calculations of Form 10-K as provided by S&P Compustat.

Table A2. Legislative Proposals to Limit Stock Buybacks.

Name& Year	Sponsors& Co-sponsors	Description
Reward Work Act (2019)	Author: Sen. Tammy Baldwin (D-WI) Cosponsors: Sen. Kirsten Gillibrand (D-NY), Sen. Bernie Sanders (I-VT), Sen. Elizabeth Warren (D-MA) Also introduced in the House by: Rep. Jesus G. "Chuy" Garcia (D-IL) and Rep. Ro Khanna (D-CA)	Repeals SEC Rule 10b-18 to end stock buybacks by removing immunity from manipulation charges. Institutes a rule that no issuer may register securities on a national exchange unless one-third of the firm's directors are chosen by employees through a one-employee, one-vote process.
Schumer & Sanders NYT Op-Ed (2020)	Authors: Sen. Chuck Schumer (D-NY) & Sen. Bernie Sanders (I-VT)	They plan to introduce a bill that would ban stock repurchases unless a firm meets the following conditions: • providing a $15 minimum wage; • providing seven days of paid sick leave; and • offering decent pensions and reliable health benefits.
Corporate Accountability and Democracy Plan	Author: Sen. Bernie Sanders (I-VT)	Obligates firms with over $100 million in revenue and with a $100 million balance sheet total to: • build up to 20 percent stock ownership by employees; • require 45 percent of the Board of Directors to be chosen by employees; and • obtain a Federal Charter that requires boards to consider the interests of all stakeholders. Repeals SEC rule 10b-18 to end stock buybacks. Establishes a $500 million Employee Ownership Bank that will assist workers with loans, guarantees, and technical assistance to purchase their own businesses via Employee Stock Ownership Plans (ESOPs) or Eligible Worker-Owned Cooperatives. Requires firms that displace labor for automation or outsourcing to share gains with workers via conveyed shares. Guarantees a Right of First Refusal via the Employee Ownership Bank. Creates Worker Ownership Centers to assist retiring small business owners in selling their firms to their employees. Requires a significant proportion of corporate boards to be composed of people from historically underrepresented groups. Has a Shareholder Democracy Component that: • States that every employee should have a right to vote in the firm and have a voice in setting their wages; • Bans actions by asset managers without explicit instructions from those whose money they manage; and • Says that savers should be able to elect representatives who set voting policy in corporations, multi-employer pensions, single-employer pensions, and 401K funds. Organizes sectoral pensions.

Name& Year	Sponsors& Co-sponsors	Description
Stock Buyback Reform and Worker Dividend Act of 2019 (S.2391)	Author: Sen. Sherrod Brown (D-OH)	Requires public companies to pay workers $1 for every $1 million they spend on dividends, special dividends, or stock buybacks. Lowers the permissible level of stock buybacks and imposes new reporting requirements. Converts the safe harbor rule to a mandatory prohibition on excessive buybacks. States that if employers fail to meet worker dividend requirements, there will be a five-year moratorium on new buybacks and a private right of action for employees.
Worker Dividend Act of 2019 (S.2514)	Authors: Sen. Cory Booker (D-NJ), Sen. Bob Casey (D-PA), and former Sen. Joe Kennedy (D-MA) (House version)	Applies to all publicly traded companies with at least $250 million in earnings in a given year. A total obligation to employees would be calculated as the lesser of the total in profits above $250 million or 50 percent of the firm's buybacks.

Appendix B. Data appendix on open-market repurchases

SEC Rule 10b-18, adopted in 1982, pertains only to *common share repurchases executed on the open market*. It does not pertain to tender offers or private transactions to purchase shares. It is through open-market repurchases (OMRs) that a company can manipulate its stock price. Our critique of stock buybacks as a legalized corporate mode of manipulating stock prices, therefore, concerns only OMRs, and hence it is common share repurchases executed on the open market that we seek to quantify in this article.

The sources of data on the number and value of its own common shares that a company repurchases are the 10-K (annual) and 10-Q (quarterly) reports on their financial condition that every U.S.-based corporation that is publicly traded on a stock market must file with the Securities and Exchange Commission (SEC). Information on share repurchases is provided in the Statement of Cash Flows and Statement of Shareholders' Equity as well as in Notes to the Financial Statements. If we hand collect data from these company financial statements, we can determine the quantity and value of OMRs that a company has executed in a given year or quarter. (Also, since 2004, as a result of a revision of Rule 10b-18 in 2003, each company reports in its 10-K and 10-Q Notes the number of shares and average price per share paid on a monthly basis.)

Hence, when we hand-collect individual company data, as we have done for the 20 companies in Table A1 of this article, the numbers represent OMRs only. In principle, for complete accuracy in reporting OMRs, we could hand-collect the data for all 500 companies in the S&P 500 database or even for the entire universe of publicly traded corporations that do 10-K or 10-Q filings. Performing that type of data collection, however, would be well beyond the resources that we and most other researchers have available, and it is obviously for that reason that subscription databases exist. In the case of stock buybacks, for large-scale aggregations, we use the Standard & Poor's (S&P) Compustat database, to which we have access through the subscriptions of our academic institutions.

There are, however, a number of problems with the way in which S&P compiles data on share repurchases for its Compustat database that render both the aggregate and individual company figures imprecise measures of stock buybacks done as OMRs.

(1) S&P sometimes makes mistakes in data entry, which we discover from time to time when we hand-collect data for the purpose of analysis of particular companies.
(2) S&P's stock buyback variable, 'Purchase of Common and Preferred Stock' (PCPS), taken from a company's Statement of Cash Flows, does not, as the variable name indicates, distinguish between the repurchase of common shares and preferred shares. But preferred shares outstanding are a very small proportion of common shares outstanding. A study for 2015 found that the value of preferred shares outstanding on U.S. stock markets was $241 billion, which was just 1.06% of the $22.71 trillion of all stock outstanding.[16]
(3) S&P's PCPS does not isolate OMRs from shares repurchased via tender offers or private transactions. We are not aware of databases on the value of tender offers or private share-repurchase transactions in the United States. They are one-off events, and our sense from our extensive experience in hand-collecting buyback data from 10-K filings is that OMRs represent the vast majority – a guestimate would be at least 95%–of all repurchases in the S&P PCPS variable.
(4) There is variation in the way in which different companies report share repurchases in the Statement of Cash Flows, for which S&P does not correct in compiling its PCPS variable. For example, in its Statement of Cash Flows, General Electric reports 'Net dispositions (purchases) of GE shares for treasury', which is the number that S&P enters as GE's PCPS. But this figure subtracts funds collected from employees from stock-based compensation plans from funds spent on stock buybacks (almost all of which are OMRs). The correct OMR figure can be found in GE's Notes to the Financial Statements. When we compile our S&P 500 database, using PCPS in the first instance, we make this correction for GE and any other company (which are very few) that we discover engages in idiosyncratic reporting of this type.

(5) S&P PCPS includes an item (using Apple's designation) 'Payments for taxes related to net share settlement of equity awards', even though in the Statement of Cash Flows it is a separate line from 'Repurchases of common stock', which is the correct line item for PCPS. In many cases, the company itself combines these two distinct pieces of information in reported repurchases, that then are entered into S&P's PCPS. This incorrect conflation of two very different types of data arose from the mid-2000s, when many companies shifted from stock options to stock awards as their prime mode of stock-based incentive pay. The main reason for this shift was the expensing of stock-based pay on 10-K and 10-Q financial statements; stock awards entail fewer shares issued to employees for the same amount of realized gains.[17] But, for employees, stock options also have the disadvantage that to exercise the option they have to pay the company the exercise price while immediately upon exercise the company withholds the employee taxes on the realized gain. These cash outlays generally compel employees to sell the shares immediately upon exercise, which is not what the company wants employees to do. Stock awards, by contrast, accrue to the employee when they vest without any cash payment to the company. But the company must still withhold employee taxes on the realized gain when the awards vest, which might also incline, and perhaps compel, employees to sell the shares immediately. To avert this pressure, the company 'repurchases' a portion of the shares that it has awarded to employees to cover the withholding taxes; hence Apple's 'Payments for taxes related to net share settlement of equity awards'. Based on our experience in hand-collecting data, the correction to the PCPS variable so that it only represents external repurchases (almost all of which are OMRS) reduces total buybacks for 466 companies in the S&P 500 Index publicly listed from 2010 through 2019 from $4.925 trillion reported in S&P PCPS to $4.829 trillion, or a reduction of 1.95%. For certain companies such as Apple and Alphabet, however, the correction to the S&P PCPS measure to capture just OMRs can be very large, especially in the presence of soaring stock prices. Hand collection eliminates these errors. Perhaps S&P will see fit to correct its erroneous data-collection protocols.

∂ OPEN ACCESS

The life and times of Edith Penrose

Jonathan Michie

The life of the late Edith Penrose was extraordinary in many ways. For readers of *the International Review of Applied Economics,* the main interest may be in *The Theory of the Growth of the Firm* – her book that has grown in importance over time (E. Penrose 1959). But as well as Edith's writings, her life too was fascinating, and wonderfully captured in Angela Penrose's book, *No Ordinary Woman* (A. Penrose 2018).

Angela is Edith Penrose's daughter in law; indeed:

> In the week Angela Penrose was given *The Theory of the Growth of the Firm* to read as part of her Philosophy, Politics and Economics degree course at Oxford she met her future husband, Perran Penrose, the son of the author, Edith Penrose.[1]

Edith Penrose's life gives a bird's eye view of much of the 20th Century including the rise of fascism in the 1930s, the Second World War, McCarthyism in America, the struggles against colonialism and imperialism, and then the challenges of economic development. This is seen through the eyes of a great economist in every sense of that term – one whose focus was absolutely on improving people's lives, and analysing emergent issues such as the oil sector, the rise of multinational enterprises, and the role of patents always through that lens of human wellbeing.

The 1930s

Economics was not one of the five Nobel Prizes established by Alfred Nobel's will in 1895. However, in 1968 an award was established by an endowment from Sweden's central bank, Sveriges Riksbank, to commemorate the bank's 300th anniversary. Officially the 'Sveriges Riksbank Prize in Economic Sciences in Memory of Alfred Nobel', this is generally referred to as the Nobel Prize in Economics, and is awarded by the Nobel Foundation. Indeed, when the organisation Promoting Economic Pluralism introduced a 'Not the Nobel Prize' for economics, to be able to recognise economists with a more pluralistic approach to the topic, the Nobel Foundation threatened to sue. (Full disclosure: I was a founding Director of Promoting Economic Pluralism, and it was my idea to call our award 'Not the Nobel Prize'.)

This is an Open Access article distributed under the terms of the Creative Commons Attribution License (http://creativecommons.org/licenses/by/4.0/), which permits unrestricted use, distribution, and reproduction in any medium, provided the original work is properly cited. The terms on which this article has been published allow the posting of the Accepted Manuscript in a repository by the author(s) or with their consent.

There is an obvious question as to why Edith Penrose was not awarded this Nobel Prize in Economics when it was introduced in 1968 – or at least, why she was not awarded it in the 1970s, 1980s or 1990s, in recognition of her pathbreaking work. I will return to this question at the end of this review article, but there is a related point to make about the gender balance – or lack of it – amongst the recipients since 1968 (with three women recipients, and ninety men), which is that Edith married David Denhardt when they were both undergraduates at Berkeley in the 1930s, and:

> ... even though Edith was a free-spirited student activist, choosing a husband at that time was effectively choosing a life. As the wife of a district attorney in a small American town she would be expected to support her husband throughout his career. Everything we know about them as a couple tells us she would have done, but David Denhardt was killed as he sought election to office on the first rung of that career. (p. 2)

This fact – of women often not having careers, due to societal pressure to prioritise domestic and child-rearing duties – explains at least in part the gender imbalance in all Nobel Prize categories. But the imbalance is worst in economics, a point to which we return to below.

In terms of Edith Penrose's biography illuminating much of the 20th Century from the 1930s onwards, she travelled to Europe 'as the Second World War broke out', to work alongside Ernest Francis Penrose, or 'Pen' as he was known, who became her second husband (p. 2):

> For nine decisive years the career and destiny of Edith and her husband Pen were intricately linked to that of John Winant; firstly whilst he was Director of the International Labour Organization in Geneva and Montreal, then in London throughout the Second World War where he was the American Ambassador to the United Kingdom, and finally as the US representative to the Economic and Social Council of the embryonic United Nations (UN) in New York. Here Edith assisted Eleanor Roosevelt in her historic role as chair of the Human Rights Commission as it drew up the Universal Declaration of Human Rights. (pp. 2–3)

In Edith's last year at Berkely she attended lectures by Pen who had arrived in 1935, and during her last semester, 'the summer of 1936, she also began working for him as an assistant, typing letters, organising courses, and helping with research'. (p. 19)

2. The Second World War

In 1938, Pen had moved from Berkely to work as an economic advisor to the International Labour Organisation (ILO) in Geneva, and in 1939 he recruited Edith to work with him at the ILO. On 7 August 1940, because of the Nazi advance and fall of France, Edith and Pen were in a contingent of ILO staff who were moved to New York (via Portugal), and then on to Montreal where forty ILO staff became located. Then in July 1941 Edith and Pen were recruited to the American Embassy in London, where they worked for almost five years. Edith's work included a report on *Food Control in Great Britain*, which concluded that:

> The purpose of food control in wartime is first to obtain an even and adequate flow of food into the channels of distribution and secondly to distribute these foods equitably to all

individuals and to all classes in the community. The task is immense and the pitfalls many, but on the whole British food control has been successful in accomplishing these ends. Most striking perhaps is the number of things generally considered administratively impracticable which, when attempted, have proved extraordinarily successful. The first requisite of any Ministry of Food is courage. (p. 72)

After the war, Edith and Pen returned to New York to work with the Economic and Social Council (ECOSOC) of the United Nations (p. 99), with Edith working particularly to support Eleanor Roosevelt, including in Eleanor Roosevelt's role as chair of the UN Commission on Human Rights (p. 108).

In January 1947 Pen resigned from the UN to become a member of the Institute for Advanced Study at Princeton – well known to anyone who saw the 2023 film Oppenheimer (about the development of the atomic bomb during the Second World War, led by Oppenheimer, who went on lead the Institute, with the film including a memorable scene with Oppenheimer talking there with Albert Einstein):

> The seven-month appointment was an essential bridge until September when he took up the position of the B. Howell Griswold, Jr. Professor of Geography and International Relations at John Hopkins University. . . . The Institute for Advanced Study purports to be 'one of the few institutions in the world where the pursuit of knowledge for its own sake is the ultimate raison d'être'. Research is never contracted or directed but eminent faculty members guide and mentor scholars. It became a refuge for scientists and academics fleeing Nazi Germany, including Albert Einstein who was professor of mathematics at the Institute until 1945 and continued to research there until his death in 1955. As Pen began his research J. Robert Oppenheimer was taking up the post of director. (p. 109)

Edith signed on to do a master's degree at the Department of Political Economy at John Hopkins, which 'was relatively small with only seven full-time faculty members but it had developed one of the best reputations in the USA' (p. 110), and in May 1948 'she submitted her essay *Discussion of Patents in Economic Doctrine* for the degree of Master of Arts' (p. 115). For her doctorate, Edith described 'the evolution of the patent system and the development of the International Convention for the Protection of Industrial Property and its provisions on patents' (p. 117):

> Signatories of the convention are bound to treat all applications for patents the same as they would their own nationals and to award priority to the first application of a patent regardless of where that patent was filed. The central argument of the thesis, analysing the economic costs and gains resulting from the rules imposed by the convention, is complex. Edith concludes that special problems arise by the international extension of the patent system and most countries lose more than they gain by accepting to abide by the rules. Questioning the alleged positive benefits of the system to social welfare she recommended the complete exemption of non-industrialized nations from the international agreement.
>
> Edith received her degree of Doctor of Philosophy and went on to publish her thesis as a book, *The Economics of the International Patent System*, in 1951. (p. 117)

Edith became a research associate of the Department of Political Economy in 1950 and a lecturer in political economy in 1951 (p. 118), and 'began the research that contributed to her book *The Theory of the Growth of the Firm*' (p. 120).

3. McCarthyism

Edith and Pen had, thus, both settled at John Hopkins, and all was set for them 'to go from strength to strength in their academic careers; they appeared to be on track to achieve all they had hoped for' (p. 120). But:

> That their hopes turned to despair, as Pen expressed it later, was due to the prevailing political climate in the USA at the time and its effect on academic institutions and freedoms. As the Second World War ended, the Cold War intensified. Anti-communism increased within the USA . . . The 'Second Red Scare', lasting roughly from 1950 to 1956, characterized by heightened political repression against communists, and the campaign spreading fear of their influence within American institutions, increasingly overshadowed Edith and Pen's years at John Hopkins. (pp. 120–121)

Again, anyone who saw the 2023 film Oppenheim will recognise this, with Oppenheim going from national hero for having led the development of the atomic bomb, to being persecuted as 'anti-American' under the McCarthyist era for his supposed political views. One academic at John Hopkins, Owen Lattimore, was particularly badly persecuted, and amongst other things was indicted by government lawyers for being a 'follower of the Communist line' and 'promoting Communist interests', to which his lawyers responded:

> The indictment is not limited to those who shift with Russia as it shifts its policy. It touches any writer whose opinion ever coincides with Russian policy at any time. Covering a period of fifteen years, as it does, and including events long antedating the cold war, it would force every British and American statesman to admit that he was a follower of the Communist line in the sense used in the indictment. (p. 129)

Edith later wrote:

> When all of this arose, I went to his defence and even took on the job of secretary of the Defence Fund . . . the kind of thing I've never done before in my life. I did not <u>know</u> then whether the charges of sympathizing etc were true or not. I felt however, that even if they were true, the attack on him was unjustified and the obvious attempt at entrapment repugnant to all sense of fair play. He denied the accusations. I have known him seven years and saw no reason to doubt his word. But I did a) read the more controversial books he has written; b) read files of correspondence etc; and c) read the full record of the hearings. I came to the conclusion that he was no communist or 'sympathizer' in any doctrinaire sense of 'fellow traveller' . . . Sometimes he said things I would wholeheartedly disagree with. It became clear to me, however, that here was a wide-ranging, not-always fully informed, sometimes wrong, sometimes superficially journalistic, but often original and clearly independent minded man. I could also see how easily a careful selection from the incredible mass of words he produced . . . could build up a case for nearly anything. It is my sincere conviction that no one who fairly and objectively read Lattimore's major works and a random selection of his minor ones could possibly call him a fellow traveller. (p. 131)

The FBI initiated a search against all the contributors to the defence fund that they could track down, including Edith. The case against Lattimore was eventually dropped, as was the FBI search to find incriminating evidence against Edith or any of the contributors to the defence fund. However, Lattimore had been suspended by John Hopkins during the McCarthyite witch hunt against him, and 'his return to John Hopkins was neither smooth nor triumphant', and he moved to the University of Leeds in England to establish a department of Chinese Studies, where he and his wife remained until 1972. (p. 140)

In 1953, Edith and Pen were called to testify before the Senate committee charged with investigating subversives, chaired by Senator Jenner:

> They came under intense pressure to provide names and were asked questions about activities in the University of California in the late 1930s. They claimed a lack of knowledge of these activities and were assured that there would be no publicity about the session. They were asked by a journalist on the *Baltimore Sun* about their experience but refused to comment.

As a result of McCarthyism in America, Edith and Pen 'began to believe they could not continue in the USA' (p. 137), and Pen arranged for a sabbatical leave in Australia on which Edith joined him, following which he wrote that:

> This journey has emphatically confirmed my sharp revulsion from the American 'way of life', notably in the last five or six years during which the whole society has been infected with the poison of witch-hunting and shocking revelations of the fundamental weakness of American culture have come to light, or rather have become evident on a greater scale than one formerly expected. (p. 147)

Following their return to John Hopkins, the Canadian diplomat E. Herbert Norman was accused by the US government of being a Soviet agent, and he 'committed suicide, leaving a note asserting his innocence, saying the forces against him were too formidable' (p. 148).

> One week before the death of Norman, the distinguished Japanese economist Schigeto Tsuru, then lecturing at Harvard on a US-Japan intellectual exchange programme, was subpoenaed ... partly because he had known Norman well as a student. (p. 148)

'Pen was outraged' (p. 148), writing that:

> My emotions were so aroused by the Norman case and the Tsuru case that I could scarcely control them enough to express myself calmly and coherently. But now I must master them enough to write some effective public protests. There is hardly anything I cling to so tenaciously as the hope that we can leave this country permanently as soon as possible... I don't wish to spend my last days as a U.S. citizen. The events of the last seven years have thoroughly alienated me from this country. The most abominable injustices and outrages are committed without significant public protest. (p. 148)

In 1957 Edith and Pen took leave of absence from John Hopkins to teach economics in Baghdad. Edith 'received the copy of the appendix for *The Theory of the Growth of the Firm* ... and planned to proofread it on the ship' (p. 151). They taught in Baghdad through to 1958, with Edith 'becoming increasingly interested in the relationship of the oil companies with the government', and also writing an article on 'The Role of Economic Analysis in Political Decisions', in which:

> She poses the question, what can the economist contribute to the questions of great political moment which will have far-reaching economic consequences? Her answer is that any political journalist can complain that government revenues are not spent quickly enough, but the 'economist knows that money is never the real problem, but rather the availability of real resources and productive services, including labor, entrepreneurial, and managerial services' [E. Penrose 1958]. The economist understands that the rate of economic advance is restricted by the scarcest of the necessary resources and his contribution is the *organization* of the use of productive services. Her observations of Iraq were drawing on her insights in *The Theory of the Growth of the Firm*. (p. 157, emphasis in the original)

In this 1958 article, Edith argues that an economist may well find that people:

> ... with the ability to undertake the organization of economic activity are in very short supply indeed. And such skills are needed as much as for state undertakings as for private undertakings. In no country are large and complex firms organized in a short period of time, because an efficient 'organism' of this kind is not created on an engineer's drawing board – it must grow, and this growth takes time. I am inclined to accept the view that the greatest obstacle to rapid economic development is the magnitude of the organizational problem and the shortage of men with appropriate training and skill to do it. (E. Penrose 1958, cited in; A. Penrose 2018, p. 157)

In the summer of 1958, Edith and Pen visited Oxford, during which the Iraqi regime was overthrown in what is variously described as a coup d'état or revolution, with the royal family executed.

> Uncertain whether they could return to Iraq Pen applied in August for a job with the UN in Libya, and his papers were submitted to the US government by the Office of Personnel of the United Nations Technical Assistance Recruitment Services, with a request for urgent action. This set in motion an investigation by the FBI which unearthed Pen and Edith's involvement with the Lattimore defence fund and the fact they had testified before the Jenner Committee in 1953. FBI agents gained access to the reports of these hearings even though they were supposedly held in secret. The final report sent to the Civil Service Commission responsible for assessing the reliability of applicants for the International Employees Loyalty Board contained Pen's testimony from those hearings and other testimony from colleagues past and present, neighbours, and employers. The FBI also discovered than in April 1936 Edith Penrose had been a speaker at a university anti-war rally, sharing a platform with a communist and a socialist. In January 1959 the Civil Service Commission indicated that the UN was no longer considering Pen for employment.[2] (p. 163)

After a brief return to Iraq, Edith was invited to Cambridge to be interviewed for a lectureship, which is one of the stranger episodes of Edith's life, and indeed in the life of the Faculty of Economics at Cambridge – and they have had a few.

> The correspondence Edith had had with the administration in Cambridge had led her to believe they intended to offer her the post. Austin Robinson had been sent a proof copy of *The Theory of the Growth of the Firm*; Joan Robinson had encouraged her application and she felt optimistic. But she did not get the post. Explanatory myths have been created – perhaps Austin did not want to appoint a woman – but Edith herself believed that Cambridge had wanted someone with a greater knowledge of the British economy and familiarity with British industry. (p. 166)

Robin Marris was then a lecturer at Cambridge and reported this:

> My administrative task was carried out after teaching hours in the department office, which was then located in Downing Street. Naturally it was my habit to read any other interesting documents concerning faculty affairs which might happen to be lying around. In 1958 one such was a full set of the galley proofs of The Growth of the Firm [sic]. Obviously I was immediately attracted. I took all the sheets home for the night and by the time I surreptitiously replaced them the next day, I had read every one. It turned out that the reason the proofs were in the office was that the department appointments committee had decided to offer Edith a Cambridge lectureship, subject to interview. The interview duly occurred; there is no record of what transpired, except that no appointment was made. A bad day for Cambridge but in my opinion a good day for Edith, who I think would have been suffocated there. (Marris, 2009, p. 62)

The bad day for Cambridge turned out to be a good day for London, as the LSE and SOAS created a joint post for Edith in 1960.

4. The theory of the growth of the firm

Chapter 10 of Angela Penrose's book on Edith is the only one not written by her – it is on *The Theory of the Growth of the Firm*, and so Angela asked her son Jago Penrose, an economist, to write it. Jago's chapter is an excellent discussion of Edith's book. He points out that Edith began with her own, fresh definitions:

> The business firm, as we have defined it, is both an administrative organisation and a collection of productive resources; its general purpose is to organise the use of its 'own' resources together with other resources acquired from outside the firm for the production and the sale of goods and services at a profit; its physical resources yield services essential for the execution of the plans of its personnel, whose activities are bound together by the administrative framework within which they are carried out. (E. Penrose 1959, p. 31, cited in Jago Penrose, pp. 182–183)

Jago Penrose argues that:

> One of the most powerful implications of Edith's theory is that knowledge creation is a key driver of economic growth, and that this process takes place *within* firms. Moreover, as firms grow so the 'smaller is the extent to which the allocation of productive resources to different uses and over time is directly governed by market forces and the greater is the scope for conscious planning of economic activity' (E. Penrose 1959, p. 51). The composition of the firm sector is therefore a key determinant of the nature of an economy's development. In the last chapter of her book Edith discusses the implications for growth of an economy dominated by big business, concluding, ultimately, that the quality and strength of that growth 'rests on the conditions that are not self-perpetuating, but may be destroyed by collusion, by the extension of financial control, and by the struggle to resolve the contradictions in a system where competition is at once the god and the devil, where the growth of firms may be efficient, and where their consequent size, though not in itself inefficient, may create an industrial structure which impedes its own continued growth' (E. Penrose 1959, p. 265) (Jago Penrose, pp. 187–188)

Jago Penrose concludes by arguing that:

> The conviction that firms control, create, and manage resources within an administrative structure overseen by flawed but motivated people and that firms affect their environment and can influence the institutional structure within which they operate governed Edith's thinking throughout her career. It informed her work on the oil industry, multinational firms – particularly those operating in developing countries – and ... her thinking on economic development. (p. 188)

5. Edith Penrose's other contributions to economics

As indicated above, Edith Penrose not only made major contributions in a range of areas – including the growth of the firm, patents, the oil industry, multinational companies, and development economics, but also her basic approach, combining theory and practice, and taking due account of history, institutions, and human behaviour, informed her work in all these areas, which made her contributions so relevant and powerful. Edith Penrose acknowledged this to some extent in the preface to a collections of her essays:

> At first glance it might seem that the three subjects dealt with in the essays written over the last twenty years could hardly be more diverse ... Oddly enough, however, these subjects are connected by the same type of historical logic that characterizes the diversification of an industrial firm: the logic in the simple principle that one thing leads to another. (E. Penrose 1971, cited in; A. Penrose 2018, p. 189)

This was what made the creation of a post for her at SOAS, initially shared with the LSE, so inspired. That readership in economics went on to be a full Chair in 1964, based solely at SOAS (p. 197). In her 1965 inaugural lecture as professor of economics, she referred to 'the economics of development' as what she had been teaching, and which was 'being established as a discipline in its own right against a background of increasing academic and governmental interest in development issues' (p. 190).

Despite her pathbreaking work in establishing development economics as a discipline, Edith Penrose remains best known for her work on the growth of the firm. The huge rise in influence of her 1959 book over the subsequent decades is due in part to the growth of management and business schools within academia, where real world analyses of firms is vitally important. It is thus not surprising that after seventeen years at SOAS, Edith was recruited to INSEAD, where she worked from 1977 to 1984, before retiring to England near Cambridge.

6. Why was Edith Penrose not awarded the Nobel Prize for economics?

Given her pathbreaking contributions, why was Edith Penrose not awarded what is known as the Nobel Prize for Economics? As noted in Section 2 above, there is a distinct gender balance against women in all the Nobel Prize subject areas, which reflects the gender imbalance in society, the economy and employment more generally, including historically. In this regard, Edith's life is a striking example, since as discussed above she looked set to take on the role of housewife, supporting her husband and his political ambitions, had it not been for his death, which resulted in her pursuing a career as an economist.

Beyond that general issue, of the gender imbalance in recipients of the Nobel Prize across subject areas, there is the question of why that imbalance is worse in economics than for any other subject area. It may be that the rather abstract approach of mainstream economics – which dominates the award – tends to be more off-putting for women than for men. Whatever the exact cause, it appears to have two effects: firstly, more men than women study economics, and secondly, of those women who do study economics, a higher proportion tend to choose areas of economics away from the mainstream, such as economic history, labour economics, or development economics. And the prize has tended to be awarded to those working in the mainstream, rather than in these other areas. Thus, when the prize was finally awarded to a woman, in 2009, it was to Elinor Ostrom, 'for her analysis of economic governance, especially the commons' – far from the mainstream.

And then there is the specific question, of why Edith Penrose was not awarded the prize, quite apart from the above factors. We will never know for sure; it will remain as mysterious as why she was not appointed to the post in Cambridge. But certainly, what is seen as her main contribution, namely *The Theory of the Growth of the Firm*, did not fit into mainstream economic analysis.

> She simply sidestepped the issue of how her work related to the mainstream ... It was strategic to depict her agenda as a focus on the *growth* of the firm rather than its static equilibrium, as a complement to the conventional theory, not an alternative grounded in a critique. In this way Edith avoided the potential costs of a Promethean quest to lead economists towards the grail of a more relevant and dynamic theory. She settled instead for mapping out a part of the story, while letting the boys continue to play with the theory of the firm, tweaking and twisting and grinding out solutions to their hearts content: a pluralistic compromise. But as feminist economics emphasizes the realistic and relevant is seldom the high ground of economics. (Best and Humphries 2001, cited on p. 283, emphasis in the original)

Notes

1. This is from the back inside cover of Penrose (2018).
2. http://foia.fbi.gov/privacy_systems/63fr8659.htm cited in Levallois (2009).

Disclosure statement

No potential conflict of interest was reported by the author.

References

Best, Michael, and Jane Humphries. 2001. "Edith Penrose: A Feminist Economist?" paper presented to the *Penrosian Legacy*, INSEAD, 11–12.
Levallois, C. 2009. "Why Were Biological Analogies in Economics 'A Bad Thing'? Edith Penrose's Battles Against Social Darwinism and McCarthyism, *Science in Context*." 163. [as cited in Penrose (2018), p. 295, note 13].
Penrose, Angela. 2018. *No Ordinary Woman: The Life of Edith Penrose*. Oxford, UK: Oxford University Press.
Penrose, Edith. 1958, June. "The Role of Economic Analysis in Political Decisions." In *Bulletin of the College of Arts and Sciences*, Vol. 3. Baghdad.
Penrose, Edith. 1959. *The Theory of the Growth of the Firm*. Oxford, UK: Oxford University Press.
Penrose, Edith. 1971. *The Growth of Firms, Middle East Oil, and Other Essays*. London, UK: Frank Cass.

Index

Note: Figures are indicated by *italics*. Tables are indicated by **bold**. Endnotes are indicated by the page number followed by 'n' and the endnote number e.g., 20n1 refers to endnote 1 on page 20.

Abdelzaher, D. 156, 159, 162
absorptive capacity: external knowledge, university-industry interaction 178–81, **179**; method of data analysis 182–5; Penrose theory 177–8; survey data collection 181–2
Acemoglu, D. 130
Ackerberg-Caves-Frazier method 30
acquisition 165
African Regional Intellectual Property Organization (ARIPO) 18, 27
Airbus 91
Alvarez, R. 133, 134, 142
Amazon 93
Amazon Web Services (AWS) 93
Annual Capital Expenditures Survey 222
Annual Manufacturing Survey 129, 136
Annual Survey of Manufactures 222
Ansoff, I. 96
Apple 92–3
Application Programming Interfaces (APIs) 93
Argyres, N. S. 225
Arno River 18
Aronson, B. 160
Arora, A. 33
as a service concept 94
Autor, D. 130
average daily trading volume (ADTV) 253–5, 257
average fixed cost (AFC) 62
average total cost (ATC) 62
average variable cost (AVC) 62

Barkema, H. 158
Barney, J. 98
Beamish, P. W. 156, 158, 162
Bell, M. 176, 180
Benavente, J. M. 133, 142
Berle, A. A. 108
Best, M. 5
beta (β)-convergence 209, **210**
biological analogies 5
Bogliacino, F. 142
Bonneuil, C. 109

Braga, C. A. O. 26
Branstetter, L. G. 26, 33
Brazilian Micro and Small Business Support Service (SEBRAE) 181
Buckley, P. 156
Bureau of Economic Analysis 203
Bureau of the Census 222
Bush, George W. 97–8
business innovation process 99
business of flight 91–2

Camisón, C. 182
capitalism 42
capital reallocation 200
captive market: motive, profit and international investments 107–9; Penrose *vs.* the mainstream 105–6; trade and technology 113–15, *114–15*, **114**
case-oriented approach 182
Casson, M. 156
Cegarra-Navarro, J. G. 9
Cepeda-Carrion, G. 9
Chatterjee, C. 33
Chemical's (CPChem) Baytown Ethylene Plant 116
Child, J. 162–4
Chile: Chilean IP use and firm performance 29–31, *29*, *31*; patents and pharmaceutical innovation 31–5, *32*; worldwide Chilean origin patent applications *32*
Chilean National Institute of Industrial Property 29
CHIPS Act 51
Choquet, P. -L. 109
client following strategy 159
Cockburn, I. M. 33
Cohen, S. D. 159
Cohen, W. M. 175, 179, 180
collective intelligence 46
Colombian National Administrative Department of Statistics (DANE) 136
Community Innovation Survey (CIS) 133, 180

INDEX

complex causality 183
Connolly, R. A. 201
consulting engineering firms (CEFs) 156
context-sensitive approach 183
Continental European countries 18
Contractor, F. 156, 162
conventional 'black box' model 13
convergence 200–2, 204
σ-convergence 207–8, *208*
cooperative alliances 162
corporate insiders 245–6, **245**, **246**
corporate repurchasers 251, **252**, 253
corporate resource allocations 242
corporate spenders NAICS **263**
corporate taxation 48
COVID-19 technology access pool (C-TAP) 51
Crépon, B. 132
Crespi, G. 133
Criscuolo, C. 133
cross-country regression 26

Daniels, John D. 162
da Rosa, Andreia Cunha 8
Davidson, W. 162
Davis, Gerald 95
Defense Advanced Research Projects Agency (DARPA) 45
disruptive technologies 236
distinctive capabilities 99
domestic firms and multinational subsidiaries 24
domestic innovation and patent system 26–7
draft job specification 237–8
Dublin-based AerCap 92
Duguet, E. 132
Dunning, J. 155, 156, 162
Dynamic Capabilities (DC) theory 223, 224
dynamic theories 214; Schumpeter's theory, entrepreneurial profit 196–7; 'The theory of the growth of the firm' 196

earnings per share (EPS) 244
East Asian countries 16
Eclectic Theory 156
Economic and Social Council (ECOSOC) 269
efficiency seeking 159–60
electrical machinery (EM) 137
employment growth and innovation **137**
EPC Membership as of 2018 *28*
era of digitalisation 14–15
Erramilli, M. K. 161–2
ethylene polymers trade balance 1995–2018 *114*
Eurasian Patent Organization (EAPO) 18, 27
European Aeronautics Defence and Space Company (EADS) 92
European Patent Convention (EPC) 27
European Patent Office (EPO) 18, 27
Exchange Act 244
external stimuli factors 158
Exxon's Corporation Baytown Ethylene Plant 116

Faronkal, nasal decongestant compound 35
Faulkner, D. 162–4
feedstock cost by region 2017 **110**
financial institutions 52–3
Financial Times (FT) 11
Fink, C. 26, 29
Fink, Larry 43
firm growth: data sources and descriptive statistics 136–8, *138*; efficiencies 142, *143*, **144**, 145; empirical strategy 138–40, **140**; external and internal causes 130; innovation and efficiency, firm-level employment 130, **131**; managerial decisions 134; micro econometric studies 132; neoclassical analysis 130; process innovation 131
firms (Penrose's theory) **153**; *see also* internationalisation strategy
first-time users of patents *31*
Flatten, T. C. 179
flight, story of: business of flight 91–2; capitalism without capital 92–4; collective intelligence 90; combinations and capabilities 98–9; economics and business strategy 96; economics of firm 96–7; entrepreneurship 97–8; Hooke, Robert 89; Icarus 89; as a service concept 94; Trevithick, Richard 90; Watt, James 89; Wright brothers 90; *see also* hollow corporation
Florentine government 18
foreign direct investment (FDI) 25–6, 155, 165
Fóres, B. 182
Franta, B. 109
Freeman, C. 134
Friedman, M. 42
From Market Fixing to Market Shaping 15
Fuzzy Set Qualitative Comparative Analysis (fsQCA) 176
Fuzzy Sets (FS) 176, *185*

Garcia, A. 133
García-Morales, V. J. 179, 182
Garnsey, Elizabeth 5
George, G. 175, 176, 179, 180
Ginarte, J. C. 26
Giuliani, E. 176, 180
global professional networks 158
Gold, E. R. 26, 35
Greenan, N. 132
Green, J. 109
gross operating surplus (GOS) 203, 222
Guellec, D. 132

Hall, B. H. 14, 19, 25, 27, 29, 132
Harrison, R. 132, 133
Hedlund, G. 162
Helmers, C. 19, 27, 29
Hercules Powder Company (HPC) 2
high absorptive capacity **187**
Hitt, M. 158
hollow corporation 94–5
Hooke, Robert 89

Hopkins, Matt 251
Hoskinson, R. 158
Hsu, C. 156, 162
human capital 138

incentives 17
independent refiners 116–18, *118*
industry and sectoral buyback activity 249,
    250, 251
industry-specific movements 204
Inkpen, A. 159, 160
Institute of Public Health 34
internalisation theory 156
Internal Rate of Return (IRR) 194
internal stimuli factors 158
International Diversification Theory 157, 161
internationalisation strategy: entry mode
    choice 161; and firm performance 166, **166**; and
    firm size 167, **168**; foreign direct investment
    (FDI) 165; home country and world economic
    growth 166–7, **167**, **168**; international
    joint venture (IJV) 162–4; merger and
    acquisition 165; qualitative analysis 167–8, **169**;
    stages 162; U-shape relationship 162
international joint venture (IJV) 162–4
International Labour Organisation (ILO) 268
international oil firms (IOCs): Braskem 120;
    decarbonisation 103–4; ethylene production
    capacity and capital investment *117*, *119*;
    forecast refinery expansion **121**; independent
    refiners 116–18, *118*; Long Lived Capital
    Stock 104; petrochemical refining 104;
    petroleum-derived feedstocks 105; policy
    implications 121–2; SABIC Annual Report 120;
    state-MNE relations 104; *see also* captive
    market; refining industry
ISP register 35
Ivus, O. 25

Jacobsen, R. 201
Jacobson, Ken 255
Jiménez-Barrionuevo, M. M. 179, 182
Jimenez-Jimenez, D. 9
Joffe, Michael 8
Johanson, J. 157
joint venture (JV) 155, 164
Jonas, Norman 94–5

Kaldor, N. 108
Kanter, R. 163
Kapczynski, A. 34
Kay, John 7
Keynes, Keynesian economics and policy 11
Kim, H. 158
Kim, L. 26
Klenert, D. 122
Knickerbocker, F. 160
knowledge intensive service sector
    industries 157–8
Kogut, B. 156, 161, 163, 165

Koka, B. R. 175
Kroc, Ray 95
Kumar, N. 26
Kundu, S. 156, 162
Kverneland, A. 162
Kyle, M. K. 33

Lachenmaier, S. 133
Lane, P. J. 175
Lanjouw, J. O. 33
Larmax-D, anti-histamine compound 35
late Edith Penrose, life of: contributions to
    economics 273–4; McCarthyism 270–3;
    1930s 267–8; Second World War 268–9; theory
    of the growth of the firm 273
Lau, Chia Huay 8
Lauterbach, R. 133, 142
law of diminishing returns 202–3
Lazonick, William 7, 9, 251, 253, 255
Leal-Rodríguez, A. L. 179
legal services 203
Lerner, J. 19, 35
Levine, L. 23
Levinthal, D. A. 175, 179, 180
Likert-type Scale Method 158–9
Long Lived Capital Stock 104
Lotti, F. 132, 133
low absorptive capacity 185
low-middle income countries 129
Lu, J. W. 156, 158, 162

macro shocks 204
Madsen, T. 161
Mairesse, J. 132, 133
managerial capabilities 3
market manipulation 244–5
market seeking 159
Martinelli, Orlando 8
Maskus, K. E. 25, 26
Mazzucato, Mariana 6–7, 15
McCarthyism 270–3
McFetridge, D. 162
McGahan, A. M. 33
McGrath, Rita 14–15
Means, G. C. 108
medical and optical instruments (MOI) 137
medium absorptive capacity 185, **187**
Michie, J. 8, 134, 176, 180
middle income countries: Chilean IP use and
    firm performance 29–31, *29*, *31*; patents and
    pharmaceutical innovation, Chile 31–5, *32*;
    regional patent systems 27–8, *28*
Miller, J. 155, 157
Miravete, E. J. 134
mission-led policy model 47
modern businesses 94
Mokyr, J. 24
Molina, L. M. 179, 182
monetary/non-monetary rewards 200
Morin, J.-F. 26, 35

Moser, P. 35
Mueller, D. 201

NASA's Apollo mission 46
National Classification of Economic Activities (CNAE) 182
National Health Service (the Sainsbury Committee) 13
National Income and Product Accounts (NIPA) 222
National Institutes of Health (NIH) 45
National Investment Banks (NIBs) 52
National Science Foundation (NSF) 45
Nell, K. S. 202
Nelson complexity index by region (2000–2019) *111*
neoclassical fallacy (Penrosian learning) 7; *Business History Review* 58; Chandlerian perspectives 60–1; description 57–8; employers and employees 60; innovative enterprise and sustainable prosperity 77–82; logic of organizational learning 58; market economy 74–7; multidivisionalization 58; 'paths of learning' project 60; productive capabilities 59; theory of 67–74, *72*; U.S. industrial firms 58; *The Visible Hand* 59; *see also* theory of innovative enterprise (TIE)
neoclassical theory 215–16; managerial capacity/talent 199; market power 198; monetary/non-monetary rewards 200; neglect of intangible assets 199; risk 198–9; standard account 197–8
Net Present Value (NPV) 194
Neubig, T. S. 21
Newcomen's steam engine 89–90
Nobel Prize in Economics 74
non-high absorptive capacity 185, **188**
non-linear dynamics 236
North American Industry Classification System (NAICS) 251

Ogram, E. W. 162
Open Door Policy 24
open-market repurchases (OMRs) 265–6
organizational learning 232–6
other transport equipment (OTE) 137
Oughton, C. 134, 176, 180
ownership advantages 160

Palladino, Lenore 9, 246
Park, W. G. 26
Past and Present (2023) 15
Patent Cooperation Treaty (PCT) 19
patent primer 18–19
patent system 17; description 19; domestic innovation 26–7; and innovation 21–3, *22*; technology transfer 25–6; *see also* middle income countries
Pathak, S. 175
Penrosian theory 13, 177–8
Penubarti, M. 25

Pernias, J. C. 134
personal protective equipment (PPE) production 251
Peters, B. 132
petrochemical refining 104, 112
petroleum-derived feedstocks 105
Pisano, G. S. 46
pluralism and multi-disciplinarity 4
Polanyi, Karl 44
Porter, M. 96, 227
potential absorptive capacity 176
Pras, B. 155, 157
Predatory Value Extraction 67
primary refining capacity by region and type *113*
process and product innovation 141–2
process innovation 128
product innovation 128, 141
professional traders 245–6, **245, 246**
profit rate 204
profit rate distribution 204; beta (β)-convergence 209, **210**; σ-convergence 207–8, *208*; descriptive statistics 205–7, *206*; lagged quantity of capital **212**; observed 205; preliminary observations 194–5; research problem 193–4; response of investment 210–11, **211**; strengths and limitations 212–13; *see also* dynamic theories; neoclassical theory
Prologis 93
public wealth funds 52
Purchase of Common and Preferred Stock (PCPS) 265

Qian, Y. 33
Qualitative Comparative Analysis (QCA) 176, 182–3
qualitative research analysis **159**
Qualls, D. 201

Radebaugh, L. H. 162
radio, television and communication equipment (RTE) 137
Raffo, J. 132
Ragin, C. C. 180, 182, 183
Ramaswamy, K. 159, 160
Rao, C. 161–2
Rapini, M. S. 178
rate of return, quantity of capital 205
rationality and biological analogies 4
realized absorptive capacity 176
Real Options Theory 156
refining capacities 1965–2019 *110*
refining industry: geographical trends 109–12, *110–11*, **110**; ownership and geographies of production 112–13, *113*
regional patent systems 27–8, *28*
regional wealth funds 52
regulatory about-face, SEC staff 254
reproducible/complementary capabilities 99
research and development (R&D) 134

Resource-Based View 223, 224; case study method 228–31; Hewlett-Packard 231–2; locus of competitive advantage 226–8; organizational learning and unlearning 232–6
Righi, H. M. 178
Rihoux, B. 180
Risk Diversification Theory 161
Robinson, J. 107
Roele, Irene 9
Rohenkohl, Júlio Eduardo 8
Rosa, A. C. 181
Rosenbaum, S. 161
Rottmann, H. 133
Rueh, Sonja 9
Ruffoni, J. 8, 181
Rugman, A. 155, 157, 161

safe harbor 255
Sakakibara, M. 227
Sampat, B. N. 34
Samuelson, Paul A. 58
Saudi Basic Industries Corporation (SABIC) 113
Saunders, K. M. 23
Schaede, U. 227
Schankerman, M. 33
School of Oriental and African Studies (SOAS) 12
Schumpeter hypothesis 98, 107–8, 196–7
Schwartz, S. 201
S-C-P approach 96
secondary patenting 34
second machine age 236
Securities and Exchange Commission (SEC) 253, 265
Securities Exchange Act of 1934 254
Shadeed, E. 26, 35
Shadlen, K. C. 34
Shandong Yulong Petrochemical Complex 118
Shuen, A. 46
simplification strategies 182
Singh, H. 165
sleeping patents 23
Small Business Innovation Research (SBIR) 45
Smith, Adam 44, 65
Solow model 203
stakeholder capitalism 43; business model 50; CHIPS Act 51; corporate taxation 48; digital companies 49; growth 49; labour's, global income 48; Obama Administration 49–50; pre-distribution approach 48; value pricing 50
state's role: carbon taxes 44; negative externalities 44; orthodox economic discourse 44; public banks 45; public purpose and mission orientation 45–8
stochastic frontier analysis 152
stock buybacks 9; corporate insiders and professional traders 245–6, **245**, **246**; description 242–3; history of policies 254–5; importance of, 2010–2019 246–8, *247–9*; industry and sectoral buyback activity

249, **250**, 251; innovation 243; legislative proposals **264**; market manipulation 244–5; policy reform proposals 255–7; theory of innovative enterprise 243–4
strategic asset seeking 160
Survey on Development and Technological Innovation in the Manufacturing Sector 129

Tallman, S. 162–4
technology licensing 25
technology transfer and patent system 25–6
Teece, D. 46
Tesco 232–6
Tetlow, Gemma 11–12
The Great Transformation 44
theoretical model 150–1
theory of innovative enterprise (TIE): AVC, AFC and ATC 62; collective 61; cost curve restructuring 65; cumulative 61–2; description 61; financial commitment 62; fixed cost 64; innovating firm 63; 'optimizing' subject 62–3; organizational integration 62; organizational-learning process 66; *Predatory Value Extraction* 67; productive capability 64; strategic control 62; uncertain 61
theory of innovative enterprise framework 243–4
The Theory of the Growth of the Firm (TTGF) 104; analogical reasoning 5; educated laymen 4; firm growth 2; internal resources and market opportunities 1; labour protection laws 3; managerial resources and capacity 3; methodology 3–5; physically describable resources 2; traditional approaches 5; UK 'productivity puzzle' 3
The Wealth of Nations 65
Thirlwall, A. P. 202
Thursby, J. G. 26
Thursby, M. 26
time decay frontier model **153**
Tobin, Damian 7–8
Torrisi, S. 23
Total Factor Productivity (TFP) 30
Transaction Cost Theory 156
Trans Pacific Partnership 33–4

UK 'productivity puzzle' 3
Unified Patent Court 19
University-Industry (UI) interaction 176–7
unlearning 232–6
UN Sustainable Development Goals (SDGs) 46
Uppsala Model 156, 157
urban wealth funds 52

Vahlne, J. 157
variable-oriented approach 182
Vermeulen, F. 158
Versiani, A. F. 179
Von Graevenitz, G. 19

INDEX

Watt, James 89
Weetman, F. 12
Wernerfelt, B. 98
Williams Act of 1968 254
Williamson, O. 155, 157
World Intellectual Property Organization
    (WIPO) 18–21, *20, 21*
Wunsch-Vincent, S. 21

The Xerox Corporation 94

Yang, L. 26

Zahra, S. A. 175, 176,
    179, 180
Zenger, T. R.
    225

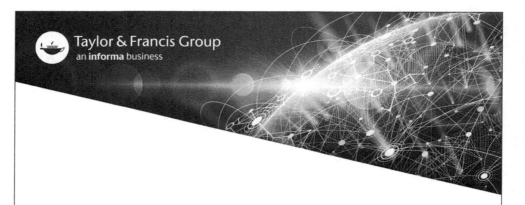

Taylor & Francis eBooks

www.taylorfrancis.com

A single destination for eBooks from Taylor & Francis with increased functionality and an improved user experience to meet the needs of our customers.

90,000+ eBooks of award-winning academic content in Humanities, Social Science, Science, Technology, Engineering, and Medical written by a global network of editors and authors.

TAYLOR & FRANCIS EBOOKS OFFERS:

- A streamlined experience for our library customers
- A single point of discovery for all of our eBook content
- Improved search and discovery of content at both book and chapter level

REQUEST A FREE TRIAL
support@taylorfrancis.com

9781032959092